PREVENTIVE
MAINTENANCE

A practical step-by-step guide to reducing equipment operating
costs and downtime and improving operating safety

FUNDAMENTAL MACHINE OPERATION

Fundamentals of Machine Operation (FMO) is a series of manuals created by Deere & Company. Each book in the series is conceived, researched, outlined, edited, and published by Deere & Company, John Deere Publishing. Authors are selected to provide a basic technical manuscript that could be edited and rewritten by staff editors.

PUBLISHER
DEERE & COMPANY, JOHN DEERE PUBLISHING
ALMON-TIAC Building, Suite 140, 1300 - 19th Street,
East Moline, IL 61244
http://www.deere.com/deerecom/Farmers+and+Ranchers/Publications
1-800-522-7448

JOHN DEERE PUBLISHING STAFF
Cindy S. Calloway, Lori J. Dhabalt

CONTRIBUTING AUTHOR AND EDITOR OF THIS 6th EDITION: *Robert H. Gunter* is a John Deere retiree with 27 years of experience in service publications including stints as factory writer, factory supervisor, and staff editor. One of his last active primary responsibilities was the training of factory writers.

ORIGINAL AUTHOR: *Louis Hathaway* was managing editor for the John Deere Service Publications staff, which publishes the Fundamentals of Machine Operation (FMO) texts and visuals. A native of Illinois, Mr. Hathaway was a technical writer and editor of agricultural machine subjects. Lou retired from Deere & Company with more than 37 years of service in April 1999.

CONTRIBUTING AUTHOR: *Frank Buckingham,* an agricultural engineer and free-lance writer of numerous articles and publications in agricultural machinery.

CONSULTING EDITOR: *Thomas A. Hoerner,* Ph.D., Professor Emeritus of Agriculture & Biosystems Engineering and Agricultural Education & Studies at Iowa State University. Dr. Hoerner had 4 years of high school agriculture teaching experience and 31 years as a teacher-educator and teacher in agricultural education and agricultural mechanics. He has authored numerous manuals, slide/cassette programs, microcomputer programs and videotapes in the agricultural mechanics area.

CONSULTING EDITOR: *Ralph J. Moens* is a teacher of vocational agricultural at the high school in Atkinson, Illinois. A part-time farmer, Mr. Moens has 18 years of experience in preparing young people for agribusiness careers.

CONSULTING EDITOR: *Keith R. Carlson* has thirteen years of experience as a high school vocational agriculture instructor. Mr. Carlson is the author of numerous instructor's guides, including the American Oil Company's "Vo-Ag Management Kits". Many of his aids have been available under the name Vo-Ag Visuals. All instructor's kits for the FMO texts are being prepared by Mr. Carlson who is presently General Manager of Agri-Education, Inc.

CONTRIBUTORS: The following persons and groups were very helpful n giving valuable literature, and technical assistance: A C Spark Plug Division; Aeroquip Corp.; American Association for Vocational Instructional materials; American Society of Agricultural Engineers, Champion Spark Plug Co., Dana Corp.; DelcoRemy, Division of General Motors; Pat Farrell, DeWitt, Iowa; Federal-Mogul Corp.; Firestone Tire & Rubber Co.; Goodyear Tire Co.; Goodrich Tire Co.; Everette Hainline, Cedar Falls, Iowa; Fred Hileman, Waterloo, Iowa; Link-Belt/FMC; Motorola Automotive Products Co.; Owatonna Tool Co.; Prestolite Co.; Rex Chainbelt; Rubber Manufacturers Assn.; Shell Oil Co.; Standard Oil Co.; Sun Electric Corp.; Sundstrand Corp.; Texaco Inc.; Union Carbide Corp.; Vickers Inc. We also wish to thank a host of John Deere people who gave extra assistance and advice on this project.

We have a
long-range interest in
Your Farming Success

FOR MORE INFORMATION

This text is part of a complete series of texts and visuals on agricultural machinery called Fundamentals of Machine Operation (FMO). For more information, or to request a free catalog, send to address above or call 1-800-522-7448.

ISBN 0-86691-267-3

CONTENTS

1 INTRODUCTION

2 ENGINE INTAKE AND EXHAUST SYSTEMS

3 ENGINE FUEL SYSTEMS

4 ENGINE LUBRICATION SYSTEMS

5 ENGINE COOLING SYSTEMS

6 ENGINE ELECTRICAL SYSTEMS

7 POWER TRAINS

8 HYDRAULIC SYSTEMS

9 OTHER COMPONENTS

10 TUNE-UP AND STORAGE

11 Troubleshooting

12 Safety

APPENDIX

INTRODUCTION

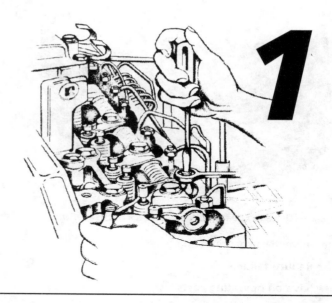

Fig. 1 — Preventive Maintenance Keeps Machines Going When Jobs are the Toughest

IMPORTANCE OF PREVENTIVE MAINTENANCE

Do you know the leading cause of premature failure in agricultural machines today? *Putting things off until tomorrow!* Yes, how many times have you heard, "I'll grease it tomorrow." Tomorrow comes and work is waiting-no time to grease it now.

Putting it off becomes a bad habit which leads to machine breakdown or high operating costs. You can make preventive maintenance a good habit. Just do one thing: *Always perform maintenance either at the end of the day or early in the morning before you go to the field.*

By knowing the fundamentals of good preventive maintenance, you can perform it efficiently and correctly. Then you will be assured of getting the most out of your equipment. And you will be pleased with your efforts and savings.

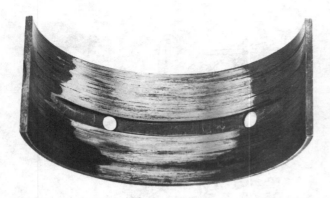

Fig. 2 — Damaged Bearing Caused by Lack of Lubrication

Preventive maintenance can do three things:

- **Reduce failures**
- **Save on operating costs**
- **Help prevent injuries**

Let's look at each of these.

REDUCE FAILURES

When the work load is heaviest, your equipment needs preventive maintenance the most. You can't afford to have your machine down when the crop has to be planted in the spring or harvested in the fall. You won't, of course, prevent the possibility of failure, but you will reduce it to a minimum.

SAVE ON OPERATING COSTS

Believe it or not, the few dollars it costs to perform preventive maintenance will pay for themselves many times over. For example, an engine tune-up can save you a possible 15 percent in fuel consumption and increase maximum power by more than 10 percent. On a 100-horsepower (75 kW) tractor, this could mean 4 or 5 gallons (15 to 19 liters) of fuel saved each day, plus a bonus of 10 extra horsepower (7.5 kW) to work with. These savings can be measured in dollars and cents. And maintenance of other components will save you even more in repairs during the life of your equipment. All these things mean more profit for you.

Preventive maintenance also provides a cumulative effect in terms of energy conservation. A properly maintained engine burns less fuel per hour; a well-cared-for machine can do more work per hour; so, fewer operating hours are required to complete needed tasks. These reductions in fuel consumption save dollars and conserve energy.

HELP PREVENT INJURIES

If your machine is not performing well, you tend to take chances to make up the time lost by poor performance. In your haste you may try to correct a malfunction without stopping or turning off the machine. Good preventive maintenance should include the checking of safety systems including guards and shields and the replacement of any damaged safety signs. Complete preventive maintenance means a safer machine to operate and less chance of injury to you and others.

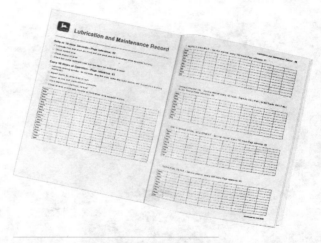

Fig. 3 — Preventive Maintenance Schedule

KEEPING RECORDS

A good way to be sure that all maintenance is performed on schedule is to keep records. A simple form like the one shown in Fig. 3 is easy to use. You can make up your own form or you may find one available from your local implement or petroleum supply dealer. Such forms are also provided in some operator's manuals.

Fig. 4 — Use Records Instead of Your Memory—It Will Pay

Follow the recommendations in your operator's manual for specific service intervals. Enter the various jobs to be performed under the "hours of operation" headings. Then check off the intervals of service after they are performed. It only takes a few minutes each day.

Keep this record in a handy place, such as near the service center of the farm.

Many machines have an hour meter which operates whenever the engine is running and shows the total hours of operation. Record the hour meter reading and watch this meter to tell when services are required.

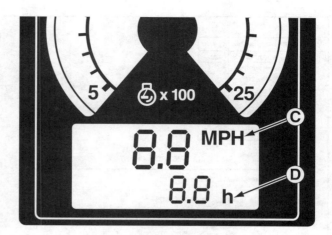

Fig. 5 — Recording Hour Meter Readings (D) Tells When Periodic Services are Needed

RECOMMENDED SERVICE INTERVALS

The American Society of Agricultural Engineers (ASAE) recommends service on machines at regular hourly intervals. These periods are commonly after 5, 10, 50, 100, 250, 500 and 1000 hours of operation. See the chart in Fig. 6 for typical service on a tractor.

The hourly intervals represent days of operation as shown below:

   5 Hours (Twice Daily)
   10 Hours (Daily)
   50 Hours (Weekly)
 250 Hours (Monthly)
 500 Hours (Bimonthly)
1000 Hours (Seasonally)

However, most farm machines are only operated 250 to 500 hours a year, so the yearly or twice-yearly services can often be combined with the other intervals and completed at the same time.

Keep in mind that the suggested intervals of service shown in this book are the *average* intervals between different machines and manufacturers. Since recommended intervals of service vary widely between machines, *refer to your operator's manual for specific instructions*. Here we are primarily concerned with the *fundamentals* of preventive maintenance and this book is not intended as a maintenance manual for specific machines.

The intervals of service are cumulative. For example: you should perform 10-hour maintenance every ten hours, including at the 50-, 100-, 250-, 500-, and 1000- hour intervals.

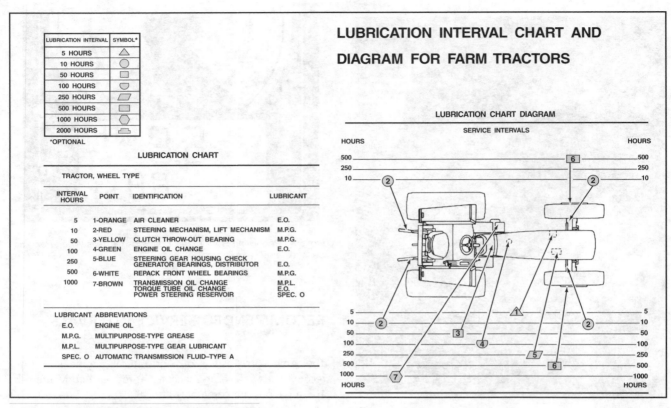

LUBRICATION INTERVAL CHART AND DIAGRAM FOR FARM TRACTORS

LUBRICATION INTERVAL	SYMBOL*
5 HOURS	△
10 HOURS	○
50 HOURS	□
100 HOURS	▽
250 HOURS	▱
500 HOURS	▭
1000 HOURS	⬡
2000 HOURS	▱

*OPTIONAL

LUBRICATION CHART

TRACTOR, WHEEL TYPE

INTERVAL HOURS	POINT	IDENTIFICATION	LUBRICANT
5	1-ORANGE	AIR CLEANER	E.O.
10	2-RED	STEERING MECHANISM, LIFT MECHANISM	M.P.G.
50	3-YELLOW	CLUTCH THROW-OUT BEARING	M.P.G.
100	4-GREEN	ENGINE OIL CHANGE	E.O.
250	5-BLUE	STEERING GEAR HOUSING CHECK GENERATOR BEARINGS, DISTRIBUTOR	E.O.
500	6-WHITE	REPACK FRONT WHEEL BEARINGS	M.P.G.
1000	7-BROWN	TRANSMISSION OIL CHANGE TORQUE TUBE OIL CHANGE POWER STEERING RESERVOIR	M.P.L. E.O. SPEC. O

LUBRICANT ABBREVIATIONS

E.O.	ENGINE OIL
M.P.G.	MULTIPURPOSE-TYPE GREASE
M.P.L.	MULTIPURPOSE-TYPE GEAR LUBRICANT
SPEC. O	AUTOMATIC TRANSMISSION FLUID–TYPE A

Fig. 6 — Typical ASAE Service Intervals for a Tractor

PROPER OPERATION TO PREVENT ABUSE

While agricultural machines are designed tough for special types of work, they were not intended to be "hot rods." They must be handled with respect. Besides causing premature wear and damage, abuse can endanger your personal safety. Although only in use a few hours, the tire in Fig. 7 shows severe, premature wear caused by the operator spinning the tires. Ignoring the recommended inflation pressure is another form of tire abuse.

Fig. 8 — Study Your Operator's Manual

Fig. 7 — Improper Operation Causes Premature Wear (Spinning Wear on Tire)

TIPS FOR GOOD MACHINE OPERATION

DO:

1. Follow suggestions in your operator's manual.

2. Perform daily (5 and 10 hour) maintenance before using machine.

3. Check the machine for damage and potential failures before starting it.

4. Run the engine until it is warm before putting it under load.

5. Let a hot engine run a few minutes without load so that it cools before shutting it off.

6. Keep bolts and nuts tight.

7. Watch the instrument panel (Fig. 10).

8. Keep the machine properly serviced.

9. See a serviceman for major repairs.

10. Operate at safe speeds.

DON'T:

1. Jump on the machine, start it, and take off with a cold engine.

2. Start the engine and turn it off before it has warmed up.

3. Jam the transmission into gear.

4. Snap or pop the clutch.

5. Spin the tires.

6. Overload the capacity of the machine.

7. Let the engine idle for long periods of time.

8. Store a machine without properly preparing it for storage.

9. Neglect to perform periodic maintenance on schedule.

10. Remove Safety shields or disable safety systems.

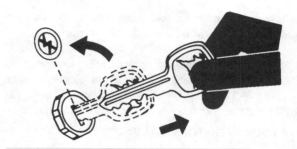

Fig. 9 — Turn Off Engine Before Servicing Machine

SAFETY RULES

Use safe procedures when performing machine maintenance. First, stop the engine (Fig. 9). Don't attempt to service your equipment when it is running, except when absolutely necessary, such as when timing the ignition or adjusting the carburetor.

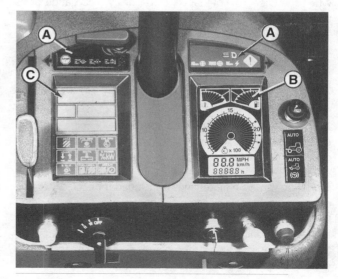

Fig. 10 — Watch Your Instrument Panel for Trouble Signs
(A-Warning Indicator Lamps; B-Tachometer; C-Performance Monitor)

Always think about what you are going to do before you do it. This is the most basic rule of safety. For example, don't remove the radiator cap until you have determined whether or not the coolant is still under pressure. Wait until it cools and the pressure drops-then remove the cap slowly.

Carefully read all safety messages in this manual and on your machine safety signs. Keep safety signs in good condition. Replace missing or damaged safety signs.

Learn how to operate the machine and how to use controls properly. Do not let anyone operate without instruction.

Keep your machine in proper working condition. Unauthorized modifications to the machine may impair the function and/or safety and affect machine life. *Be ure to read Chapter 12, "Safety"*, before performing any work on your machine.

STUDY YOUR OPERATORS MANUAL

Read your operator's manual carefully before attempting to operate or service your machine (Fig. 8). Follow the safety rules and you may avoid injury to yourself or others. Safe operation also reduces accidents which could damage equipment and require costly repairs or replacement. Where they apply, safety suggestions are included in this book.

WATCH YOUR INSTRUMENT PANEL

When you drive a machine, glance at the instrument panel from time to time (Fig. 10). The gauges and lights will tell you the condition of various engine systems and will signal you when they need maintenance. Don't delay! If a gauge gives you a warning, maintenance or repair is probably overdue and should be performed at once.

COVERAGE IN THIS BOOK

This book will cover not only tractors, but all engine-powered machines, such as self-propelled combines, windrowers, hay cubers, and forage harvesters.

Typical preventive maintenance is included for each system on a typical machine. For example, Chapter 2 will cover "Engine Intake and Exhaust Systems." Other chapters will cover lubricating, cooling, and electrical systems, as well as power trains, hydraulics, and other components such as cab air conditioning and accessories.

Although diesel engines presently outnumber gasoline engines in sales of new equipment, thousands of gasoline engines are still used regularly on combines, tractors, and other machines. Preventive maintenance is equally important on old as well as new equipment. Therefore, significant coverage is provided here for both engine types.

This book is not intended for making you, the reader, into a mechanic. Rather it is designed to give you a better understanding of the importance of preventive maintenance and the steps of performing maintenance jobs on farm machines. It is your responsibility to follow through and actually perform these steps and those in your operator's manual. Only then will you get the full benefits of this book.

TEST YOURSELF

QUESTIONS

1. Name three major benefits of good preventive maintenance.

2. What are the economic advantages of preventive maintenance?

3. Why should you refer to your operator's manual when performing maintenance?

4. What are the two most important things you must do before starting your machine each day?

5. What is the most basic rule of safety?

ENGINE INTAKE AND EXHAUST SYSTEMS

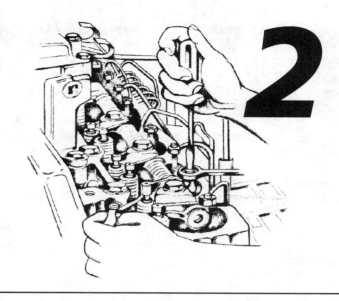

INTRODUCTION

An engine must "breathe" to create energy just as you do (Fig. 1). The intake and exhaust systems are the breathing apparatus of an engine. They carry the fuel-air mixture into the engine and remove the exhaust gases after combustion (Fig. 2).

INTAKE SYSTEM

The intake system supplies the engine with clean air of the proper quantity and temperature for good combustion.

The intake system has five basic parts:

- **Air cleaners**

- **Turbocharger (if used)**

- **Air inlet**

- **Intake manifold**

- **Intake valves**

AIR CLEANERS filter dust and dirt from the air passing through them enroute to the carburetor (Fig. 3). Pre-cleaners prevent larger particles from reaching the air cleaner and lengthen service intervals.

TURBOCHARGERS (or Superchargers) increase power by forcing more air or fuel-air mixture into the engine cylinders than the engine could draw in by itself.

AIR INLET supplies fuel mixed with incoming air in the proper ratio for combustion, and also controls engine speed. (On spark-ignition engines, this mixture come from the carburetor. On diesel engines, air only is provided, with fuel injected later at the engine cylinders.)

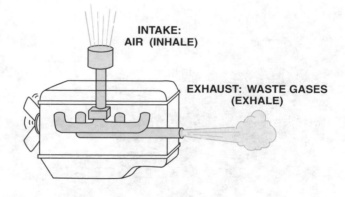

Fig. 1 — An Engine Must "Breathe"

INTAKE MANIFOLDS transport the fuel-air mixture (pure air in diesel engines) to the engine cylinders.

INTAKE VALVES admit the air or fuel-air mixture to the engine cylinders for burning. They are normally opened and closed by linkage from the engine camshaft.

EXHAUST SYSTEM

The exhaust system collects the exhaust gases after combustion and carries them away. This is really three jobs: (1) Removing heat; (2) Muffling engine sounds; (3) Carrying away burned and unburned gases.

The exhaust system has three basic parts:

- **Exhaust valves**

- **Exhaust manifold**

- **Muffler**

EXHAUST VALVES open to release the burnt gases from the cylinder after combustion. The valves are normally opened and closed by the camshaft.

The EXHAUST MANIFOLD collects the exhaust gases and conducts them away from the cylinders.

The MUFFLER reduces the sound of the engine during the exhaust period.

A more detailed explanation of the intake and exhaust systems follows.

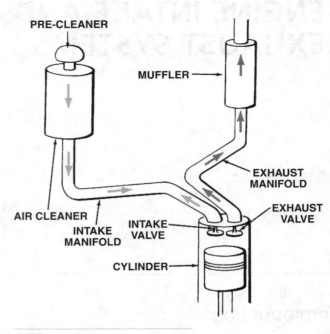

Fig. 2 — Intake and Exhaust Systems

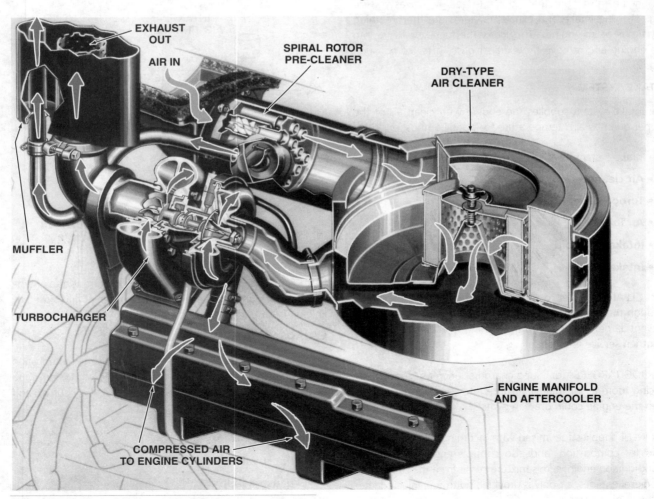

Fig. 3 — Intake and Exhaust System of a Typical Modern Engine

AIR CLEANERS AND AIR DUCTS

INTRODUCTION

The average engine mixes 9,000 to 10,000 gallons (liters) of air (by volume) with every gallon (liter) of fuel it consumes. Turbocharged engines use even more air. This amount of air can contain enough dirt to wear out the engine prematurely if the air is unfiltered, or if the air intake system leaks.

An air cleaner must have the capacity to hold material taken out of the air so that the engine can operate for a reasonable period before cleaning and servicing are necessary.

Multiple air cleaner installations are sometimes used where engines are operated under extremely dusty conditions or where two small air cleaners must be used in place of a single large cleaner.

Fig. 4 — Good Air Cleaner Maintenance Keeps Engines Going When Conditions are Toughest

HOW DIRTY AIR CAN DAMAGE ENGINES

Consider these facts:

In some dusty environments, an engine can be ruined:

1. If an air hose comes off for only a few hours.

2. If a mere pinhole leak in a hose is left for a full season.

Keep this in mind when you think of air cleaning systems.

Agricultural engines operate in some very tough conditions (Fig. 4) and this makes air cleaner service doubly important.

TYPES OF AIR CLEANERS

The major types of air cleaners are:

- **Precleaners**
- **Dry element air cleaners**
- **Oil bath air cleaners**

Let's examine these more closely.

Precleaners

Precleaners (Fig. 5) are usually installed at the end of a pipe extended upward into the air from the air cleaner inlet. This places them in an area relatively free of dust.

Fig. 5 — Precleaner and Prescreener

Precleaners remove larger particles of dirt or other foreign matter from the air before it enters the main air cleaner. This relieves much of the load on the air cleaner and allows longer intervals between servicing.

Most precleaners have a *prescreener* (Fig. 5) which prevents lint, chaff, and leaves from entering the air intake. However, the prescreener can become plugged quickly under some conditions, thus preventing air from entering the air cleaner.

Dry-Element Air cleaners

Two major types of dry-element cleaners are used at the present time (Fig. 6).

Dry-element air cleaners are built for two-stage cleaning:

1) *Precleaning*

2) *Filtering*

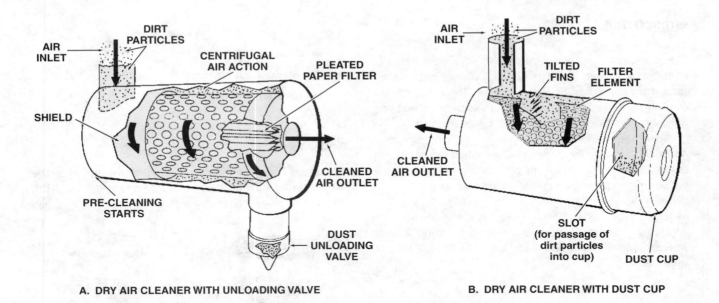

A. DRY AIR CLEANER WITH UNLOADING VALVE

B. DRY AIR CLEANER WITH DUST CUP

Fig. 6 — Dry Element Air Cleaners—Two Types

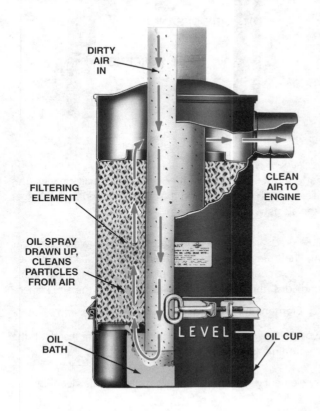

Fig. 7 — Medium-Duty Oil Bath Air Cleaner

The first stage (precleaning) directs the air into the cleaner at high speed so that it sets up centrifugal rotation (cyclone action) around the filter element.

The cleaner shown in Fig. 6A directs the air into the *precleaner* so it strikes one side of the metal shield. This starts the centrifugal action which continues until it reaches the far end of the cleaner housing. At this point, the dirt is collected into a dust cap, or dust unloader, at the bottom of the housing.

The cleaner shown in Fig. 6B conducts the air past *tilted fins* which start the centrifugal (cyclone) action. When the air reaches the end of the cleaner housing, the dirt passes through a slot in the top of the cleaner and enters the dust cup.

In both types, *this precleaning action removes from 80 to 90 percent of the dirt particles* and greatly reduces the load on the filter.

The partially cleaned air then passes through the holes in the metal jacket surrounding the pleated paper filter. *Filtering* is done as the air passes through the paper filter. It filters out almost all of the remaining small particles. This is the second stage of cleaning.

Some heavy-duty cleaners use a spiral rotor device for precleaning the air as shown in Fig. 3. Others have a small safety element built into the unit in case the main element fouls.

If the air cleaner has a *dust cup* (Fig. 6B) it should be emptied daily. If an *automatic dust unloader* is used in place of a cup (Fig. 6A), it is usually recommended that it be checked at least once daily to make certain it doesn't become clogged. The dust unloader is a rubber duck bill device that is held closed by engine suction while the engine is running. When the engine stops, the flaps open so dirt can drop out. Check the flaps regularly to see that they close during operation so precleaner will work properly to give longer filter life.

Some dry-element cleaners are equipped with a *vacuum gauge* or *restriction indicator* to show when the filter needs cleaning (see inset, Fig. 13). The indicator is attached to the intake manifold of the tractor. *As the dirt accumulation builds up on the filter, air flow is restricted.* This increases the suction in the intake manifold and causes the indicator to show red. To maintain engine operating efficiency, it is important that the filter be serviced at once.

Oil Bath Air Cleaners

Medium-duty oil bath air cleaners (Fig. 7) draw air down a center tube where it strikes the surface of oil in a partly filled cup. The impact causes a mixture of air and oil spray to be carried up into the element of baffles and wire mesh. The separating element breaks up the dust-laden air and fine dust particles are trapped by the oil film. The particles are then washed down as the oil later drains back into the cup. Clean air continues through the element and on to the engine.

The washing down of the oil keeps the filter element fairly clean.

The major services are (1) to keep the oil cup filled to the proper level with the correct weight of oil, and (2) to replace the oil when it gets dirty or thickens, reducing its ability to clean particles from the air.

However, at least once each year, the air cleaner should be disassembled and the filter element cleaned in solvent.

NOTE: Today's detergent oils may hold the dirt in suspension. For this reason the need for oil cup service cannot be determined by the layer of dirt which has settled into he bottom of the cup. Instead, see if the oil has thickened due to dirt.

Some medium-duty air cleaners are fitted with an oil trap. This trap catches the oil which otherwise would be thrown out of the cleaner when the engine backfires.

Heavy-duty oil bath air cleaners (Fig. 8) operate the same as medium-duty ones. They are used on larger engines, especially diesels, because these engines use more air.

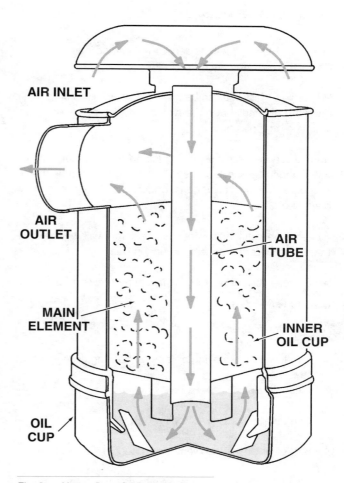

Fig. 8 — *Heavy-Duty Oil Bath Air Cleaner*

IMPORTANCE OF SERVICE

Air cleaner efficiency depends upon your performing proper maintenance and service.

Oil bath cleaners must be properly maintained or the oil cup will become filled with sludge, preventing the screens and elements from cleaning the air properly. This will restrict air flow to the engine (the same effect as choking the engine) and may allow dirty air to enter. Restricted air flow through the air cleaner will eventually cause incomplete combustion, increased carbon formation, and crankcase oil dilution.

Clean air and unrestricted air flow help conserve fuel and enable the engine to produce more power per unit of fuel burned.

Leaks in the connecting pipes, loose hose connections, or damaged gaskets which allow dust-laden air to enter the engine defeat the purpose of the air cleaner. Always check for dust paths in the air intake and around the ends of the filters. *Remember: Dirty air going directly into an engine cylinder is abrasive and will cause premature wear of moving parts.*

AIR CLEANER SERVICES

"How do I know when to service my engine's air cleaner?" Check the operator's manual.

No hard and fast rule can be given for servicing an air cleaner since this depends upon the type of cleaner, condition of air, and type of application.

Normal service intervals are designated by the manufacturer, but frequent inspection can tell whether or not this is adequate for the conditions under which the engine is operating.

A cleaner operating in severe dust conditions will require more frequent service than one operating in clean air.

Always refer to your operator's manual for service information.

Materials Needed

For oil-bath air cleaners:

1. Wrenches for removing air cleaner housing (if required).

2. Cleaning cloths.

3. Container to catch waste oil.

4. Bucket of cleaning solvent (not gasoline).

5. Clean oil of the same viscosity used in the crankcase.

For dry-element air cleaners

1. Goggles or glasses for eye protection.

2. Wrenches for removing air cleaner (if required).

3. Compressed air source (not over 30 psi; 205 kPa of pressure).

4. Bucket of warm water with a nonsudsing detergent.

5. Water source (not over 40 psi; 275 kPa of pressure).

Servicing Precleaners

Every 10 hours, check the precleaner bowl. If dirt has built up to the line, remove the bowl (Fig. 9) and empty it.

If the unit has a pre-screener (see Fig. 5), check it daily. Blow or brush off any chaff or other foreign matter.

If the precleaner unit is allowed to clog, a greater load is placed on the main air cleaner.

Servicing 0il Bath Air Cleaners

Every 10 hours of operation, check the oil cup for correct oil level and for dirt accumulation.

NOTE: Under extremely dirty conditions, check the oil cup twice daily.

Service the air cleaner as follows:

1. *Loosen oil cup and remove from filter (Fig. 10).*

   Don't try to remove cup with engine running. This allows unfiltered air to enter directly.

Fig. 9 — Emptying Precleaner Dust Bowl

2. *Check depth of sediment deposit in outer chamber.*

   If *sediment* in the outer compartment is about 1/2 inch (12 mm) deep, proceed with the remaining steps. (Some manufacturers recommend cleaning when 1/4 inch (6 mm) of dirt has accumulated. Check your operator's manual for recommendations.)

   If the *oil has thickened,* even though the dirt depth may not be as high as 1/2 inch (12 mm), change the oil. Thickened oil acts as a choke on your engine causing it to use more fuel. Fuel consumption may increase as much as a gallon (4 liters) or more per hour.

   There is also a possibility of drawing dirt-laden oil into the carburetor, then into the engine, where it acts as a grinding compound causing extremely fast wear.

Fig. 10 — Removing Oil Cup from Air Cleaner

With today's high-detergent oils, dirt may never settle to the bottom of the cup, so watch for thick oil as your signal that the oil needs to be changed.

If there is *water in the cup,* you will probably find the air intake cap has been removed allowing rain to enter. Proceed with cleaning the cup and be sure to replace air intake cap. Water interferes with effective air cleaning action.

3. *If cup needs cleaning, dispose of dirty oil properly, scrape and then wash inner and outer cups with clean diesel fuel (Fig. 11).*

 CAUTION: Don't use gasoline or other highly flammable liquids such as naptha or benzene which could explode or catch fire and burn.

Remove all caked dirt from bottom of cup.

Also clean dirt from tray (if used). See Fig. 11.

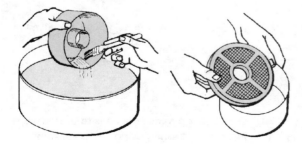

1. **CLEAN OIL CUP IN DIESEL FUEL**   2. **REMOVE DIRT FROM TRAY (IF USED)**

Fig. 11 — Cleaning Oil Cup and Tray

4. *Check air intake pipe (air stack) for dirt accumulation.*

This will not need cleaning often, but it is good practice to check it each time the oil cup is serviced.

If dirty, swab it out with your cleaning material. The more dirt you allow to accumulate in the stack, the more it acts as a choke to air flow and increases fuel consumption.

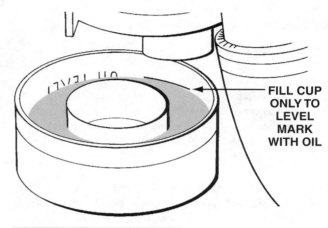

FILL CUP ONLY TO LEVEL MARK WITH OIL

Fig. 12 — Fill Oil Cup to Level Mark

5. *Refill cup with oil to "oil level" mark (Fig. 12).* Most operator's manuals recommend the same weight as used in the engine crankcase.

If you us an *oil that is too heavy,* the washing action is lessened. It also acts as a choke on the engine and increases fuel consumption.

Oil that is too light will pull into the engine. This lowers the oil Level in the cup until the cleaner is not efficient. With diesel engines, the oil is used as fuel, causing the engine to run wild. When this happens, you have no control of engine speed.

Don't use old crankcase oil. It may contain unburned fuel which evaporates quickly and lowers the oil level in the cup. It also contains dirt which limits washing action.

An additive oil can be used, but it is of no particular benefit for this purpose.

Don't overfill the oil cup. On spark-ignition engines it increases fuel consumption and cause loss of power. On diesel engines, the oil may be drawn into the engine and used as fuel, causing the engine to run wild.

6. *Replace oil cup (and screen tray, if used) and tighten clamp.*

7. *Check air duct between cleaner and carburetor (or intake manifold on diesel engines) for holes or loose clamp connections.*

Air entering the engine here bypasses the air cleaner. Dirt particles pass directly to the engine, causing rapid wear.

8. *Check air inlet screen, or precleaner, and remove trash if necessary.*

Oil-Bath Cleaning

At least once each year, completely disassemble and clean the air cleaner system. This is vital for long engine life.

Over long periods, dirt collects in the air cleaner center tube and in the lower part of the filter element. Dirt chokes off the air supply to the engine. Cleaning the system at least once each year pays off in reduced fuel consumption and more engine horsepower.

Swab out the center tube with a cloth soaked with diesel fuel. If the filter element is dirty, wash it in diesel fuel or solvent. Drain all parts and wipe dry. Then reassemble the air cleaner.

When assembling, be sure all hoses and gaskets are in good condition and that all connections are tight.

Servicing Dry-Type Air Cleaner

If the dry air cleaner has a dust cup, empty it daily. If an automatic dust unloading valve (Fig. 16) is used in place of a dust cup, check it daily for clogging.

Service the dry air cleaner element every 50 hours or at the following times:

1. *Units with restriction indicator: Clean element* whenever indicator glows or signals a restriction. (Some indicators may stick, so watch conditions and hours of operation carefully.)

2. *Units without indicator:* Clean element at recommended intervals-more often during dusty or unusual operation.

NOTE: Avoid too-frequent cleaning of dry-type air cleaners as cleaning always presents the danger of damaging the filter element.

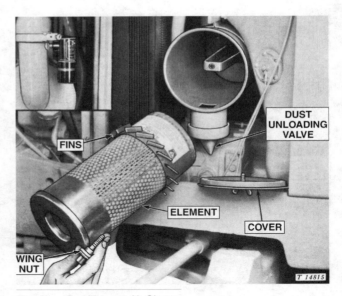

Fig. 13 — Dry-Element Air Cleaner

When the engine smokes too much or loses power, there may be a restriction in the dry air cleaner.

Dusty Element: Remove filter element and tap element *gently* on heel of hand to remove dust. Rotate element while tapping it. **Never tap element on hard surface** such as wheel of machine, as this may dent it and create an opening for dirty air.

Patting The Element   Blowing Out The Element

Fig. 14 — Cleaning the Dry Element

 CAUTION: Wear goggles or glasses to protect eyes from dust and dirt when using compressed air.

If tapping does not remove the dust, use a compressed air cleaning gun (pressure not to exceed 30 psi; 250 kPa) to clean the element (Fig. 14). Blowing from inside to outside, direct clean, dry air up and down the pleats.

IMPORTANT: Be careful not to rupture the element. Do not try to clean off outside of air cleaner with an air hose as it may clog it.

To clean with water: First blow out dirt with compressed air as described above. Then attach garden hose to cleaning gun and flush remainder of dirt from inside to outside of element. *Be sure to allow element to dry before installing it.* (It is a good idea to have two elements on hand in case one is damaged. Also, the completely dry element can then be installed each time.)

Oily or Sooty Elements: Blow out the dust with compressed air or flush with clean water. Soak and gently agitate element in a solution of lukewarm water and commercial filter element cleaner or an equivalent nonsudsing detergent (Fig. 15).

Rinse element thoroughly with clean water from hose (Fig. 15) having maximum pressure of 40 psi (275 kPa) or less. Shake excess water from element and allow it to air dry (requires 24 hours or longer). Protect from freezing.

IMPORTANT: Never wash a dry element in fuel oil, gasoline, or solvent. Never use compressed air to dry the element.

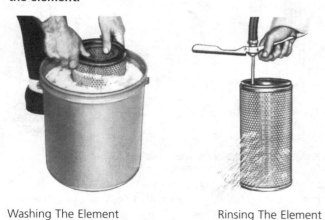

Washing The Element   Rinsing The Element

Fig. 15 — Washing and Rinsing the Dry Element

After cleaning the element, inspect it for damage by placing a light inside it. Discard any element that shows the slightest damage.

Inspect filter element gasket for damage. Replace element if gasket is damaged or missing.

IMPORTANT: Replace the filter element:

*   **If damaged.**

*   **After a recommended service period (such as one year or six washings).**

*   **When attempts to clean it fail.**

Thoroughly clean inside of cleaner body with a clean, damp cloth. Install element in cleaner body, gasket and fin end first. Be sure gasket is in place.

Draw cover tight on cleaner. *Reset restriction indicator (if used).*

Servicing Secondary Element

Some large engines have a secondary element in case the primary element ruptures and fails. Normally these elements are not cleaned, only replaced once each season. However, check the condition of the secondary element during service. If it is very dirty, the primary element has probably failed and both elements must be replaced to maintain efficient engine operation.

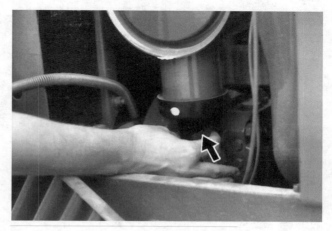

Fig. 16 — Dry Air Cleaner Dust Unloading Valve

Servicing Dust Unloading Valve (If Used)

Every 10 hours, inspect rubber dust unloading valve (if used) (Fig. 16). Squeeze the rubber end of the valve to make sure it is still open and free of clogging. Be sure valve closes when engine is running. This prevents dirt from being sucked into the engine through the valve. Clean the valve if necessary. Replace if cracked or worn.

Checking Air Cleaner Connections

Every 500 hours of operation, make a general check of all connections from the air cleaner to the engine (Fig. 17). Remove the hood or cowl if necessary. Tighten any clamps on hoses or tubes to prevent dirty air from entering engine through loose connections.

This concludes our air cleaner service story. Remember that dry air cleaners are as effective as oil bath types, but they do require careful handling and more inspection for breaks or holes which could allow dirty air to harm the engine.

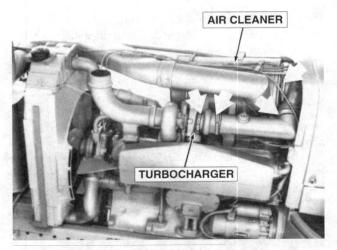

Fig. 17 — Checking Air Cleaner Connections

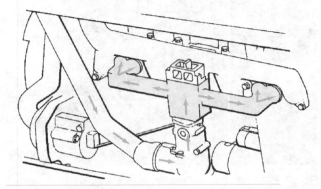

Fig. 18 — Typical Intake Manifold (Spark-Ignition Engines)

INTAKE MANIFOLD

On gasoline engines, the fuel-air mixture is carried from the carburetor to the engine intake valves by the manifold (Fig. 18).

Diesel engine intake manifolds are similar to spark ignition engine manifolds except that they do not require heat (to vaporize fuel) and are usually located on the side of the engine opposite the exhaust manifold.

LP-gas fuel vaporizes at normal temperatures so a mixing valve and converter are used instead of a carburetor.

Even though heat transfer from the exhaust manifold is not required to vaporize fuel, a similar intake system (following the carburetor) can be used for LP-gas as for gasoline systems.

Fig. 18 illustrates a typical gasoline engine manifold. Heat is supplied either by having the exhaust manifold touch the intake manifold at various spots or by having exhaust passages built into the intake manifold.

SERVICING INTAKE MANIFOLDS

Every 50 hours, tighten the bolts and check the intake manifold for restrictions or air leaks.

TURBOCHARGERS

The power delivered by an internal combustion engine is determined by the amount of fuel and air which can be compressed into each cylinder. The more the fuel-air mixture, the more power the engine develops.

The **turbocharger** is a type of air pump and gives the engine a higher overall compression pressure than it would normally have (Fig. 19).

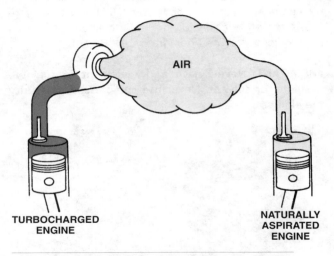

Fig. 19 — Turbocharger Compress More Air into Engine for Greater Combustion and Power

It does this by taking intake air, compressing it, and forcing it into the engine cylinders (Fig. 20).

Pumping air into an engine also aids in getting exhaust gases out. This too results in more efficient combustion.

Some engines are designed and built for turbocharging. If an engine is not equipped with a turbocharger, it may be damaged if one is added. Be sure to check with your dealer before you try to turbocharge an engine yourself.

SERVICING TURBOCHARGERS

IMPORTANT: Turbochargers operate at speeds of 40,000 to 130,000 rpm or more. This means they must have adequate lubrication at all times and air must be clean to avoid excessive wear.

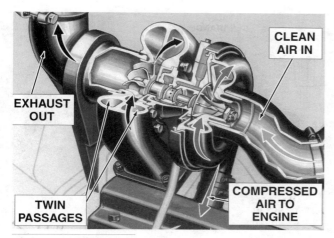

Fig. 20 — A Turbocharger

IMPORTANT: Clean air is vital to turbochargers as dirty air can pit the rotary vanes and alter its balance.

Periodically make the following inspections:

1. Inspect the mounting and connections of the turbocharger to be certain they are secure and there is no leakage of oil or air.

2. Check the engine crankcase vent to be sure there is no restriction to air flow.

3. Operate the engine at approximate rated output and listen for unusual turbocharger noise. If a shrill whine (other than normal) is heard, stop the engine immediately. The whine means that the bearings are about to fail. Have the turbocharger removed for inspection.

Do not confuse the normal whine heard during "run down" as the engine stops with a bearing failure during operation.

Other unusual turbocharger noises could mean improper clearance between the turbine wheel and housing. In these cases, a serviceman should remove the turbocharger for inspection.

4. Check the turbocharger for unusual vibration while engine is operating at rated output. If necessary, have the turbocharger removed for inspection.

5. Check engine under load conditions. Excessive exhaust smoke indicates an incorrect fuel-air mixture. This could be due to engine overload or turbocharger malfunction.

INTAKE AND EXHAUST VALVES

The valves let fuel and air in and exhaust gases out of each engine cylinder during the combustion cycle.

OPERATION OF VALVES

You, as a machine operator, should understand how the intake and exhaust **valves** work.

The engine must take in fuel-air and expel spent gases at precise intervals. The *valves* do this job by opening and closing the intake and exhaust ports to the cylinder.

The sequence of valve operation for a typical fourstroke cycle engine is shown in Fig. 21. Each cylinder has two valves-intake and exhaust.

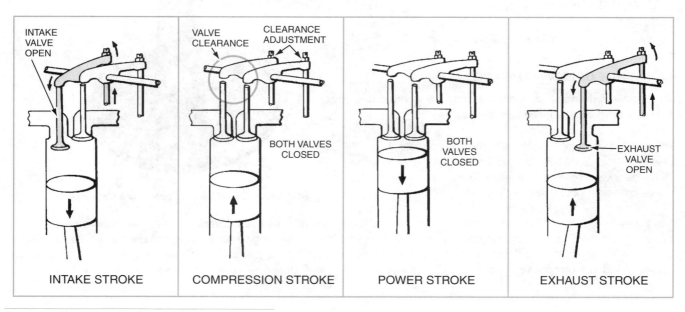

Fig. 21 — Valve Operation in a Four-Stroke Cycle Engine

1. During the intake stroke, the intake valve opens as shown, allowing the fuel-air mixture to enter the combustion chamber.

2. During compression and power strokes, both valves are closed to seal in the combustible mixture,

3. During the exhaust stroke, the exhaust valve opens, allowing gases to be exhausted.

4. At the end of the exhaust stroke, the intake valve opens, beginning another cycle.

The camshaft (Fig. 22) is turned by the engine crankshaft. A lobe (cam) on the camshaft causes the cam follower and push rod to push the valve open. The spring closes the valve when the cam allows the push rod and cam follower to return to the low side of the cam. Cam movements are designed to open or close the valves at the right moment.

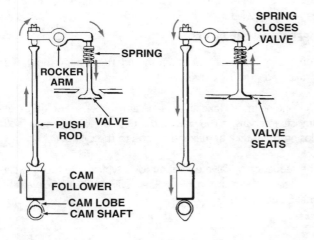

Fig. 22 — Typical Valve Operating Mechanism

IMPORTANCE OF VALVE CLEARANCE

If proper valve maintenance is not performed, the engine will not work efficiently and may be damaged.

When valves are properly adjusted, there is normally a small clearance between the valve stem and the end of the rocker arm (This clearance is sometimes referred to as "valve clearance," "valve lash" or "tappet clearance.")

Valve clearance allows for the heat expansion of valve operating parts. Without clearance, the heated parts would cause the valves to stay partly open during operation and engine would lose compression and power (Fig. 23).

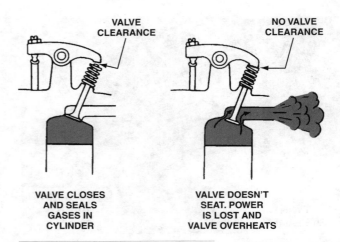

Fig. 23 — Importance of Valve Clearance

This valve clearance is small, varying from approximately 0.006 inch to 0.030 inch (0. 15 to 0.75 mm). The engine manufacturer recommends a definite clearance for each engine model. The valve clearance may vary, depending on the engine model and whether the engine should be hot or cold during adjustment (some engines run hotter than others).

Too little valve clearance throws the valves out of time. This causes valves to open too early and close too late. Also, valve stems may lengthen from heating and prevent valves from seating completely (Fig. 23). Hot combustion gases rushing past the valves cause overheating because the valves seat so briefly or so poorly that normal heat transfer into the cooling system does not have time to take place. This causes burned valves (Fig. 24).

Fig. 24 — Valve Burned from too Little Valve Clearance

Too much valve clearance causes a lag in valve timing which throws the engine-out of balance. The fuel-air mixture is late entering the cylinder during the intake stroke. The exhaust valve closes early and prevents waste gases from being completely removed.

The valves themselves also become damaged. When valve clearance is properly adjusted, the camshaft slows the speed of valve movement as it closes. But with too much clearance, the valves close with great impact, cracking or breaking the valve (Fig. 25) and scuffing the cam and follower.

IMPACT BREAK

Starting Point of Break

Fig. 25 — Valve Broken from too Much Valve Clearance

Summary: Why Proper Valve Adjustment Is Important
- *The engine will use fuel more efficiently.*
- *The engine will start more easily.*
- *Maximum power will be achieved.*
- *Valves will give longer service.*
- *Overheating of the engine is less likely to occur.*

TOOLS AND MATERIALS NEEDED

To make valve clearance adjustments, the following is needed:

1. Set of box-end wrenches (inch or metric, as required).

2. Set of open-end wrenches (inch or metric, as required).

3. Spark plug wrench (inch or metric, as required).

4. Feeler gauge (inch or metric, as required).

5. Torque wrench and socket set (inch or metric, as required).

6. Screwdriver

7. Clean cloths

8. Bucket of cleaning solvent (*not* gasoline).

9. Container for nuts and cap screws.

10. New gasket to replace old valve cover gasket.

PREPARING FOR VALVE TAPPET ADJUSTMENTS

Check valve tappet adjustments every 2000 hours of operation, or at intervals indicated in your operator's manual. Before adjustments can be made, you must determine how you are going to make them. Some manufacturers recommend that valve adjustments be made by an authorized dealer or trained mechanic. Read your operators manual, or obtain a technical service manual for your engine for step-by-step procedures. Many agricultural engines are enclosed under fuel tanks and engine shrouds. Often these parts must be removed before the valve cover or rocker arm cover can be removed to obtain access to the valves (Fig. 27).

NOTE: If you are adjusting valves for the first time, have someone help you, or practice on an older engine or a small engine until you become proficient.

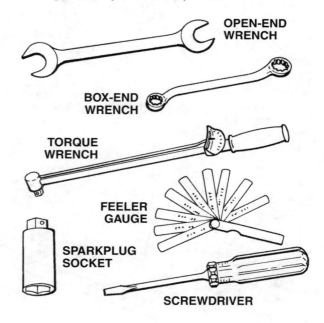

OPEN-END WRENCH

BOX-END WRENCH

TORQUE WRENCH

FEELER GAUGE

SPARKPLUG SOCKET

SCREWDRIVER

Fig. 26 — Tools Needed for Adjusting Valve Tappet Clearances

Let's assume that you must remove parts which interfere with removal of the valve cover.

1. Remove parts as necessary (Fig. 27).

2. Clean dirt from the valve cover and from around the spark plugs.

3. Remove the nuts or cap screws which hold the cover in place.

4. Carefully remove the valve cover (Fig. 28). Strike the cover on one side and then on the other with the palm of your hand. Don't worry about damaging the gasket because you should replace it with a new one each time the cover is removed.

 CAUTION: If these precautions are not followed, the engine could start during valve adjustment and cause serious injury to you.

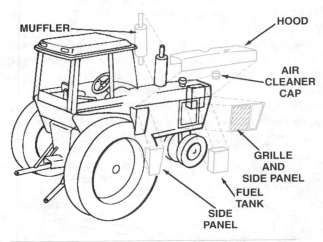

Fig. 27 — Parts that May Need to be Removed Before Valve Cover is Removed

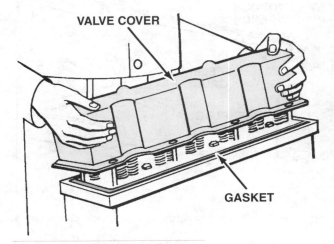

Fig. 28 — Removing Engine Valve Cover

5. To prevent accidental starting of the engine during valve adjustment, take the following precautions:

   a. Disconnect the center terminal wire to the distributor (Fig. 29).

   b. OR, remove spark plugs.

   With *diesel engines,* shut off the fuel supply to the injection pump.

ADJUSTING VALVE TAPPET CLEARANCE

Since most manufacturers recommend that the valve clearance adjustment be made when the engine is stopped, we will cover procedures for adjusting valves with the engine cold. Refer to your operator's manual for recommendations.

Unless your operator's manual gives a shortcut, you must rotate the engine crankshaft each time a different pair of valves is to be adjusted. We will show adjustment of valves using this method, which works for all engines.

1. **Retorque Cylinder Head**

   Check the tightness of the cylinder head nuts or bolts with a torque wrench (Fig. 30). Refer to the operator's manual or service manual to determine the proper torque to apply and the sequence. Do this *before* adjusting valves because valve clearance may be changed if you tighten the head after adjustment of the valve clearance.

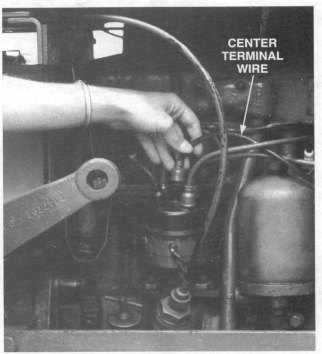

Fig. 29 — Disconnecting Center Terminal Wire to the Distributor

2. **Set No. 1 Cylinder At TDC**

   Turn the crankshaft slowly until piston in number one cylinder is at top dead center (TDC) of its compression stroke. Use one of the methods described below to determine this position. Usually, the number one cylinder is next to the radiator on vertical engines, or next to the flywheel on horizontal engines.

To rotate the crankshaft use one of the following methods: "Bump" the engine with the starter, turn the crankshaft with a special tool, or if the spark plugs are removed, you may be able to turn the fan enough to rotate the crankshaft.

With the piston in the correct position (TDC) of the compression stroke, both the intake and exhaust valves are closed. The cam followers are riding on low sides of the cam lobes.

There are two methods for determining when number one piston is at TDC of compression stroke:

a. *For both spark-ignition and diesel engines,* you can proceed as follows:

Refer to your operator's manual to determine correct timing marks. Several markings may be present. As you turn the crankshaft to top dead center (TDC), watch the intake valve on he number one cylinder. When it closes, turn the crankshaft one-half turn. The TDC mark should be in line with the pointer. Check both the intake and exhaust rocker arms of cylinder number four (or number six if a six-cylinder engine). Both arms should be "rocking" (exhaust valve closing and intake valve opening) when the number one piston is at TDC.

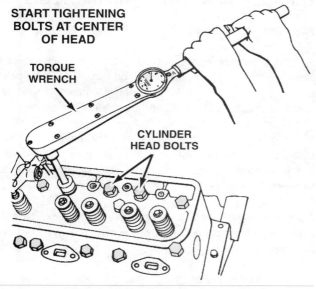

START TIGHTENING BOLTS AT CENTER OF HEAD

TORQUE WRENCH

CYLINDER HEAD BOLTS

Fig. 30 — Tightening Cylinder Head Bolts Before Adjusting Valves

b. *For spark-ignition engines only,* you can proceed as follows:

To prevent engine from starting, remove spark plugs. Be sure the coil wire is inserted into the center of the distributor. Position number one spark plug wire about 1/4 inch from the engine block. Turn the crankshaft slowly until a spark jumps the gap.

Place your thumb over the spark plug opening and crank the engine until you reach the end of the compression stroke-when no further pressure is felt. The piston should now be at TDC. (A special whistle can also be used. By inserting it in No. 1 cylinder port, a whistle is heard when TDC is reached.)

3. **Select Feeler Gauge**

Select the correct feeler gauge thickness according to your operator's manual. Both the intake and exhaust valves may require the same clearance; however, on some engines the exhaust valve requires more clearance than the intake valve because it normally runs hotter.

4. **Check Clearance With Feeler Gauge**

Insert the gauge between the valve stem and the rocker arm of both valves (Fig. 31). If the two valves require different clearances, be certain to identify which valve is the exhaust and which is the intake. Your operator's manual or technical manual will show this.

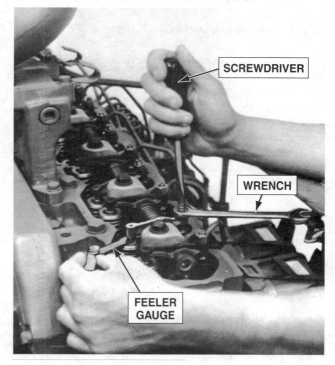

SCREWDRIVER

WRENCH

FEELER GAUGE

Fig. 31 — Adjusting Valve Clearance

As you slide the gauge in and out of the clearance, you should feel a slight drag if the gap is correct. Check with the next size thicker and thinner gauges. The thicker gauge should be difficult to insert, and the thinner gauge should be easy to insert.

If the clearances are correct, proceed with step 8.

If the clearance requires adjusting, proceed with the steps that follow.

5. **Adjust Two Valves**

   a. Loosen the lock nuts on the two rocker arm adjusting screws (Fig. 31).

   b. Turn adjusting screws until feeler gauge slips with a slight drag.

   c. Hold the adjusting screws from turning and tighten the lock nuts. Recheck the clearance as described in step 4. You may have to readjust the clearance.

6. **Determine Which Cylinder Fires Next**

   The firing order will tell you this. Usually the firing order appears on the side of the engine. If it does not, refer to your operator's manual. Fig. 32 shows the firing order for most agricultural engines.

7. **Set Next Cylinder At TDC**

   Turn the crankshaft until the next cylinder to fire is at top of its compression stroke. With 2- and 4-cylinder engines, turn the crankshaft one-half turn. With a 6-cylinder engine, turn the crankshaft one-third turn. (On 8-cylinder engines turn one-fourth turn.) Fig. 32 shows that this much rotation will bring the next piston into correct position.

8. **Adjust Valve Clearance**

   Adjust valve clearance following the same procedures as used on the number one cylinder.

9. **Set Remaining Valve Clearances**

   Proceed in the same manner as above with the remaining cylinders, rotating the engine for each pair of valves.

NOTE: For 8-cylinder engines, the firing order is 1-8-4-3-6-5-7-2. These engines, such as V-8's, can normally be adjusted as follows: Place engine in No. 1 TDC position. Then adjust the following valves. Exhaust-1, 3, 4, 8. Intake-1, 2, 5, 7. Crank the engine one revolution , to No. 6 TDC position, then adjust all remaining valves: Exhaust-2, 5, 6, 7. Intake-3, 4, 6, 8.

REASSEMBLY AFTER VALVE ADJUSTMENTS

1. Clean and install spark plugs (see page 107).

2. Before installing valve cover, start engine to check lubrication of rocker arms. You may have to install some of the parts you removed if they are required to run the engine. Be certain an ample supply of oil is being delivered to all rocker arms. If your operator's manual recommends that you check the valve clearances again with the engine thoroughly heated, do this now. A different set of clearances must be used because as the engine heats, the valve stems lengthen and less clearance is needed.

3. Position new gasket on the cylinder head.

4. Install valve cover. Be certain that the gasket fits properly under the edges of the valve cover or oil will leak by and increase oil consumption.

5. Install all remaining parts.

EXHAUST MANIFOLDS AND MUFFLERS

EXHAUST MANIFOLDS

Exhaust manifolds receive burned gases from each cylinder and carry them away from the engine (Fig. 33). Some heat from the exhaust manifold on gasoline engines is used to maintain the intake manifold at the proper temperature.

The exhaust ports in the engine and the passages in the exhaust manifold are large to allow free flow and expansion of the hot escaping gases. This is important because it permits better removal of gases or scavenging of the engine cylinders.

Note: Usually the number one cylinder is next to the radiator on vertical engines, or next to the flywheel on horizontal engines.

If any burned gases are left in the cylinders following the exhaust stroke, the amount of fuel-air mixture which can be taken in on the next intake stroke is limited. This reduces engine power and increases fuel consumption.

The only maintenance required for the exhaust manifold is to keep the attaching bolts tight (check every 500 hours).

MUFFLERS

There are two common types of mufflers:

- **Straight-through**
- **Reverse-flow**

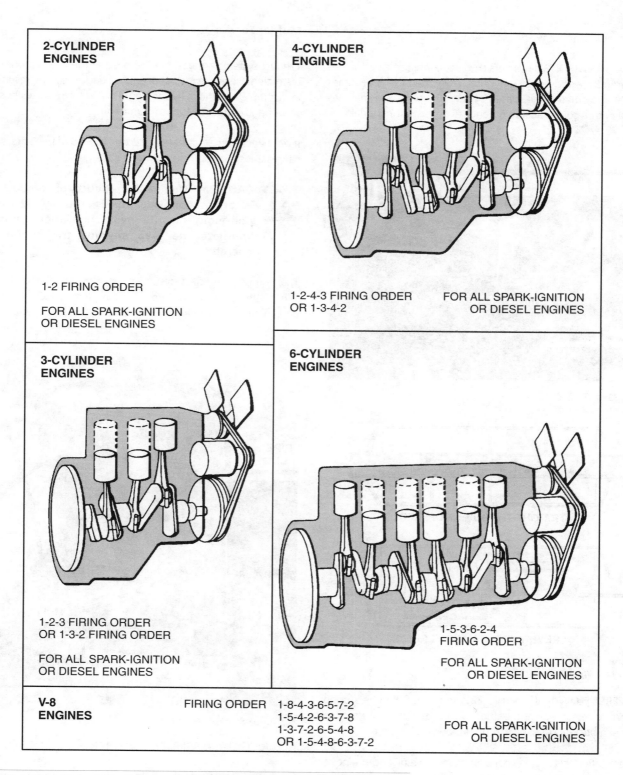

2-CYLINDER ENGINES

1-2 FIRING ORDER

FOR ALL SPARK-IGNITION OR DIESEL ENGINES

4-CYLINDER ENGINES

1-2-4-3 FIRING ORDER OR 1-3-4-2

FOR ALL SPARK-IGNITION OR DIESEL ENGINES

3-CYLINDER ENGINES

1-2-3 FIRING ORDER OR 1-3-2 FIRING ORDER

FOR ALL SPARK-IGNITION OR DIESEL ENGINES

6-CYLINDER ENGINES

1-5-3-6-2-4 FIRING ORDER

FOR ALL SPARK-IGNITION OR DIESEL ENGINES

V-8 ENGINES

FIRING ORDER 1-8-4-3-6-5-7-2
1-5-4-2-6-3-7-8
1-3-7-2-6-5-4-8
OR 1-5-4-8-6-3-7-2

FOR ALL SPARK-IGNITION OR DIESEL ENGINES

Fig. 32 — Firing Order 2-, 3-, 4-, 6-, and 8-Cylinder Engines (For Modern Farm Machines)

Let's look at these types.

STRAIGHT-THROUGH mufflers (Fig. 34) consist of a perforated inner pipe enclosed by an outer pipe roughly three times larger in diameter. The space between the pipes is sometimes filled with a sound-absorbing and heat-resistant material.

Fig. 33 — Exhaust Manifold

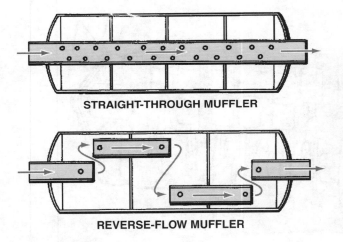

Fig. 34 — Two Types of Mufflers

REVERSE-FLOW mufflers (Fig. 33) are hollow chambers using short pieces of pipe and baffles to force the exhaust gases to travel a back-and-forth path before being discharged.

The muffler acts as an expansion chamber, reducing the noise of the spent gases. It also serves as a spark arrester, to reduce fire hazards when operating near combustible material.

Muffler Service

Exhaust systems are designed to provide the least amount of restriction. Excessive restrictions cause back-pressure, resulting in incomplete cylinder scavenging. This, in turn, causes loss of power and increased fuel consumption.

It has been estimated that each 2 psi (14 kPa) of back pressure causes a loss of about four engine horsepower.

 CAUTION: One of the products of combustion is carbon monoxide. This is a deadly, odorless, poisonous gas. To avoid inhalation of gas, ventilate the area anytime the engine is operating.

The complete exhaust system must also be free of leaks. When they do occur, repair them immediately. This is particularly true when the engine is in a machine equipped with a cab or other enclosure.

Fig. 35 — Spark-Arresting Muffler

CLEANING SPARK-ARRESTING MUFFLERS

Spark-arresting mufflers should be cleaned every 50 hours of operation. Park the machine in an area where the possibility of fire is not a hazard.

Remove pipe plug from muffler (Fig. 35) to provide an outlet for loosened particles and start the engine. Run the engine from slow to fast idle two or three times to blow out deposits.

Stop engine and replace plug.

WEATHER CAPS FOR MUFFLERS

Some engines have a hinged cap on the muffler or exhaust pipe which closes when the engine stops to protect against rain and weather. Rain water can rust the engine valves or damage the turbocharger. Check frequently to see that the cap opens fully when the engine starts and closes tightly when it shuts off. A cap that doesn't open can cause excessive heat that can burn the hood.

CRANKCASE VENTILATION

During normal operation, unburned fuel vapor and water vapor are created in the engine. If allowed to condense, these vapors become contaminating liquids that drain into he crankcase. The purpose of the ventilation systems is to circulate fresh air through the engine to carry away these harmful vapors.

Fig. 36 — Crankcase Vent Tube

As with all ventilating systems, the must be:

- *An air inlet*
- *An air and vapor outlet*
- *A means of circulating air between the two*

The most common types of crankcase ventilation are: oil filler caps, vent tubes, manifold vent, and circulating pump systems.

OIL FILLER CAP VENT

The oil filler cap is probably the most common inlet. A small air cleaner built into the cap filters the air as it is drawn into the system. Some systems use the main air cleaner as the inlet.

CRANKCASE VENT TUBES

The use of a vent tube is one means of circulating the air through the system (Fig. 36). As the machine moves, the air moving past the tube opening creates a lower pressure than that at the breather. Air in the engine naturally flows to this low pressure area, and the tube becomes an outlet for the system. Some vent tubes use a wire mesh screen to filter oil particles out of the vapor.

INTAKE MANIFOLD VENT

On some engines, the intake manifold circulates the air and is also the vent outlet. In this type of ventilation system a tube connects the crankcase to the intake manifold. The intake vacuum draws the air through the engine, into the manifold, then into the cylinders, and out the exhaust system. A ventilation valve is used to regulate the flow of air into the manifold.

VENT SYSTEM WITH CIRCULATING PUMP

Another type of system uses a vane or impeller pump circulate the air. The air is taken from the main air cleaner and pumped through the engine. The outlet can be either a vent tube or the intake manifold.

AIR EMISSION CONTROLS

Future developments will probably mean that more agricultural engines will have pollution control devices which route crankcase vapors back to the carburetor or manifold for burning. This will reduce the emission of raw vapors into the atmosphere.

SERVICING THE VENTILATION SYSTEM

Every 50 hours, service the ventilation system. Begin with the inlet. If the oil filler cap is the inlet, clean it with a solvent. If the main air cleaner is the inlet, service it regularly as recommended by the engine manufacturer.

If the system uses a ventilating valve, service it regularly. Some manufacturers recommend cleaning the valve with solvent, while others recommend replacing the valve rather than cleaning it.

If a vent tube is used in the system (Fig. 36), periodically remove and clean it with a solvent. If a filter is used with the vent tube, be sure to clean it, too.

Keeping the engine clean and free of caked-on dirt and oil also helps in crankcase ventilation and general engine cooling.

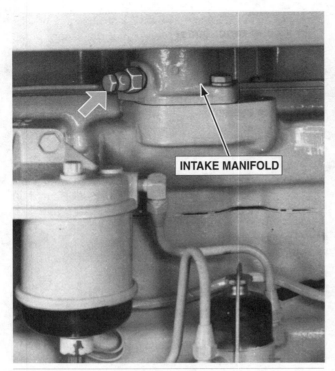

Fig. 37 — Manometer or Gauge Connection Point (Diesel Engine)

Fig. 38 — Testing Manifold Depression With a Vacuum Gauge (Spark-Ignition Engine)

TESTING AIR INTAKE SYSTEM

When the air flow into the engine is restricted, there is more vacuum or suction in the cylinders. This can cause oil to be drawn in around the valve stems and pistons and so increase oil consumption.

Complete air cleaner service will usually correct the air flow restriction to the engine. However, if a restriction is still suspected, use the tests which follow.

INTAKE VACUUM TEST (DIESEL ENGINES)

Test as follows:

1. Warm up the engine.

2. Connect the gauge to the intake manifold (Fig. 37).

3. Set engine speed at fast idle and note the reading on the gauge. *Too high a reading means that there is a restriction in the air intake system.* Check the engine technical manual for correct specifications.

4. If a restriction is shown by this test, have a serviceman inspect the engine.

MANIFOLD DEPRESSION TEST (SPARK-IGNITION ENGINES)

Use a vacuum gauge calibrated in inches of mercury to perform this test.

1. Connect the vacuum gauge to the intake manifold (Fig. 38).

2. Warm up the engine and operate it at idle speed.

3. Note the reading on the vacuum gauge. Check the engine technical manual for exact specifications.

4. Interpret the gauge reading as given below.

Judging Test Results

- *If the reading is steady and low,* loss of power in all cylinders is indicated. Possible causes are late ignition, bad valve timing or loss of compression at valves or piston rings. A leaky carburetor gasket will also cause a low reading.

- *If the needle fluctuates steadily,* a partial or complete loss of power in one or more cylinders is indicated. This can be due to an ignition defect, or loss of compression due to stuck piston rings or a leaky cylinder head gasket.

- *Intermittent needle fluctuation* indicates occasional loss of power due to an ignition defect or a sticking valve.

- *Slow needle fluctuation* is usually caused by improper carburetor idle mixture adjustment.

- *A gradual drop in the gauge reading* at idle engine speed indicates back pressure in the exhaust system due to a restriction.

Be very careful in analyzing abnormal readings since the gauge readings can indicate more than one thing. An air cleaner restriction is the most common cause, but this should be corrected before making the above test. If a problem still exists, have a serviceman inspect the engine.

Fig. 39 — Checking Engine Compression With a Pressure Gauge

TESTING ENGINE COMPRESSION

Weak compression results in loss of horsepower and poor engine performance. This is even more true in diesel engines, which depend upon the heat of compression to ignite the fuel in the cylinders.

If you suspect a compression loss, check the engine compression as follows:

1. Warm up the engine to operating temperature and then shut off the engine.

2. Remove the spark plugs or injection nozzles.

3. Connect a pressure gauge to the cylinder port (Fig. 39).

4. On **spark-ignition engines,** be sure that both carburetor throttle and choke valves are in the wide open position. Disconnect the ignition coil-to-distributor wire at the distributor. Ground the wire by placing it in contact with some part of the engine.

5. On **diesel engines,** the air intake system has no throttle valve, so merely be sure that the engine speed control is in the "stop" position.

6. Turn the engine with the starter until the pressure gauge registers no further rise in pressure. It is a good practice to count the number of compression strokes (indicated by movement of the gauge needle) and check each cylinder with the same number of strokes. The engine must be at full cranking speed to get a good reading.

7. Check the pressure reading against the engine technical manual.

8. If the compression is very low, apply oil to the ring area of the piston through the openings. Do not use too much oil to avoid getting oil on the valves. Then check the compression again.

9. Judge the compression readings as given below.

JUDGING COMPRESSION READINGS

All cylinder pressures should be about the same-this is most important. Variations are usually limited to about 10 percent of the full reading.

If compression is too low, the engine must be reconditioned before a tune-up can be effective.

If compression in one cylinder is higher than the others, the other cylinders need reconditioning.

Altitude affects compression pressures. Normally there is about a 4 percent loss for every 1000 feet (300 m) of altitude above sea level. Pressures given are normally for about 1000 feet (300 m) above sea level.

Compression pressures are affected by the **cranking speed** of the engine. Therefore, be sure the batteries are in good condition and fully charged when making a compression test.

If it appears that engine service is needed, take the engine to a qualified serviceman for inspection.

TEST YOURSELF

QUESTIONS

1. Place an I by the parts of the Intake system, an E by the parts of the Exhaust system, an N by the parts that are Not a part of either system, and a B by parts of Both systems.

   a._____ muffler   d._____ air cleaner
   b._____ gasoline   e._____ manifold
   c._____ turbocharger   f._____ carburetor

2. The intake system supplies the engine with clean air of proper (quantity) (temperature) (mixture) (all of these) .

3. Which of the following does not apply to dry element air cleaners?
   a. Clean off outside of element With an air hose.
   b. Tap element on a hard surface to remove surface dust.
   c. Wash element in any good detergent.
   d. Use compressed air to dry element.

4. Match the items below:
   A. Too little valve clearance.
   B. Too much valve clearance

   1. Will cause cracking or breaking of the valve.
   2. Will cause the valves to burn.

5. (Fill in blank.) During the_____stroke you can measure the valve clearance.

6. The valve clearance for intake and exhaust valves would need to be checked in the operator's manual since they may be different.
   True _____   False _____

7. Air cleaners may contain oil.
   True _____   False _____

8. What is the firing order for a 4-cylinder engine?

9. (Fill in blank.) If you identified the end of the compression stroke on an engine, you would say the cylinder is at _____.

10. (Fill in blanks.) What are the two types of mufflers?_____ and_____.

ENGINE FUEL
SYSTEMS

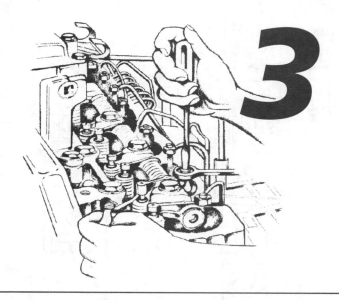

3

INTRODUCTION

Dirt and water are the major enemies of the engine fuel system.

However, today's engines need quality fuels and these fuels will remain reasonably clean if handled properly.

In addition, good maintenance will help keep the fuel system free of dirt and water and will guarantee longer life and smoother operation.

HOW ENGINES USE FUELS

Gasoline, diesel and LP-Gas engines require fuels with certain qualities. This is because of the difference the way the fuel is ignited in each type.

If you're not familiar with the major types of engines and how they use fuels, study Figs. 2 and 3. They show the operating principles of spark-ignition (carburetor) and diesel engines.

In the FOUR-STROKE CYCLE engine (Fig. 2), the are four strokes of the piston, two up and two down, during each cycle. Then it starts over again on another cycle of the same four strokes. This cycle occurs during *two* revolutions of the crankshaft. Most engines today operate on the four-stroke cycle.

Gasoline and diesel engines ignite their fuel in different ways as shown in Fig. 3.

Fig. 1 — Modern Engines Require Quality Fuels from a Clean Source

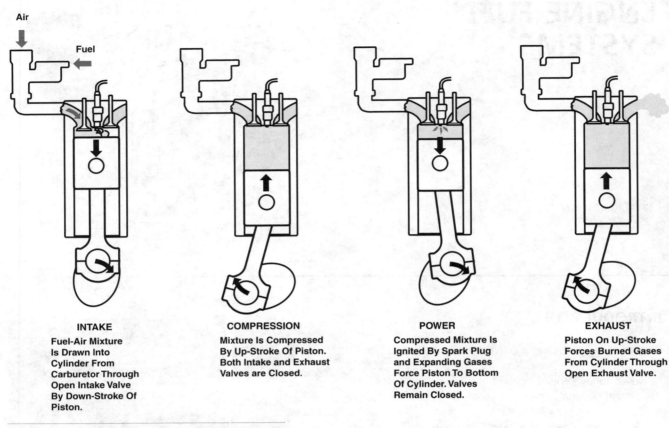

INTAKE

Fuel-Air Mixture Is Drawn Into Cylinder From Carburetor Through Open Intake Valve By Down-Stroke Of Piston.

COMPRESSION

Mixture Is Compressed By Up-Stroke Of Piston. Both Intake and Exhaust Valves are Closed.

POWER

Compressed Mixture Is Ignited By Spark Plug and Expanding Gases Force Piston To Bottom Of Cylinder. Valves Remain Closed.

EXHAUST

Piston On Up-Stroke Forces Burned Gases From Cylinder Through Open Exhaust Valve.

Fig. 2 — How a Four-Stroke Cycle Gasoline Engine Works

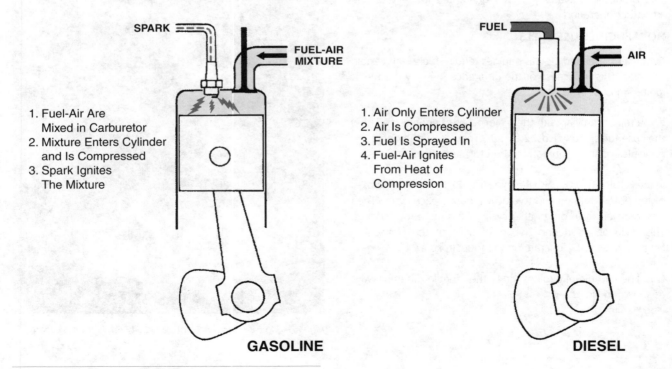

1. Fuel-Air Are Mixed in Carburetor
2. Mixture Enters Cylinder and Is Compressed
3. Spark Ignites The Mixture

GASOLINE

1. Air Only Enters Cylinder
2. Air Is Compressed
3. Fuel Is Sprayed In
4. Fuel-Air Ignites From Heat of Compression

DIESEL

Fig. 3 — Spark-Ignition (Gasoline) and Diesel Engines Compared

COMPRESSION RATIOS AND OCTANE RATINGS OF SPARK-IGNITION FUELS

Fuel	Engine Compression Ratio (approx).	Approx. Octane No.	
Kerosene, No. 1 fuel oil*	4.0 to 1	0- 30	(Motor Method)
"Farm Tractor Fuel"**	4.7 to 1	45- 70	(Motor Method)
Gasoline (low grade)	5.0- 6.0 to 1	70- 75	(Research Method)
Gasoline (regular)	7.0- 8.5 to 1	88- 94	(Research Method)
Gasoline (premium)***	9.0-10.0 to 1	About 100	(Research Method)
LP-Gas: Butane	7.8 to 1	95-100	(Research Method)
Propane	8.75 to 1	110-115	(Research Method)

*Well adapted to magneto ignition because of longer spark duration.

**Standard name used in place of a number of other terms such as: distillate or power fuel.

***Not normally used in farm and industrial machines.

In **gasoline engines,** fuel and air are mixed *outside* the cylinders, in the carburetor and manifold. The mixture is forced in due to the partial vacuum of the pistons' intake stroke.

In *diesel engines,* there is no premixing of air and fuel outside the cylinders. Air only is drawn through the intake manifold and compressed in the cylinders. Fuel is then sprayed into the cylinder and mixed with air as the piston nears the top of its compression stroke.

Gasoline engines use an electric spark to ignite the fuel-air mixture, while diesels use the heat of the compressed air for ignition.

COMPRESSION AND FUELS

Compression ratio is the total volume inside the engine cylinder when the piston is at the bottom of its stroke, compared to the volume when the piston is at the top-closest to the cylinder head (Fig. 4). Note that a common compression ratio for gasoline engines is 8-1, while a 16-1 ratio is common for diesels.

Each fuel has limits on how much it can be compressed and still burn properly. *The fuel required for each type of engine is governed by the compression ratio of the engine.* Fuel is formulated according to the design of the engine in which it is to be used.

The table at right gives the compression ratios and octane ratings expected with modern fuels. The cetane number or ratings of diesel fuels are a measure of the fuel's ignition value and are a prime factor in fuel-engine performance.

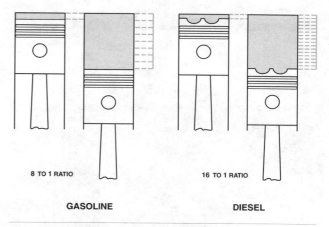

8 TO 1 RATIO — 16 TO 1 RATIO

GASOLINE — DIESEL

Fig. 4 — Compression Ratios Compared for Gasoline and Diesel Engines

SELECTING FUELS

The selection of fuel for your engine will affect the maintenance required and the performance you can expect. By choosing quality fuels you can be assured that you will get the proper octane or cetane rating plus beneficial additives and clean fuel.

SELECTING FUEL FOR GASOLINE ENGINES

Your assurance of getting a fuel with an adequate anti-knock quality is indicated by its bold type number rating. The operator's manual tells you what the minimum octane rating should be for your engine. Compare it with the octane rating of the fuel supplied by your dealer.

Fuels with the least tendency to knock have higher octane numbers. The names "premium," "regular," and "low-grade" are rough comparative measures of octane ratings. Most farm and industrial machines use regular grade-88 to 94 octane. If your operator's manual recommends an octane number within the regular range, don't use low-grade (70 to 75 octane) fuel. You can use premium-grade gasoline, but there is usually no advantage because most machine engines are not designed (lack the compression ratio) to secure the benefits of the higher octane rating.

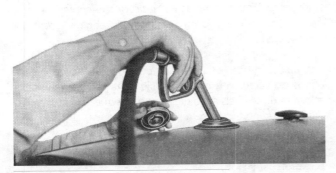

Fig. 5 — Use Only a Good Grade of Gasoline

HEAVY LP-GAS TANK HOLDS HIGH PRESSURES

Fig. 6 — LP-Gas Engines Have High-Pressure Fuel Tanks

Additives have become essential ingredients of modern gasolines. They are used to raise octane number and to combat surface ignition (anti-knock), spark plug fouling, gum formation, rust, carburetor icing, deposits in the intake system, and intake valve sticking.

Gasohol, a mixture of 90 percent unleaded gasoline and 10 percent ethanol (grain alcohol), is available in many areas as a substitute for gasoline. Gasohol burns cleaner and may provide better mileage in motor vehicles compared to straight gasoline. However, some engine manufacturers have not approved of the use of gasohol in certain engines. So, always be sure the fuel is compatible before using it in an engine or the warranty may be voided. Also, in engines used infrequently, water may combine with the alcohol and cause serious corrosion or damage to some engine components.

IMPORTANT: Never use non-leaded gasolines unless your operator's manual specifies they can be used in your machine engine. Non-leaded fuel can damage some agricultural engines.

SELECTING FUEL FOR LP-GAS ENGINES

LP-Gas is short for "liquefied-petroleum gas." It is sometimes indicated as "LPG."

Most LP-Gas used in engines today is all propane or a mixture of mostly propane with some butane.

LP-Gases must be stored and handled in high-pressure containers to keep them in liquid form (Fig. 6). Butane boils at approximately +33°F (1°C), while propane boils at - 44°F (-42°C). When confined to a closed container, the pressure varies with the outside temperature. Butane develops pressure of 37 psi (255 kPa) at 100OF (38°C), while propane develops pressure of 195 psi (1350 kPa) at the same temperature.

An LP-Gas engine is similar to a gasoline engine, but the LP-Gas engine is designed with a higher compression ratio about 7.8:1 to as high as 10:1. Also, LP-Gases have a high octane rating ranging from about 95 for butane to as high as 125 for propane.

There is very little that can be done about,selecting LP-Gas fuel except to deal with a reliable distributor. You are entirely dependent on him to supply fuels that are relatively free of sulfur compounds and other contaminants which may cause difficulties such as filter plugging, valve failures, etc. For cold weather operation, your dealer should give you a different blend (more propane) than for warm weather.

SELECTING FUEL FOR DIESEL ENGINES

You may have heard a saying, "Diesel engines will burn anything." It is true that they will burn a wide variety of fuels; in fact, powdered coal was the first fuel used for diesel engines.

From this you may gain the wrong impression-that selecting fuel for your diesel engine is simply supplying anything it will burn; but diesel fuel selection is far more critical than this.

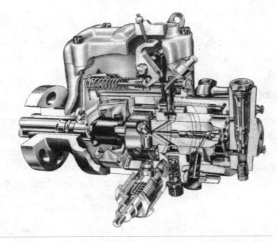

Fig. 7 — Precision Diesel Components Require Clean Fuel

Knowing how a diesel engine works will help you to understand why certain grades of fuel must be used in them. The operating principles for a 4-stroke cycle diesel engine as compared to a gasoline engine are shown in Fig. 3.

Note that there is no spark plug to start the diesel fuel burning. Instead, the air is compressed until it is so hot that fuel injected into it will start burning spontaneously.

The compression ratios for diesel engines are much higher than for spark-ignition engines. This extra compression of the air provides enough heat (900° to 1200°F; 480° to 650°C) so that the fuel is ignited by heat alone when sprayed into the cylinder. Note in Fig. 5 that the compression ratio for a diesel engine is 16:1. This compares with the compression ratios of about 8:1 in gasoline engines.

The average compression ratio for diesel tractors is approximately 16.3:1. The ratios vary from as low as 14:1 to as high as 20:1.

Diesel Fuel Grades

The two major grades of diesel fuels are:

- **No. 1-D Diesel Fuel**

- **No. 2-D Diesel Fuel**

Both fuels (or "fuel oils") are used in high-speed diesel engines on the farm or ranch. Their differences are explained below.

GRADE NO. 1-D FUEL

Grade No. 1 -D is a higher class of *volatile* fuel oils from kerosene to the intermediate distillates. These fuels are for use in high-speed engines with variable loads and speeds, and also for extremely cold weather and high altitude operation.

GRADE NO. 2-D FUEL

Grade No. 2-D is the class of distillate gas oils of *lower volatility*. These fuels are for use in high-speed engines with relatively high loads and more uniform speeds, or in engines not requiring fuels having the higher volatility or other properties specified for Grade No. 1-D.

Remember that engine design and operation materially affect the grade of fuel best suited for an engine.

RECOMMENDED DIESEL FUEL GRADES FOR AGRICULTURAL MACHINES

The following is a typical recommendation from a diesel tractor operator's manual.

Type of Engine Service	Surrounding Air Temperature	Diesel Fuel Grade No.
Light load, low speed, considerable idling.	Above 80°F (25°C) Below 80°F (25°C)	2-D 1-D
Intermediate and heavy load, high speed, minimum of idling.	Above 40°F (5°C) Below 40°F (5°C)	2-D 1-D
At altitudes above 5,000 feet.	All	1-D

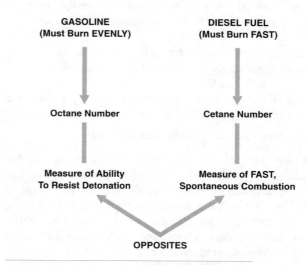

Fig. 8 — Octane and Cetane Numbers are Opposite

Cetane Number

The method of determining the ignition quality of diesel fuel is similar to that used for determining the antiknock quality of gasoline. However, for diesel fuels this is called **cetane number** instead of octane. These qualities are opposites as shown in Fig. 8.

In general, *high-cetane* fuels permit an engine to be started at lower air temperatures, provide faster engine warmup without misfiring, reduce varnish and carbon deposits, and help eliminate engine knock.

However, *too-high cetane* numbers may lead to incomplete combustion and exhaust smoke if the ignition delay period is too short to allow proper mixing of the fuel and air within the combustion space.

Diesel fuels marketed in the United States range from 33 to 64 in cetane number. A typical high-speed engine on a farm tractor or combine calls for diesel fuel with a cetane of "40 minimum." However, higher cetane fuels are specified for some cold weather or high altitude operations.

Knock In Diesel Engines

In **diesel engines,** knock is due to the fuel igniting TOO SLOWLY (Fig. 9). It should start to burn almost as soon as it is injected (A). If there is much delay, a fuel build-up results which burns with explosive force (B) and causes knocking.

By contrast, in **spark-ignition engines,** where the fuel-air charge is mixed and then compressed before ignition takes place, knock is caused by the fuel burning TOO RAPIDLY.

Good diesel fuel provides for early spontaneous burning. By contrast, good gasoline fuels avoid this spontaneous action.

The difference between octane numbers (gasoline) and cetane numbers (diesel fuel) are shown in Fig. 8.

Diesel Fuel Compared With Furnace Fuel

The question is often asked, *"Are diesel fuel and furnace fuel the same?"* It is possible for your fuel supplier to have one fuel that he supplies for both diesel-engine use and heating purposes. Where there is one dominant use, such as home heating compared to limited diesel fuel use, the dealer may not be justified in stocking a separate diesel fuel. So he purchases fuel from his supplier to meet the specifications for both fuels. The refiner can meet this demand because the specifications for both fuels are broad enough that they overlap.

If a dealer is supplying big quantities of fuel for both heating and diesel engines, he will normally stock two fuels. In this case the furnace oils usually contain more of the heavy cracked distillates which are quite satisfactory for furnaces, *but are not suitable for diesel engines* (especially with light intermittent loads) and do not generally meet standards.

FUEL AND COLD WEATHER STARTING

The higher the cetane number, the easier your engine will start on diesel fuel. However, in very cold weather, some diesel engines need a starting aid such as ether which has a cetane rating of 85 to 96 and is highly volatile (Fig. 10). Cylinder block heaters and manifold air heaters are other cold weather starting aids.

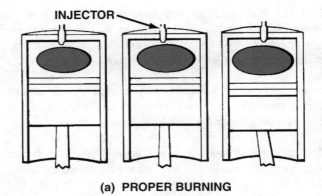

(a) PROPER BURNING

(Fuel Charge Ignites Early and Burns Evenly To Overcome Knocking)

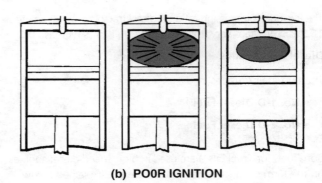

(b) POOR IGNITION

(Ignition Of Fuel Charge Is Delayed, Followed By A Small Explosion)

Fig. 9 — In Diesel Engines Knock is Due to Fuel Igniting too Slowly

IMPORTANT: Spray ether into an engine ONLY while cranking with the starter. Ether is highly explosive and can damage the engine if too much is sprayed in before cranking.

 CAUTION: Never use ether in a diesel engine equipped with glow plugs or a manifold air heater.

STORING FUELS

The importance of proper fuel storage cannot be stressed too highly. Many engine difficulties can be traced to dirty fuel and fuel that has been in storage too long.

To keep the fuel system in its most efficient condition, keep all dirt, scale, water, and other foreign matter out of the fuel, and avoid storing fuel for a long period of time.

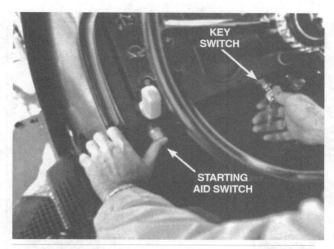

Fig. 10 — Starting a Diesel Engine in Cold Weather Using Ether Starting Fluid

Fig. 10 — Refuel the Machine at the End of Each Day

Fuel should be stored in a convenient place outside of buildings.

Each state has its own laws regarding the handling, storage and use of fuels. It is important that you become acquainted with and obey fuel handling regulations for your own safety and for insurance purposes.

Proper storing and handling of fuels can affect your safety, how easily your machine starts, and how much maintenance your fuel system requires.

A complete discussion of the storage and safe handling of fuels is given in the John Deere Fundamentals of Service (FOS) manual on "Fuels, Lubricants, and Coolants."

SULFUR IN FUEL

Sulfur in fuel will combine with water and form harmful sulfuric acid in engines. Changing oil more often is the best way to remove the acid. Avoiding high sulfur fuel also helps to reduce the acid problem. *In general, NEVER use diesel fuel with a sulfur content greater than one percent.*

REFUELING MACHINES

Proper refueling of your machine is more than just filling the tank with fuel. The time and method of refueling are important because of their influence on:

- **Keeping out moisture**
- **Keeping out dirt**
- **Avoiding fire hazards.**

Most operator's manuals suggest that you *fill the fuel tank at the end of the day or whenever you finish using the machine.* This keeps moisture from accumulating in the tank.

Most water in fuel comes from moisture condensing inside the fuel tank. This is true of all fuels except LP-Gas.

Here is why: As fuel is used, air is drawn in. Much of the time the air contains considerable moisture. The warmer the air the more moisture it can hold. At the end of the day, the fuel tank is full of warm moist air which, when cooled at night, deposits moisture on the sides of the tank. As it collects, it runs into and under whatever fuel is left in the tank. (No air enters an LP-Gas tank.) This is shown in Fig. 12.

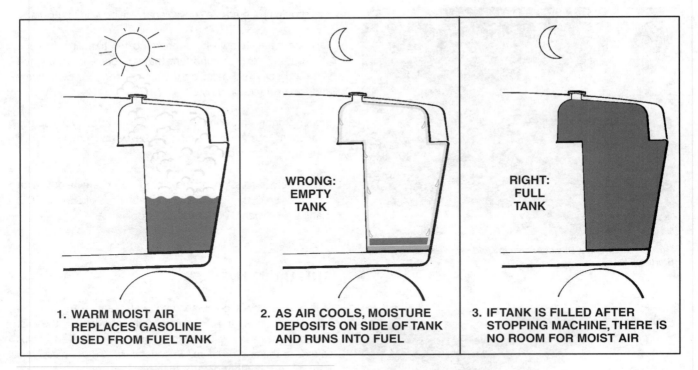

	WRONG: EMPTY TANK	RIGHT: FULL TANK
1. WARM MOIST AIR REPLACES GASOLINE USED FROM FUEL TANK	2. AS AIR COOLS, MOISTURE DEPOSITS ON SIDE OF TANK AND RUNS INTO FUEL	3. IF TANK IS FILLED AFTER STOPPING MACHINE, THERE IS NO ROOM FOR MOIST AIR

Fig. 12 — Why Fuel Tanks Should be Filled at the End of Each Day

Water doesn't do much damage to the tank. Most tanks have a protective coating that helps prevent rust. But in a *spark-ignition engine,* any moisture that gets past the sediment bowl in the feed line from the tank, moves into the fuel pump (if the machine has one) and then into the carburetor. Any sulfur present in the fuel combines with water and attacks the metal parts. In cold weather, water that has collected in the sediment bowl or fuel line may freeze and cause starting trouble.

Diesel fuel and water mix rather readily and the water is slow to settle out-much slower than with gasoline. Yet if water gets to the injection pump, it causes galling and sticking of the finely-machined pump parts. Next is an expensive repair job.

By filling the tank immediately after the machine is used, there is a period of several hours during the night that allows time for most of the water already in the fuel to collect at the bottom of the tank. This is why it is recommended that water be drained from the sediment bowl before starting the engine each day.

Dirt is an equally bad actor in a *carburetor.* It often closes or partly closes the small openings (orifices) that allow the right amount of fuel to mix with incoming air. In *diesel engines,* it speeds the wear of the close-fitting plungers in the injector pump.

Fire hazards exist when handling any kind of fuel. But with gasoline and LP-Gas the risk is somewhat greater. There are two reasons:

(1) Either fuel vaporizes at temperatures around zero. Only a small amount mixed with air (6 percent or less of gasoline vapor) will explode if exposed to a spark or flame.

(2) Since the vapors are heavier than air, they settle to a low spot and remain there unless ventilated out.

Kerosene and fuel oil don't vaporize readily until the temperature reaches 110°F (45°C) or more. This makes them less of a hazard than gasoline, unless you spill them on a hot manifold or other hot surfaces. Then they vaporize readily. With so much vapor present, a spark or flame will readily ignite it.

Consequently, if your machine is hot and you haven't time to wait 4 or 5 minutes for it to cool, wait and refuel the next morning. The risk of water in your fuel tank becomes less important than the risk of fire or explosion from refueling a hot engine.

Refueling of machines is discussed as follows:

- **Refueling with liquid fuels**
- **Refueling with LP-Gas**

We will now explain each one.

REFUELING WITH LIQUID FUELS

When *filling* a fuel tank with *gasoline, kerosene or diesel fuel:*

1. *Check against fire hazards.*

   Shut off engine and turn off all electrical switches to lessen the danger of a spark.

   Allow engine to cool if extra hot. Be sure there are no open flames and that no one is smoking.

2. *Check mouth of container or hose nozzle for dirt. Remove any dirt with a clean cloth.*

   Be sure to use closed containers if you are hauling fuel to the field (Fig. 13). There is less chance of dirt and moisture entering the fuel tank if you fill your machine directly from an overhead supply tank or pump (Fig. 13).

   Use only authorized gasoline containers; these are painted red. Paint your kerosene, distillate or diesel fuel containers green.

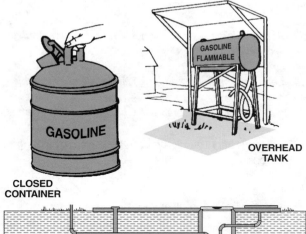

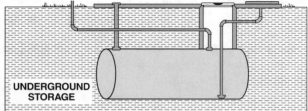

Fig. 13 — Fuel in Storage Containers

3. *Remove dust and loose dirt from fuel tank cap and area around tank opening.*

 CAUTION: Never smoke while filling a fuel tank.

4. Fill fuel tank almost full.

   Leave space in neck of opening for fuel to expand if heated; this helps avoid overflow and possibility of fire.

   Don't move fuel drums as the movement can agitate the fuel causing water and dirt to mix with it.

   With diesel fuel, leave 3 or 4 inches of fuel in the bottom of the storage tank as a safeguard against moisture and dirt.

   If your *fuel supply is low* in the supply tank, you run a risk of drawing off both dirt and water into your fuel tank. Rather than take this risk, line a clean funnel with a chamois and filter the fuel through it. The chamois removes both dirt and water.

   Let fuel stand at least 10 hours after supply tank is filled before fueling machines to permit any dirt in the fuel to settle out.

5. *Replace fuel tank cap tightly.*

   Make it a practice to check the opening in the fuel tank cap occasionally. If it becomes clogged, a vacuum tends to develop in the fuel tank and fuel won't feed into the carburetor satisfactorily.

REFUELING WITH LP-GAS

> **CAUTION: Check to make sure engine is turned off and that there is no smoking or flames nearby. These precautions are extremely important. It is difficult to know when you have an LP-Gas leak. The gas is invisible and the odor is not as easy to detect as with gasoline. In other respects, it has about the same hazards as when filling a gasoline tank.**
>
> **Never attempt to fuel your machine inside a building or over a pit. There is too much danger of gas pocketing and providing conditions for an explosion.**

As we discussed earlier, LP-Gas is a petroleum gas commonly made up of propane and butane (some is all propane). At ordinary temperatures it changes to a gas, and in order to keep it in liquid form it must be kept under pressure. For this reason, the method of filling the machine fuel tank is different than with other fuels.

Note in Fig. 14 there are two hose lines extending from the storage tank to the machine fuel tank.

The reason for the two lines is shown in Fig. 14. One line delivers liquid fuel from the supply tank to the machine tank, while the second line allows vapor to flow from the machine tank back to the supply tank. In this way no air enters either tank and there is no loss of pressure due to escaping gas vapor.

 CAUTION: Don't ever attempt to fill the tank without a vapor-return hose line. While it is true that it can be done by allowing vapor to escape to open air, this practice violates all safety regulations. It is extremely dangerous and fire or explosion is almost certain if continued over a period of time.

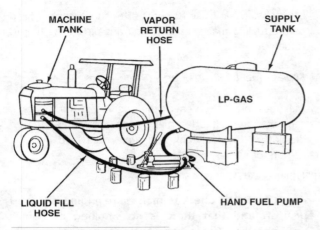

Fig. 14 — Refueling With LP-Gas

As long as the level of the liquid in the supply tank is above the level of the liquid in the machine tank, it will flow by gravity from the storage to the machine tank. If the storage tank is lower than the machine tank, a hand-operated or motor-operated pump is used to pump the liquid from the supply tank (Fig. 14).

IMPORTANT: A different set of valves is used for filling the fuel tank from those used when operating the machine. Check your operator's manual for details on fueling your type of machine. In general, the procedures are as follows.

1. *Remove dust caps (covers) from machine fuel-tank connections and hose ends.*

   Valves inside the tank keep liquid and gas from escaping.

   The vapor return valve is built somewhat differently from the filler valve. It has one check valve and an excess flow valve on the end. The excess-flow valve closes in case

there is a rapid movement of gas from the tank such as might happen if a hose should break.

2. *Attach vapor-return line to vapor-return connection on machine and open hand valve (Fig. 15).*

   When this valve is opened, pressure is equalized between the storage tank and tractor tank. This is necessary for the liquid to flow into the tractor tank.

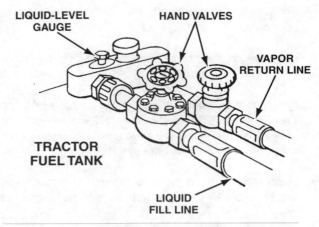

Fig. 15 — Hand-Operated Valves on Hoses Which Connect to Machine Tank

3. *Attach liquid-fill hose to connection on machine tank and open valve (Fig. 15).*

4. *Operate pump if storage tank is below level of machine.*

5. *Watch fuel gauge to determine when tank is 75 percent full.*

   This step is important in order to keep from overfilling the fuel tank.

   Your gauge may be of the *float type;* if so, it shows the percentage of liquid fill in your tank at all times.

   Some gauges are of the *tube type.* To determine percentage of fill with this type of gauge, level of liquid is checked by rotating tube inside tank. It is connected to a dial handle on the gauge.

6. *Check fuel overflow valve until liquid appears.*

   Open this valve momentarily, then close until liquid appears. This shows when liquid has reached proper level in tank. Don't leave this valve open during the filling

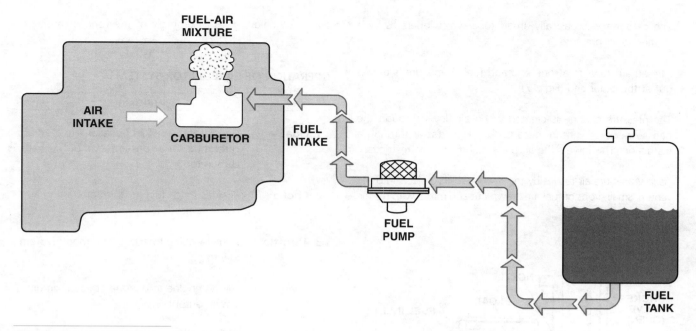

FUEL-AIR
MIXTURE

AIR
INTAKE

CARBURETOR

FUEL
INTAKE

FUEL
PUMP

FUEL
TANK

Fig. 16 — Gasoline Fuel Systems

process. As discussed earlier, this is extremely dangerous and violates all codes and laws regarding proper and safe handling of LP-Gas tanks.

 CAUTION: When the hoses are disconnected from the machine tank, a small amount of liquid fuel is lost. Continue to avoid smoking or lighting a match until the fuel has had time to vaporize and be ventilated away from the machine.

7. *Close both line valves and disconnect from machine tank.*

The machine fuel tank is now around 80 to 85 percent full. This still leaves room for vapor at the top and provides for expansion of the fuel in case of heat.

8. *Replace dust caps.*

A safety-relief valve is mounted on your tank to relieve pressure in case you overfill and the pressure gets too high for safety.

GASOLINE FUEL SYSTEMS

The gasoline fuel system supplies a combustible mixture of fuel and air to power the engine.

The gasoline fuel system (Fig. 16) has three basic parts:

- **Fuel Tank**
- **Fuel Pump**
- **Carburetor**

The FUEL TANK stores the gasoline for the engine.

The FUEL PUMP moves fuel from tank to carburetor.

A fuel pump is needed only with force-feed supply systems. When fuel tank is above the engine, gravity moves fuel to the carburetor.

The CARBURETOR does two jobs: (1) atomizes fuel for the engine, and (2) provides proper fuel-air ratio.

Most systems also have a fuel sediment bowl and strainer below the tank outlet, or it may be part of the fuel pump.

OPERATION

How do these parts work together as a team?

Operation of the basic system is shown in Fig. 16.

The *fuel pump* draws fuel through a line from the tank and forces it to the *float chamber* of the, carburetor, where it is stopped.

The *carburetor* is basically an-air tube which operates by a change in air pressure.

Filtered air flows in at one end and fuel-air-mixture is drawn out at the other end (Fig. 17).

The pressure change is created when air flows through the narrow neck, or venturi, because air moves faster through a restriction. This lowers the air pressure beyond the restriction.

As low-pressure air rushes by the nozzle which projects into the venturi, small drops of fuel are drawn out and mixed with the air.

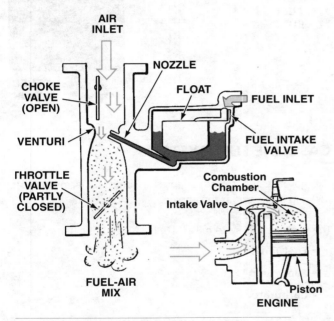

Fig. 17 — Basic Carburetor at Part Throttle or Low Power

At the same time, the engine's intake stroke creates a partial vacuum which draws the fuel-air mixture into the combustion chamber of the cylinder as shown in Fig. 17.

The fuel-air mixture must pass the *throttle valve* which opens or closes to let the right volume of fuel-air into the engine. This is controlled as the operator sets the engine speed or by the governor's action.

The *choke valve* also controls the supply of fuel to the engine. When starting the engine in cold weather, for example, it can be partly closed, forming a greater vacuum. This vacuum causes more fuel and less air to be drawn into the combustion chambers. The richer mixture burns easier, providing extra power in the cylinders for the harder job of starting.

The operation of the carburetor at part throttle or low power is shown in Fig. 17; operation at full throttle or full power is shown in Fig. 18.

The chart below gives a summary of the various carburetor systems.

OPERATION OF CARBURETOR SYSTEMS

System	Function
1. **Float**	...Controls flow of fuel from tank to carburetor for a constant level of fuel in carburetor.
2. **Choke**	...Creates a rich fuel mixture for starting a cold engine.
3. **Throttle**	...Allows engine to accelerate smoothly from idle to high speeds.
4. **Load**	...Allows engine to operate at its maximum power output.
5. **Idle**	...Allows engine to operate economically at idle speeds when power is not needed.

IMPORTANCE OF SERVICE

When the fuel system is operating properly, the maximum in fuel economy and horsepower is achieved.

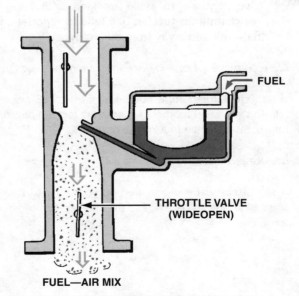

Fig. 18 — Basic Carburetor at Full Throttle or Full Power

If too rich a mixture is used, fuel consumption may be increased by 10 percent or more. A too-rich mixture can also cause carbon deposits to accumulate in combustion chambers.

Too lean a mixture reduces power and may cause valve burning from extra-hot, slow-burning gases.

Always keep the fuel tank and filter clean to prevent dirt, rust or other foreign matter from clogging the carburetor and filters. Moisture in the fuel can cause rust and poor engine operation.

TOOLS AND MATERIALS NEEDED

1. Wrenches (inch or metric, as required).
2. Screwdriver.
3. Container of cleaning solvent (not gasoline).
4. Goggles or glasses for eye protection.

ADJUSTING THE GASOLINE CARBURETOR

 CAUTION: Gasoline is flammable. To avoid injury, do not smoke or allow any flame near the area. Also do not allow gasoline to spill onto any hot surface, such as a hot manifold.

Check and make carburetor adjustments every 250 hours of engine operation, or as needed.

Before making any carburetor adjustments, check the following:

1. Remove the strainer screen from the carburetor (if it has one) (Fig. 19) and clean the screen in solvent or replace it if it is dirty. Reassemble screen in solvent if it is dirty. Reassemble screen after cleaning.

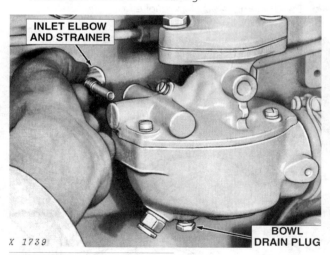

Fig. 19 — Carburetor Fuel Strainer

2. Check for air leaks at manifold connections and carburetor gaskets. With the engine running, squirt a few drops of oil over suspicious areas. If oil is drawn into the manifold, air is leaking into the manifold. Tighten fittings and check again. If leaks persist, replace gaskets.

The carburetor can't be adjusted properly if the screen is clogged or the manifold is leaking.

Adjusting Idling Speed

The idle adjusting screw (Fig. 20) determines how completely the throttle valve closes. This controls the idling speed of the engine.

To adjust the idling speed, proceed as follows:
1. Start the engine and allow it to warm to operating temperature.
2. Set the speed-control lever at the completely closed position.
3. Turn the idle speed adjusting screw clockwise to increase speed, counterclockwise to decrease speed.

Check your operator's manual for proper idling speed and the recommended point for measuring it. Depending on the engine, the speed may vary from 300 to 800 rpm. If the engine has a tachometer, use it. But setting the speed by sound is not a good way because you could be off several hundred rpm. On some engines the idling speed can be measured at the power take-off shaft by using a portable tachometer or speed counter and a watch. An electric tachometer connected to the ignition system can also be used for checking speed.

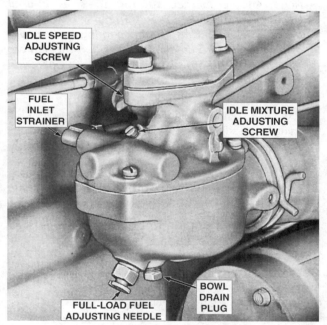

Fig. 20 — Adjusting Points on Typical Carburetor

Adjusting Idling Fuel-Air Mixture

The idle-mixture adjusting screw (Fig. 20) adjusts the fuel-air mixture while the engine is idling.

Your operator's manual may indicate a setting of so many turns from the completely closed position. If your carburetor is a little dirty, however, this may not be close enough. Use the following procedures to get a finer adjustment:

1. With the engine at normal operating temperature, set the speed-control lever in the idling position.

2. Turn the idle-mixture adjusting screw (Fig. 20) clockwise slowly until the engine begins to "roll" or shake. This decreases the air flow and causes a richer mixture on some engines and decreases fuel flow on other engines, resulting in a leaner mixture. The engine isn't getting the correct fuel-air mixture when it idles roughly.

3. Turn the adjusting screw counterclockwise until the engine begins to run smoothly. Do this slowly so that the engine has a chance to adjust to the changing mixture. You may have to change the direction you are turning the screw several times until you are certain that the best setting has been achieved. This is when the engine runs the smoothest.

NOTE: Another method is to turn the screw in until the engine runs rough. Then turn the screw out until the engine again runs rough, counting the number of turns. Now turn the screw in one-half the number of turns for the best setting for smooth operation and economy.

Some two-cylinder engines have an idling screw for each cylinder. To adjust these, short the spark plug on one cylinder while adjusting the idle mixture on the other.

NOTE: If the engine is not affected by one or two complete turns of the adjusting screw, something may be wrong. The float valve in the carburetor may be leaking, the fuel level may be too high, or deposits in the manifold around the throttle valve may be restricting air flow. See your dealer if you can't correct the problem.

4. Recheck the idle speed after the idle fuel is set as the mixture could change the speed. Generally, idle speed and idle fuel should be set together.

Adjusting Load Fuel-Air Mixture

The valve which controls the fuel for full-load or highs speed conditions is called "main adjusting needle", "power adjusting needle", or "full-load fuel adjusting needle" (Fig. 20). Many later model engines do not have this adjustment (are preset at factory).

To make this adjustment, the engine must be up to full operating temperature. Adjust the load fuel-air mixture as follows:

1. Run the engine at full throttle and provide a constant load on the engine, if possible. *A dynamometer and flow meter is best, but you can make the adjustment without these by trial and error.* See Chapter 10 for dynamometer procedures.

If you make the adjustments without load, follow up with a final check to make sure the adjustment is satisfactory under load.

 CAUTION: Do not try to adjust the carburetor while your machine is in motion. You may seriously injure yourself and cause an accident which could injure someone else nearby.

2. Turn the full-load adjusting screw clockwise until the engine begins to lose power.

This indicates that you have reached the border line on the lean side of the mixture as shown by (A) in Fig. 21. At this setting, your engine will have high fuel efficiency, but it would not be developing its maximum horsepower. The temperature of the exhaust would be too high also. This could lead to burned valves.

3. Turn the adjusting screw counterclockwise (or out) until the engine gives off black smoke from the exhaust.

This indicates that the fuel-air mixture is too rich as shown by (B) in Fig. 21. You will get satisfactory horsepower, but fuel efficiency will be low.

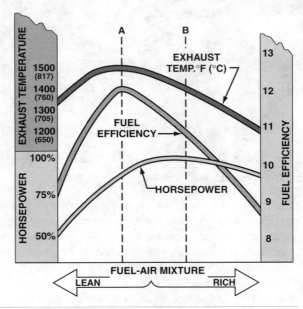

Fig. 21 — Relationship of Exhaust Temperature, Fuel Efficiency and Horsepower to Different Fuel-Air Mixtures

4. Turn the screw clockwise until engine runs smoothly and at full speed. Turn the screw slowly so that the engine will have time to adjust.

NOTE: The same method as shown in "NOTE" under step 3 of idle fuel adjustment can also be used here.

5. Check this adjustment by accelerating the engine quickly while under load.

If you were not able to adjust the engine under load, you should now operate the tractor to determine how it accelerates under load.

The engine should accelerate quickly when you move the speed control lever suddenly. If the engine backfires, the mixture is too lean. If dark-colored smoke comes from the-exhaust, the mixture is too rich.

MAINTENANCE TIPS FOR CARBURETORS

Carburetor adjustment is part of maintenance, but repair of the carburetor requires special knowledge and tools. If you do service the carburetor, the tips listed below will help you.

1. Always **service** the carburetor at these times:

   a. After engine valve grinding or major engine overhaul.

   b. Every year or at the beginning of each season on seasonal machines. At this time, clean the carburetor, repack the shaft, check the bearings, and replace the seals and gaskets.

2. Always **adjust** the carburetor at the following times.

   a. During engine tune-up

   b. After major overhaul of the engine

   c. Whenever the carburetor has been removed for service.

   d. Anytime the engine idles badly or requires speed adjustment

3. Repair kits are provided for many carburetors. When repairing, be sure to use ALL of the new parts in the kit not just those which **appear** worn.

4. Clean all parts thoroughly when repairing the carburetor. Use a carburetor cleaning solution for removing varnish like deposits from all metal parts and rinse them in solvent.

5. Never use small wires or drills to clean out jets or orifices. This may enlarge or burr the precision bores and upset the performance of the carburetor.

6. Never use compressed air to clean a completely assembled carburetor. To do so may cause the metal float to collapse.

7. To test a metal float for leaks, immerse it in hot water. If air bubbles escape from the float, replace it. Do not attempt to repair a float unless recommended.

8. Always drain the carburetor before any long storage period. Many carburetors have a drain plug in the fuel bowl.

9. Most carburetors are vented to avoid vapor lock. Be sure the vent is kept clean and open.

10. Never turn adjusting needles too tightly against their seats as you may damage them.

11. Use special tool kits, when available, to recondition the carburetor.

12. Be sure to tighten the screws which hold the throttle disk in place. If loose, suction from the engine may draw screws into the combustion chamber.

13. Always check the height of the float when assembling the carburetor. See the machine technical manual for the correct height. If the float is badly bent or warped, replace it. Use a special float bending tool to adjust the float when recommended.

SERVICING GASOLINE SEDIMENT BOWL AND FUEL STRAINER

Most agricultural machines are equipped with a combination sediment bowl and fuel strainer (Fig. 22).

NOTE: In extremely trashy or dry conditions, some manufacturers recommend replacing glass sediment bowls with metal bowls to reduce possibility of a bowl breaking and causing a fire.

Most sediment bowls should be visually checked every 10 hours for dirt and water deposits. However, actual service intervals vary widely and some manuals say "periodically".

The tools and materials needed to clean these parts are:

1. Container of cleaning solvent (not gasoline)

2. New gaskets (where used)

3. Clean, lint-free rags

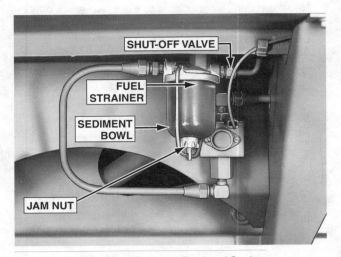

Fig. 22 — Gasoline Fuel Sediment Bowl and Strainer

To clean the sediment bowl and strainer, proceed as follows:

1. Shut off fuel supply line at fuel tank or sediment bowl.

2. Remove sediment bowl gasket and strainer screen (Fig. 23).

3. Wash screen in cleaning solvent. If screen is difficult to clean, remove varnish or gum deposits with a carburetor cleaner solvent.

4. Clean sediment bowl with cloth dampened in cleaning solvent. Wipe bowl dry and remove any lint remaining in bowl.

5. Drain sediment from bottom of fuel tank, or open fuel valve and observe fuel as you catch it in a container. This should remove dirt or water from the tank and fuel line. If the vent hole in the fuel tank cap is plugged, the flow will be slow. Clean the cap, if clogged, in solvent.

6. Reassemble sediment bowl, strainer or filter and gasket (Fig. 23) and tighten the jam nut. (On some systems you must let fuel run into the bowl before tightening it completely.)

7. Open the fuel valve. Start the engine and check for fuel leaks.

8. Reassemble the sediment bowl, strainer or filter and gasket (Fig. 23).

9. Tighten the bowl against gasket. (On some systems you must let fuel run into bowl before tightening it airtight.)

10. Open the fuel valve. Start the engine and check for leaks.

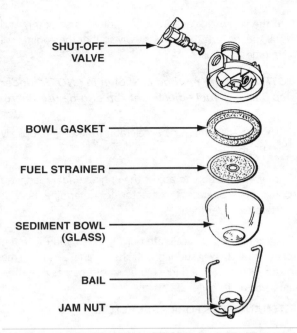

Fig. 23 — Servicing Gasoline Fuel Sediment Bowl and Strainer

LP-GAS FUEL SYSTEMS

LP-Gas vaporizes very easily. In fact, it normally remains a liquid only when under pressure. Therefore, it must be kept in strong tanks.

LP-Gas is vaporized *before* it reaches the carburetor, while gasoline remains a liquid until this point. This is the basic difference between the two systems.

OPERATION

In most systems, the fuel is drawn from the tank as a pressurized *liquid* and then vaporized (Fig. 24).

Vapor is taken from the top of the tank only for starting the engine. This is done because in a cold engine there is not enough heat to convert liquid fuel to vapor. Once the engine is started and warmed up, it can be switched to liquid withdrawal again.

PARTS OF LP-GAS FUEL SYSTEM

The LP-Gas fuel system (Fig. 24) has four basic parts:

• **Pressurized Fuel Tank**

• **Fuel Strainer**

• **Converter**

• **Carburetor**

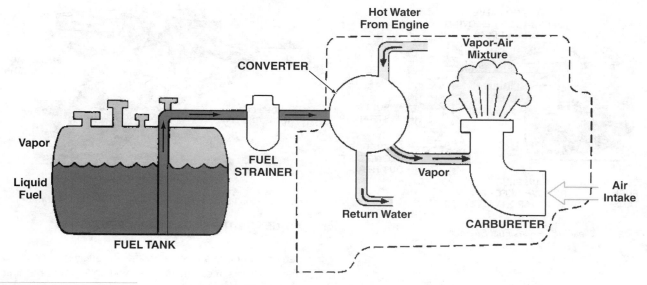

Fig. 24 — LP-Gas Fuel System

The PRESSURIZED FUEL TANK stores the liquid fuel under pressure. A space for vapor is left at the top of the tank.

The FUEL STRAINER cleans the liquid fuel. It normally has a solenoid valve which permits flow only when the engine ignition is turned on.

The CONVERTER changes the liquid fuel to vapor by warming it and then lowering the, pressure of the vapor.

The CARBURETOR mixes the fuel vapor with air in the proper ratio for the engine.

IMPORTANCE OF SERVICE

The LP-Gas fuel system requires maintenance similar to the gasoline system. To achieve the maximum fuel economy and horsepower, you must perform periodic service to keep the system operating correctly.

As with gasoline fuel systems, if the carburetor is not adjusted correctly, fuel consumption can be excessive or power can be lost.

Clean fuel is not a major problem with LP-Gas; however, don't neglect it. Small particles of dirt or gummy residues can lodge in the finely machined valve openings and damage the seats when valves are closed. This can cause dangerous gas leaks or plugging of the lines. Plugging can be detected by frosting of the filter or line at the point of stoppage.

CLEANING THE LP-GAS FUEL STRAINER

Clean the LP-Gas strainer as recommended. Intervals vary from every 100 hours to yearly. However, if the strainer clogs, frost will form on the outside of the metal strainer.

The tools and materials needed to clean the filter are:

1. Set of wrenches (inch or metric, as required).

2. Container of solvent (not gasoline)

3. New gaskets (where used)

4. Clean, lint-free cloths

5. Source of air pressure

To clean the strainer, proceed as follows:

1. Close liquid and vapor valves at fuel tank (see Fig. 25).

2. Remove the drain plug from the strainer (Fig. 25).

 CAUTION: Never open vapor valve in the vicinity of a flame as a spark or explosion could result. Also, be sure there is plenty of ventilation.

3. Open the vapor valve at tank *slowly*. This should blow accumulation of moisture and sediment from the strainer bowl.

4. Close the vapor valve and reinstall the plug.

This procedure will clean some of the contamination from the strainer bowl, but to clean the filter completely, it must be removed.

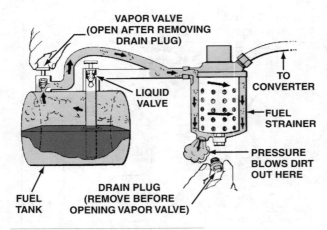

Fig. 25 — Cleaning LP-Gas Fuel Strainer

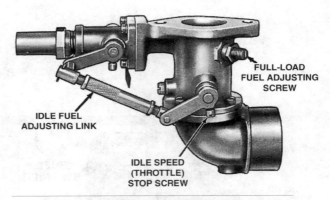

Fig. 26 — Adjusting Points on a Typical LP-Gas Carburetor

For complete cleaning of strainer:

1. Be sure that both the vapor and liquid supply valves are closed.

2. Loosen the drain plug in the bowl slowly so that any pressure build-up can be relieved.

3. Loosen the nut or bolt holding the filter bowl and remove bowl, gasket and filter element.

4. Wash the filter in solvent if the filter is washable. Replace disposable filters with new ones.

5. If a disk-type filter is to be reinstalled, finish drying the filter by blowing air through one end. This forces out any particles from inside the filter element.

6. Clean sediment bowl with a cloth dampened with the cleaning solution. Wipe the bowl dry and be sure no lint remains in the bowl.

7. Install gasket, filter and sediment bowl and tighten nuts or bolts to hold filter in place.

8. Open the fuel supply valves at tank and check for leaks. Brush on a soapy-water solution around connections. If bubbles are present, tighten connections. If tightening does not correct the problem, replace the necessary parts.

ADJUSTING THE LP-GAS CARBURETOR

Refer to your operator's manual for specific instructions. Some manufacturers recommend that you take your machine to your local dealer for this service. However, many LP-Gas carburetors can be adjusted as follows:

1. Warm up the engine fully.

2. Adjust the idle speed at the throttle stop screw (Fig. 26). Normally adjust with the throttle disk closed and try to get the slowest engine idling speed without stalling or "roughening." See your operator's manual for recommended idle rpm.

3. Adjust the idle fuel mixture at the adjusting link (Fig, 26). With the engine at slow idle, turn the link until the engine begins to stall. Then turn the link the other way until the engine idles smoothly.

4. If necessary, readjust the idle speed (step 2).

5. Adjust the full-load fuel mixture per the specification. For safety, load the engine but keep the engine stationary (as with a dynamometer). With a tractor you can use the tractor to power a grinder or other PTO driven unit. With self-propelled machines such as cotton pickers or combines, the harvesting mechanism can provide the engine with a. load.

IMPORTANT: Never let an LP-gas engine run with the fuel mixture "too lean." LP-Gas burns hotter than gasoline and will allow the engine to develop maximum horsepower. However, this lean burning will result in burned valves and pistons.

Be sure the throttle is wide open. Turn the full-load fuel adjusting screw until the engine starts to lose power. Then back it out until the engine picks up speed and runs smoothly.

Fig. 27 — LP-Gas Converter

NOTE: This adjustment has no effect unless the engine is at full throttle under load and the throttle disk is wide open.

SERVICING THE LP-GAS CONVERTER

The converter (Fig. 27) is constructed so that it will seldom cause trouble, providing clean fuel is used in the tank and clean, soft water in the cooling system.

If the converter frosts up when the engine is cold, it is probably due to a leaking high-pressure valve caused by dirt under the valve seat.

If frosting occurs when the engine is hot, it is probably due to poor coolant circulation through the heat exchanger—or a restriction in the high-pressure valve.

To check the converter for leaks, turn on the ignition switch without starting the engine and open the vapor withdrawal valve. Then remove the radiator cap and check the coolant for bubbles, which would mean that the converter has a leaking gasket.

For converter service, see your dealer.

SERVICING LP-GAS FUEL TANK, VALVES AND GAUGES

Be sure that you are familiar with all rules and regulations before servicing LP-Gas equipment.

Two rules are important here:

1. *Never service the fuel tank except to remove and install valves or gauges.*

2. *Never service the valves or gauges except to remove and install them or to replace caps or dust covers. Your dealer should perform all major LP-Gas service.*

Replacing Parts

If a valve or gauge is damaged or worn and must be replaced, first empty all fuel from the tank to remove the pressure. If possible, *do this outdoors by running the engine until all fuel is exhausted.* If not possible, consult your local LP-Gas distributor for the approved method in your locality for emptying the tank.

 CAUTION: Never use an open flame to test for gas leaks.

When replacing a valve, use a small amount of Permatex or similar sealer on the threads. Install the valve and tighten securely. Test for leaks by using soapy water.

For other information, see your machine dealer.

DIESEL FUEL SYSTEMS

The prime job of the diesel fuel system is to inject a precise amount of atomized and pressurized fuel into each engine cylinder at the proper time (Fig. 28).

Combustion in the diesel engine occurs when this charge of fuel is mixed with hot compressed air. No electrical spark is used (as in gasoline engine).

The major parts of the diesel fuel system are:

- **Fuel Tank—stores fuel**
- **Fuel Transfer Pump-pushes fuel through filters to injection pump**
- **Fuel Filters-clean the fuel**
- **Injection Pump-times, measures, and delivers fuel under pressure to cylinders**
- **Injection Nozzles-atomize and spray, fuel into cylinders**

These parts in a basic system are shown in Fig. 28.

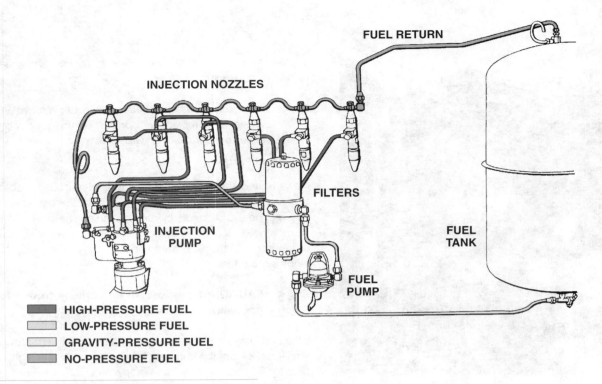

FUEL RETURN

INJECTION NOZZLES

FILTERS

INJECTION PUMP

FUEL TANK

FUEL PUMP

■ HIGH-PRESSURE FUEL
■ LOW-PRESSURE FUEL
■ GRAVITY-PRESSURE FUEL
■ NO-PRESSURE FUEL

Fig. 28 — Diesel Fuel System (Distributor Type Shown)

OPERATION

In operation, fuel flows by gravity pressure from the FUEL TANK to the Transfer Pump (Fig. 28).

The TRANSFER PUMP pushes the fuel through the FILTERS, where it is cleaned.

The fuel is then pushed on to the INJECTION PUMP where it is put under high pressure and delivered to each Injection Nozzle at the exact time needed.

The INJECTION NOZZLES atomize the fuel and spray it into the combustion chamber of each cylinder.

Various kinds of injection systems are used on different engines. All systems have a low-pressure side and a high-pressure side as shown in Fig. 28. The low pressure side is from the fuel tank to the injection pump. The high pressure side is from the injection pump to the injectors. The high pressure created by, the injection pump forces the fuel through the injectors, making a fine mist as fuel is sprayed into the cylinders.

The injection pump times and meters the injection of fuel into each cylinder at the precise moment for good combustion. Note that one type of injection system has a combination injection pump and nozzle which is actuated by a rocker arm similar to those that operate the intake and exhaust valves.

Most diesel fuel systems have a fuel return line which returns excess fuel from the injectors or from the injection pump to the fuel tank. The excess fuel is used on some systems to help cool and lubricate the pump and injectors.

Filter systems vary from one filter to three filters. If there is only one filter (Fig. 29) it must be serviced regularly and carefully because there are no other filters to help clean the fuel.

Additional filters, such as second-stage and third-stage filters, are often used to assure that water and dirt particles will be removed from the fuel (Fig. 30). Second- and third-stage filters also require careful attention, but at longer intervals.

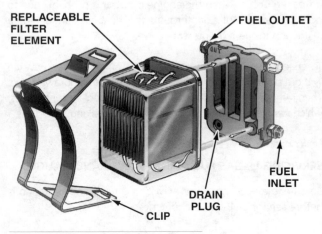

REPLACEABLE FILTER ELEMENT

FUEL OUTLET

DRAIN PLUG

CLIP

FUEL INLET

Fig. 29 — Single-Stage Diesel Fuel Filter

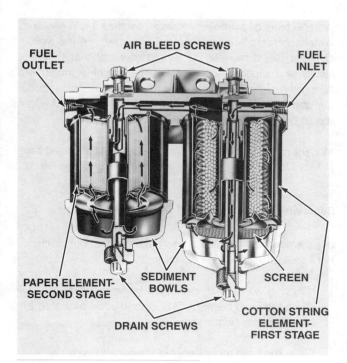

FUEL OUTLET

AIR BLEED SCREWS

FUEL INLET

PAPER ELEMENT-
SECOND STAGE

SEDIMENT
BOWLS

SCREEN

DRAIN SCREWS

COTTON STRING
ELEMENT-
FIRST STAGE

Fig. 30 — Two-Stage Diesel Fuel Filter

IMPORTANCE OF SERVICE

The diesel fuel system requires careful service in order to keep it operating properly. *The injection pump and nozzles are precision parts which can be damaged by small particles of dirt or other contaminants.* Any damage to these parts is costly to repair. If dirt enters the injection pump, the pump will wear and poor fuel delivery will result. Dirt will also clog the injector nozzles and make them inoperable. Water is another enemy: it can rust these precision parts.

The injection pump and injector nozzles have very finely machined parts, with clearances as small as 0.0001 inch (0.0025 mm). These parts are necessary to develop and use the high pressures required at the nozzle tips so the engine will operate properly and efficiently.

Check with your machine dealer for service of injector parts. Not all dealers are equipped to service these precision machined parts and it may be necessary for the manufacturer to service them

It is not possible to eliminate all moisture and dirt particles from the fuel. However, dirt and moisture can be reduced by good maintenance so that your engine will give thousands of hours of operation without repair to the injection pump or the injectors.

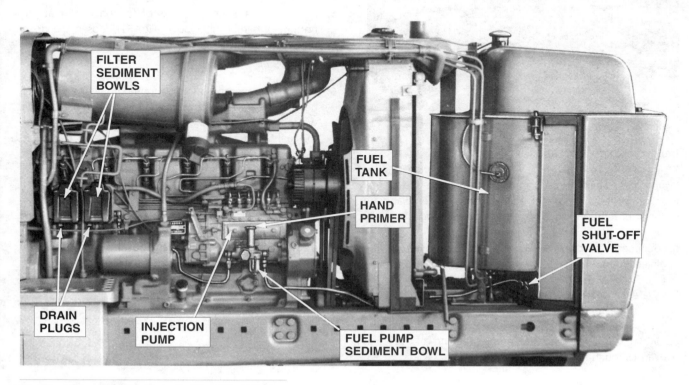

FILTER
SEDIMENT
BOWLS

FUEL
TANK

HAND
PRIMER

FUEL
SHUT-OFF
VALVE

DRAIN
PLUGS

INJECTION
PUMP

FUEL PUMP
SEDIMENT BOWL

Fig. 31 — Removing Daily Deposits From Diesel System

SERVICING THE DIESEL FUEL SYSTEM

Because servicing the injection pump and injector nozzles require special tools and equipment, you should be mainly concerned with the other components, on the low-pressure side, such as the fuel filters, fuel sediment bowl and fuel tank. If these units are properly serviced, little trouble should be experienced with the injection pump and nozzles.

Tools and Materials Needed

To service the low-pressure side of the system, the following tools and materials are needed.

1. Clean, lint-free cloths
2. Container of cleaning solvent (not gasoline)
3. Container to catch waste fuel
4. Set of wrenches (inch or metric, as required)
5. Small, soft bristle scrub brush
6. Replaceable filters, if needed

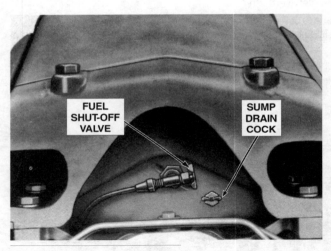

FUEL SHUT-OFF VALVE

SUMP DRAIN COCK

Fig. 32 — Drain for Fuel Tank Sump

Importance of Water and Dirt Removal

Water and sediment can seriously damage a diesel fuel injection system. So, diesel engines have rather elaborate systems for removing such impurities from the fuel.

a. Sediment grinds away the finely fitted parts of the injection pump.

b. Water causes the parts to rust (a very small amount of rust can cause serious damage).

c. Water interferes with the proper feeding of fuel and causes rough running of the engine.

Water is more of a problem in diesel fuel than it is in gasoline. Water separates from gasoline rather readily; but the weight of diesel fuel is so near the weight of water that they mix readily and separate slowly. With the machine motionless during the night, water has time to separate from the diesel fuel and settle to the bottom of the tank. The trapped water should be removed from the system each morning.

Machine manufacturers take advantage of this situation and have provided for removing the water as shown in Fig. 31 and Fig. 32.

Removing Daily Deposits of Water and Sediment

Use the directions in the operator's manual for your machine. Here are instructions for a typical unit.

1. If there is water or an excess of foreign matter in the fuel pump sediment bowl (Fig. 31), close the fuel tank shut-off valve and remove the sediment bowl.

2. Clean the bowl and strainer in solvent and wipe dry.

3. Install the bowl and strainer, using a good gasket.

4. Open the shut-off valve and bleed the filters by working the hand primer on the injection pump (see "Bleeding System," later).

5. If there is water or an excess of foreign matter at the bottom of a fuel. filter bowl (Fig. 31), loosen the drain plug for that filter and drain the water or foreign matter from the filter. Bleed the filters.

6. If water was present in the fuel pump bowl or a fuel filter bowl, drain all the water from the fuel tank to prevent the water from plugging the filter. A sump at the bottom of the fuel tank traps the water.

7. To drain the fuel tank sump, open the drain cock (Fig. 32).

Normally, only the fuel pump sediment bowl and the filter sediment bowls need to be checked every day. If they are clean, the system should be okay. If they are dirty, perform all the maintenance steps given above.

Servicing Fuel Filters

Refer to your operator's manual for the filter change interval. Normally, a first-stage filter should be changed every 500 hours, and the second-stage filter every 1000 hours, or each season. The condition of your fuel will determine whether or not you have to change more frequently.

Service the filters as follows:

1. Be sure fuel shut-off valve (Fig. 32) is turned off. Clean outside of filter and area surrounding filter.

2. Drain fuel from filter if the filter has a drain.

3. Remove filter or filter bowl. Filters may be held in place with one or more stud bolts or a clip (Fig. 33), or be of the spin-on type.

4. If the filter is not the disposable type, clean it in a pan of cleaning solvent (not gasoline).

Fig. 33 — Removing Diesel Fuel Filter

5. Inspect it for ruptures or damage. Replace element if it is not in excellent condition. Always replace a disposable filter (such as the one shown in Fig. 33).

6. Clean inside of filter bowl or body (unless it is a self-contained unit). Use a brush or lint-free cloth for cleaning. Be sure that it is absolutely clean.

7. Install cleaned filter or new disposable filter element. Be sure to use new gaskets where separate gaskets are used. Secure filter to filter body.

8. Replace or clean the second-stage filter if necessary. (The dual filters shown in Fig. 33 are replaced in pairs.)

9. Replace the drain plug or tighten the drain valve (if opened).

10. Open the fuel shut-off valve.

11. Bleed the fuel filters (see below).

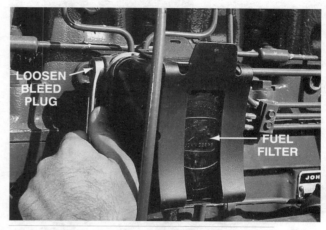

Fig. 34 — Bleed Plug for Removing Air from Fuel Filters

Bleeding Air From Fuel System After Service

Each time you drain the fuel lines or filters, air is left in them. Unless removed, this air may form an air lock when you try to start the engine. This will prevent a normal supply of fuel from reaching the injection pump, and the engine may not start or may run poorly.

Before bleeding air, be sure fuel tank is nearly full to provide enough fuel and pressure to bleed the system.

Bleed air from the system as follows:

1. If you have changed more than one filter, bleed the filter closest to the fuel tank first.

2. Open bleed plug or plugs on top of filters (Fig. 34).

3. Open fuel supply valve. This will force air through the bleed plug and replace the air in the lines and filters with fuel (on gravity-flow systems). Some systems are equipped with a hand priming pump or lever to be used in removing air (Fig. 35). Push the hand primer several strokes until fuel free of air bubbles escapes from the bleed plug hole at the filters.

Fig. 35 — Hand Priming Pump for Bleeding Air from System

4. Close bleed plug after all air is removed from filters.

5. If air lock is still present (the engine may not start or will run poorly), you will also have to bleed the injection lines (Fig. 36). (Normally, you can bleed half the injection lines and the others will bleed themselves by running the engine until it runs smoothly).

Fig. 36 — Bleeding Injection Lines at Injectors (If Necessary)

 CAUTION: Escaping diesel fuel under pressure can penetrate the skin, causing injury. Before disconnecting lines, be sure to relieve all pressure. Before applying pressure again, be sure that all connections are retightened after bleeding. If an accident occurs, see a doctor immediately. Any fluid injected into the skin must be removed within a few hours or gangrene may result. Doctors unfamiliar with this type of injury should reference a knowledgeable medical source.

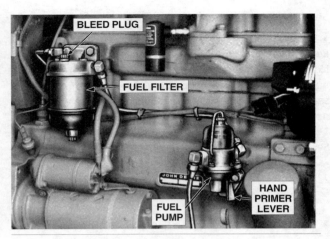

Fig. 37 — Bleeding Air from Diesel Fuel System (Alternate System)

6. Loosen injection line nuts *only one turn* to avoid excessive spray. Use two wrenches as shown in Fig. 36 to avoid bending or twisting fuel line.

7. Crank the engine with the starter until fuel without foam flows around the connectors.

8. Carefully tighten the line connectors only until snug and free of leaks.

9. Start the engine and run it until it runs smoothly. This will bleed the other injectors.

NOTE. Some diesel fuel systems have a separate fuel pump with primer (Fig. 37). On these systems, loosen filter bleed plugs and pump out air using primer lever on pump. Then bleed air from lines if necessary.

Servicing Of Diesel Injection Pumps And Nozzles

Injection pumps and nozzles require special tools and equipment, so *go to your dealer or service center for all adjustments and repair of precision injection units.*

ENGINE GOVERNORS

The governor is a device which automatically controls the speed of the engine under varying loads (Fig. 38).

Governors do these jobs:

- **Maintain a selected speed**
- **Limit the slow and fast speeds**
- **Shut down the engine when it overspeeds**

Fig. 39 shows how the governor keeps the engine at a constant speed when the machine is going uphill or downhill.

The governor on the engine automatically regulates speed at whatever setting you select on the speed control (throttle) lever.

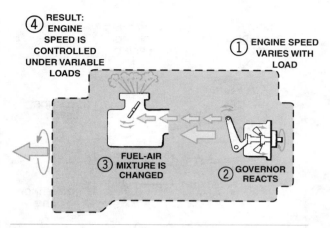

Fig. 38 — Governing System (Gasoline Engine with Centrifugal Governor Shown

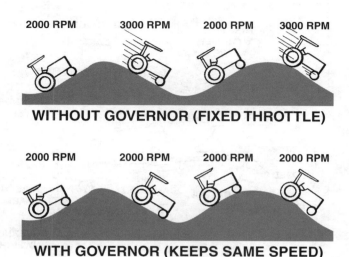

WITHOUT GOVERNOR (FIXED THROTTLE)

WITH GOVERNOR (KEEPS SAME SPEED)

Fig. 39 — What the Governor Does for the Machine Engine

Most operator's manuals give detailed instructions on how to adjust the governor for high no-load speed. However, some manuals have no governor adjustment and others warn against making any adjustments.

Some engines have governors with the adjustments sealed inside the governor housing to discourage operators from making adjustments.

Since there is some question about whether operators should adjust governors, this discussion does not include procedures for doing the job. But it is intended to help you understand how a governor works, and the importance of proper governor adjustment. This understanding will be helpful whether you service it, or have it done by a competent serviceman.

IMPORTANCE OF GOVERNOR ADJUSTMENT

Machine manufacturers test their engines and select a maximum speed for each model that provides satisfactory power in relation to fuel consumption, wear and other factors. The speed selected varies with different makes and models. The maximum idle speed recommended for your machine is given in the operator's manual. It is the one you normally use for checking your governor.

Your operator's manual may also give a full-load speed. It will be less than the high-idle speed even though the speed control lever is in the same position. As load is added, there is some loss of engine speed that the governor does not recover. For example, an engine that has a high no-load speed of 2700 revolutions per minute (rpm) may have a full-load speed of 2500 rpm. The speed loss is different with different engines.

- *If a machine is operated much faster than the top speed specified, wear increases rapidly.*

- *If the engine is operated much slower than the manufacturer recommends, there is less power available and operating costs increase.*

If only one high no-load speed is given, the governor is usually considered as being in satisfactory adjustment if the top engine speed is within 20 rpm (faster or slower) of that speed. However, some manuals will indicate a speed range such as 2500 to 2600 rpm. The governor is considered to be in proper adjustment if the high idle speed is within this range.

OPERATION OF GOVERNOR

After you set the speed control lever, the job of the governor is to adjust the amount of fuel-air mixture (fuel only for diesel engines) that the engine receives so the engine speed remains approximately the same even though the load varies. Consequently, the governor must be sensitive to speed changes. Fig. 39 shows a simplified governor control. Note that the governor is mounted on the engine camshaft where it is directly affected by any slight change in engine speed.

On **carburetor (spark-ignition) engines,** the governor controls the fuel-air mixture by opening and closing the throttle (butterfly) valve. When you open the *speed-control lever* (Fig. 40), tension is exerted on the *governor control spring.* The spring tension turns the *governor lever clockwise,* opening the *throttle valve.* More fuel-air mixture can enter the engine, causing it to speed up.

But when the engine speeds up, centrifugal force acts on the *flyweights* pushing them outward (Fig. 40). They are hinged so that when they move outward, the governor *drive plate* is pushed out. This rotates the *governor arm* which, in turn, moves the *governor lever* in a counter-clockwise direction. As a result, the butterfly valve tends to close. This would slow the engine speed except for the tension of the *governor control spring.* But a balance is reached immediately between the force of the flyweights and the tension of the governor control spring. This balance holds the throttle valve at the proper position to maintain a constant engine speed.

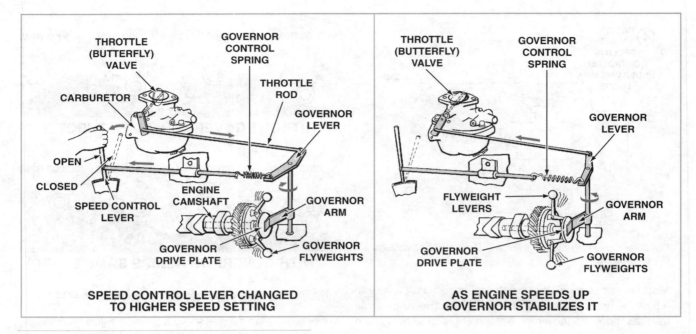

| SPEED CONTROL LEVER CHANGED TO HIGHER SPEED SETTING | AS ENGINE SPEEDS UP GOVERNOR STABILIZES IT |

Fig. 40 — Operation of Governor in Controlling Engine Speed

Let's assume *more load is put on the engine.* The engine speed slows, centrifugal force is reduced on the flyweights and they pull in. This removes some of the pressure on the *drive plate* against the *governor arm,* allowing spring tension to turn the *governor lever* in a clockwise direction (Fig. 40). The throttle valve opens further, allows more fuel-air mixture into the engine and increases horsepower output (lugging power) without increasing engine speed.

With the throttle valve open further, more fuel-air mixture is fed to the engine. Engine speed tends to increase but any increase in speed causes the flyweights to move out, overcoming enough spring tension to set up a new balance between the governor and the governor control spring which keeps the engine speed constant.

At higher engine speeds your machine has the capacity to meet a wide range of power demands. This is why it is important to set the speed control lever at high enough speed to take care of the maximum power needed for a job. When you do this, the engine is ready to start lugging the instant the governor action feeds more fuel into it. If your setting is too low, there is not enough tension on the governor spring to allow the engine to come up to full power.

GOVERNING OF DIESELS

The operating principle of the governor on a **diesel engine** is the same as that for a spark-ignition engine, except the diesel engine governor controls only the fuel going to the engine. This is done by various means, such as: an arrangement that shortens or lengthens the stroke of the injection pump to meet varying load conditions ((Fig. 41); or a master valve that meters the fuel supply to meet the varying power demands.

The built-in centrifugal governor in a typical diesel injection pump is shown in Fig. 41.

Fig. 41 — Governor in Diesel Injection Pump

MAINTAINING THE GOVERNOR

A governor in proper condition will respond quickly to a change in load conditions and will maintain, the correct engine speed without surging. Note the delicate balance that exists between the governor control spring and the governor flyweights. If the spring loses tension, if the governor parts wear or if any of the linkage that connects the mechanism starts to bind, the governor will not work properly.

Check the operator's manual for guidance on whether you should attempt to adjust it or take it to a serviceman.

TEST YOURSELF

QUESTIONS

1. (Fill in blank.) Gasoline fuels with higher octane ratings have the least tendency to produce _____ in the engine.

2. Match the two items at left with the definitions at right.

   A. No. 1-D Diesel Fuel

   B. No. 2-D Diesel Fuel

   1. Used in high-speed engines in services involving relatively high loads and uniform speeds.

   2. Used in high-speed engine in services involving frequent and relatively wide variations in loads and speeds.

3. What causes knock in diesel engines?

   A. The fuel igniting too slowly.

   B. The fuel igniting too fast.

4. In what order should the following carburetor (gasoline) adjustments be made?

   A. Load fuel-air mixture

   B. Idling fuel-air mixture

   C. Idling speed

5. Name the four basic parts of an LP- Gas fuel system.

6. Name two gases that are combined to make LP-Gas.

7. What is the number one enemy of the diesel fuel system?

8. Name the three jobs of the engine governor.

9. What are the three basic parts of the low pressure fuel system on a diesel?

10. What part of a diesel fuel system will require the most service by the operator?

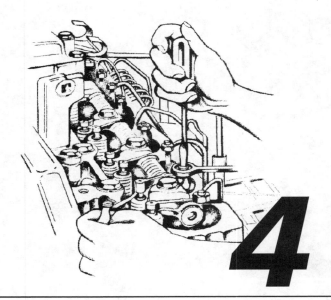

ENGINE LUBRICATION SYSTEMS

4

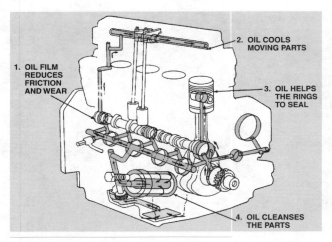

1. OIL FILM REDUCES FRICTION AND WEAR

2. OIL COOLS MOVING PARTS

3. OIL HELPS THE RINGS TO SEAL

4. OIL CLEANSES THE PARTS

Fig. 1 — Lubricating System on Typical Engine

INTRODUCTION

When agricultural engines were first used, you could have lubricated the engine with an oil can and a single type of oil. Most oil was supplied in three grades—light, medium and heavy.

But in today's high-speed engines, all this has changed. Speeds, pressures, and temperatures have all increased.

Special oils have been developed for each type of engine, for each type of machine, and for each season.

As a result, lubrication has changed from a simple chore to a science of preventive maintenance.

WHAT ENGINE OILS MUST DO

To keep today's engines running, engine oils must:

- **Reduce friction and wear**
- **Cool moving parts**
- **Help seal the cylinders**
- **Keep the parts clean**

To do these jobs, engine oil must also:

1. *Keep a protective oil film on moving parts.*

2. *Resist high temperatures.*

3. *Resist corrosion and rusting.*

4. *Prevent ring sticking.*

5. *Prevent sludge formation.*

6. *Flow easily at low temperatures.*

7. *Resist foaming.*

8. *Resist breakdown after prolonged use.*

Fig. 2 — Effect of Poor Maintenance—Piston Oil Control Ring Plugged by Oil Sludge

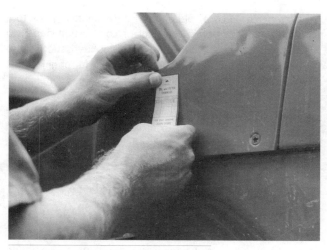

Fig. 3 — Record All Oil and Filter Changes

IMPORTANCE OF SERVICE

CHANGING ENGINE CRANKCASE OIL

Oil loses many of its good lubricating qualities as it gets dirty and its additives wear out. Acid formations, sludge, varnish, and engine deposits contaminate oil and make it unfit for continued use. This in turn can harm vital engine parts (Fig. 2).

On the other hand, just because crankcase oil is black, doesn't mean it's time for an oil change. Additives in the oil are supposed to clean and hold deposits in suspension for removal when the oil is drained.

Changing the oil at a time BEFORE the additives wear out will protect the engine against sludge. For the operator, this time is practically impossible to determine. That's why the best policy is to follow the manufacturer's recommendations on oil and filter changes.

New or rebuilt engines require oil and filter changes after a specified *break-in period.* Performing this service on time is very important, since foreign materials accumulate in the oil at a faster rate during initial operation than when the engine is broken in.

When changing the oil and filter on any engine, always warm up the engine first. This way the contaminants and foreign materials are mixed with the oil and are drained out with it.

Replacing some oil filters requires installing new gaskets or sealing rings. Be sure the sealing surfaces on the engine and filter are clean.

After installing the filter and filling the engine with oil, run the engine and check for possible filter leaks.

Keep a maintenance record of all oil and filter changes to be sure of regular engine service. Some operator's manuals provide a chart for such record keeping, or use a sticker on the cab window or hood as a reminder (Fig. 3).

PREVENTING CONTAMINATION OF OIL

Oil contamination will reduce engine life more than any other factor. Some sources of contamination are obvious while others are not.

Let's review some of these sources of contamination and what can be done about them.

1. The most obvious source of contamination is the *storing and handling of the oil* itself. Store lubricants in a clean, enclosed storage area. Keep all covers on and cap the spouts on containers when not in use. These practices not only keep dirt out of the oil, but also reduce condensation of water caused by atmospheric changes.

2. Another obvious source is *dust that is breathed into the engine* with combustion air. It is very important that the air cleaner be cleaned or replaced regularly (see Chapter 2).

3. A major source of contamination is a cold engine. When the engine is cold, its fuel burning efficiency is greatly reduced. Partially burned fuel blows by the piston rings and into the crankcase. Oxidation of this fuel in the oil forms a very harmful varnish which collects on engine parts.

   To help prevent this, be sure the thermostat is working to provide fast engine warm-up (see Chapter 5). An overchoked or misfiring engine will also create contamination from unburned fuel.

Water created by a cold engine contaminates the oil too. Water vapor, a normal product of combustion, tends to condense on cold cylinder walls. This condensation is also blown by the rings into the crankcase. The engine must warm up before this condensation problem is eliminated.

Water not only causes rusting of steel and iron surfaces, but it can combine with oxidized oil and carbon to form sludge. This sludge can very effectively plug oil screens and passages.

Contamination from a cold engine can be prevented by:

(a) Properly warming up the engine before applying a load.

(b) Making sure the engine is brought up to operating temperature each time it is used.

(c) Using the proper thermostat in the cooling system to warm up the engine as quickly as possible.

4. *Antifreeze* can be another sludge-forming source of contamination. It can also dilute the oil. To guard against antifreeze contamination:

(a) Tighten cylinder head bolts to specified torque during an overhaul.

(b) Periodically check the cooling system for internal leaks (see Chapter 5).

(c) Guard against detonation and improper use of starting fluids in diesel engine (both can result in head gasket damage).

Other problems can also cause oil contamination:

5. *Oxidation* is not an obvious source of contamination, but is is a very real one. Oxidation occurs when the hydrocarbons in the oil combine with oxygen in the air to produce organic acids. Besides being highly corrosive, these acids create harmful sludges and varnish deposits.

6. *Carbon* particles are another contaminant created by the normal operation of the engine. The particles are created when oil around the upper cylinder walls is burned during combustion. Excessive deposits can cause the piston rings to stick in their grooves.

7. *Engine wear* creates contaminants. Tiny metal particles are constantly being worn off bearings and other parts. These particles tend to reduce the oil's effectiveness.

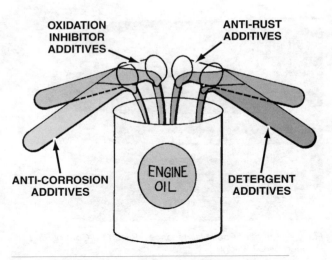

Fig. 4 — Good Quality Oil Already has Important Additives

All sources of contamination cannot be eliminated. **What, then, can be done to protect the engine?**

Start by using a good-quality oil with the proper **additives** (Fig. 4). Additives are put in the oil for a specific reason, based on the service expected for the oil.

Here are some of the important additives:

ANTI-CORROSION ADDITIVES protect metal surfaces from corrosive attack. These work with oxidation inhibitors.

OXIDATION INHIBITOR ADDITIVES keep oil from oxidizing at high temperatures. They prevent the oil from absorbing oxygen, thereby preventing varnish and sludge formations.

ANTI-RUST ADDITIVES prevent rusting of metal parts during storage periods, downtime, or even overnight. They form a protective coating which repels water droplets and protects the metal. These additives also help to neutralize harmful acids.

DETERGENT ADDITIVES help keep metal surfaces clean and prevent deposits. Particles of carbon and oxidized oil are held suspended in the oil. The suspended contaminants are then removed from the system when the oil is drained. Black oil is evidence that the oil is helping to keep the engine clean by carrying the particles in the oil rather than letting them accumulate as sludge.

However, remember that *additives eventually wear out.* To prevent any problems, drain the oil before the additives are completely depleted. Your, operator's manual will tell you when you should change oil. However, watch both the hours of operation and the elapsed time. Some additives in oil lose their effectiveness after a period of time, even if the engine has not been operated much.

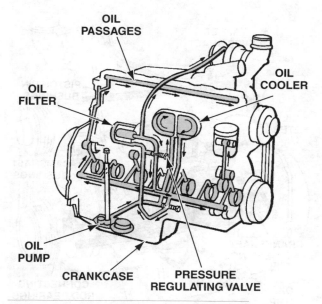

Fig. 5 — Major Parts of Engine Lubricating System

Also service engine oil filters at recommended intervals. This is usually at the same time the crankcase oil is drained and replaced.

If you use quality oil of the type recommended for the engine, other additive compounds should normally *not* be added to the engine crankcase.

Buy oil only from the manufacturer of your engine or from a reliable oil supplier. Be wary of claims of "miracle" additives, or oils which "won't wear out." Such oils could damage your engine and void the engine warranty.

Finally, keep the fuel, cooling, ignition, intake, and exhaust systems in good condition so that the fuel is efficiently burned.

OPERATION OF LUBRICATION SYSTEM

The major parts of the system are:

- **Oil Pump**
- **Crankcase**
- **Oil Cooler (if used)**
- **Oil Filter**
- **Pressure Regulating Valve**
- **Pressure Gauge**

The OIL PUMP pushes oil through the system (Fig. 5). A reserve of oil is stored in the CRANKCASE for circulation through the system. At the OIL FILTER, dirt is taken out of the oil to help keep it clean. OIL PASSAGES take the oil to engine

parts where they can provide lubrication and cooling and carry away dirt and deposits. Pressure of the oil is regulated by the PRESSURE REGULATING VALVE, which is usually adjustable. After oil moves through the whole system it comes back to the crankcase reservoir again. Finally, the PRESSURE GAUGE tells the operator if engine oil pressure is normal.

The system described above is a full force feed type. Let's now look at the major types of systems.

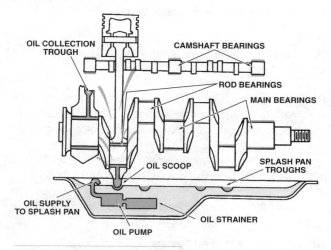

Fig. 6 — Circulating Splash System

TYPE OF SYSTEMS

An engine lubricating system may be classified as:

- **Circulating Splash**
- **Internal Force Feed and Splash**
- **Full Internal Force Feed**

The type of system used depends largely upon the size and design of the engine.

Circulating Splash System

In the *circulating splash system* an oil pump supplies oil to a splash pan located under the crankshaft (Fig. 6). As the connecting rods revolve, scoops on the ends of the rods dip into troughs in the splash pan, creating the oil splash.

The splashing oil lubricates the moving parts nearby. Other parts are lubricated more by oil mist than by the oil splash itself. This mist is created as the connecting rods spin.

The *circulating splash system* must have:

1. Proper oil level in the pan

2. Suitable oil for good splashing

There must be enough oil in the troughs of the splash pan for the connecting rods to splash. The oil pump must be working properly to provide this oil.

Because the oil must splash and flow freely, heavy oil will not work. Use only oil of the viscosity recommended by the engine manufacturer.

This system is used mainly on smaller engines.

Internal Force Feed and Splash System

In the *internal force feed and splash system,* the pump forces oil directly to a main oil gallery in the engine block rather than to a splash pan.

From the main oil gallery, the oil is forced through passages to the main bearings, connecting rod bearings, camshaft bearings, rocker arm shaft, filter, and pressure sending unit.

The oil escaping from the bearings creates a mist which also lubricates the upper cylinder walls, pistons, and pins.

Pressure of the lubricating oil can usually be adjusted in these systems.

Full Internal Force Feed System

The *full internal force feed system* goes one step farther than the system above. Oil is forced not only to the crankshaft bearings, rocker arm shaft, filter and pressure sending unit, but also to the piston pin bearings.

The piston pin bearings are lubricated through drilled passages in the connecting rods (Fig. 7). The cylinder walls and pistons are lubricated by oil escaping from the piston pin bearings or the connecting rod bearings.

The force feed system has one prime need: GOOD OIL PRESSURE.

Sufficient oil pressure is required to pump the oil long distances and through many passages. The required pressure for most engines is 25 to 40 psi (170 to 275 kPa), but it may go as high as 65 psi (450 kPa). If the oil pressure drops too low on the gauge or if you receive a low pressure warning, shut off the engine immediately and determine the cause.

Oil pressure is normally adjusted at a pressure regulating valve (shown in Fig. 7).

This type of system is widely used in today's agricultural engines.

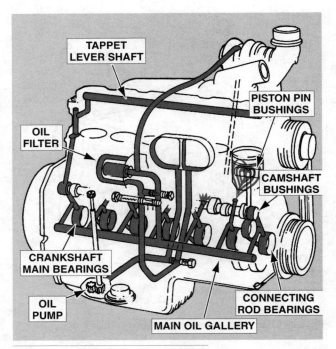

Fig. 7 — *Full Internal Force Feed System*

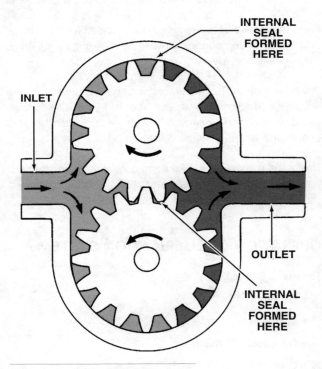

Fig. 8 — *Engine Oil Pump in Operation*

OIL PUMP

Pumps for engine lubrication are usually gear types, mechanically driven by the engine. Usually the pump is driven from the camshaft or from the crankshaft. In some large engines, an electric motor is used to drive the auxiliary pump.

The pumps push oil through the system and also trap it so that normal pressure can be built up in the system.

The common *external gear pump* has two gears in mesh, closely fitted inside a housing (Fig. 8). The drive shaft drives one gear, which in turn drives the other gear. The machined surfaces of the outer housing are used to seal the gears.

As the gears rotate and come out of mesh, they trap inlet oil between the gear teeth and the housing. The trapped oil is carried around to the outlet chamber. As the gears mesh again, they form a seal which prevents oil from backing up to the inlet. The oil is forced out at the outlet and sent through the system.

OIL FILTERS AND FILTRATION SYSTEMS

Oil contamination reduces engine life more than any other factor. To help combat this, oil filters are designed into all modern engine lubricating systems.

Let's look first at the two basic types of filters, then at two types of filtering systems.

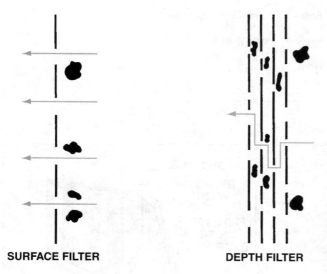

SURFACE FILTER   **DEPTH FILTER**

Fig. 9 — Surface and Depth Filters Compared

Types of Filters

Filters are classified as either *surface*-type filters or *depth*-type filters depending on the way the oil moves through them (Fig. 9).

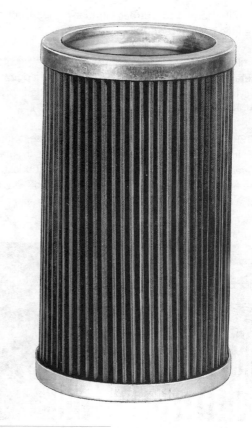

Fig. 10 — Wire Mesh Filter

Fig. 11 — Metal Edge Filter

SURFACE FILTERS have a single surface that catches and removes dirt particles larger than the holes in the filter. Dirt is strained or sheared from the oil and stopped outside the filter as oil passes through the holes in a straight path. Many of the large particles will fall to the bottom of the reservoir or filter container, but eventually enough particles will wedge in the holes of the filter to prevent further filtration. Then the filter must be cleaned or replaced.

A surface filter may be made of fine wire mesh (Fig. 10), stacked metal or paper disks, metal ribbon wound edgewise to form a cylinder (Fig. 11), cellulose material molded to the shape of a filter, or accordion pleated paper (Fig. 12).

DEPTH FILTERS, in contrast to the surface type, use a large volume of filter material to make the oil move in many different directions before it finally gets into the lubrication system. The filter made of cotton waste shown in Fig. 13 is an example of a depth filter.

Fig. 13 — Depth Filter (Cotton Waste Type)

Now let's look at the complete filtration system.

Types Of Filtration Systems

There are two types of oil filtering systems. They are:

(1) By-pass system.

(2) Full-flow system.

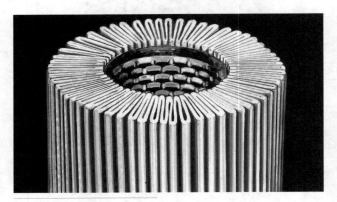

Fig. 12 — Pleated Paper Filter

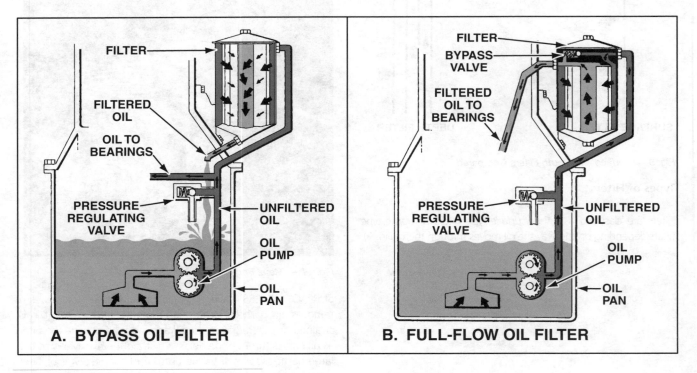

Fig. 14 — Two Types of Engine Oil Filters Compared

Both are shown in Fig. 14. Note in Fig. 14A that in the *by-pass system* only a portion of the oil moves through the filter as it leaves the pump. The rest goes directly to the engine bearings. With this type only about 1/10th to about 1/30th of the oil is by-passed through the filter at any one time. As the filter becomes contaminated, less of the oil goes through and more goes around.

With the *full-flow system,* as shown in Fig. 14B, all of the oil moves through the filter unless it is partly or completely blocked because of a dirty filter or cold oil. In that case, oil pressure builds up in the filter until the bypass valve is forced open, permitting unfiltered oil to flow around the filter and directly to the engine bearings. This protects the engine against loss of needed oil.

The full-flow filter, as part of an internal force-feed system, is used on most modern agricultural engines.

OIL COOLERS

Lubrication systems of many engines use an oil cooler to help remove the heat created by the engine. Most coolers are the oil-to-water cooling type, using engine coolant to dissipate unwanted heat from the engine crankcase oil.

The oil cooler may be mounted inside the crankcase or on the outside of the engine block.

The full-flow filter as part of an internal force-feed system is used on most modern agricultural engines.

Operation Of Oil Cooler

As shown in Fig. 15, coolant circulates around the plates in the cooler, while the engine oil flows inside the plates. Heat from the oil is conducted through the plates to the coolant, which carries it to the radiator for dissipation.

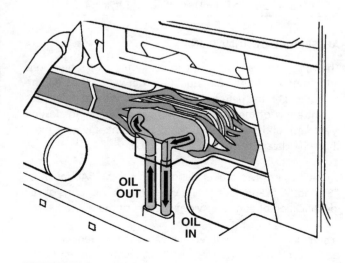

Fig. 15 — Operation of Engine Oil Cooler

Another cooler (not shown) uses a small radiator core. The oil is pumped through the core and coolant is circulated around it.

A bypass valve is used with some oil coolers to assure circulation of the oil if the cooler should become clogged.

SELECTING ENGINE OILS

If you are to receive the best performance possible from a machine, you must use lubricants of the highest quality. The savings to be gained with lower-quality oils are at best small in relation to your over-all operating costs.

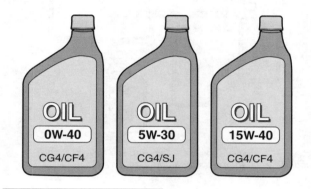

Fig. 16 — Selecting an Engine Oil

How can you be assured of obtaining an oil of high quality and one that's right for the job?

First, follow your operator's manual recommendations for engine oil (Fig. 16). Second, choose oil from a reliable supplier—a reputable brand of oil.

To select the proper oil, you must be able to identify it. Descriptions such as "viscosity" and "service classification" are used to identify types of engine oils.

The Society of Automotive Engineers (SAE) has established the **Viscosity** designation which is a measure of the *fluidity of an oil at a given temperature.*

The American Petroleum Institute (API) established the **Service Classification** designation which identifies the *engine service design of the oil.*

Let's look at how oils are rated by these two organizations.

SAE VISCOSITY

As we stated, SAE rates the oil viscosity—or ability to flow at a given temperature. The lighter or more fluid oils intended for winter use are specified at OF (-18°C) and carry a 5W,

1OW, or 20W symbol. Heavier oils for warmer operation are specified at 210°F (99°C) and carry SAE 30 and 40 symbols.

Oils vary in viscosity as temperatures change—becoming more fluid as temperatures increase and less fluid as temperatures decrease. The temperature effect on viscosity is not the same for all oils, and a measure of this is often important to the user.

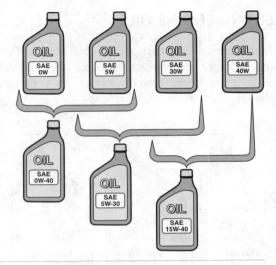

Fig. 17 — A Multi-Viscosity Oil Can Replace Several Single Viscosity Oils (When Recommended)

Some oils are compounded to behave as light oils at cold temperatures and as heavier oils at high temperatures. These oils are called **multi-viscosity oils** and include, for example, 5W-30 (Fig. 17). One multi-viscosity oil can replace several single-grade oils. Multi-viscosity oils are preferred as they give protection at both high and low temperatures.

SAE viscosity numbers are widely used as a means of identifying and classifying lubricating oil, and today are found on practically all cans or drums of oil marketed in the United States (Fig. 18).

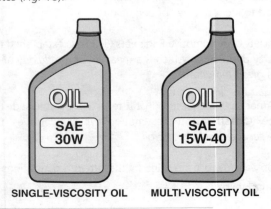

SINGLE-VISCOSITY OIL   **MULTI-VISCOSITY OIL**

Fig. 18 — Viscosity is Marked on Oil Containers

Each number indicates a permissible range or limit of viscosity at specified temperatures. No attempt is made to define the oil's quality, additive content, performance value or suitability for specified service conditions. Therefore, the SAE viscosity should not be the only factor considered when selecting an oil.

Fig. 19 shows one equipment manufacturer's oil viscosity recommendations for four-cycle diesel engines operating at various temperature levels. Note the upper temperature limits recommended for multiviscosity oils in industrial equipment applications.

API Service Designations For Engine Oils

SAE Letter	API Identification
SC	1964-67 Gasoline Engine Warranty Service
SD	1968-71 Gasoline Engine Warranty Service
SE	1972 Gasoline Engine Warranty Service
SF	1980 Gasoline Engine Warranty Service
SG	1989 Gasoline Engine Warranty Service
OB	Moderate Duty Diesel Engine Service
CC	Moderate Duty Diesel & Gasoline Engine Service
CD	Severe Duty Diesel Engine Service 1
CE	Severe Duty Diesel Engine Service 2
CF-4/EG-4	Severe Duty Diesel Engine Service 3

API SERVICE DESIGNATIONS

The API system is an attempt to clarify the oil specifications and better define oil qualities between the engine manufacturer, the petroleum industry, and the customer. It is a joint effort of the API, ASTM (American Society for Testing Materials), and SAE organizations. Lubricants meeting more than one classification can be so marked.

The API chart gives a brief designation for the SAE family of "S" and "C" designations and what it means in terms of API identification of engine service expected of the oil.

A summary of all current recommendations, current common names, and new Performance Classifications is given in the following chart. The U.S. Army also has military (MIL) specifications which parallel some of the API designations.

SUMMARY OF CURRENT EQUIPMENT MANUFACTURER RECOMMENDATIONS—ENGINE OILS

Application	Oil Recommendations		Comments
	API Performance Classification	Common Current Name	
Gasoline Engine, Passenger Car	SE[1] SF[1] SG/SH/SJ[1]	—	Meet warranty requirements of passenger car manufacturers.
Gasoline Engine, Truck, Bus and Off Highway	CC/CD/CE/CF4/CGH4[1] SE[1] SF[1] SG/SH/SJ[1]	MIL-B —	Principally concererned with heavy duty, some applications may require improved low temperature performance of SF adn SE.
Diesel Engine, Truck, Bus and Off Highway	CB CC CD[2] CE[2] CF-4/CG-4	Supplement 1 MIL-B Series 3 (S-3)	Recommendation of performance level involves consideration of engine design factors as well as application.

1. *Oils meeting the performance requirements of MIL-L-46152B meet the performance requirements of SE, CC, and SF. Oils meeting military specification MIL-L-46167A may be used as arctic oils.*
2. *Oils meeting the performance requirements of MIL-L-2104C or MIL-L-2104D meet the performance requirements of both CD and CE. Oils meeting military specification MIL-L-46167A may be used as arctic oils.*

Fig. 19 — Engine Oils

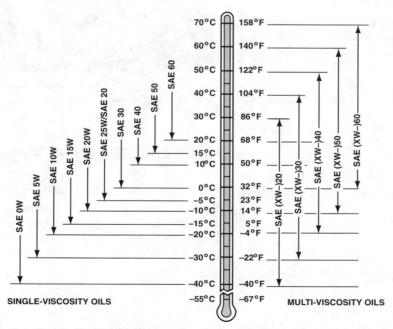

Cold weather oil blends (0W, 5W, 10W) that do not have the listed minimum industry performance (CF-4, ACEAE2), are limited to 100-hour drain intervals.

Fig. 20 — Typical Oil Viscosity Recommendations at Various Temperature Levels (Diesel and Gasoline Engines)

Fig. 20 shows one equipment manufacturer's oil viscosity recommendations for four-cycle gasoline engines operating at various temperature levels.

AGRICULTURAL VS. AUTOMOTIVE ENGINE OILS

Agricultural machines operate almost continuously under full loads, at constant speeds, over long periods of time (Fig. 21).

By comparison, automotive and light truck engines have lighter loads and more idling and stop-and-go driving conditions.

As you can see, each application is very different. For this reason, engineers have recently developed engine oils specifically for off-the-road farm and industrial machines.

If the operator's manual recommends a special engine oil, the engine will probably perform better with that oil than with any other—use it if at all possible.

STORING AND HANDLING ENGINE OILS

Use care in storing and handling oil to keep out dirt and moisture.

Store oil inside whenever possible—in clean, closed cabinets or rooms. It is best to keep oil relatively warm in the winter. Rapid changes in temperature can draw water into oil barrels if stored outside.

If stored outside, lay barrels on their sides. If they cannot be laid on their sides, tilt them slightly, and turn the barrel so that the bung is at the high side, away from any water which might collect.

Keep oil bungs drawn tight. Use wooden mallets to make sure.

Rinse oil containers and funnels in fuel after use. Cover them to keep out dirt, or store them upside down.

When adding oil, clean all dirt from around the filler cap before removing it. (Do the same before unscrewing an oil filter or a filter cap.)

Fig. 21 — Agricultrual Machines Don't Work Like Automobiles— and May Need Special Engine Oils

SERVICING THE LUBRICATING SYSTEM

You must service the engine lubricating system regularly to prevent premature wear and engine damage. This service consists mainly of checking crankcase oil level daily and changing the oil and filter at the proper intervals.

CHECKING CRANKCASE OIL LEVEL (DAILY)

Check the crankcase oil level **daily** (Fig. 22).

Don't check the oil level while the engine is running. Try to allow 10 minutes for oil to drain down after engine is stopped.

Remove the dipstick as shown and wipe dry with a clean cloth. Then insert fully and withdraw to check oil level.

Look at the top and bottom marks, which may be labeled "FULL" and "ADD". (Some manufacturers make the dipstick short so that when no oil shows it is time to add.)

Add oil if needed. If oil is down to lower mark, add recommended oil (usually one quart [one liter]) to fill to upper mark on dipstick.

Be sure oil and container are clean.

Don't overfill; this can cause oil consumption and foaming.

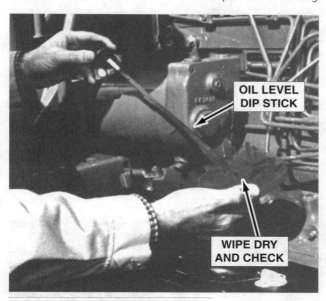

Fig. 22 — Check the Engine Oil Level Daily

CHANGING CRANKCASE OIL AND FILTER

The oil in the crankcase of your engine should be changed every 250 hours or as recommended (refer to your operator's manual for specific times). Periods vary from 60 to 300 hours. Changing the oil filter is usually recommended at the same time. Be sure to change the oil and the filter more often if operating in extremely dirty or dusty conditions.

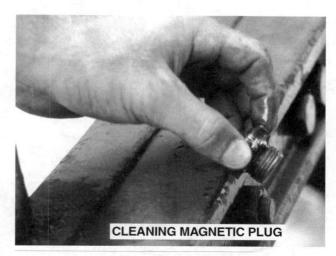

CLEANING MAGNETIC PLUG

Fig. 23 — Removing Engine Crankcase Drain Plug

Tools and Materials Needed

1. Wrenches for crankcase drain plug and filter cap if needed (inch or metric, as required).

2. Clean, lint free cloths.

3. Cleaning solvent (not gasoline).

4. New oil of grade and type recommended to your engine and anticipated temperature.

5. New oil filter cartridge

6. Container to catch waste oil.

Procedure For Changing Engine Oil and Filter

To change the oil in the crankcase, proceed as follows:

1. Operate the engine until it is thoroughly heated. This permits the oil to drain more completely. More contaminants are removed while the oil is still agitated. If the oil is drained while cold, contaminants may remain in the engine.

2. Shut off the engine and remove the drain plug (Fig. 23). Magnetic drain plugs may have metal particles on them. Strike the plug against a solid object to remove the particles. Be careful not to damage threads.

3. Allow the oil to drain for several minutes (Fig. 24). This permits oil to drain completely from various parts of the engine.

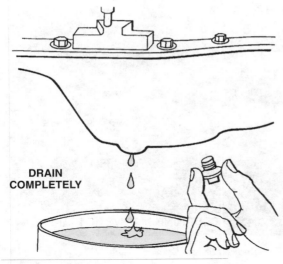

DRAIN COMPLETELY

Fig. 24 — Allow Crankcase to Drain Completely

4. Wipe dirt from filter and surrounding area.

5. Loosen filter bowl or cover and remove (Fig. 25). (If the filter has a drain plug, remove the plug and allow the filter to drain before removing.)

   IMPORTANT: Engine must be stopped while filter is removed.

6. Remove old filter cartridge and discard it.

7. Clean inside of filter bowl and base with solvent (not gasoline) (Fig. 26) if the same bowl is used again.

FILTER BOWL

USE CLEANING SOLVENT NOT GASOLINE

Fig. 26 — Clean Inside of Filter Bowl and Base

8. Replace and tighten drain plugs in the crankcase and filter if removed.

9. Install new filter gasket, if supplied with filter. With a "spin-on" filter, apply a light film of engine oil or grease to the gasket or sealing ring (Fig. 27) before installing it. This will prevent tearing the seal as it is tightened.

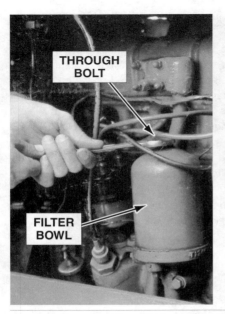

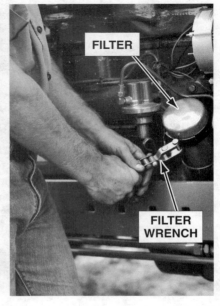

THROUGH BOLT

FILTER BOWL

FILTER

FILTER WRENCH

Fig. 25 — Removing Three Kinds of Engine Oil Filters

10. Install new filter cartridge. Do not tighten too much as seals can be damaged. With spin-on filters, turn the filter until the seal contacts the base, then tighten no more than an extra one-half turn (Fig. 27). This keeps from overtightening which distorts the seal and causes leaks. On vertical-mounted filters, pre-fill the filter with new oil before installing.

IMPORTANT: Be sure the new filter is an exact duplicate of the one recommended by the engine manufacturer.

Fig. 27 — Clean Oil Container and Filling Equipment

11. If separate filter bowl is used, replace it and tighten. Do not over-tighten.

12. Fill crankcase with new oil. Use the proper amount of oil. Do not overfill. Clean tops of oil cans and use a clean funnel or spout (Fig. 28). Use the viscosity and type of oil recommended in your operator's manual.

13. Start the engine and operate it for a few minutes. This gives the oil an opportunity to coat and protect parts and fill the oil filter.

14. Check for oil leaks around the drain plug and the filter (Fig. 29). Also check the pressure gauge on control console to make certain that the oil pump is working properly.

15. Check oil level on the dipstick, after allowing engine to set for a few minutes. If oil is not to the "full" line, add more until it reaches that level. *Do not over fill;* this can cause oil consumption and oil foaming.

Fig. 28 — Check for Oil Leaks After Installing Engine Filter

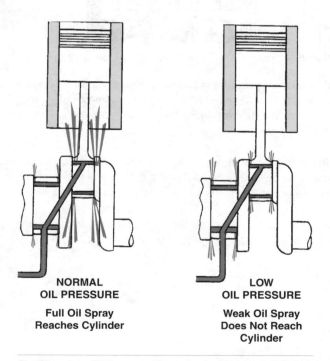

NORMAL OIL PRESSURE

Full Oil Spray Reaches Cylinder

LOW OIL PRESSURE

Weak Oil Spray Does Not Reach Cylinder

Fig. 29 — Low Oil Pressure Means Lack of Engine Lubrication

TESTING ENGINE OIL PRESSURE

The modern engine must have full oil pressure or not enough lubricating oil will reach vital engine working parts (Fig. 29).

All modern engines with pressurized lubricating systems have an oil pressure gauge on the operator's console (Fig. 30). Watch this gauge for proper oil pressure. Once the engine is started and running, this gauge should read in the normal range (or go out if it is a glowing indicator). If not, stop the engine at once and find the cause.

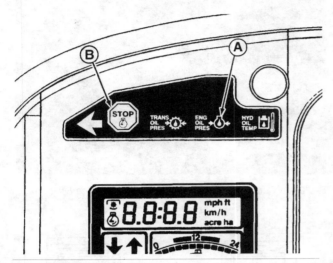

Fig. 30 — Engine Oil Pressure Gauge (A) On Operator's Console

If engine oil pressure is too low, crankcase oil level may be down, oil may be too thin, oil pump or engine bearings may be worn, the gauge may be bad, or the pressure valve may only need adjustment.

Too-high oil pressure is not as common, but can be caused by crankcase oil that is too heavy, a defective pressure gauge, or a stuck regulating valve or one that is out of adjustment.

Anytime the oil pressure is too high or low, stop the engine and install a master gauge to check it as follows:

HOW TO TEST ENGINE OIL PRESSURE

1. Before checking the engine oil pressure, always check the condition of the oil filter. A dirty filter will drop the pressure reading.

2. Also check the oil level in the crankcase. Low oil level may show up as low oil pressure. .

3. Many engines have tapped holes in the block as oil pressure test points. On other engines, the oil pressure sending unit hole is used for testing.

4. Install a master gauge as shown in Fig. 31.

5. Start and run the engine at fast-idle speed.

6. When the engine is warmed up to operating temperature, record the pressure reading on the gauge. Compare this reading with the specifications for the engine.

7. If master gauge indicates pressure is satisfactory, but gauge on operator's console still reads high or low, replace oil pressure sensor and/or gauge which are often supplied as a single unit.

8. Adjust engine oil pressure if necessary.

Fig. 31 — Checking the Engine Oil Pressure

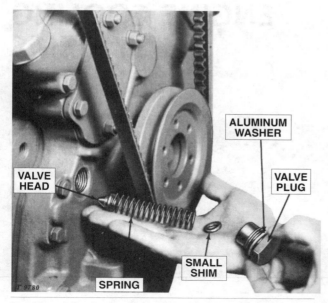

Fig. 32 — *Adjusting Engine Oil Pressure (Shim-Adjusted Valves)*

Some regulating valves are adjusted by an adjusting screw (Fig. 32). Normally, turn the screw *in* to increase the spring tension and the pressure setting. Turn the screw *out* to decrease the pressure setting.

Shims and washers are used for adjusting pressure in some regulating valves (Fig. 32).

To lower pressure, shims are removed to decrease the tension of the spring and allow the valve to open at a lower setting.

Recheck pressure on master gauge. If okay, remove gauge and install plug.

If the oil pressure problem continues, have a serviceman inspect the engine.

TEST YOURSELF

QUESTIONS

1. What four functions must engine oil perform to keep engines running?

2. (Fill in blank.) The Society of Automotive Engineers established the SAE _____ designation which is a measure of the fluidity of an oil at a given temperature.

3. When the crankcase oil is black, it is time for an oil change.
   True _____   False_____

4. Oil additives hardly ever wear out.
   True _____   False_____

5. (Fill in blank.) "Oil _____ will reduce engine life more than any other factor."

6. Name the three types of lubricating systems.

7. (Fill in blanks.) The two basic types of oil filtration systems are _____ and _____ .

8. How often should the engine crankcase oil level be checked?

9. Why should an engine be warmed up before draining the oil?

10. Tighten oil filters as tight as possible or they may leak.
    True _____   False_____

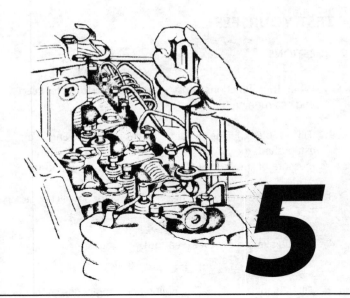

ENGINE COOLING SYSTEMS

5

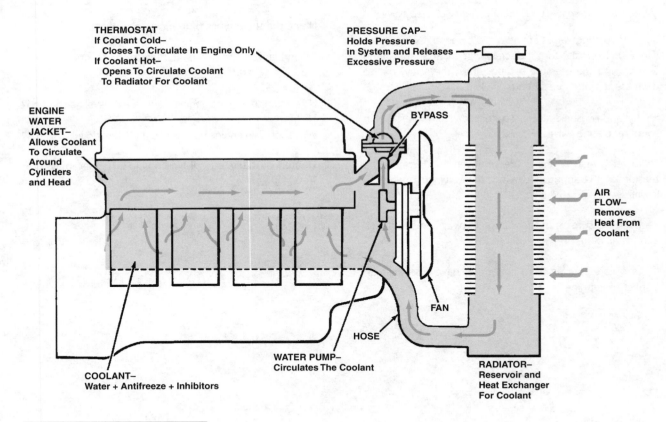

THERMOSTAT
If Coolant Cold–
  Closes To Circulate In Engine Only
If Coolant Hot–
  Opens To Circulate Coolant
  To Radiator For Coolant

PRESSURE CAP–
Holds Pressure
in System and Releases
Excessive Pressure

ENGINE
WATER
JACKET–
Allows Coolant
To Circulate
Around
Cylinders
and Head

BYPASS

AIR
FLOW–
Removes
Heat From
Coolant

FAN

HOSE

WATER PUMP–
Circulates The Coolant

RADIATOR–
Reservoir and
Heat Exchanger
For Coolant

COOLANT–
Water + Antifreeze + Inhibitors

Fig. 1 — Basic Engine Cooling System

INTRODUCTION

If a liquid-cooled engine were run without its coolant, the pistons and bearings would soon *weld* to their mating parts and the engine would be damaged beyond repair.

JOBS OF COOLING SYSTEM

The engine cooling system does two things:

- **Prevents overheating**
- **Regulates temperatures**

OVERHEATING could "burn up" the engine parts. Some heat is necessary for combustion, but the engine generates too much. So the cooling system is designed to carry off the excess heat.

REGULATING TEMPERATURES keeps the engine at the best heat level for each operation. Just after starting, the engine must be warmed faster, while during peak operations, the engine must be cooled and kept at a constant temperature.

PARTS OF COOLING SYSTEM

A liquid cooling system (Fig. 1) consists of the following:

- **Radiator and Pressure Cap**
- **Fan and Fan Belt**
- **Coolant Pump**
- **Engine Coolant Jacket**
- **Thermostat**
- **Connecting Hoses**
- **Liquid or Coolant**
- **Coolant Filter-Conditioner (if used)**

Now we will see how these parts function in the complete system.

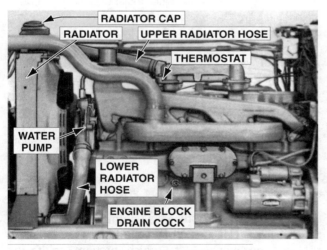

Fig. 2 — Liquid Cooling System On Modern Engine

OPERATION OF COOLING SYSTEM

The RADIATOR is one of the major components of any liquid cooling system (Fig. 1). It is here that heat in the coolant is released to the atmosphere. The radiator also provides a reservoir for enough liquid to operate the cooling system efficiently.

Coolant from the engine enters the radiator by way of the top tank, then passes down through a series of small tubes surrounded by fins and air passages. Cooled liquid reaching the bottom tank is picked up by the water pump to repeat the complete cycle.

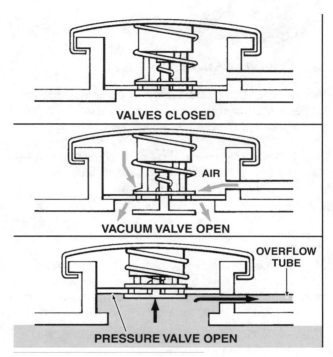

Fig. 3 — Pressure Control Radiator Cap

The RADIATOR CAP (Fig. 3) provides pressure control of the cooling system. With a pressure cap, the boiling point of the coolant can be raised (a 7 psi [50 kPa] cap raises the boiling point of water from 212° to about 230°F, or approximately 100° to 110°C). This allows the engine to operate at higher temperatures for better efficiency.

A *pressure valve* (Fig. 3) in the cap permits the escape of coolant or steam when the pressure reaches a certain point.

The *vacuum valve* in the cap opens to prevent a vacuum in the cooling system when the system cools.

The FAN forces cooling air through the radiator to more quickly dissipate the heat being carried by the coolant into the radiator. The fan is generally driven by a belt from the engine crankshaft, although some engines may use an electrically powered fan.

The COOLANT PUMP circulates the coolant through the cooling system (Fig. 4). The pump draws hot coolant from the engine block and forces it through the radiator for cooling. When the pump fails to circulate the coolant, heat is not removed from the engine and overheating will occur.

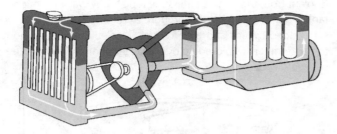

Fig. 4 — Coolant Pump is Heart of Cooling System

The THERMOSTAT provides automatic control of engine temperature at the correct level. This is necessary in order to get the best performance from an engine.

During warm-up the thermostat remains closed (Fig. 5, right). The water pump circulates the coolant through the engine coolant jacket only, by way of the bypass.

This quickly warms the engine to its operating temperature before the thermostat opens (Fig. 5, left).

When the thermostat opens (usually at 180°F to 190°F; 82° to 88°C), hot coolant flows from the engine to the radiator and back. An engine operating at a temperature lower than recommended will use more fuel, have less power, and have increased cylinder wear.

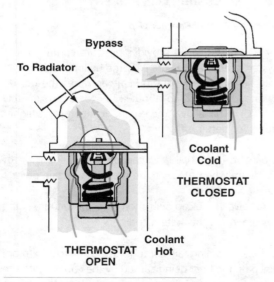

Fig. 5 — Thermostat for Cooling System

The COOLING SYSTEM HOSES are flexible because they stand up under vibration better than rigid pipes.

A COOLANT FILTER-CONDITIONER (used on some engines) contains chemicals which soften the water, maintain a proper acid/alkaline condition, prevent corrosion, and suppress cavitation erosion.

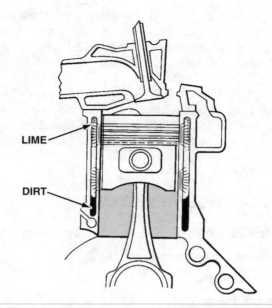

Fig. 6 — Mineral Deposits from Using Water Alone as a Coolant

The COOLANT or liquid which circulates in the system to absorb and release heat will be covered next.

COOLANTS

The primary purpose of the liquid coolant circulating through the engine is to absorb and dissipate the excess heat created by the engine.

While water was once used as a coolant in early engines, it is not recommended today. *Use water only in an emergency situation. Drain the cooling system and refill with antifreeze as soon as possible.*

An antifreeze solution is the recommended coolant for both gasoline and diesel engines even in geographical areas where freeze protection is not necessary.

COOLANT FOR MODERN DIESEL ENGINES

IMPORTANT: Some diesel engine manufacturers recommend a specific coolant containing supplement coolant additives (SCA's) which prevent cavitation (corrosive pitting) of the cylinder liners. There are restrictions to the alternatives for these specified coolants. SCA's wear out and must be periodically replaced. ALWAYS consult the machine manual when dealing with a diesel engine.

In general, use water as a coolant only in an emergency situation. Drain the water from the cooling system and refill with the recommended coolant as soon as possible.

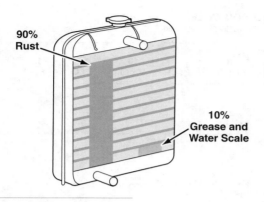

90% Rust

10% Grease and Water Scale

Fig. 7 — Rust in Clogging Material

WATER AS A COOLANT

Water, by itself is not a satisfactory coolant. Without inhibitor additives it will rust, corrode, and leave deposits in the engine coolant jacket and cause the radiator to plug (Fig . 6). Without an antifreeze solution, it Will freeze at 32°F (0°C).

The best water for coolant is clean soft water-distilled water or rain water is the best source. Most ground water is to hard and contains minerals which form scale in the engine. Artificially softened water is better, but there are still dissolved minerals in it. Even distilled water, while the purest of all, needs inhibitors.

The problem is that *all* waters tend to either corrode or form deposits. Waters that have been softened may tend to corrode metal parts, while harder tap waters tend to form deposits.

The safest rule is to add commercial **inhibitors** to the water even in summer to prevent rust, corrosion, and deposits.

Usually when the radiator becomes clogged, up to 90 percent of the material is rust (Fig. 7).

ANTIFREEZE

Antifreeze is mixed with water to produce a coolant solution. The prime characteristic of the solution is that it will not freeze. If a coolant freezes, it, will expand and may crack the engine block or head and create leaks. It may also weaken the radiator and hoses. During operation of the engine, freezing can prevent circulation of the coolant causing the engine to run hot.

An effective antifreeze solution will:

1. *Prevent freezing at the lowest expected temperature.*

2. *Flow readily at all temperatures.*

3. *Inhibit rust and corrosion of system parts.*

4. *Will be chemically stable.*

5. *Conduct heat readily.*

6. *Resist foaming.*

7. *Have a higher boiling point than water (Fig. 8).*

8. *Provide lubrication for pump and seals.*

9. *Will not expand too much.*

10. *Will not have an unpleasant odor.*

Types of Antifreeze

The two types of antifreeze used in engine coolant solutions today are:

- **Ethylene glycol base**
- **Propylene glycol base**

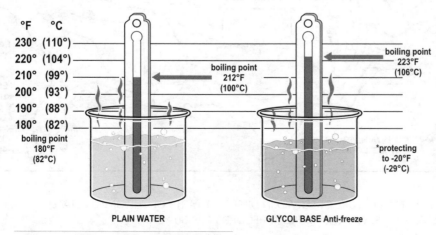

°F	°C
230°	(110°)
220°	(104°)
210°	(99°)
200°	(93°)
190°	(88°)
180°	(82°)

boiling point 180°F (82°C)

boiling point 212°F (100°C)

boiling point 223°F (106°C)

*protecting to -20°F (-29°C)

PLAIN WATER

GLYCOL BASE Anti-freeze

Fig. 8 — Shielded Metal Arc Welding (SMAW)

FREEZING PROTECTION TABLE

FULL STRENGTH "PERMANENT" ANTIFREEZE REQUIRED

Quarts

COOLING SYSTEM CAPACITY QUARTS (LITERS)	1 °F (°C)	2 °F (°C)	3 °F (°C)	4 °F (°C)	5 °F (°C)	6 °F (°C)	7 °F (°C)	8 °F (°C)	9 °F (°C)	10 °F (°C)	11 °F (°C)	12 °F (°C)	13 °F (°C)
5 (4. 7)	16° (- 9.0°)	-12° (-22.0°)	-62° (-52.0°)										
6 (5.7)	19° (- 7.0°)	0° (-17.5°)	-34° (-36.5°)										
7 (6.6)	22° (- 5.5°)	7° (-14.0°)	-17° (-27.0°)	-54° (-47.5°)									
8 (7.6)	23° (- 5.0°)	11° (-12.0°)	- 7° (-14.0°)	-34° (-36.5°)	-69° (-56.0)								
9 (8.5)	24° (- 4.5°)	14° (-10.0)	0° (-17.5°)	-21° (-29.5°)	-50° (-45.5°)								
10 (9.5)	25° (- 4.0°)	16° (- 9.0°)	4° (-15.5°)	-12° (-24.5°)	-34° (-36.5°)	-62° (-52.0°)							
11 (10.4)	26° (- 3.5°)	18° (- 8.0°)	8° (-13.5°)	- 6° (-21.0°)	-23° (-31.0°)	47° (-44.0°)							
12 (11.4)		19° (- 7.0°)	10° (-12.0°)	0° (-17.5°)	-15° (-26.0°)	-34° (-36.5°)	-57° (-49.5°)						
13 (12.3)		21° (- 6.0°)	13° (-10.5°)	3° (-16.0°)	- 9° (-23.0°)	-25° (31.5°)	-45° (-43.0°)	-66° (-55.5°)					
14 (13.2)			15° (- 9.5°)	6° (-14.5°)	- 5° (-20.5°)	-18° (-28.0°)	-34° (-36.5°)	-54° (-47.5°)					
15 (14.2)			16° (- 9.0°)	8° (-13.5°)	0° (-17.5°)	-12° (-24.5°)	-26° (-32.0°)	-43° (-41.5°)	-62° (-52.0°)				
16 (15.1)			17° (- 8.5°)	10° (-12.0°)	2° (-16.5°)	- 8° (-22.0°)	-19° (-28.5°)	-34° (-36.5°)	-52° (-46.5°)				
17 (16.1)			18° (- 8.0°)	12° (-11.0°)	5° (-15.0°)	- 4° (-20.0°)	-14° (-25.5°)	-27° (-33.0°)	-42° (-41.0°)	-58° (-50.0°)			
18 (17.0)			19° (- 7.0°)	14° (-14.0°)	7° (-14.0°)	0° (-17.5°)	-10° (-23.5°)	-21° (-29.5°)	-34° (-36.5°)	-50° (-45.5°)	-65° (-54.0°)		
19 (18.0)			20° (- 6.5°)	15° (- 9.5°)	9° (-13.0°)	2° (-16.5°)	- 7° (-22.0°)	-16° (-26.5°)	-28° (-33.5°)	-42° (-41.0°)	-56° (-49.0°)		
20 (18.9)				16° (- 9.0°)	10° (-12.0°)	4° (-15.5°)	- 3° (-19.5°)	-12° (-24.5°)	-22° (-30.0°)	-34° (-35.5°)	-48° (-44.5°)	-62° (-52.0°)	
21 (19.9)				17° (- 8.5°)	12° (-11.0°)	6° (-14.5°)	0° (-17.0°)	- 9° (-23.0°)	-17° 27.0°	-28° (-33.5°)	-41° (-40.5°)	-54° (-47.5°)	-68° (-55.5°)
22 (20.8)				18° (- 8.0°)	13° (-10.5°)	8° (-13.5°)	2° (-16.5°)	- 6° (-21.0°)	-14° (-25.5°)	-23° (-31.0°)	-34° (-36.5°)	-47° (-44.0°)	-59° (-50.5°)
23 (21.8)				19° (- 7.0°)	14° (-10.0°)	9° (-13.0°)	4° (-15.5°)	- 3° (-19.5°)	-10° (-23.5°)	-19° (-28.5°)	-29° (-34.0°)	-40° (-40.0°)	-52° (-46.5°)
24 (22.7)					15° (- 9.5°)	10° (-12.0°)	5° (-15.0°)	0° (-17.0°)	- 8° (-22.0°)	-15° (-26.0°)	-24° (-31.0°)	-34° (-36.5°)	-46° (-43.5°)

(Note: Celsius temperatures above are rounded to nearest 0.5°

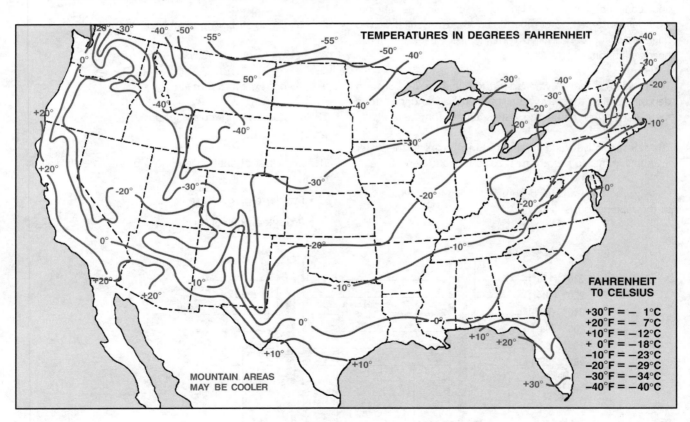

LOWEST TEMPERATURE OBSERVED IN DIFFERENT PARTS OF THE UNITED STATES.
BASED ON U. S. WEATHER BUREAU RECORDS FOR 50 YEARS.

Fig. 9 — Freezing Protection Tables

CAUTION: Glycol base antifreezes can be fatal if swallowed by humans or animals. Always store containers safely away from children and pets. Clean up spilled antifreeze at once.

Operating characteristics of the two glycol base antifreezes are similar. Ethylene glycol antifreeze contains a *YELLOW* dye. Propylene glycol antifreeze, often referred to as "low -tox," contains a *PURPLE* dye. While antifreezes will not boil away, they will wear out or become contaminated. Most antifreezes are recommended for only one or at most two seasons before they are replaced.

Freezing Protection For Coolant

When you add antifreeze, protect for the lowest expected temperatures. The map in Fig. 9 show the lowest temperature observed in various parts of the United States during the past 50 years (from U.S. Weather Bureau records).

Check your operators manual for this system capacity of your engine. Then use the chart in Fig. 9 to find how much full-strength "permanent" antifreeze is required to protect to the lowest expected temperature. For example, a tractor operating in Northern Illinois should be protected to approx. -25°F (-32°C). If the tractor cooling system had a 20 quart (75 liter) capacity, then 10-quarts (or 37 liters) of permanent antifreeze would be needed.

Install and maintain a 33 to 50 percent solution (0°F; -18°C freezing protection) for corrosion protection. A 50 percent solution will provide protection to -34°F (-36°C). (A 68 percent solution will protect to about 90°F; -68°C).

Because of the nature of ethylene glycol, a greater concentration of antifreeze will actually give *less* protection. Examples of this are that an 80 percent solution will provide protection to -57°F (-50°C) and a 100 percent solution provides protection only to -9°F (-23°C).

IMPORTANCE OF SERVICE

The cooling system absorbs about 1/3 of the heat energy developed by the engine fuel. Another 1/3 of the heat energy is used for power, and the remaining 1/3 is dissipated through exhaust gases and crankcase oil. If the cooling system fails to remove its share of the heat the engine may be severely damaged.

In Fig. 10 you can see some of the problems of a poorly maintained cooling system. These problems not only affect the cooling system but other parts of the engine and could result in costly damage.

Damage From Engine Too Hot

If these problems *cause the engine to run too hot,* the following damage may result:

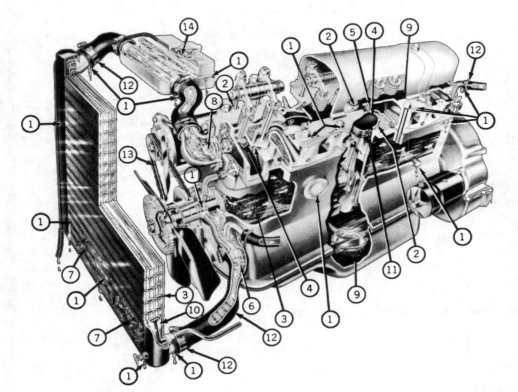

① **External Leakage**
② **Internal Leakage**
③ **Rust Deposits**
④ **Heat Cracks**
⑤ **Exhaust Gas Leakage**
⑥ **Air Suction**
⑦ **Clogged Air Passages**
⑧ **Stuck Thermostat**
⑨ **Sludge Formation in Oil**
⑩ **Transmission Oil Cooler**
⑪ **Heat Damage**
⑫ **Hose Failure**
⑬ **Worn Fan Belt**
⑭ **Pressure Cap Leakage**

Fig. 10 — Maintenance Problems of the Engine Cooling System

1. LET SYSTEM COOL

2. TURN CAP ONLY TO STOP TO RELEASE PRESSURE

3. THEN REMOVE CAP SLOWLY

Fig. 11 — Checking Coolant Level

- *Burned Valves and Spark Plugs*
- *Scored Pistons*
- *Lubrication Failure*
- *Excessive Engine Wear*
- *Engine Knock, Detonation or Preignition*

Damage From Engine Too Cold

If the engine runs too cold, the following may result:

- *Unnecessary Wear*
- *Poor Fuel Economy*
- *Crankcase Dilution by Fuel*
- *Fouled Spark Plugs*
- *Sludge formation in crankcase*

SERVICING THE COOLING SYSTEM

To maintain the engine cooling system properly, check the coolant level daily and perform other periodic maintenance as explained below.

TOOLS AND MATERIALS NEEDED

1. Commercial *flushing* compound if cooling system is in good condition.

   Commercial *cleaning* compound if there is much scale and rust present.

2. Soft distilled water.

3. Clean container to catch drained coolant.

4. Adjustable pliers.

5. Screwdriver.

6. Wrenches (if needed, inch or metric, as required).

7. Goggles or glasses for eye protection.

SERVICES TO BE COVERED

Maintenance of the cooling system will be covered as follows:

- **Checking coolant**
- **Preventing leaks**
- **Preventing corrosion**
- **Flushing or cleaning system**
- **Filling system with coolant**
- **Coolant pump lubrication**
- **Checking fan belt Let's discuss each subject in detail.**

Let's discuss each subject in detail.

CHECKING COOLANT

Checking Coolant Level

 CAUTION: When checking the coolant level, wait until the coolant temperature has cooled well below the boiling point before removing the pressure cap (Fig. 11). Then loosen the cap only to the first stop to relieve pressure before removing the cap completely.

The coolant level should be 1/2 to 2 inches (12 to 48 mm) below the neck of the radiator tank, depending on the system (Fig. 12). Follow the engine manufacturer's recommendations. *Never overfill the system.* A pressurized system needs space for heat expansion without overflowing. As the coolant expands with heat, any excess coolant will overflow and this wastes antifreeze. Continued overfilling can dilute the antifreeze concentration and there will no longer be adequate freeze protection.

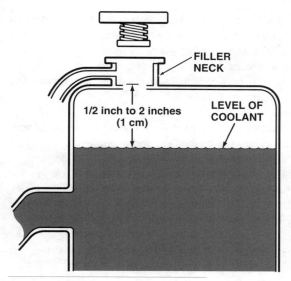

FILLER NECK

1/2 inch to 2 inches (1 cm)

LEVEL OF COOLANT

Fig. 12 — Proper Level of Engine Coolant

Check the radiator cap and gasket. If in doubt, replace the cap with an exact duplicate (see "Testing Radiator Cap" later in this chapter).

Check for leaks around the radiator, hoses, and hose clamps.

Remove trash from the radiator or radiator screen.

If you have water under pressure, use a hose as shown in Fig. 13. Direct the stream against the radiator from the side next to the engine. Be sure to get the radiator clean as mud will make the problem worse if it is not all flushed out.

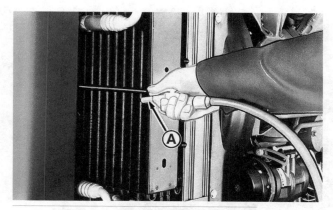

Fig. 13 — Removing Trash from Radiator or Screen

When operating in trashy, conditions such as in corn harvesting, check the radiator hose for trash several times a day.

IMPORTANT. Never pour hot water into a cold engine or cold water into a hot engine that is not running. You may crack the head or the cylinder block. Do not operate the engine without coolant for even a few minutes.

CHECKING ANTIFREEZE SOLUTIONS

There are three methods for checking the freeze point of antifreeze solutions:

- *Hydrometer*
- *Test strips*
- *Refractometer*

The hydrometer (Fig. 14) must have a thermometer and a correction table to be accurate as the density of a liquid changes with the temperature.

Test strips measure the freeze point by changing color when emmersed in the solution. The color change is the result of a chemical reaction between the strip and the antifreeze solution. Follow the instructions provided with the test strips.

Some engine manufacturers recommend using a refractometer to measure the freeze point of the solution. Follow the instructions furnished with the refractometer.

If the freeze point does not provide protection for the lowest expected temperature, drain some solution from the system and refill with fresh solution. If it is time for a seasonal change, drain, flush, and refill the entire cooling system.

Fig. 14 — Checking Freezing Protection Using a Hydrometer

PREVENTING LEAKS

Leaks in the cooling system can mean a loss of valuable coolant. A serious leak could cause the engine to overheat and become damaged.

If antifreeze solution leaks into the engine crankcase (Fig. 15), it can dilute the oil until the engine's lubrication fails. When coolant mixes with oil, it forms sludge and gum which retard lubrication and cause sticking of valves, valve lifters or piston rings.

To prevent leakage of coolant into the crankcase, check the cylinder head joints periodically to be sure the gasket is okay and the cap screws are tightened to specifications.

Watch oil level in the crankcase. If oil level rises, either coolant or unburned fuel is entering the crankcase. Determine the problem and make corrections immediately.

Cooling system leaks can be caused by other problems: Loose cylinder head and other gasket joints, loose hose clamps, fracture of radiator solder, corroded water tubes in the radiator, and rotten hoses and gaskets.

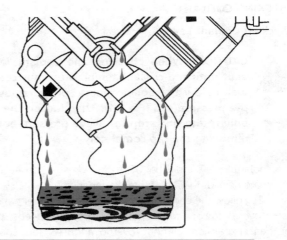

Fig. 15 — Coolant Leaking into the Crankcase Can Cause Lubrication Failure

Stop-Leak Products

To stop small leaks, at least temporarily, stop-leak compounds can sometimes be used. The main problem is that they give a sense of false security. For example, stop-leak may prevent seepage at a hose connection through the *inner* lining, but eventually the hose will rot and burst, losing coolant and overheating the engine.

Also, stop-leak compounds *will not* correct a leaking cylinder head gasket because of the heat and pressures.

Stop-leak compounds can also lead to radiator clogging if water tubes already contain deposits which act as a strainer. If coolant level gets too low, some stop-leak ingredients may harden in the upper radiator and block it.

However, stop-leak compounds are recommended for preventive maintenance in some engines.

Before using a stop-leak, check your operators manual. Some manufacturers do not recommend them. If used, the compound must be compatible with the antifreeze and the inhibitors, and it must be added correctly and in the right quantity.

NOTE: Do not use coolant system stop-leak additives if the engine is equipped with a coolant filter-conditioner. The stop-leak compound will plug the filter.

NOTE: Some antifreezes now contain stop-leak additives. If this type of antifreeze is approved by the engine maker, no further stop-leak compound is needed in the system.

Air Leaks Into Cooling System

Air mixing with the coolant in the system speeds rusting and corrosion. It may also cause foaming, overheating, and overflow loss of coolant.

Air leaks into the coolant may be caused by:
- *Leak in the system*
- *Turbulence in top radiator tank*
- *Too-low coolant level*

Exhaust Gas Leaks Into System

A cracked head or a loose cylinder head joint allows hot exhaust gas to be blown into the cooling system under combustion pressures, even though the joint may be tight enough to keep liquid from leaking into the cylinder.

The cylinder head gasket itself may be burned and corroded by escaping exhaust gases.

Exhaust gases dissolved in coolant destroy the inhibitors and form acids which cause corrosion, rust, clogging, and damage to rubber parts.

Excess pressure may also force coolant out the overflow pipe.

Either bubbles or an oil film present in the coolant is a sign of blow-by in the engine cylinders (Fig. 16).

NOTE: *Make this test quickly, before boiling starts, since steam bubbles give misleading results.*

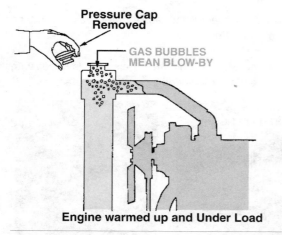

Pressure Cap Removed

GAS BUBBLES MEAN BLOW-BY

Engine warmed up and Under Load

Fig. 16 — *Checking for Exhaust Gas Leakage that May Indicate Blow-By*

PREVENTING CORROSION AND DEPOSITS

Three types of corrosion can attack the parts of the cooling system:
- **Chemical corrosion**
- **Electrolytic corrosion**
- **Erosive corrosion**

CHEMICAL CORROSION is a direct chemical reaction between the coolant and the metal parts of the system. This may be caused by acids in the coolant or various oxidizing agents. An example is the formation of rust on iron parts by the water and oxygen reacting with the metal.

ELECTROLYTIC CORROSION is a reaction between two different metals joined together, in contact with a solution which conducts electricity. This action is the same as that of a dry-cell battery which produces current by converting a metal into salt. When selecting an antifreeze, be sure that it is not a good conductor, such as a salt solution.

EROSIVE CORROSION is the mechanical abrasion from particles such as rust, scale, and sand as they circulate rapidly through the system with the coolant.

The result of corrosion on metal surfaces is that heat transfer is reduced.

Good engine coolants contain rust and corrosion inhibitors. The inhibitors, however, wear out and must be periodically replaced by adding liquid coolant conditioner to the cooling system.

IMPORTANT: Some diesel engines require a specific coolant containing supplemental coolant additives (SCA's) which must be periodically replaced. ALWAYS consult the machine manual for coolant and SCA replacement recommendations.

Preventing Cooling System Deposits

Lime and mineral deposits can be reduced by using distilled or filtered rain water when mixing with the coolant concentrate.

Mineral deposits form rapidly at hot spots in the engine (see Fig. 6).

Because heat transfer is reduced, deposits can lead to overheating, knocks, and eventually engine damage.

Using Coolant Filter-Conditioners

Note: *Later engines may use the conditioner additives in the coolant itself rather than a filter-conditioner.*

Coolant filter conditioners (Fig. 17) soften water and remove dirt. The filter-conditioner may be the spin-on type as in Fig. 17. To change the filter, unscrew the *canister from the engine and discard it. Install a new filter as a replacement.*

Another type of filter-conditioner contains a replaceable filter element with a sump at the bottom where dirt settles after it collects in the filter. The sump can be drained periodically to remove accumulated dirt and sediment.

The spin-on type filter contains two elements. The outer paper element filters out rust, scale, or dirt particles in the coolant. The inner element releases chemicals into the coolant to soften the coolant, maintain a proper acid/alkaline condition, prevent corrosion, and suppress cavitation erosion.

The chemicals released into the coolant by the inner element forms a protective film on the surface of the cylinder liner. The film acts as a barrier against collapsing vapor bubbles and reduces the quantity of bubbles formed.

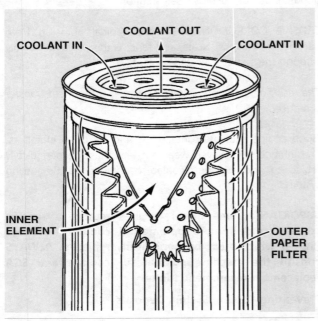

COOLANT OUT
COOLANT IN   **COOLANT IN**
INNER ELEMENT
OUTER PAPER FILTER

Fig. 17 — Coolant Filter-Conditioner Softens and Cleans Coolant

FLUSHING OR CLEANING THE SYSTEM

Always flush the system before installing antifreeze. Rust and other deposits in the system can shorten inhibitor life (and also reduce cooling efficiency). When draining the system, if the coolant contains rust and scale, *clean the system with an acid-base cleaner.* Be sure to follow the manufacturer's instructions.

It is also important to follow the engine maker's instructions when flushing or cleaning their system. For example, some alkaline cleaners can corrode aluminum engines or radiators.

For heavy deposits in the system, more drastic cleaning with an acid-base cleaner may be needed. Allow the solution to remain in the system for two to three hours at operating temperatures and then drain. To neutralize the acid, flush the system with water and lye solution. After running the engine for a while, drain the system and *flush it again* with clear water to remove all traces of the lye water. *This is a very important step.*

In severe cases, the radiator must be removed and boiled in a tank cleaner. This is normally done in a commercial radiator shop.

Flushing The System

Incomplete flushing, such as hosing out the radiator, closes the thermostat and prevents thorough flushing of the engine coolant jacket.

For complete flushing, take the following steps:

1. Drain old coolant from the system.

2. Fill the system completely with soft (distilled) water.

3. Run the engine long enough to open the thermostat (or remove the thermostat).

4. Open all drain plugs to again drain the system completely. (Most systems have at least two drains. See Fig. 18). Some also have a drain at the engine oil cooler (if equipped). Unless all drains are opened, some coolant will be left in the system.

   Clean out the radiator overflow tube and remove insects and dirt from radiator air passages, radiator grille and screens.

   Also check the thermostat, radiator pressure cap, and the cap seat for dirt or corrosion.

5. Replace coolant filter-conditioner element (if used) with new element recommended by engine manufacturer.

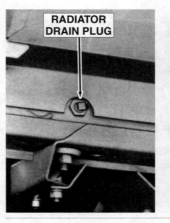

RADIATOR DRAIN PLUG
ENGINE DRAIN PLUG

Fig. 18 — Cooling System Usually Has at Least Two Drains

FILLING SYSTEM WITH COOLANT

IMPORTANT: For diesel engines, consult the machine manual for specified coolant containing the proper supplemental cooling additives (SCA's) or alternative coolant and additives.

After flushing the system, refill with a complete coolant (containing antifreeze, additives, and soft water) or a recognized brand of antifreeze and soft water.

If not using a complete coolant, see Fig. 9 for antifreeze dilution table for freezing protection for the lowest temperature expected.

After adding coolant, run the engine for a few minutes until it reaches normal operating temperature. This will allow the thermostat to open and will assure that the solution has circulated through the entire system for full protection against freezing.

Recheck the cooling system for leaks and to be sure it is filled to the proper level.

COOLANT PUMP LUBRICATION

In most engines, the water pump is driven by the same shaft as the cooling fan. Usually, the shaft bearings are factory-lubricated and sealed and require no further lubrication. However, some older fan and pump units must be lubricated periodically through a grease fitting (often with a special grease). Here it is important that coolant does not leak into the bearings (Fig. 19).

Other pumps are lubricated by additives in the coolant. For this reason, most permanent antifreezes already contain a water pump lubricant; so do most inhibitors that are used with plain water. In this case, it is doubly important to *change the coolant or add inhibitors at regular intervals.* Check the operators manual for the exact intervals and procedures as well as the label on the additives used.

Fig. 19 — Coolant Pump with Corroded Bearing and Shaft

CHECKING FAN BELT

The fan belt should be neither too tight nor too loose.

Too tight a belt puts an extra load oil the fan bearings and shortens the life of the bearings as well as the belt.

Too loose a belt allows slippage and lowers the fan speed, causes excessive belt wear and leads to overheating of the cooling system.

The condition of the fan belt and its tension should be checked periodically. Adjust fan belt tension as specified by the manufacturer (Fig. 20).

Fig. 20 — Checking Fan Belt Tension

TESTING OF COOLING SYSTEM

In addition to regular maintenance, several tests will tell you the condition of the cooling system. These are:

- **Testing system pressure**
- **Testing radiator cap**
- **Testing thermostat**

Make these tests whenever the condition of the system components is in doubt. If the tests show major troubles, have the faulty parts replaced.

TESTING SYSTEM PRESSURE

Because most modern cooling systems are pressurized, all of the components must be tight and in good condition before the system can operate properly.

Overheating and loss of coolant will result unless pressure in the system is maintained.

Test the pressure in the entire cooling system as follows:

Install a *pressure tester* on the radiator according to the manufacturer's instructions (Fig. 21). *Avoid applying too much pressure.*

With the tester installed, carefully inspect the radiator, water pump, hoses, drain cocks and cylinder block for leakage.

Mark all leaks plainly to help locate them when repairs are made by a serviceman.

Fig. 21 — Testing the Cooling System Pressure

TESTING RADIATOR CAP

The pressure cap is vital to correct pressure build-up in the cooling system.

Use a reliable tester to test the radiator cap (Fig. 22). The pressure valve should open at a certain pressure (see engine technical manual for specifications).

If the pressure valve does not open as specified or leaks before reaching opening pressure, replace the gasket or the whole cap as necessary.

Be sure that both the cap and radiator are free from leaks.

TESTING OF THERMOSTAT

The thermostat must work properly to control the engine temperature at its best level.

Test the thermostat as follows:

1. Suspend the thermostat and a thermometer in a container of water (Fig. 23). Do not let them rest against the sides or bottom.

Fig. 22 — Testing the Radiator Cap

2. Heat and stir the water.

3. The thermostat should begin to open at the temperature stamped on it, plus or minus 10°F (5°C). It should be fully open (approximately 1/4-inch; 6 mm) at 22°F (12°C) above the specified temperature.

4. Remove thermostat and observe its closing action.

5. If the thermostat is defective, discard it.

6. Be sure to replace with an exact duplicate of the original thermostat. Notice the temperature stamped on it.

IMPORTANT: Never operate the engine without a thermostat.

A thermostat tester can also be used to test the thermostat, if available.

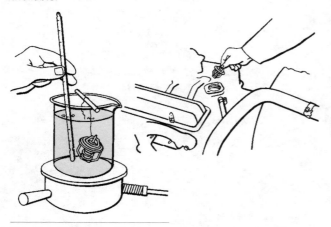

Fig. 23 — Testing the Thermostat

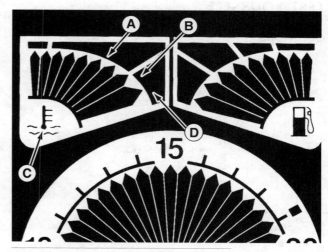

Fig. 24 — Engine Coolant Temperature Gauge
   A—Normal Temperature
   B—Warning Temperature
   C—Coolant Temperature Symbol
   D—Alarm Temperature

WATCHING THE COOLANT TEMPERATURE GAUGE

All modern engines have a coolant temperature gauge to tell the operator if the engine is operating at a normal temperature (Fig. 24). Watch this gauge during operation. Once the engine is warmed up, the needle should stay in the "normal" range. If the needle goes over into the red "warning" zone, stop the engine at once. Allow engine and radiator to cool and then check for low coolant level or other causes.

Other machines may have an indicator light which glows red when the engine is too hot.

NEVER STOP A HOT ENGINE

When an engine has been working hard, the pistons, turbocharger, and other parts are very hot and should be allowed to cool gradually to prevent seizing and permanent damage.

IMPORTANT: Allow a hot engine to idle for a few minutes before shutting it down.

This will prevent the engine from running after the ignition is turned off. Above all, it will keep the hot pistons and other parts from stewing and cooking in their own oil films, producing deposits. Another problem is that a red-hot valve, open when the engine stops, may warp and later burn.

NOTE: If overheating is accompanied by an indication of low oil pressure (signal light or gauge reading) stop the engine at once. Running the engine without enough oil could cause more damage than stopping a hot engine.

TEST YOURSELF

QUESTIONS

1. What are the two functions of the cooling system?

2. Why isn't water by itself a satisfactory coolant?

3. Which two of the following is best for a cooling system?
   A. Tap water   B. Well water
   C. Distilled water   D. Rain water

4. When a radiator becomes plugged, what is the major cause?

5. A 50 percent solution of antifreeze will protect against freezing to:
   A. 0°F (-18°C)   B. -15°F (-26°C)   C. -34°F (-37°C).

6. The cooling system absorbs (1/4-1/3-1/2) of the heat energy developed by the engine fuel.

7. The thermostat keeps the engine from overheating.
   True _____   False_____

8. It is all right to remove the radiator cap when the coolant is hot if the cap is removed slowly.
   True _____   False_____

9. Never pour _____ water into a cold engine or _____ water into a hot engine.

10. (Fill in the blank.) "Either bubbles or an oil film present in the coolant is a sign of _____ in the engine cylinders."

ENGINE ELECTRICAL SYSTEMS

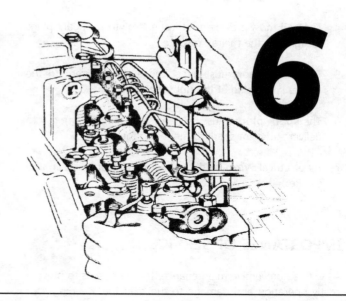

6

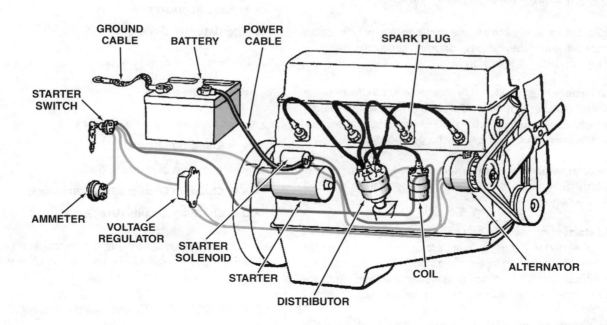

Fig. 1 — *Engine Electrical Systems and Components (Spark-Ignition Engine Shown)*

INTRODUCTION

If the engine is hard to start or lacks good performance, it could be caused by the engine *electrical systems*. Poor maintenance of the engine's starting, charging and ignition circuits is one of the chief causes of these problems.

Engine electrical systems and components are shown in Fig. 1. The charging circuit is shown in blue, while the ignition circuit is shown in red.

For the engine to run properly, the following conditions must be present:

1. The **battery** must be fully charged to provide enough power to start the engine.

2. The **alternator** (or generator) must be able to recharge the battery when needed.

3. The **starter** must crank the engine fast enough to start the engine.

4. The **coil** must provide electrical energy to the spark plugs for igniting the fuel-air mixture.

5. The **distributor** must direct the electric current to the proper spark plug at the right moment.

6. The **spark plugs** must be clean and gapped correctly to deliver sufficient spark to ignite the fuel properly.

7. All electrical **wires and connections** must be clean and secure.

IMPORTANCE OF SERVICE

As with all preventive maintenance, the purpose is to prevent costly operation and damage to the machine. Keeping your engine's electrical systems properly serviced is just as important as any other maintenance job.

Listed below are some of the components which require attention and the results of not servicing them as recommended:

The **battery** must be kept fully charged and filled with water. It must also be kept clean. Failure to maintain the battery properly can result in brief battery life. The battery can become shorted out and lose its charge.

The **alternator** or **generator** requires periodic inspection of its brushes to insure that sufficient charge is being put back into the battery.

The **starter** brushes must also be inspected regularly to insure that the starter is not draining excessive current from the starting circuit (caused by excessive cranking). The engine will be difficult to start with too little electrical power. Also, the starter must be checked for signs of overheating.

The **distributor** must be timed correctly to direct current to the spark plugs at the proper moment for good combustion. If the timing is late, extremely hot exhaust gases are created which can warp or burn the valves. If the timing is early, power is wasted and severe "knock" (pre-ignition) can damage the pistons, valves and bearings. Also, poor timing increases fuel consumption.

The breaker points and condenser must be maintained for good current delivery to the spark plugs.

The **spark plugs** must be clean and gapped correctly to provide sufficient spark to ignite the fuel properly. If the plugs are oil fouled or have deposits on them, the plug will not fire with a good spark and the fuel will not burn completely. Loss of power and fuel economy will result. The spark plug **wiring** must also be in good condition—clean, free of cracks and shorts.

OPERATION OF ELECTRICAL SYSTEMS

The complete engine electrical system consists of three circuits:

- **Charging Circuit**
- **Starting Circuit**
- **Ignition Circuit**

Let's look at these circuits briefly.

CHARGING CIRCUIT

The charging circuit includes:

- *Battery*
- *Voltage Regulator*
- *Alternator (or Generator)*

The charging circuit does two jobs:

1. Recharges the battery

2. Generates current during operation

Types of Charging Circuits

There are two kinds of charging circuits:

- **A.C. Charging Circuits (Use Alternators)**
- **D.C. Charging Circuits (Use Generators)**

Both circuits generate an alternating current (a.c.). The difference is in the way they rectify the a.c. current to direct current (d.c.) for use by the engine.

A.C. CHARGING CIRCUITS have an *alternator* and a *regulator* (Fig. 2).

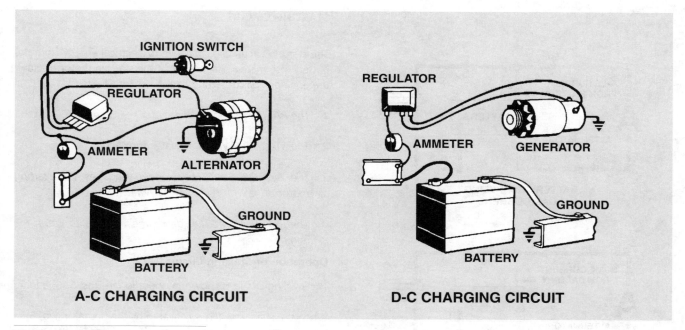

IGNITION SWITCH

REGULATOR

AMMETER

ALTERNATOR

BATTERY

GROUND

A-C CHARGING CIRCUIT

REGULATOR

AMMETER

GENERATOR

BATTERY

GROUND

D-C CHARGING CIRCUIT

Fig. 2 — Two Types of Charging Circuits

The *alternator* is really an a.c. generator. Like the generator, it produces a.c. current but rectifies it electronically using diodes. Alternators are generally more compact than generators of equal output, and supply a higher current output at low engine speeds. They have replaced generators on most modern engines.

The *regulator* in a.c. charging circuits limits the alternator voltage to a safe, preset value. Transistorized models are used in many of the modern circuits.

D.C. CHARGING CIRCUITS have a *generator* and a *regulator* (Fig. 2).

The *generator* supplies the electrical power and rectifies its current mechanically by using a commutator and brushes.

The *regulator* has three jobs: (1) opens and closes the charging circuit; (2) prevents overcharging of the battery; (3) limits the generator's output to safe rates so as not to damage the electrical system.

Operation of Charging Circuit

All charging circuits operate in three stages:

- *During starting-battery supplies all load current*
- *During peak operation-battery helps alternator (or generator) supply load current*
- *During normal operation-alternator (or generator) supplies all current and recharges battery*

In both charging circuits, the *battery* starts the circuit when it supplies the spark to start the engine. The engine then drives the alternator (or generator) which produces current to take over the operation of the ignition, lights and accessory loads in the whole system.

The battery also helps out during peak operation when the electrical loads are too much for the alternator (or generator).

But once the engine is started, the alternator (*or generator*) is the "workhorse" which produces current for the ignition and accessory circuits.

The alternator (or generator) supplies this current as long as the engine is speeded up. When the engine slows down or stops, the battery takes over part or all of the load.

Operation of the charging circuit during the three stages is illustrated in Fig. 3.

The top illustration shows operation while starting the engine when the battery must supply the current.

The middle diagram shows what happens during peak electrical loads when the battery only helps the alternator (or generator).

The lower diagram shows the system during normal operation when the alternator (or generator) supplies all power for loads and also recharges the battery.

Detailed operation and maintenance will be covered later in this chapter.

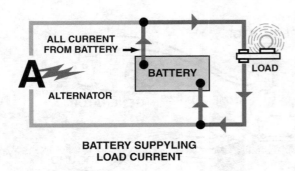

**BATTERY SUPPLYING
LOAD CURRENT**

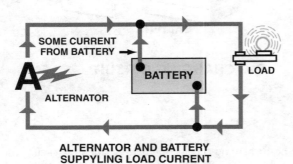

**ALTERNATOR AND BATTERY
SUPPLYING LOAD CURRENT**

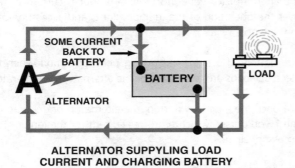

**ALTERNATOR SUPPYLING LOAD
CURRENT AND CHARGING BATTERY**

Fig. 3 — Charging Circuit in Operation—Three Stages (Alternator or Generator)

STARTING CIRCUIT

The starting circuit (Fig. 4) converts electrical energy from the battery into mechanical energy at the starting motor to crank the engine. A basic starting circuit has four parts:

1. *The BATTERY supplies energy for the circuit.*

2. *The STARTER SWITCH activates the circuit.*

3. *The MOTOR SWITCH (solenoid) engages the starting motor drive with the engine flywheel.*

4. *The STARTING MOTOR drives the flywheel to crank the engine.*

Operation of Starting Circuit

The starting circuit is shown in operation in Figs. 5, 6, and 7.

When the starter switch is activated by the operator (Fig. 5), a small amount of electrical energy flows from the battery to the solenoid and back to the ground circuit.

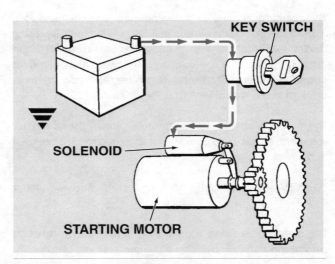

Fig. 5 — Starting Circuit in Operation: (1) As The Starter Switch is Activated

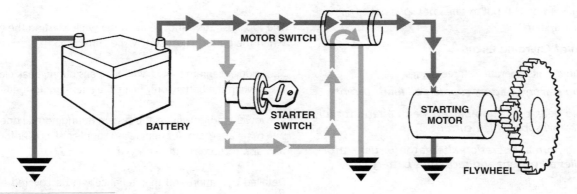

Fig. 4 — Basic Starting Circuit

As the solenoid gets this power from the battery, it moves the solenoid plunger and engages the pinion with the flywheel (Fig. 6). The plunger also closes the switch inside the solenoid between the battery and starting motor, completing the circuit and allowing a large amount of electrical energy to flow into the starting motor.

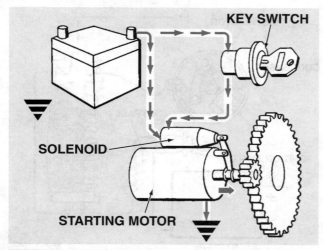

Fig. 6 — Starting Circuit in Operation: (2) Starting Motor Engages Flywheel

The starting motor takes the electrical energy from the battery and converts it into rotary mechanical energy to crank the engine (Fig. 7).

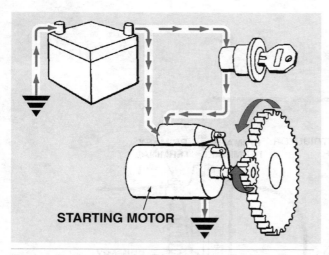

Fig. 7 — Starting Circuit in Operation: (3) Starting Motor Cranks Engine

But remember that the battery is the only source of power for starting the engine.

In this typical system, we have used a solenoid switch as an example. Motors can also use other types of switches, such as manual or magnetic.

IGNITION CIRCUIT (Spark-ignition Engines)

The ignition circuit creates the spark which ignites fuel-air mixture to power gasoline or LP-Gas engines.

To do this, the ignition circuit must:

(1) Step up low voltage to high voltage surges

(2) Time these surges to the engine cycle

The ignition circuit (Fig. 8) has these parts:

- **Ignition Coil**
- **Condenser**
- **Distributor**
- **Spark Plugs**
- **Ignition Switch**

The COIL transforms the low voltage from the battery to a high voltage for producing a spark.

The CONDENSER aids in collapsing the magnetic field in the coil to produce a high voltage. In doing this it also protects the distributor points against arcing.

The DISTRIBUTOR does three things: 1) Opens and closes the primary circuit, causing the coil to produce high voltage surges. 2) Times these surges to engine rotation, and 3) Directs each high-voltage surge to the proper spark plug.

The SPARK PLUGS ignite the fuel-air mixture within each cylinder of the engine.

The battery is the initial power source for the voltage in the ignition circuit, while the IGNITION SWITCH turns on the circuit when it cranks the engine.

Operation Of Ignition Circuit

The ignition circuit must take low voltage from the battery and create high voltage to fire the spark plugs. It must do this very accurately and very rapidly—100 or more times per second. This is why maintenance is so important.

The PRIMARY CIRCUIT is the path for low-voltage current from the power source. Note the primary circuit in Figure 8 is the darkest shown. It includes these parts:

1) *Ignition Switch*

2) *Coil Primary Winding*

3) *Distributor Contact Points*

4) *Condenser*

The SECONDARY CIRCUIT is the high-voltage path for current stepped up by the coil. Note this circuit in Figure 8 is shown in blue. It includes these parts:

1) *Coil Secondary Winding*

2) *Distributor Rotor*

3) *Distributor Cap*

4) *Spark Plug Wires*

5) *Spark Plugs*

Now let's take these circuits and see how they work.

To simplify, let's divide the operation into two parts—before the distributor points open and after they open.

Before the engine is started, the distributor points are normally closed (Fig. 9).

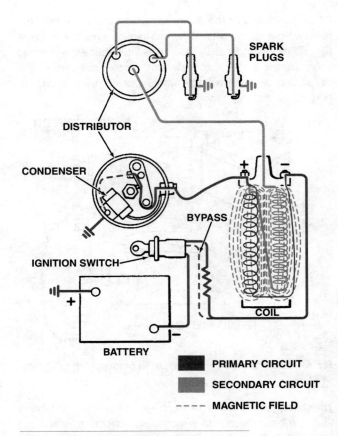

	PRIMARY CIRCUIT
	SECONDARY CIRCUIT
- - - -	MAGNETIC FIELD

Fig. 8 — Ignition Circuit (Spark-Ignition Engines)

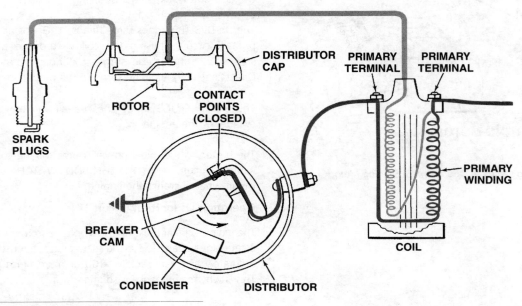

Fig. 9 — Operation Before the Distributor Points Open

OPERATION BEFORE THE DISTRIBUTOR POINTS OPEN

When the ignition switch is turned on, current flows from the battery into the primary windings of the coil as shown in red. This current creates a magnetic field around the winding.

From the primary winding, the current—at low voltage—simply travels through the closed distributor points and back to ground. This is why the battery can be completely discharged if the switch is left on when the engine is not running.

OPERATION AFTER THE DISTRIBUTOR POINTS OPEN

As the engine rotates in starting, it drives the distributor shaft and the breaker cam.

When the breaker cam opens the distributor points, the second phase of ignition begins (Fig. 10).

As the points open, they open the primary circuit and divert the flow of current to the condenser, which stops flow in the primary circuit.

Stopping this flow causes the magnetic field around the primary winding to collapse very quickly.

This collapse induces a voltage in the primary winding which causes current to flow. The current in the primary circuit is absorbed by the condenser thus giving the current a place to flow rather than arc the breaker points.

In this case, the collapsing field further collapses across the *secondary* winding and induces voltage in it also.

But because the secondary is a much "stronger" winding (has more turns in proportion to the primary winding), a higher voltage is induced there—or 4,000 to 20,000 volts.

This surge of high voltage "pushes" current through the secondary winding and the high-tension terminal into the distributor cap as shown in red in Fig. 10.

The rotor inside the distributor cap turns to a spark plug terminal, directing the voltage "surge" to the correct plug through insulated cables.

At the spark plug, current flows down the center electrode, jumps the gap, and creates the spark.

This whole cycle happens from 50-150 times a second, depending on the speed of the engine.

NOTE: In a "bypass" ignition system (shown in Fig. 8), there are two primary leads from switch to coil. When the switch is turned to start, full battery voltage flows through the dotted red line, resulting in a holter spark for first ignition. When the ignition switch-is released, primary current flows through the solid line and resistor to the coil. In a 12-volt system, the resistor reduces voltage by half and allows use of a 6-volt coil. This gives longer life to the distributor points and aids in faster starting.

This completes the basic operation of electrical circuits. Now we will cover maintenance for each component.

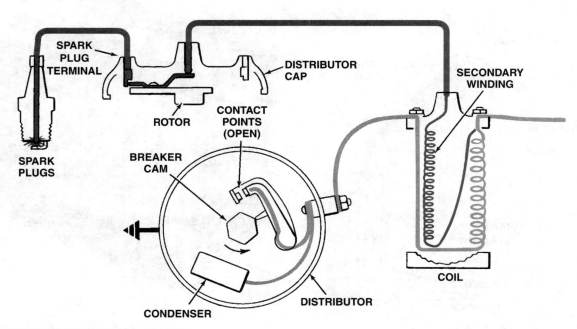

Fig. 10 — Operation After the Distributor Points Open

ELECTRONIC IGNITION CIRCUITS

The components of an electronic ignition system are much the same as the mechanical system just described. The main difference is the electronic ignition uses a solid state ignition control unit with a reluctor and sensor to time the spark delivery eliminating the breaker points and condenser arrangement.

There really isn't much maintenance on electronic ignition systems except keeping connections clean and tight and setting the air gap between the sensor and reluctor (more on this later in this chapter).

SERVICING THE BATTERY

Battery maintenance is simple, but it is important that service be performed regularly or the battery will soon fail.

Before we discuss how to service the battery, let's look at how it works. Then it will be easy to understand why the battery requires periodic maintenance.

HOW A BATTERY WORKS
Construction

The battery is made up of a number of individual *cells* in a hard rubber case (Fig. 11).

The basic units of each cell are the positive and the *negative plates*.

These plates hold the active materials in flat grids. Charged negative plates contain spongy lead (Pb) which is grey in color. Charged positive plates contain lead peroxide (PbO2) which has a chocolate brown color.

A *plate group* is made by welding a number of similar plates to a plate strap (Fig. 11).

Plate groups of opposite polarity are interlaced so the negative and positive plates alternate. Negative plate groups normally have one more plate than the positive groups. This keeps negative plates exposed on both sides of the interlaced group.

Each plate in the interlaced plate group is kept apart from its neighbor by porous separators as shown in Fig. 11. The separators allow a free flow of electrolyte around the active plates. The resulting assembly is called an *element*.

After the element is assembled, it is placed in a cell compartment of the battery case.

Hard-top batteries (Fig. 12) have cell connectors which pass through the partitions between cells. The connectors and partitions are sealed so that electrolyte will not transfer between cells. This improves battery performance, since the cell connections are shorter and the cover is more acid-tight.

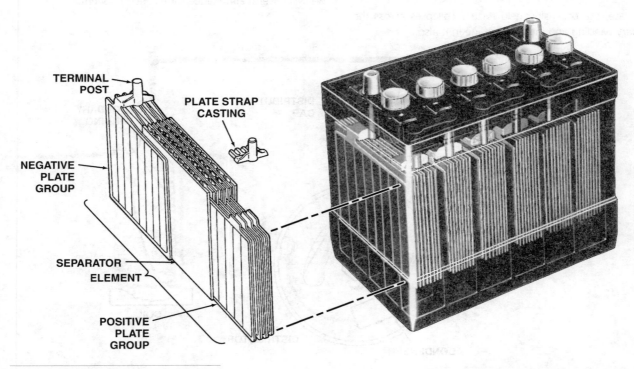

Fig. 11 — Construction of a Storage Battery

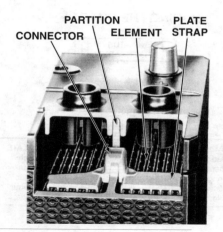

PARTITION CONNECTOR   PLATE STRAP   ELEMENT

Fig. 12 — Hard-Top Battery with One-Piece Cover

The main battery terminals are the *positive* and *negative* posts. The positive terminal is larger to help prevent the danger of connecting the battery in reverse polarity.

Vent caps are located in each cell cover. The caps have two purposes: 1) They close the openings in the cell cover through which the electrolyte level is checked and water is added; 2) They provide a vent for the escape of gases formed when the battery is charging.

Each cell in a storage battery has a potential of about two volts. Six-volt batteries contain three cells connected in series, while 12-volt batteries have six cells in series (Fig, 13, top diagram).

For higher voltages, combinations of batteries are used. An example is where two 12-volt batteries are connected in series to serve a 24-volt system (Fig. 13, bottom diagram).

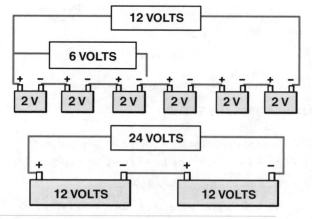

Fig. 13 — Battery Cells and Batteries Connected in Series

Operation Of Battery

The battery produces current by a chemical reaction between the active materials of the unlike plates and the sulfuric acid of the electrolyte (Fig. 14).

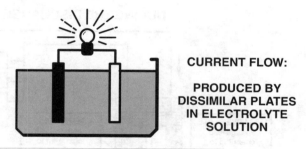

CURRENT FLOW:

PRODUCED BY DISSIMILAR PLATES IN ELECTROLYTE SOLUTION

Fig. 14 — How a Battery Produces Current Flow

While this chemical reaction is taking place, the battery is *discharging*. After most of the active materials have reacted, the battery is *discharged*. It must then be recharged before use.

We'll discuss these two cycles, but first let's see what the electrolyte is made of.

ELECTROLYTE SOLUTION

 CAUTION: Battery electrolyte is a highly corrosive acid and should be handled with extreme care. If electrolyte comes in contact with any part of the body, immediately flush the contaminated area with fresh clean water and seek medical attention immediately. Always wear eye protection when working around batteries. Keep sparks, lighted matches, and open flames away from the top of the battery. Battery gas can explode.

The *electrolyte* in a fully charged battery is a solution of concentrated sulfuric acid in water (Fig. 15). It has a specific gravity of about 1.270 at 80°F (27°C)—which means it weighs 1.270 times more than water. The solution is about 36% sulfuric acid (H_2SO_4) and 64% water (H_2O) as shown.

The voltage of a battery cell depends upon the chemical difference between the active materials and also upon the concentration of the electrolyte.

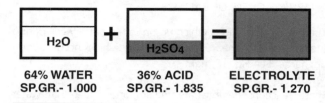

H_2O	+	H_2SO_4	=	
64% WATER SP.GR.- 1.000		**36% ACID SP.GR.- 1.835**		**ELECTROLYTE SP.GR.- 1.270**

Fig. 15 — Battery Electrolyte

DISCHARGE CYCLE OF BATTERY

When the battery is connected to a complete circuit, current begins to flow from the battery. The *discharge* cycle begins (Fig. 16, left).

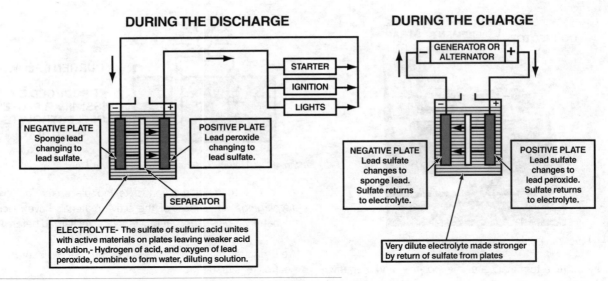

DURING THE DISCHARGE

STARTER
IGNITION
LIGHTS

NEGATIVE PLATE
Sponge lead changing to lead sulfate.

POSITIVE PLATE
Lead peroxide changing to lead sulfate.

SEPARATOR

ELECTROLYTE- The sulfate of sulfuric acid unites with active materials on plates leaving weaker acid solution,- Hydrogen of acid, and oxygen of lead peroxide, combine to form water, diluting solution.

DURING THE CHARGE

GENERATOR OR ALTERNATOR

NEGATIVE PLATE
Lead sulfate changes to sponge lead. Sulfate returns to electrolyte.

POSITIVE PLATE
Lead sulfate changes to lead peroxide. Sulfate returns to electrolyte.

Very dilute electrolyte made stronger by return of sulfate from plates

Fig. 16 — Chemical Action in Battery During Discharge and Charge Cycles

This current is produced by a chemical action as shown in the diagram. Study this process to become familiar with the reactions in the battery during discharge.

Note that the material in the positive plates and negative plates becomes similar chemically during discharge, as the lead sulfate accumulates. This condition accounts for the loss of cell voltage, since *voltage depends upon the difference between the two materials.*

As the discharge continues, dilution of the electrolyte and the accumulation of lead sulfate in the plates eventually brings the reactions to a stop. For this reason the active materials never are completely exhausted during discharge.

When the battery can no longer produce the desired voltage, it is said to be *discharged.* It must be recharged by a suitable flow of direct current from some external source before it can be put back in service.

CHARGING CYCLE OF BATTERY

The chemical reactions which go on in the battery cell during the *charge* are the reverse of those which occur during discharge. See Fig. 16, right.

These reactions demonstrate the important fact that water actually takes part in the chemistry of a lead-acid storage battery.

The purity of water for battery use has always been a controversial subject, but it always resolves to the fact that distilled water is the best.

Water with impurities hurts the life and performance of a battery. This is because minerals and other impurities build up on the battery plates, reducing the surface area.

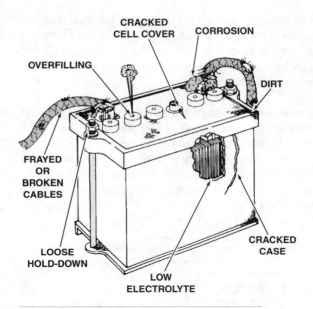

CRACKED CELL COVER   CORROSION

OVERFILLING

DIRT

FRAYED OR BROKEN CABLES

LOOSE HOLD-DOWN

LOW ELECTROLYTE

CRACKED CASE

Fig. 17 — Things Which Affect the Life of a Battery

MAINTAINING THE BATTERY

To receive the maximum life from the battery, you must:

• *Check the Electrolyte Level Every 50 Hours*

• *Clean the Battery Every 250 Hours*

• *Check the Battery Electrical Condition Every 250 Hours*

• *Charge the Battery When Needed*

Fig. 17 shows a poorly maintained battery. This unit will soon fail completely and all these problems could likely have been avoided by good maintenance.

Fig. 18 — Removing Vent Caps to Check Battery Electrolyte Level

Checking The Electrolyte Level

Every 50 hours of operation, remove all caps from vent wells (Fig. 18). The electrolyte level should be to the bottom of the filler neck—so that the tops of the battery plates are covered (Fig. 19).

 CAUTION: GAS FROM BATTERY ELECTROLYTE IS FLAMMABLE. Keep all sparks and flames away from the battery. If the battery has been charging, hydrogen gas is present. This gas will explode in the presence of a spark or flame and possibly cause serious injury to you or others nearby.

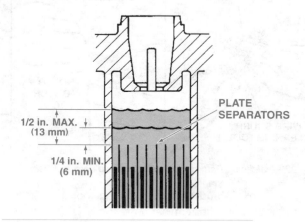

Fig. 19 — Proper Level of Electrolyte in Battery Cells

If any of the cells require water, fill them with distilled water. Use a battery syringe shown in Fig. 20 to avoid overfilling. If distilled water is not available use clean rain water (better than softened water)-Replace caps.

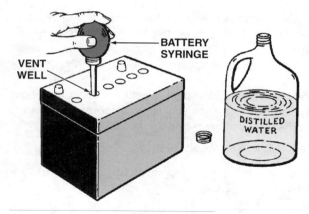

Fig. 20 — Adding Distilled Water to Battery

Battery Don'ts

Don't overfill. When the battery is being charged, the electrolyte will overflow through the vents in the caps and onto the top of the battery. This provides a path for leakage of electricity and will also cause corrosion and deterioration of the metal parts.

Don't use hard water. The minerals in hard water will leave deposits on the plates and interfere with the chemical action of the battery.

Don't add acid to the battery unless electrolyte is lost by spilling. To operate properly, a battery must have the correct proportions of acid and water.

Don't add water to the battery just before checking specific gravity. If the level is too low, add necessary water and operate in circuit for a few hours to mix water and electrolyte, then check.

Don't add water to the battery in freezing weather unless it will be operated immediately to allow proper mixing of water with electrolyte.

Cleaning the Battery

Your battery requires cleaning regularly to prevent dirt, moisture and corrosion from robbing it of its charge.

While the battery is charging, acid spray is carried out of the battery with the hydrogen gas created by the chemical action of the electrolyte. This acid settles on the top of the battery and provides a damp surface for dust and dirt to cling. Posts and terminals become corroded also.

The small amount of acid is enough to provide an electrical path to the metal frame or to the opposite terminal. This will cause the battery to slowly discharge.

Corroded terminals also prevent the generator from recharging the battery when needed. Your battery loses its charge due to the poor contact of the cables and terminals caused by a film of corrosion.

Periodically wipe off the battery with a damp cloth about every 250 hours or when very dirty. If corrosion is present, clean the battery as given below.

TOOLS AND MATERIALS NEEDED

To clean a battery, the following tools and materials are needed.

1. Bristle Brush

2. Wire Brush and Sandpaper (or Battery Clamp and Post Cleaning Tools)

3. Small Paint Brush

4. Large Common Screwdriver

5. Battery Clamp Puller

6. Box-End Wrenches (To Fit Terminal Bolts)

7. Baking Soda

8. Container of Water

9. Light Grease or Petroleum Jelly

HOW TO CLEAN BATTERY

To clean the battery, proceed as follows:

1. Remove *ground* strap or cable from battery terminal post (Fig. 21). This prevents short circuits caused by accidentally grounding the other terminal with a too. Use a battery clamp puller if available.

   Don't pound on terminal; you may crack the battery top or loosen the post.

TO REMOVE CLAMP, LOOSEN BOLT AND CAREFULLY SPREAD JAWS OF CLAMP. USE CLAMP PULLER IF AVAILABLE.

Fig. 21 — Removing Battery Terminal Clamp

2. Remove the other battery cable.

3. Wipe off the clamps with a cloth. Dip the clamps into a mixture of baking soda and water (two tablespoons of soda to a pint [65 mL per liter] of water). This will clean off some of the corrosion and acid.

4. Clean the inside of the clamps with a round wire brush cleaning tool (Fig. 22), or roll a small piece of sandpaper around your finger (grit side out) and clean the inside of the clamps. Wipe the clamps clean with a dry cloth.

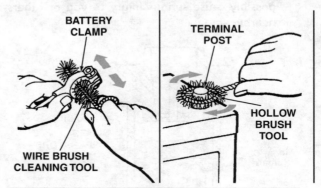

Fig. 22 — Cleaning Battery Cable Clamps and Terminal Posts

5. Use a hollow-brush terminal cleaning tool to scrub the corrosion from the terminal posts (Fig. 22). (A stiff wire brush can be used if no tool is available.)

6. Use a bristle brush to remove loose dirt and corrosion particles from the top of the battery (Fig. 23).

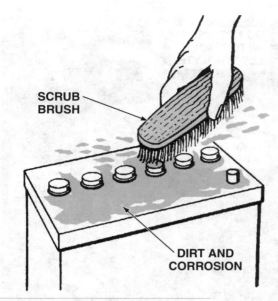

Fig. 23 — Removing Dirt with a Bristle Brush

7. Brush a fresh mixture of baking soda and water on top of battery and posts (Fig. 24). This will neutralize the acid. Apply solution until foaming stops.

NOTE: Do not allow any of the solution to enter the breather holes in the caps. The baking soda will weaken the acid in the electrolyte. Also be sure caps are securely tightened before cleaning.

Fig. 24 — Neutralizing Acid Deposits

8. Flush off residue with clean water (Fig. 25). Protect battery caps from direct stream of water to avoid flushing dirt into the battery through the vent holes.

If battery is on machine, also flush off surrounding areas with water.

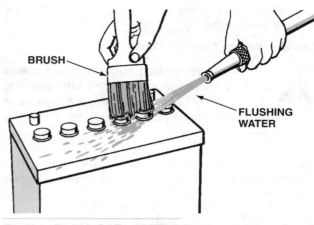

Fig. 25 — Flushing Off Top of Battery

9. Dry the top of the battery with a clean cloth.

10. Inspect the battery for any damage which may require repair or replacement (See Fig. 17).

11. Attach nongrounded cable to proper battery terminal. Be sure the correct connection is made or you may damage the generator or alternator. (Most batteries have terminals of different sizes to avoid mix-ups).

12. Then attach ground cable to the opposite terminal. This will avoid accidental grounding of the other terminal.

IMPORTANT: Do not pound the clamps in place. You may break the seal around the battery posts or crack the battery cover.

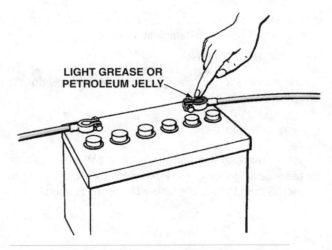

Fig. 26 — Applying Protective Coat of Grease to Terminals

13. Apply a coating of light grease or petroleum jelly (Fig. 26) to the terminals and clamps to protect them against further corrosion.

14. Examine the breather holes in the top of each battery cap to be sure they are open.

Checking Battery Electrical Condition

 CAUTION: Never short across battery terminal posts to check for a spark. This tells you very little about the condition of the battery and an explosion may occur when hydrogen gas is present.

Several devices are available to check the battery more accurately and safely. These include: *hydrometer, voltmeter, charger-tester.*

Because the *hydrometer* is the most commonly used and least expensive, we will cover use of it only.

Checking Specific Gravity

The state of battery charge is indicated by the specific gravity or weight of the battery electrolyte.

The strength of the electrolyte varies directly with the state of charge of each cell.

To find out how much energy is available from the battery, you need only find out what percentage of sulfuric acid remains in the electrolyte. One of the simplest and most reliable ways to do this is to measure the specific gravity or weight of the solution.

Specific gravity can be measured very quickly by means of a battery hydrometer with a thermometer for temperature correction.

Hydrometers are calibrated to-measure specific gravity correctly at an electrolyte temperature of 80°F.

USING THE HYDROMETER

To check the specific gravity of the electrolyte, do the following:

1. Remove battery caps.

2. When checking specific gravity of a battery which has been gassing freely, allow sediment to settle or gas to escape from the sample before taking the reading.

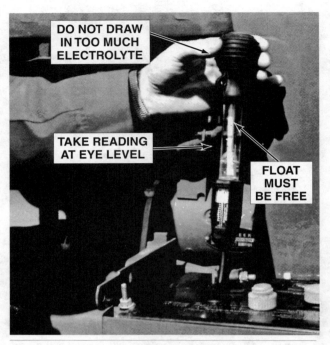

DO NOT DRAW IN TOO MUCH ELECTROLYTE

TAKE READING AT EYE LEVEL

FLOAT MUST BE FREE

Fig. 27 — Checking Specific Gravity of a Battery with a Hydrometer

3. Insert the hydrometer into one of the cell openings (Fig. 27). Squeeze the bulb and slowly release it to draw electrolyte into the barrel.

If the electrolyte level is too low to fill the hydrometer, add water to the battery. Operate the engine for a few hours to mix the water and electrolyte so that an accurate reading can be taken.

Hold the hydrometer vertically so the float does not touch the sides. Apply or release some pressure on the bulb until the float in the hydrometer rides freely in the barrel. If the float tends to touch the side of the barrel, shake the hydrometer gently. If the float continues to stick or touch the sides, flush the inside of the hydrometer with soap and water and rinse well before further testing.

If the indicator scale inside the float appears wet or stained, the float probably leaks and your reading will not be accurate.

4. Leave the hydrometer nozzle in the battery cell to avoid spilling acid on the battery or yourself. Be sure your eye is at the level of the liquid when the reading is taken. Readings taken at an angle may be false.

Note the reading indicated by the level of the electrolyte position on the scale.

5. *The specific gravity should read from 1.215 to 1.270* (corrected for 80°F; 27°C electrolyte temperature).

For Fahrenheit Temperatures

To determine a corrected specific gravity reading when the temperature of the electrolyte is other than 80°F: *ADD* to the hydrometer reading four gravity points (0.004) for each 100 *ABOVE* 80°F.

SUBTRACT four gravity points (0.004) for each 10° *BELOW* 80°F.

This compensates for expansion and contraction of the electrolyte at temperatures above or below the standard.

For example, a specific gravity reading of 1.234 is obtained when electrolyte is at 120°F (See Fig. 28). Since this reading was taken with the electrolyte temperature 40° above the standard, a total of 16 (4x4) gravity points (0.016) is added, giving a corrected reading of 1.250.

As a further example, suppose a reading of 1.282 is obtained at 0°F. This reading was taken with the electrolyte temperature 80° below the standard. Therefore, a total of 32 (8 x 4) gravity points (0.032) is subtracted, giving a corrected reading of 1.250 (which is satisfactory).

For Celsius Temperatures

To determine a corrected specific gravity reading when the electrolyte temperature is other then 27°C: *ADD* to the hydrometer reading seven gravity points (0.007) for each 10° ABOVE 27°C.

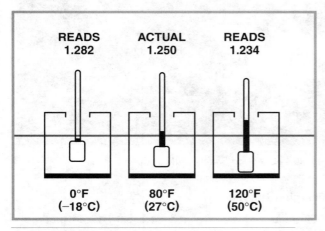

READS 1.282	ACTUAL 1.250	READS 1.234
0°F (−18°C)	80°F (27°C)	120°F (50°C)

Fig. 28 — Correcting Specific Gravity Readings to Allow for Temperature Variations

SUBTRACT seven gravity points (0.007) for each 10° BELOW 27°C.

For example, if a specific gravity reading of 1.234 is obtained when electrolyte is at 49°C (See Fig. 28), the electrolyte temperature is 22°C above the standard. A total of 16 (2.2 x7) gravity points (0.016) is added, giving a corrected reading of 1.250.

Then, suppose a reading of 1.282 is obtained at -18°C. This reading was taken with the electrolyte temperature 45°C below the standard. Therefore, a total of 32 (4.5 x 7) gravity points (0.032) is subtracted, giving a corrected reading of 1.250 (which is satisfactory).

6. Return the electrolyte to the cell from which it was taken.

 CAUTION: Sulfuric acid in battery electrolyte is poisonous. It is strong enough to burn skin, eat holes in clothing, and cause blindness if splashed in eyes. If you spill acid on yourself, flush your skin with water, apply baking soda or lime to help neutralize the acid, and flush your eyes with water for 10-15 minutes. Get medical attention immediately.

7. Check the remaining cells in the same manner as above.

8. Install battery caps and flush the hydrometer with clean water.

9. Compare the temperature-corrected readings with the chart and descriptions below to determine condition of the battery.

**Specific Gravity
Reading (Adjusted)** | **State of Charge**

1.260 Sp. Gr	100% Charged
1.230 Sp. Gr	75% Charged
1.200 Sp. Gr	50% Charged
1.170 Sp. Gr	25% Charged
1.140 Sp. Gr	Very Little Useful Capacity
1.110 Sp. Gr	Discharged

The table above shows the state of charge of a typical battery at various specific gravity readings.

IF SPECIFIC GRAVITY IS LESS THAN 1.215

When the specific gravity reading is less than 1.215 (after correction for temperature), the battery may be in satisfactory condition although its state of charge is low. Charge the battery before making further tests. (See following in this chapter for details.)

IF SPECIFIC GRAVITY IS ABOVE 1.270

When the specific gravity reading is above 1.270 (after correction for temperature), the battery may be in satisfactory condition although it is above full charge. In use, its specific gravity should return quickly to the normal 1.215-1.270 range. Make further tests to be more certain of the battery condition.

VOLTAGE CHART	
ESTIMATED ELECTROLYTE TEMPERATURE	MINIMUM REQUIRED VOLTAGE UNDER 15 SEC. LOAD (USE 1/2 THESE VALUES FOR 6 VOLT BATTERIES)
70°F (21°C)& ABOVE	9.6
60°F (16°C)	9.5
50°F (10°C)	9.4
40°F (4°C)	9.3
30°F (-1°C)	9.1
20°F (-7°C)	8.9
10°F (-12°C)	8.7
0°F (-18°C)	8.5

Fig. 29 — Voltage Chart

IF MORE THAN 0.050 VARIATION BETWEEN CELLS

A difference of more than 50 specific gravity points (0.050) between cells indicates an unsatisfactory battery condition. This may be due to an internal defect, short circuit, improper activation, or deterioration from extended use. The battery should normally be replaced.

NOTE: Specific gravity readings do not always give a true indication of the state of charge of a battery. If water has been added recently or acid has been lost through accident or leakage, the reading will indicate a lower state of charge than is actually the case. Therefore, never use specific gravity readings alone to decide the condition of a battery. If unsure of the tests, take the battery to your dealer for further testing.

ADJUSTABLE LOAD TEST

The following instructions are intended as guidelines. When available, the instrument manufacturer's instructions should be followed.

1. Disconnect battery cables starting with ground cable.

2. Measure temperature of a center cell. If instrument has an integral temperature compensator, use attached probe. Cover battery with a wet cloth.

3. Connect voltmeter and load test leads to appropriate battery terminals. Make certain terminals are free of corrosion.

4. Connect current transducer (if necessary) to appropriate lead.

5. Apply test load equivalent to 50% of Cranking Performance rating of battery for 15 seconds.

6. Read the voltage (Fig. 30) at 15 seconds, then remove the load.

7. Determine minimum voltage required at electrolyte test temperature from chart (Fig. 29) above.

8. If test voltage is above minimum, return battery to service.

9. If test voltage is below minimum, replace battery.

Fig. 30 — Checking Battery State of Charge

Charging The Battery

The amount of electrical current a battery can produce is limited by the amount of chemical reaction which can take place within it.

When chemical reaction in a battery has ended through defect or long use, the battery is discharged and can no longer produce a flow of electrical current.

The battery can be recharged, however, by causing direct current from an outside source to flow through it in a direction opposite to that in which it flowed out of the battery.

During discharge, current flows from the positive (+) terminal of the battery, through the circuit, and back into the battery at the negative (-) terminal (Fig. 31).

Within the battery, current flow is from the negative to the positive terminal.

To recharge the battery, this flow of current is reversed as shown, restoring the chemicals in the battery to their active state.

The battery then becomes charged and ready to produce electrical current again. The chemical action which takes place within a battery during the discharging and charging was explained earlier in this chapter.

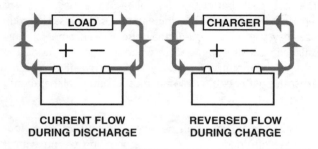

CURRENT FLOW DURING DISCHARGE   **REVERSED FLOW DURING CHARGE**

Fig. 31 — Current Flow During Discharge and Charge of Battery

Batteries can be recharged in two ways:

- **Fast Charging**

- **Slow Charging**

Because most operator-owned chargers are "trickle" chargers, we will only discuss slow charging here.

 CAUTION: A battery produces gasses which can explode. Keep sparks, lighted matches, and open flames from the top of the battery.

SLOW CHARGING

IMPORTANT: If after using a fast charger for three minutes, the electrolyte in a sulfated battery will bubble and produce excessive gasses. The charging rate must be reduced to protect the battery from damage. Reduce the charging rate until the electrolyte produces comparatively few bubbles. If badly sulfated, the battery must be slow charged.

Be sure to follow the manufacturer's instructions for using the charger. The battery charger shown in Fig. 32 will fast or slow charge and can also be used as a booster battery.

NOTE: Be sure to remove the battery cell caps while charging to allow gas to flow freely from battery.

Charge the battery at a low rate (7% of the battery ampere-hour rating or less) for an extended period of time until fully charged.

A battery is considered fully charged when three consecutive hydrometer readings, taken at hourly intervals, show no rise in specific gravity.

The normal slow-charging period is from 12 to 24 hours.

If a battery's specific gravity has not reached the normal full-charge range (1.215 to 1.270) within 48 hours of slow charging, replace the battery.

Badly sulfated batteries, however, may take from 60 to 100 hours to recharge completely.

Fig. 32 — Battery Charger

Connecting Booster Batteries

Cold weather starting can be made easier by connecting an additional battery (equal voltage) in PARALLEL with the original battery.

 CAUTION: A battery produces gasses which can explode. Make sure all switches are turned off and make the last connection or the first disconnect away from the battery receiving the boost.

The first jumper cable should connect the positive (+) terminal of the booster battery to the positive (+) terminal of the original battery. The second jumper cable should first be connected to the negative (-) terminal of the booster battery and then to the frame of the machine with the battery being boosted. NEVER REVERSE THE CONNECTIONS.

Always break the connection at the booster battery first.

Some portable battery chargers can be used as a booster battery (Fig. 32).

IMPORTANT: Never use booster cable from a 12-volt battery to a 6-volt system as it may damage system.

SELECTION OF BATTERIES FOR REPLACEMENT

When replacing batteries, be sure to replace the battery with one at least equal in size to the original.

For cold weather starting, the battery must be powerful enough for the cranking job.

Fig. 33 shows how the load on the battery gets bigger when it is colder. At -20°F (-30°C), the battery has only 30% of its full cranking capacity. At the same time, greater load is put on the battery by the colder engine when starting.

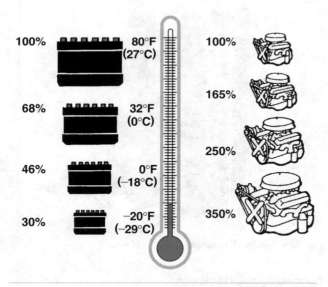

Fig. 33 — How Cold Weather Affects the Battery and the Engine When Starting

In effect, *at cold temperatures the battery is "smaller" while the engine is "larger".*

If the replacement battery is smaller than the original, the engine will surely be harder to start in cold weather.

There are many times in the heat of summer when engines are just as hard to start as in the winter especially when an air conditioner is added to the engine load. Therefore, use the same method of matching battery power to the engine in hot areas as you would in colder climates.

Other Factors In Battery Selection

When replacing batteries, be sure to replace the battery with *one at least equal* in size (ampere-hours rating) to the original.

A *larger* battery than the original may be needed if added accessories put a larger load on the battery.

An extra-output alternator may be the answer in cases where electrical loads are excessive or when operating mostly at slower speeds. This will help keep the battery charged and increase its service life.

The cheapest battery is not always the best buy for replacement. For example, three batteries in the same group size may vary in price, but they also vary in ampere-hours rating, in construction, and in warranty period. Divide the price by the months of warranty, and you may find the most expensive batteries are really the most economical, per month of expected service.

A final word on replacing batteries: One out of every four batteries returned for warranty has nothing wrong with it except that it is discharged. *Be sure to trouble shoot the battery before you replace it.*

SAFETY RULES FOR BATTERIES

1. To avoid injury from a spark or short circuit, DISCONNECT THE BATTERY GROUND STRAP (Fig. 34) when working on any part of the electrical system or engine. This will also prevent accidental starting.

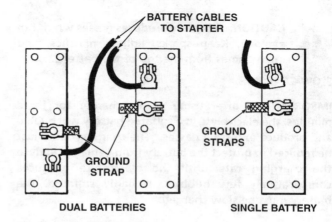

Fig. 34 — Installation of Typical Batteries

2. Disconnect the battery cable (Fig. 34) before fast charging the battery in the machine. This is especially important with a.c. charging systems where the alternator can be damaged.

3. When removing the battery, disconnect the battery ground strap first. When installing the battery, wait until last to connect the ground strap.

4. Never reverse the polarity of the battery connections. In general, systems with a.c. charging have negative grounds (-), while systems with a.c. charging can have either, positive (+) or negative (-) grounds. Reversing the polarity may damage some components and wiring in the system.

5. DO NOT ATTEMPT TO POLARIZE THE ALTERNATOR on a.c. circuits after connecting the battery. No polarization is needed. Any attempt to do so may damage the alternator, regulator, or circuits. However, if your machine has a *generator*, it should be polarized (see later under "Generator Service").

6. If booster batteries are used to start an engine, connect the (+) terminal of the booster battery to the (+) terminal of the dead battery with a jumper cable. Then, connect the second cable to the (-) terminal on the booster battery. Make the last (-) connection to a good ground on the machine with the dead battery. Disconnect in reverse order.

7. Do not attempt to recharge or jump-start a frozen battery. Check for ice in each cell of the battery.

8. When using booster batteries, prevent fire hazards as follows: a) When possible, use cables with a switch in the line. b) Always "rock" the connector clips to make, sure they are making good contact. c) Always put the machine in PARK. d) Never jump start by touching connectors to the starter motor. The machine can suddenly lurch and crush you.

9. Don't lay tools down by a battery. An accidental nudge and a tool can contact a battery terminal, and short circuit the battery.

10. GAS FROM BATTERY ELECTROLYTE IS FLAMMABLE: Keep sparks and flame away from the battery. When charging the battery, gas is created rapidly. Be sure the room where batteries are charged is well ventilated.

11. BATTERY ACID IS HARMFUL ON CONTACT

If battery electrolyte spills:

1. Remove affected clothing.

2. Rinse affected skin with clear water for 10 or 15 minutes.

3. Flood eyes with clear water for 10 or 15 minutes. Force the eyes open so water can flush them.

4. Then, see a doctor.

5. Don't use any medication or eye drops unless prescribed by a physician.

MAINTENANCE-FREE BATTERIES

Maintenance-free batteries operate similar to the conventional style battery. The construction is somewhat different than other batteries. The plates in maintenance-free batteries are made of lead-calcium which reduces gassing by as much as 97 percent over conventional batteries with lead-antimony plates.

Maintenance-free batteries are vented but most do not have vent caps. This reduces acid spillage and thus reduces the potential for corrosion on the battery terminals.

The vent strip may be removed from the top of some maintenance free batteries to expose the electrolyte. A hydrometer can then be used to check the battery and water may be added if necessary. However, because of the reduced gassing in maintenance-free batteries with lead-calcium plates, additional water normally is not required for the life of the battery.

Most maintenance-free batteries with lead-calcium plates are activated, charged, and ready for service when shipped from the factory. Because of a low rate of discharge, they have a longer shelf life than conventional wet-charged batteries. A maintenance-free battery may have a shelf life of 12 months or longer, depending on storage temperature.

SERVICING SPARK PLUGS

Fouled or damaged spark plugs can rob a spark-ignition engine of power and economy. For example, if spark plugs are badly fouled, the power and fuel lost in only a few weeks can pay for a new set of plugs.

SPARK PLUG OPERATION

A spark plug has two electrodes separated by a gap (Fig. 35). High voltage current from the distributor enters the top of a spark plug, travels down the center electrode, and jumps the gap at the bottom to make a spark.

The width of the spark plug gap is vital to both the size of the spark and to proper timing of the ignition.

HEAT RANGE OF PLUGS

The heat range of a spark plug is as important as the gap setting.

The term *heat range* refers to the plug's ability to transfer the heat at the firing tip to the cooling systems of the engine. This is determined by the *distance the heat must travel.*

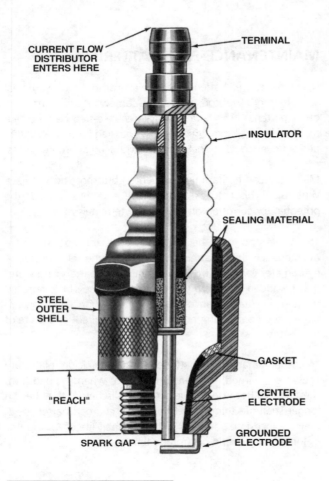

Fig. 35 — *Spark Plug Construction*

As shown in Fig. 36, the end of a plug insulator that has a long nose or cone is further from the cooling system. Therefore, heat at the end will travel further. This type of plug will then run *hot.*

In contrast, the end of a short insulator cone is closer to the cooling system and heat will transfer faster. This plug will then operate *cooler.*

Engine design and operating conditions will decide which type of spark plug—hot or cold—should be used. Generally, an engine which operates at fast speeds or heavy loads, and thus hotter, will require a *colder* plug so that the heat will

transfer faster. On the other hand, a *hotter* plug will be used in an engine that operates at low or idle speeds most of the time. For normal engine operations, a plug that falls somewhere between hot and cold is used.

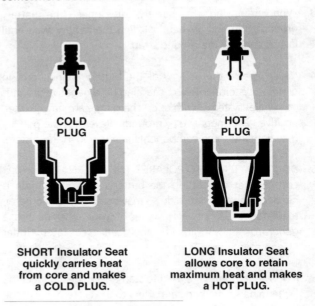

SHORT Insulator Seat quickly carries heat from core and makes a COLD PLUG.

LONG Insulator Seat allows core to retain maximum heat and makes a HOT PLUG.

Fig. 36 — *Heat Range of Spark Plugs*

The heat range of a plug is usually shown by a number on the plug. A higher number (such as "18") is hotter than a lower one (such as "15").

When the correct heat range is used, the plugs operate at the proper temperatures to burn themselves free of carbon.

If plugs operate too hot, preignition will occur.

If plugs operate too cold, fouling will result.

TOOLS AND MATERIALS NEEDED

To service spark plugs, the following tools and materials are needed:

1. Spark plug socket wrench

2. Pan of cleaning solvent (not gasoline)

3. Wire brush

4. Blade-type file

5. Wire-type plug gap gauge (inch or metric, as required)

6. Set of new plug gaskets (if available)

7. Torque wrench (inch or metric, as required)

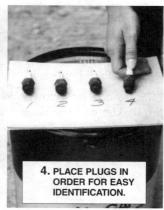

1. PULL UP ON CONNECTOR ONLY TO REMOVE WIRE

2. HOLD SOCKET WRENCH STRAIGHT WHILE LOOSENING PLUG.

3. REMOVE DIRT FROM AROUND PLUGS BEFORE REMOVING.

4. PLACE PLUGS IN ORDER FOR EASY IDENTIFICATION.

Fig. 37 — Removing Spark Plugs

REMOVING SPARK PLUGS

Spark plugs should be removed and serviced every 500 hours, or sooner if recommended in the operator's manual.

Observe these practices when removing plugs:

1. Pull the wire from the plug by grasping the terminal, *not* by pulling on the wire (Fig. 37 left).

2. Use a deep-well socket (Fig. 37) to loosen the spark plug. (A special spark plug socket with rubber insert is even better.) Hold the socket straight to prevent breaking the insulator.

3. After loosening the plug but before removing it, always clean the area around the spark plug by blowing, wiping, or brushing (Fig. 37). (Be sure to protect your eyes.) This will prevent dirt from falling into the cylinder after removal.

4. Remove the plugs and place them in order to match the cylinder each came from (Fig. 37, right). The condition of the spark plug can tell you a lot about the operation of a particular cylinder. Also remove the plug gaskets (if used).

ANALYZING CONDITION OF SPARK PLUGS

Check the condition of all spark plugs removed-even if you are replacing them. The appearance of the plug's firing end can tell you whether your engine is using too much oil, overfueling, misfiring, or overheating. Condition of plugs may also warn you of a wrong grade of fuel or an incorrect spark plug.

Study the chart at the right to become familiar with, spark plug conditions and what they mean.

SERVICING OF SPARK PLUGS

Spark plug service has three basic jobs:

- **Inspection**
- **Cleaning**
- **Gap adjustment**

Most engine manufacturers recommend a specific time interval for ignition services. Follow this timetable very closely.

Inspecting Spark Plugs

When inspecting the plugs, look for the abnormal wear shown in the Spark Plug Condition Chart.

Then decide whether to recondition or replace the plugs.

Remember, if one plug is replaced, all the plugs should be replaced to get the full advantage of new plug performance and economy. This does not apply, of course, if unusual conditions cause premature failure to just one in a fairly new set of plugs.

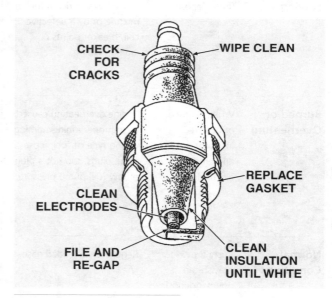

CHECK FOR CRACKS

WIPE CLEAN

REPLACE GASKET

CLEAN ELECTRODES

FILE AND RE-GAP

CLEAN INSULATION UNTIL WHITE

Fig. 38 — Spark Plug Maintenance

Normally, replace the whole set of plugs after long intervals of use. Normal wear can double the voltage requirements of a spark plug even in a short period of time.

Cleaning Spark Plugs

NOTE: Do not use a power wire brush to clean the plugs. Most makers of plugs do not recommend this.

1. Badly fouled plugs should be replaced. It is doubtful if sand blasting or liquid cleaning will remove all the deposits from such plugs.

2. If the plugs have moderate deposits, you may take them to your dealer for machine cleaning. However, if a sandblast machine is used to clean the plugs, some engine manufacturers void the warranty on the engine.

3. Clean wet, oily plugs with a cleaning solvent which dissolves petroleum deposits (but *not* gasoline).

4. Clean the threads with a wire hand brush.

5. To allow room for filing, bend the ground electrode away from the center electrode.

SPARK PLUG CONDITION CHART					
Condition	**Identification**	**Caused By**	**Condition**	**Identification**	**Caused By**
Oil Fouling	Wet, Sludgy deposits.	Excessive oil entering combustion chamber worn rings and pistons, excessive clearance between valve guides and stems, or worn or loose bearings.	**High Lead Deposits**	White, powdery through deposits.	Highly leaded gasoline (premium gasoline).
Gas Fouling	Dry, black, fluffy deposits.	Incomplete combustion caused by too rich a fuel-air mixture or by a defective coil, breaker points or ignition wiring.	**Carbon Fouling**	Hard, baked on black carbon.	Too cold a plug. Weak ignition, defective fuel pump, dirty air cleaner, too rich a fuel mixture.
Burned or Overheating	White, burned, or blistered insulator nose and eroded electrodes	Engine overheating caused by improper ignition timing, wrong type of fuel, loose spark plugs, too hot a plug, or low fuel pump pressure.	**Silicone Deposit**	Hard and scratchy.	Formed when fine sand particles combine with anti-knock compounds in fuel. Most common in dusty areas. The plugs cannot be cleaned.
Normal Conditions	Rusty brown to grayish-tan powder deposit and are minor electrode erosion.	Regular or unleaded gasoline.	**Splashed Fouling**	Splattered deposits.	Deposits from misfiring loosend when normal combustion chamber deposits restored after new plugs are installed. During high-speed run, these deposits are thrown into plug.

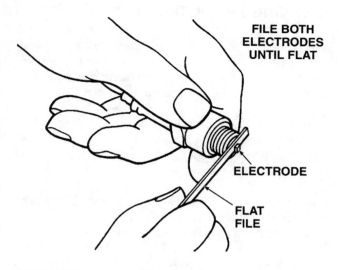

FILE BOTH ELECTRODES UNTIL FLAT

ELECTRODE

FLAT FILE

Fig. 39 — Filling Spark Plug Electrodes Until Flat

6. File both electrodes (Fig. 39) until they have flat bright surfaces (like a new plug). However, remove as little material as possible.

These flat surfaces reduce the voltage required to fire the plug consistently. Rounded electrodes require higher voltages to fire the plug.

7. Bend ground electrodes back to original position.

8. Clean or blow metal filings from plug.

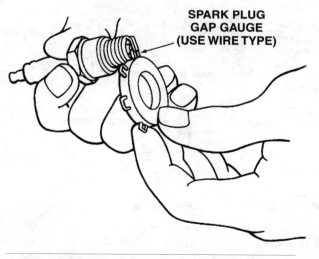

SPARK PLUG GAP GAUGE (USE WIRE TYPE)

Fig. 40 — Checking Spark Plug Gap (With Wire-Type Gauge)

Gap Adjustment of Spark Plugs

1. Whether the plug is new or used, always check the gap before you install the plug (Fig. 40). Refer to your operator's manual for the correct gap (usually .020, .025, or .030 inch; 0.5, 0.6 or 0.8 mm).

2. Don't use a flat gauge to check the spark plug gap. A flat gauge doesn't give an accurate indication of the true gap. A wire gauge will fit the contour of irregular surfaces.

3. Bend the ground electrode, as necessary, with a gap setter (usually part of the spark plug gauge). See Fig. 41. Check the gap with the proper thickness gauge.

IMPORTANT: Never bend the center electrode, Doing so may crack or break the insulator tip.

Fig. 41 — Adjusting Spark Plug Gap

INSTALLING SPARK PLUGS

As stated earlier, spark plugs are cooled by the coolant in the passages of the engine head. For this reason, be sure the area around each spark plug post is absolutely clean before installing plugs. New spark plugs may result in some increase in power and decrease in fuel consumption.

1. Install the plugs and tighten with your fingers. Be sure to use a gasket—unless the plug has a tapered seat (gaskets aren't required for this type of plug).

You should use new gaskets when installing plugs. Old gaskets will be flattened by tightening; however, they may still be usable.

A properly tightened gasket conducts almost 50 percent of the heat flow from the plug to the engine head and coolant.

2. Tighten plug with a spark plug socket and torque wrench. The operator's manual will tell how much torque to apply. For example, the average 14 mm threaded plug is usually tightened to about 25 ft-lbs (34 N•m) torque.

If the plug is not tight enough against the gasket, the plug will overheat.

However, if the plug is too tight against the gasket, the porcelain insulator may break. Also, the plug could be distorted and change the gap between the electrodes.

3. Check the condition of the spark plug wires before reinstalling. If the insulation is cracked or extremely soft, replace the wires. Defective insulation will allow electrical leaks and misfiring.

   Check the plug connectors for looseness and bad fit. If the connectors are not repairable, replace the wires.

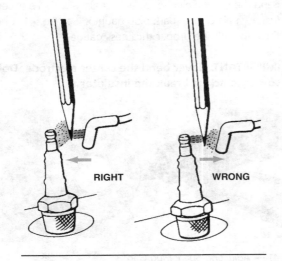

Fig. 42 — Checking Polarity at the Spark Plug

4. Check the polarity of the spark at the spark plug (Fig. 42).

   To check the polarity, hold the metal connector of the spark plug wire about 1/4 inch (6 mm) from the spark plug terminal (Fig. 42). Insert the point of an ordinary lead pencil as shown.

   If the spark feathers on the plug side, the polarity is correct.

   If the spark feathers on the connector side, the polarity is reversed. To correct, interchange the primary wire connections on the ignition coil.

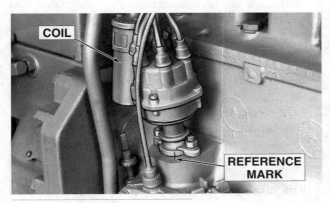

Fig. 43 — Ignition Distributor and Coil

SERVICING THE DISTRIBUTOR

As we have discussed earlier, the *distributor* controls the spark plug operation and engine timing on sparkignition engines. Therefore, maintenance of the distributor is important to maintain the efficiency and power of the engine.

Badly pitted or burned breaker points, for example, can cause hard starting and misfiring at the spark plugs. A poorly timed engine can also cause poor fuel economy, loss of power, and possible damage to the engine.

If the timing is late, the fuel-air mixture does not burn completely, valves will burn, fuel is wasted, and power is lost. If the timing is too early, pre-ignition occurs.

You should perform maintenance of the distributor every 500 hours or less of operation; refer to your operator's manual.

Your engine may be equipped with either a *conventional* ignition system or a *transistorized* system. We will discuss their differences later, but now let's examine the distributor, which is part of both systems.

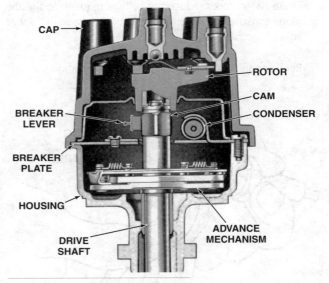

Fig. 44 — Cutaway View of Distributor

OPERATION OF THE DISTRIBUTOR

As the distributor drive shaft turns, the breaker cam lobe pushes the breaker lever rubbing block. This action opens the contact points, stopping the current flow in the coil primary circuit. See at left in Fig. 45, below.

The collapsing field and the resulting high-voltage surge in the coil's secondary winding forces current into the center terminal of the distributor cap as shown in red. The distributor rotor picks up this current and delivers it to the proper spark plug to fire the engine.

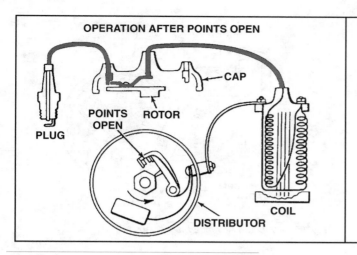
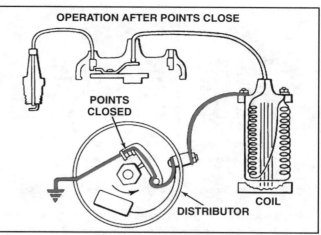

Fig. 45 — Basic Operation of the Distributor and Coil

Meanwhile, the distributor cam lobe has moved away from the rubbing block and spring tension brings the points back into contact (see at right in Fig. 45). The primary circuit is again complete and current flows until the next lobe opens the points. The cycle then repeats itself.

In this way a spark is created as each lobe of the cam opens the contact points. The entire cycle for each spark takes place at a very high speed.

CONDENSER OPERATION

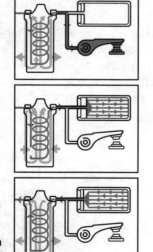

① Steady, straight current flow through coil primary, points closed.

② As points open, induced voltage produces current in the primary to flow into the condenser, creating a voltage difference between the insulated foil sheets.

③ Drained condenser foil sheets now have lower voltage charge than adjacent grounded sheets, so current flow again reverses as shown until all coil energy is used up.

Fig. 46 — Operation of Condenser

In a mechanical ignition, the condenser (capacitor) receives and stores electrical current briefly, while the contact points are opening (Fig. 46). With the current flowing into the condenser while the contact points open, the current can't arc across the points and burn them.

But, a condenser can only hold so much. When it is fully charged, it discharges its current in one burst. Since the points are fully open by this time, the burst of current flows back to the coil. At the coil, the burst of current collapses the magnetic field and induces a tremendous voltage in the secondary circuit. This voltage flows to the spark plug and jumps the spark plug gap producing the ignition spark for the engine.

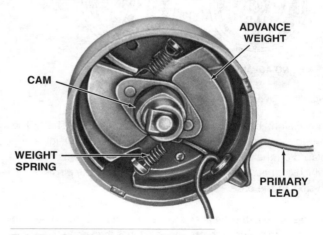

Fig. 47 — Centrifugal Advance Mechanism

Centrifugal Advance on Distributor

Basically, an *advance* mechanism (Fig. 47) is a device which times the ignition spark to occur at a certain tim determined by engine speed. Why is a spark advance necessary?

The distributor must deliver the spark to the engine when it is most effective. The most effective time is determine by the position of the piston and the time required to ignite the fuel-air mixture in the engine cylinder.

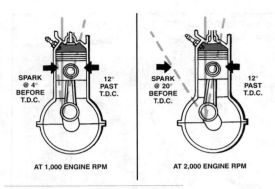

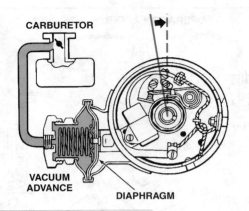

Fig. 48 — Spark Timing of the Engine

Fig. 50 — Vacuum Advance Mechanism

What the advance mechanism does is adjust the tributor timing to allow for speed changes so that the spark will occur at the right time even though the engine speed changes (Fig. 48).

The most common advance mechanism is the *centrifugal advance* (Fig. 49). This device has two weights, weight base, and two springs.

Vacuum Advance on Distributor

For greater fuel economy, an extra advance mechanism is used on some distributors. This is the *vacuum advance* (Fig. 50).

A vacuum can develop in the engine intake manifold, allowing less fuel and air into the cylinder. Since a lean fuel-air mixture will burn slower, ignition must take place sooner in the cycle than even the centrifugal advance can provide. So a vacuum advance is used to advance the spark still further.

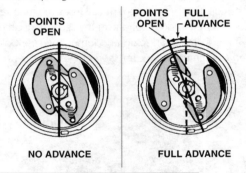

Fig. 49 — Operation of Centrifugal Advance

The weight base is part of the distributor drive shaft. The springs are connected to the base, while the weights are placed on the base. The distributor breaker cam has two pins which connect it to the springs and weights. The pins also set in slots in the base.

At idle speeds the breaker cam is "pinned" to the base and rotates with the drive shaft. The cam lobes then open the points at a preset time—such as 4 degrees before top dead center.

As the engine speeds up, centrifugal force throws the weights out against spring tension (Fig. 49). This turns the breaker cam so the cam lobes are now striking the breaker lever earlier. Therefore, the contact points open ahead of time.

The higher the speed, the farther the weights are thrown out. And the farther the weights are thrown, the more they turn the breaker cam and the more the spark is advanced.

When the engine slows down, the springs return the breaker cam and weights to their original position, thus retarding the spark timing.

The vacuum advance uses an air-tight diaphragm connected to an opening in the carburetor by a vacuum passage (Fig. 50). The diaphragm is connected by linkage to the distributor housing or the breaker plate.

When a vacuum at the intake manifold draws air from the diaphragm chamber, it causes the diaphragm to rotate the distributor breaker plate in the opposite direction of drive shaft rotation. This moves the breaker lever to contact the breaker cam lobes sooner and thus advances the spark.

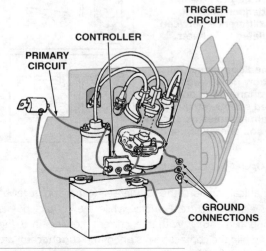

Fig. 51 — Simplified Electronic Ignition

ELECTRONIC IGNITION

The components of an electronic ignition system (Fig. 52) are much the same as the components of a mechanical ignition system.

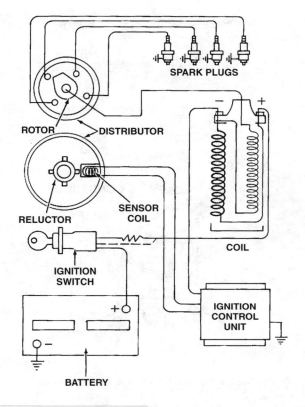

Fig. 52 — An Electronic Ignition

The main difference in the two systems is that the electronic battery system uses a solid state ignition control unit with a reluctor and sensor to time spark delivery in place of breaker points and a condenser.

When the ignition switch is turned on, battery current flows through the switch to the coil and through the primary winding to the ignition control unit. A strong electromagnetic field is developed around the winding in the sensor coil (Fig. 53).

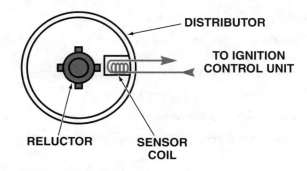

Fig. 53 — Sensor and Reluctor

When one of the reluctor projections enters the magnetic field around the sensor coil its presence is sensed, and the sensing element in the ignition control unit breaks the primary circuit. Breaking the primary circuit collapses the electromagnetic field around the primary coil windings. This collapsing field induces a high voltage in the secondary coil. The voltage is routed to the distributor rotor (Fig. 54) through the high tension lead. If timed correctly, the rotor, at that moment, is in position to contact the wire to the correct spark plug. The current flows to the spark plug, and jumps the spark plug gap to make the ignition spark. The entire cycle then starts over to fire the next spark plug in order.

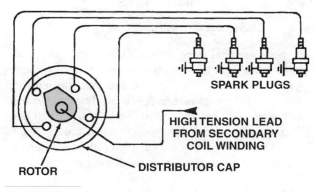

Fig. 54 — Rotor

ELECTRONIC IGNITION MAINTENANCE

The ignition control unit is sealed and requires no maintenance. There is no service to be performed on the sensor coil and reluctor with the exception of setting the air gap. To set the air gap:

1. Loosen the sensor coil adjusting screw.

2. Align one of the reluctor teeth with the sensor.

3. Insert a nonmagnetic feeler gauge, usually about .008 inch (0.2 mm), between the reluctor tooth and sensor. Move sensor against the feeler gauge and, tighten the screw.

The rest of the system requires the same maintenance as a mechanical ignition system.

CHECKING CONDITION OF DISTRIBUTOR

1. Clean outside of distributor housing and cap before removing cap. Use a small amount of cleaning solvent if necessary. Do not use water; it may cause short circuits. Do not allow any dirt to enter distributor. A clean cap will help prevent electrical shorts or crossfiring during operation.

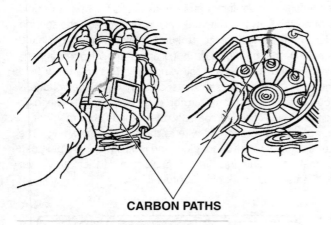

CARBON PATHS

Fig. 55 — Carbon Paths on Distributor Caps

2. Remove cap and wipe interior clean with a dry cloth. Dust, moisture or oil deposits must be removed. If carbon paths are present, (Fig. 55) the cap must be replaced. These paths are caused by electricity flowing between terminals or between terminals and a ground. Accumulation of dirt and moisture cause these paths to form. Once the path is formed, it will continue to conduct current and eventually burn through the cap.

Check to see if ventilator holes are open. If ozone gas (created by sparking between the rotor and terminals) is trapped, moisture will combine with the gas to form an acid which will corrode metal parts.

3. Inspect the distributor cap for chips or cracks.

Replace the cap if it is cracked. If the carbon button in the center of the cap is worn excessively, chipped or cracked, replace the cap.

4. Remove the rotor (Fig. 56) and clean it. Inspect for cracks or excessive burning of the metal strip. Replace the rotor if these signs of damage are present.

5. If a dust cover is used, remove it and check the condition of the felt seal. If the seal is worn, replace the seal. Dirt may enter past a worn seal and cause rapid wear of the cam lobes or rubbing block on the points.

6. Check the centrifugal advance mechanism (See Fig. 47). Turn the distributor shaft in the direction of normal rotation. It must rotate freely for a short distance and return to its original position when released. If it doesn't, have it checked by a service.shop.

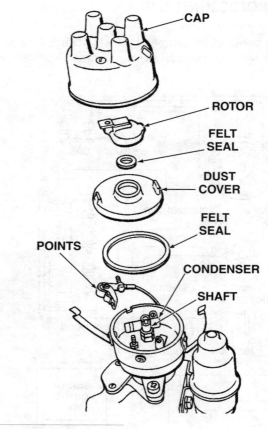

CAP

ROTOR

FELT SEAL

DUST COVER

FELT SEAL

POINTS

CONDENSER

SHAFT

Fig. 56 — Distributor Rotor

7. Inspect the contact surfaces of the breaker points.

It the surfaces are rough but show only slight pitting and metal deposits (Fig. 57, A), file them smooth with an ignition file (B). Keep the surfaces parallel and flat. Do not use sandpaper or emery cloth; particles may become imbedded in the contact surfaces and cause the points to burn. Be sure that a large area of contact is maintained between the surfaces. Remove just the high spots; all pits do not need to be completely removed.

If the points are badly pitted with very rough surfaces (Fig. 57, C), replace them. See "Replacing Breaker Points" on the following page.

Burned points may be caused by any one of the following reasons:

- *Oil or Foreign Material on the Contact Surfaces*
- *Condenser of Improper Capacity*
- *Incorrect Gap Adjustment*
- *Poor Alignment of Contact Surfaces*

If the breaker points must be replaced, proceed as given on next page.

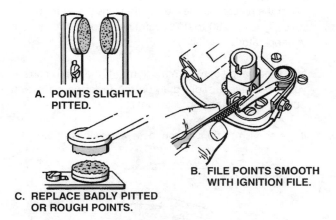

A. POINTS SLIGHTLY
   PITTED.

B. FILE POINTS SMOOTH
   WITH IGNITION FILE.

C. REPLACE BADLY PITTED
   OR ROUGH POINTS.

Fig. 57 — Checking and Reconditioning Breaker Points

CHECKING THE CONDENSER

If in doubt about the condition of the breaker points or ignition voltage, remove the condenser and test it with a condenser tester, if available (Fig. 58). The condenser should be tested for grounds, short, resistance, and proper capacity for system (per service manual specifications). Use instructions furnished with the tester units to make the tests.

REPLACING BREAKER POINTS

When replacing breaker points, be sure that you replace the condenser at the same time. Condensers are not expensive and you will be assured that a new one will operate properly.

To replace breaker points:

1. Remove breaker arm and spring (Fig. 59).

   Disconnect the condenser lead and the breaker arm spring from the primary terminal.

   If the breaker arm is separable from the breaker point bracket, pull it off.

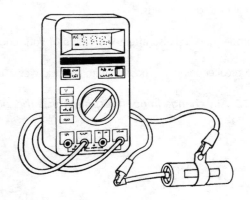

Fig. 58 — Testing the Condenser with a Condenser Tester

If the breaker arm is riveted to the stationary breaker point bracket, remove the bracket together with the breaker arm.

2. Clean and then lubricate the cam with special cam lubricant. Use a very small amount of lubricant about the size of a small match head. Distribute the lubricant around the cam. Petroleum jelly or multi-purpose grease or crankcase oil is not sufficient. They melt when hot or become stiff in cold weather. In either case, the breaker points may not function properly.

   If the top of the cam has a wick (Fig. 59), apply a few drops of clean SAE 20 oil to the wick.

3. Remove the condenser (Fig. 59).

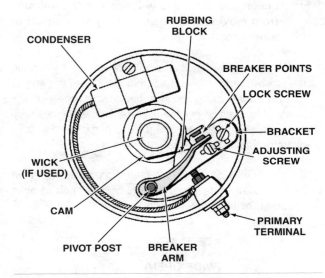

Fig. 59 — Typical Mounting for Distributor Breaker Point Assembly

4. Install new condenser and breaker points in the reverse order of disassembly. Apply a drop of clean SAE 20 oil around the breaker-arm pivot post. Be sure all electrical connections are tight.

   IMPORTANT: Never allow lubricant to get on the breaker point contacts.

Now we can adjust the breaker points.

ADJUSTING BREAKER POINTS

1. First check the alignment of the breaker points (Fig. 60). If points are misaligned, the results will be excessive burning, pitting, and uneven wear of points.

   If necessary, loosen lock screw and adjust at adjusting screw (see Fig. 59).

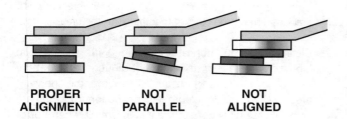

PROPER ALIGNMENT   **NOT PARALLEL**   **NOT ALIGNED**

Fig. 60 — Alignment of Distributor Breaker Points

2. Turn the engine crankshaft until the distributor cam opens the breaker points to their widest position (Fig. 61).

 CAUTION: When cranking the engine, be sure the transmission is in park or neutral and the brakes are set. This will prevent the machine from moving and causing injury to yourself or others nearby.

Crank the engine by "bumping" the starter, by turning the fan by hand (remove spark plugs to allow the engine to turn easier) or by using a heavy screwdriver in the flywheel housing to pry the flywheel (some engines have a slot or special rotating tool for this purpose). See your operator's manual for other suggestions.

If the cam lobe is close to opening the points, you might be able to turn the advance mechanism enough to open the points to their widest position.

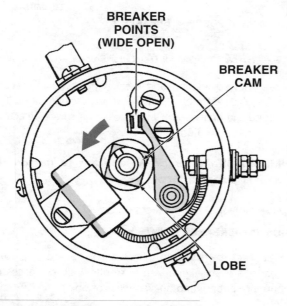

BREAKER POINTS (WIDE OPEN)

BREAKER CAM

LOBE

Fig. 61 — Breaker Points at Widest Position

3. Check the point gap for proper spacing using a blade-type feeler gauge (Fig. 62).

Select the proper thickness of feeler gauge (varies from .010 to .028 inch; 0.250 to 0.700 mm) per recommendations in your operator's manual.

Insert the gauge between the points. If the gap is correct, you should feel a slight drag on the feeler gauge as you pull it between the contact points.

If the gap is too tight or too loose, proceed with Step 4.

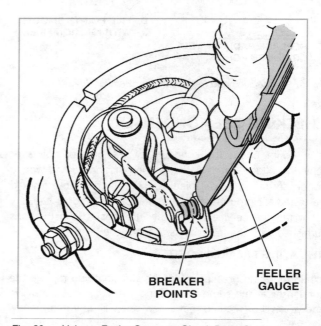

BREAKER POINTS   **FEELER GAUGE**

Fig. 62 — Using a Feeler Gauge to Check Point Gap

4. Loosen lock screw on the stationary point bracket (Fig. 63).

5. Adjust the points for proper spacing. An adjusting screw (Fig. 63) or screwdriver slot provides the means of adjustment.

   If you set the points too close, they will rapidly burn and pit.

   If you set the points too wide, they will cause a weak spark at higher engine speeds.

   Improper gap will also affect the timing of your engine.

6. Lock breaker points into position with the lock screw (Fig, 63).

NOTE: Any change in point setting affects the ignition timing.

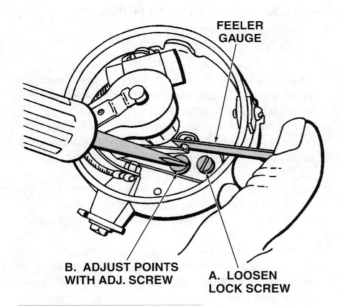

Fig. 63 — Adjusting Breaker Point Gap

7. Recheck the gap and wipe the points clean with a strip of paper or clean cloth (Fig. 64). *Points must be absolutely clean. Any particle will cause rapid burning of points.*

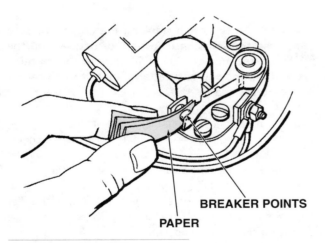

Fig. 64 — Cleaning Contract Surfaces

By rechecking the gap, you can be assured that the gap wasn't changed when you tightened the locking screw.

An alternate way to check the gap on old points is shown in Fig. 65. This method is more accurate on worn points as it is not affected by rough point surfaces. Indicator is placed beside breaker arm as shown to measure how far it opens.

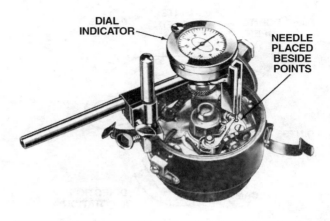

Fig. 65 — Checking Point Gap with Dial Indicator (Alternate Method)

CHECKING CAM ANGLE (DWELL)

The *cam angle* is the number of degrees that the breaker cam rotates from the time the points close until they open again (Fig. 66). As the cam angle increases, the point gap decreases, and vice versa.

Too little cam angle can cause engine to misfire at high speed.

Too much cam angle allows the points to close for too long, causing burned points.

Use the dwell meter on a distributor tester (if available) to check the cam angle. Then adjust the points to the specified dwell angle.

If the cam angle reading on the meter varies more than two degrees, look for a worn drive shaft or bushings.

If the cam angle and point gap cannot both be set to specifications at the same time, check for these problems:

- *Improper spring tension*
- *Wrong contact point assembly*
- *Worn breaker cam*
- *Points not following cam at high speeds*
- *Bent distributor drive shaft*

Now we're ready to assemble the distributor.

8. Reassemble the distributor in the reverse order of disassembly. Be sure that the rotor does not come in contact with the condenser lead wire or it could short out the condenser.

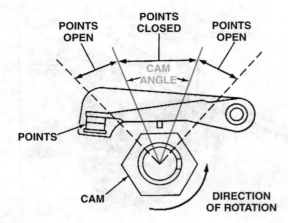

Fig. 66 — Distributor Cam Angle (Dwell)

9. Check the condition of the wires leading to the spark plugs and coil. Be sure connections are tight, the nipples seal over the terminals and the insulation is not soft or cracked. Replace wires if they show damage.

Because you have replaced the points or readjusted them, you must check or retime the ignition. Remember we said that the breaker point gap affects timing.

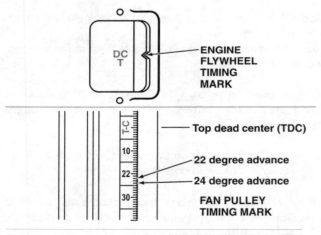

Fig. 67 — Typical Engine Timing Marks (Spark-Ignition Engine)

TIMING THE IGNITION CIRCUIT

Two methods of timing are available:

- **Breaker Point Method**
- **Timing Light Method**

Of the two methods above, the *timing light method* is more accurate than the breaker point method. However, we will demonstrate both methods.

Timing Ignition By Breaker Point Method

To time the engine by this method:

1. Locate the timing marks on the engine flywheel or fan pulley (Fig. 67). Your operator's manual should tell you where they are and which ones to use. Usually there are several marks before and after TDC (top dead center). If the marks are difficult to see, mark over them with chalk or paint to make them more visible.

2. Remove distributor cap so that you will be able to see the distributor rotor rotate when you crank the engine. You will need to know the direction of rotation for step 9.

3. Remove or loosen No. 1 spark plug. If you loosen the spark plug two or three turns, you will be able to hear air escape when the No. 1 piston is on its compression stroke. If you have someone helping you, remove the plug and place your thumb over the spark plug hole so that you can feel the air pressure as the compression stroke begins.

4. Crank the engine until No. 1 piston starts its compression stroke. Step 3 describes how to determine when the compression starts.

 CAUTION: When cranking the engine, be sure the transmission is in park or neutral and the brakes are set. This will prevent the machine from moving and causing injury to yourself or others nearby.

Crank the engine by "bumping" the starter, by turning the fan by hand (remove spark plugs to allow the engine to turn easier) or by using a heavy screwdriver in the flywheel housing to pry the flywheel (some engines have a slot or special turning tool for this purpose). See your operator's manual for other suggestions. (A special starter cable is sometimes available for engaging the starter while working close to the engine.)

Look for which way the distributor rotor turns as you crank the engine. You will need this information for step 9.

5. Place the distributor end of the coil high-tension wire 1/8-inch (3 mm) from the engine (Fig. 68). Turn ignition switch on. A spark will jump the gap as the distributor points start to open.

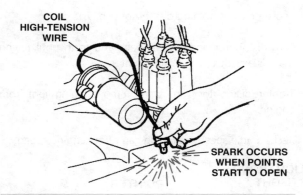

COIL
HIGH-TENSION
WIRE

SPARK OCCURS
WHEN POINTS
START TO OPEN

Fig. 68 — Checking for When Distributor Points Start to Open

6. Continue to rotate the crankshaft until the proper timing marks appear aligned with the timing pointer. See your operator's manual to determine which markings to use.

If the spark jumps the gap when the proper timing marks are aligned, the timing is correct. Reassemble the distributor. Replace spark plugs and tighten.

If timing is not correct, proceed with the remaining steps.

7. Reestablish proper positions of No. 1 piston and timing marks as described in steps 4 and 5.

8. Loosen clamps holding distributor to engine block (Fig. 69).

9. Turn the distributor body slowly in the direction the rotor normally turns (Fig. 69). You observed the rotation of the rotor in step 4. This procedure retards the time the breaker points open and makes sure the points are completely together.

10. Now, turn the distributor body slowly in the opposite direction until the points start to open and the spark jumps the gaps (see Step 5 above).

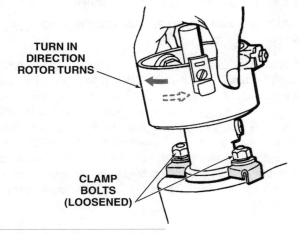

TURN IN
DIRECTION
ROTOR TURNS

CLAMP
BOLTS
(LOOSENED)

Fig. 69 — Turning Distributor Body

11. Tighten distributor clamps and reassemble distributor. The ignition is now timed.

12. Be sure the spark plugs are installed and properly tightened. Also, reconnect spark plug wires.

13. Start the engine to determine if it operates satisfactorily. If the engine is misfiring or backfires, you may have reconnected some of the spark plug wires incorrectly.

To check sequence of spark plug wires:

A. Identify which wire and distributor terminal leads to No.1 cylinder. This connection should be correct since you just finished timing the engine with it.

B. Determine the firing order of the engine either from numbers appearing on the engine or from your operator's manual.

C. Remove all spark plug wires from the distributor except No. 1.

D. Insert spark plug wires in the distributor cap in the order that the cylinders fire. Proceed around the cap in the same direction in which the rotor turns.

14. The engine should now run properly. If it doesn't, something else may be wrong. Review the steps you performed when timing the engine; perhaps you did something incorrectly. If you can't determine what is wrong, see your local service shop.

Timing Ignition By Timing Light Method

To time the engine with a timing light:

1. Locate the timing marks on the flywheel or fan pulley (see Fig. 67) just as you did in the previous method. However, you will probably use a different mark—see the operator's manual.

2. Connect the timing light to the No. 1 spark plug and make any other connections recommended by the timing light manufacturer (see Fig. 70). Three types of timing lights are available:

   • *Two-Wire Leads*

   • *Three-Wire Leads*

   • *110-Volt Powered*

   The TWO-WIRE TYPE has one lead connected to the No. 1 spark plug and the other to a ground connection.

   The THREE-WIRE TYPE is connected with one lead to the No. 1 spark plug and the other two to the battery terminals.

The110-VOLT TYPE has a lead which is connected to the No. 1 spark plug and the power cord plugs into a 110 volt receptacle.

Be sure to read the instructions included with the timing light so that you make the proper connections.

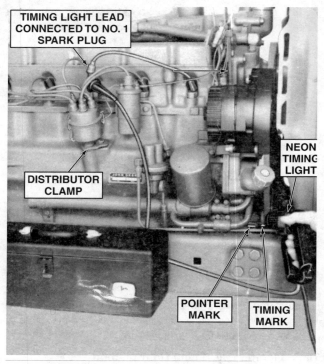

Fig. 70 — Timing the Distributor with a Timing Light

3. Determine the correct engine operating speed for making timing adjustments according to your operator's manual.

4. Chalk the proper timing mark so that it is easy to see.

5. Start the engine and adjust it to the proper speed.

 CAUTION: Be careful to avoid getting your hand or the timing light leads caught in any drive belts or the fan blades.

6. Aim the timing light (Fig. 70) at the marking or pointer near the flywheel or crankshaft fan pulley (wherever the timing marks appear).

Be sure you aim the timing light so that it is aligned with the pointer mark and the centerline of the crankshaft (Fig. 71). This will assure you of a correct reading.

If the proper timing mark doesn't align exactly with the pointer, proceed with the following steps.

7. Loosen clamps holding distributor (Fig. 70).

8. Turn distributor body slowly back and forth until timing mark is exactly opposite the pointer.

9. Tighten distributor clamps and remove timing light from engine.

10. Recheck idle speed, as timing can affect engine speed.

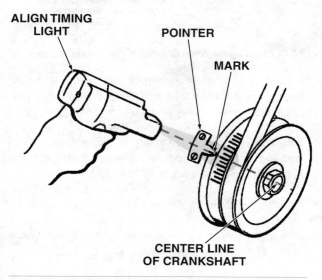

Fig. 71 — Be Sure to Align Timing Light with Pointer Mark and Center of Crankshaft

SERVICING ALTERNATOR (OR GENERATOR) AND STARTING MOTOR

The alternator (or generator) and starter will normally require little attention. But it is important that they receive service when required or you will have trouble starting your engine and these components may become damaged.

OPERATION OF ALTERNATOR, GENERATOR, AND STARTER

The **alternator** (a.c. charging circuits) operates continuously while the engine is running Fig. 72). A regulator controls the alternator output as required to charge the battery or supply other electrical components on the engine or machine with power. The alternator is more efficient than the older style generator and it produces an alternating current which flows back and forth. This current must be "rectified" (made to flow in one direction) to be usable by the electrical systems. This is done by electronic "check valves" called diodes within the alternator.

The alternator has two advantages over a generator:

- *Produces a higher output at lower engine speeds*

- *Simple construction requires less maintenance*

Fig. 72 — Alternator (A.C. Generator)

The **generator** (d.c. charging circuits) (Fig. 73) serves the same purpose as the alternator. But, because it is less efficient, it is found mostly on older machines. The generator has been replaced by the alternator on most modern engines.

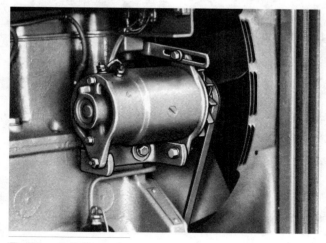

Fig. 73 — D.C. Generator

The **starting motor** (Fig. 74) engages the flywheel when the engine is to be cranked for starting. As soon as the engine starts, the starting motor disengages. Running the starter without pause for more than 20 or 30 seconds will cause overheating and damage to the starter. It is designed to handle heavy loads for short periods of time only.

Fig. 74 — Starting Motor and Solenoid

Most alternators do not require any periodic service except to check electrical connections and belt tension. However, read the following alternator and voltage regulator precautions to avoid damaging these components.

If your alternator, generator or starting motor requires more service than is given in the following procedures, take it to your local service shop.

Precautions For Alternator and Voltage Regulator

Disconnect the battery ground strap from the battery when working on or near the alternator or regulator.

This will prevent damage that might occur if the terminals are accidentally shorted.

When the batteries are connected, observe the following precautions. Failure to observe them will probably result in damage to the alternator, regulator or both.

1. NEVER ATTEMPT TO POLARIZE THE ALTERNATOR OR REGULATOR. Never ground a terminal or connect a jumper wire to any alternator terminals.

2. If electrical problems are encountered, **before** disconnecting the battery or alternator from the circuit, check for proper polarity. If polarity was incorrect the alternator has probably been seriously damaged. Have it repaired by a qualified service shop.

3. Before installing a battery or alternator, BE SURE OF PROPER POLARITY. Turn off all switches and accessories. Then, before connecting the battery ground strap, momentarily touch it to the battery post. No sparks should occur. If there are sparks, recheck all connections and installation procedures.

4. The alternator field terminal or the field circuit between the alternator and the regulator must never be grounded under any circumstances.

5. The alternator output terminal must never be grounded under any circumstances.

6. NEVER disconnect or connect any alternator wires with batteries connected or with alternator operating. Do not operate the alternator on open circuit. The high voltage resulting from open circuit operation will result in damage to the alternator, regulator, or electrical system.

7. Always connect additional batteries to each other in the correct polarity: POSITIVE to POSITIVE and NEGATIVE to NEGATIVE.

8. **IMPORTANT: Disconnect cables from positive battery terminals when charging batteries.**

SERVICING THE ALTERNATOR (OR GENERATOR) AND STARTER

The generator and starter require similar service; therefore, we will cover both components later with the same discussion.

Fig. 75 — Adjusting Generator Belt Tension

Checking Alternator (or Generator) Belt Tension

Every 250 hours or as recommended, check the alternator (or generator) belt tension (Fig. 75).

Flex the belt with a firm push midway on the side of the belt and measure with a ruler. If belt tension is specified in pounds (kg) rather than inches (mm) of flex, use a spring scale or belt tension gauge to measure tension.

If necessary, loosen the mounting bolt as shown and adjust the belt. Then tighten the bolt and recheck the tension.

NOTE: When a new belt is installed, always recheck the tension after a few hours of operation. This is when the initial "stretch" takes place.

Also note the condition of the belt. Excessive wear, fraying, or slack mean the belt should be replaced with an exact duplicate from your dealer.

IMPORTANT: Be sure belt is not too tight as it may wear out alternator (or generator) bearings faster. A small amount of flex is needed in the belt.

Check the condition of the generator and starter every 500 hours or when your operator's manual recommends attention. Almost all generators and starters have sealed bearings so that lubrication is not required. However, some have oil cups for bearing lubrication every 250 hours.

Lubricating Generator Oil Cups (if Used)

Every 250 hours or as recommended, add specified engine oil to front and rear oil cups on generator (Fig. 76). Most generators are sealed, but some have oil cups as shown. Only 8 or 10 drops of oil are required. *Do not over lubricate!* This can damage inner parts more than lack of lubricant.

Fig. 76 — Lubricating Generator Oil Cups

Also check for excessive dirt around generator housing and wipe off if necessary.

Servicing Generator And Starter

To service the generator and starter, proceed as follows.

Tools and Materials Needed

1. Screwdriver

2. Open-End Wrenches (inch or metric, as required)

3. Clean Cloth and Solvent (not gasoline)

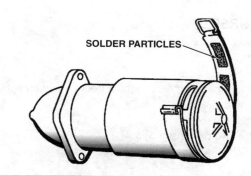

Fig. 77 — Overheated Starter or Generator

Removal And Inspection

1. Remove the generator or starter to inspect it.

2. Wipe dirt and grease from the housing. Use a cloth dampened with solvent if necessary.

3. Remove cover band or end plate, whichever provides access to the brushes and commutator.

4. Inspect for signs of overheating. If solder has been thrown against the band (Fig. 77) or against the inside of the housing, the unit requires expert repair. Take it to a service shop.

5. If other problems are evident, take one of three steps:

    a. Take the generator or starter to a service shop.

    b. Follow servicing recommendations in the technical service manual for that engine.

    c. Follow servicing procedures in Fundamentals of Service, ELECTRICAL SYSTEMS.

Polarizing Generator

If any wire leads were disconnected from the starter or generator while servicing, polarize the generator before starting the engine. See the operator's manual for details. Reverse polarity can create high current and damage the ignition system.

On externally grounded (type A) generator:

1. Reconnect the proper wires and terminals.

2. Touch short jumper wire (Fig. 78) momentarily between the terminals marked "BAT" and "GEN" (sometimes marked "ARM").

On internally grounded (type B) generator:

1. Momentarily touch the ends of the "BAT" wire and "FLD" wire together (Fig. 79).

2. Reconnect proper wires and terminals.

NOTE: A flash or arc will be noted when the lead is removed in either case. This polarizes the generator. On high-voltage generators, insulate the brushes. Failure to polarize the generator will result in a burned out generator if the polarity is wrong.

IMPORTANT: Do not attempt to polarize an ALTERNATOR system. Alternators do not require polarization and any attempt to do so will damage the alternator.

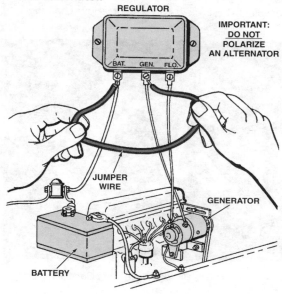

Fig. 78 — Polarizing Externally Grounded (Type A) Generator

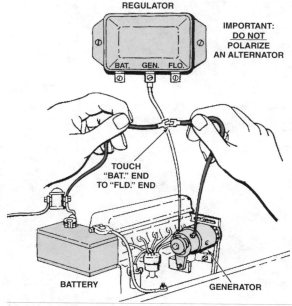

Fig. 79 — Polarizing Internally Grounded (Type B) Generator

WATCHING GAUGES DURING OPERATION

When operating a machine, glance at the electrical gauges from time to time. They will tell you if the electrical system is charging properly.

The voltmeter shown in Fig. 80 tells the operator it the battery is being charged and also tells the charged condition of the battery itself. Once the engine is running, the voltmeter needle should stay in the white "normal" range.

Indicator lights are used on some-mac hine consoles. These glow to warn of a low charging rate.

Fig. 80 — Voltmeter Tells Battery Charge and Condition

When starting the engine, the electrical indicator lights will glow, but they should go out after the engine has been running for a few seconds.

TEST YOURSELF

QUESTIONS

1. Which of the following are results of poor engine timing?
   ___A. Burned valves
   ___B. Worn breaker points
   ___C. Excessive oil consumption
   ___D. Excessive fuel consumption

2. The condition of the spark plugs affects timing.
   True_____   False_____

3. What are the *three* basic circuits in an engine electrical system?
   1. _____
   2. _____
   3. _____

4. What causes a dirty battery to lose its charge?

5. What makes battery charging a potential safety hazard?

6. An engine that runs at fast speeds, heavy loads and hot temperatures, requires a hotter spark plug.
   True_____   False_____

7. Which of the following are *not* causes of spark plug failures?
   ___A. Burned breaker points
   ___B. Cracked distributor cap
   ___C. Cracked plug insulation
   ___D. Carbon deposits on the electrodes
   ___E. Incorrect spark plug gap

8. What is a sure sign that a generator or starter has overheated?

9. (Fill in the blank.) After performing electrical service on the generator, always _____ it before starting the engine.

10. Match the items below with their proper description:
   ___A. If you set the   ___1. They will cause a weak
        breaker points   spark at higher speeds.
        too close ...
   ___B. If you set the.   ___2. They will rapidly burn
        breaker points   and pit.
        too wide..

POWER TRAINS

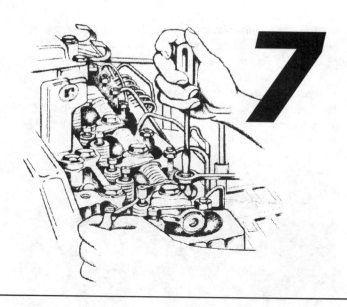

INTRODUCTION

The power train (Fig. 1) has to absorb tremendous forces in today's farm machines. These components also operate under severe conditions: from the freezing cold of winter to the searing heat of summer—and from engine-staggering loads to rough, start-and-stop operation.

Because the clutch, transmission, and final drives receive such severe use, important periodic maintenance is required to provide transmission of power for the life of the machine (Fig. 2).

Fig. 1 — Power Train in Farm Tractor

The lubricant used in the power train, whether it is hydraulic fluid or gear oil, becomes contaminated by dust, rust, moisture and metal particles. All of these elements can cause severe damage to gears, bearings, and valves when the power train maintenance is neglected.

Because the transmission lubricant is so important, let's discuss it first.

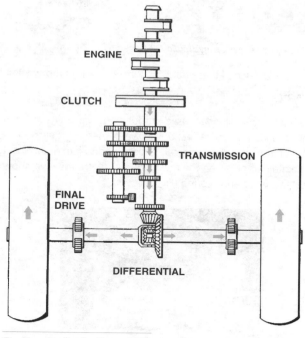

Fig. 2 — Parts of a Power Train

SELECTING TRANSMISSION LUBRICANTS

Three basic types of transmissions are used today. Each requires specific types of lubricants. Below is a description of each type of transmission and its lubrication requirements.

• **Sliding gear transmissions** require *gear oils* to provide lubrication under extreme pressure conditions.

- **Automatic transmission** (including torque converters and hydrostatic transmissions) require *automatic transmission fluids* to provide a medium to transmit power, lubricate and transfer heat.

- **Hydraulic assist transmissions** require *transmission-hydraulic fluids* to provide a medium to transmit power, lubricate and transfer heat from both the transmission and hydraulic system of the machine (Fig. 3).

Fig. 3 — Transmission-hydraulic Oil Reservoir

Let's look at each of these transmission lubricants in more detail.

GEAR OILS

The relatively small gears used in today's power trains result in higher loads and more friction between meshing gears. This makes lubrication more critical. Unless a good film of lubricant is maintained between the meshing gear teeth, they will show excessive wear and scoring (Fig. 4).

NORMAL WEAR

SCORING WEAR

Fig. 4 — Normal Gear Wear and Scoring Wear

In spur gear units (Fig. 5), where tooth pressures are relatively light, a simple gear oil is often adequate. However, special gears, such as spiral bevel and worm gear units (Fig. 5) can wear very rapidly unless the correct gear oil is used.

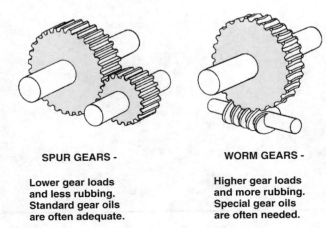

SPUR GEARS -

Lower gear loads and less rubbing. Standard gear oils are often adequate.

WORM GEARS -

Higher gear loads and more rubbing. Special gear oils are often needed.

Fig. 5 — Gear Oils Must Match the Gear Load

For these higher loads, the gear oil must have special "anti-friction" and "anti-weld" agents. Oils containing these additives are known as *extreme pressure* or *hypoid* lubricants.

To select the proper gear oil you must know:

1. *Viscosity requirements*

2. *Service classification requirement*

Viscosity Classification

The Society of Automotive Engineers (SAE) gear oil classification is based on the viscosity of an oil.

While the SAE numbers of gear oils are higher than the SAE numbers of engine crankcase oils, gear oils are not necessarily that much higher in viscosity. To avoid confusion, higher numbers are assigned to gear oils (Fig. 6). For example, SAE 80 gear oil actually has about the same viscosity as SAE 20 engine oil.

Multi-grade gear oils are presently available from some suppliers in grades of SAE 75/80 and SAE 80/90.

Some manufacturers recommend engine crankcase oils for use in standard transmission service, while some transmissions may use SAE 50 engine oil as an alternate for SAE 90 gear oil. As a result of this, some gear oil containers are marked SAE 50-90 indicating that the viscosity requirements of SAE 50 *engine* oil are also met.

Service Classification

The American Petroleum Institute (API) designates gear lubricants by the types of service for which they may be suitable. *This is not a rating of performance.*

API GL-1 oil is the lowest service, adequate for lower gear speeds and pressures, while GL-5 oil is for the hardest service.

As the "GL" number rises, so does the type of service.

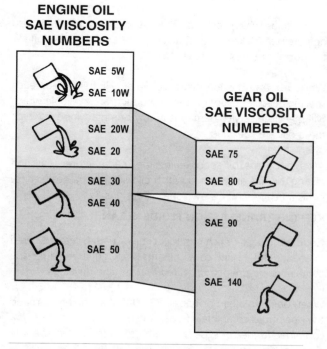

ENGINE OIL SAE VISCOSITY NUMBERS

SAE 5W	
SAE 10W	
SAE 20W	
SAE 20	
SAE 30	
SAE 40	
SAE 50	

GEAR OIL SAE VISCOSITY NUMBERS

SAE 75	
SAE 80	
SAE 90	
SAE 140	

Fig. 6 — Higher SAE Viscosity Numbers are Assigned to Gear Oils (To Avoid Confusion)

For example, GL-5 oil is rated for harder service than GL-4.

Lubricants indicated for API Service GL-4 and GL-5 are applicable for use in non-automatic transmissions and final drives, and are generally available locally.

API Service GL-6 is an obsolete designation which may have been specified for some older machines. If so, consult your machine dealer or a reputable oil supplier for the proper substitute.

Fig. 7 — Distillation Plant for Distilling Crude Oil

Refer to your operator's manual for recommended gear oils—the suggested viscosity and service classification should be designated.

AUTOMATIC TRANSMISSION FLUID

Inside an automatic transmission, the lubricant must perform specific functions under severe conditions. These are:

1. Protect heavily-loaded helical and spiral gears with an oil film cushion.

2. Perform as a non-foaming fluid in transmitting power.

3. Operate as a hydraulic fluid between -30° and +300°F (-35° and 150°C).

4. Act as a wet clutch and transmission lubricant to provide smooth, silent engagement, without slipping.

5. Resist oxidation under conditions of heat and aeration, while at the same time be compatible to all metals, rubber seals, gaskets, adhesives, facings, and liners in the system.

Automatic transmission fluids are designed to perform under a variety of conditions. Because of this, three popular types of fluids are used in most automatic transmissions today:

- *Type F (Ford Motor specification)*
- *DEXRON II (General Motors specification)*
- *Detroit Diesel Allison C-3*
- *John Deere Hydrostatic Fluid*

Do not mix these fluids. Although these fluids are physically compatible, their built-in frictional properties are different to meet different transmission design requirements. Mixing alters the properties of the fluids and should be avoided. Follow the machine manufacturer's recommendations in selecting fluids.

Some special components may require different qualities from an automatic transmission fluid. Torque converters and hydrostatic transmissions are among these.

Torque Converter Fluids

Automatic transmission fluids, Type A and Suffix A, have proven satisfactory for torque converters in heavy-duty trucks, buses, and off-the-road machines.

More recently, the specification has been replaced by DEXRON II from General Motors, and Type F from Ford Motor.

However, torque converters may require different qualities from an automatic transmission fluid.

Hydrostatic Drive Fluids

Hydrostatic drives can use automatic transmission fluids, but may require different qualities in the fluid.

Always follow the exact fluid recommendations in the machine operator's manual.

TRANSMISSION-HYDRAULIC FLUIDS

Some farm and industrial manufacturers have designed machines with a common reservoir for both the transmission and hydraulic systems (Fig. 8). This means that the same lubricating fluid has to serve the gear train as well as the precision hydraulic system.

This requires special fluids, and these have been developed:

- *John Deere Hy-Gard Fluid*
- *International Harvester Hy-Tran Fluid*
- *Allis-Chalmers Power Fluid 821*
- *Case TCH and TFD Fluids*
- *Ford M2C53-A and M2C134-A Fluids*

These fluids are referred to as *four-way oils* because of the wide range of services they must perform.

Their key properties are:

1. Have high oxidation stability for long life and protection.

2. Have low pour point for low temperature service, particularly during cold starting.

3. Have high viscosity index for best viscosity under various operating temperatures.

4. Contain extreme pressure additives for increased load carrying and wear protection under heavy and shockloads.

5. Contain rust and corrosion inhibitors.

6. Are compatible with all types of seals.

7. Contain foam suppressors.

Some fluids which serve as transmission-hydraulic fluids also operate wet brake or wet clutch systems and require additives to control clutch or brake chatter.

While no transmission-hydraulic fluid will fully meet each specific need for every machine, products are available which will meet the service demands in any one machine for which these oils are specified.

Always use the oil specified by the manufacturer. Through testing, he has determined which oil will give the best service in his machine and his own special designs.

KEEPING TRANSMISSION FLUIDS CLEAN

Good lubricants, which come in cans or barrels, are delivered clean and free from contaminants. It is generally after the containers are opened or stored that trouble develops.

When opening a can or barrel, BE SURE that the area around the opening is completely free of dust, dirt, lint, or water. *If a container, funnel, or hose is required to fill the system, be sure that it is spotless.*

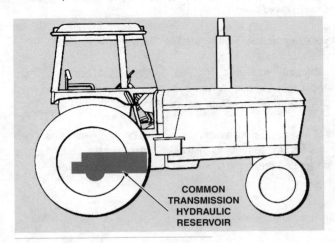

Fig. 8 — *Transmission-Hydraulic Systems*

When possible, always store barrels indoors, or at least under cover, and be sure the, bung is tight. If barrels are stored in the sun without a tight bung, the fluid will expand forcing some air

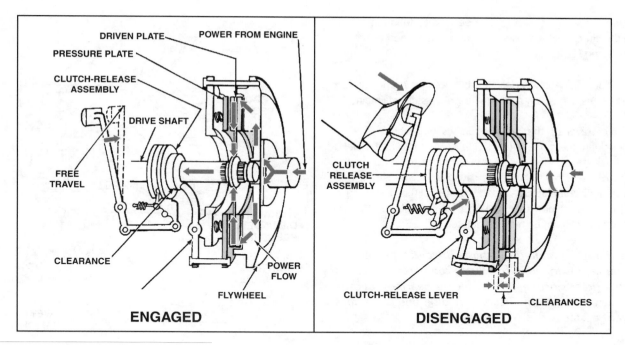

Fig. 9 — Operation of Standard Dry-Disk Clutch

from the bung. Then as the fluid cools off, the fluid contracts, drawing rain, dew, or other moisture into the barrel and fluid.

The harmful effects of water in lubricants have already been discussed (Chapter 4). For this reason, keep the bungs in barrels as tight as possible, and tip the barrels so that water cannot collect around the bung.

OPERATION OF POWER TRAINS

To help, understand why maintenance is important, we will briefly look at how the various power trains work.

Operation of the following components will be covered:

- **Clutch**
- **Mechanical transmission**
- **Hydraulic assist transmission**
- **Mechanical front wheel drive (MFWD)**
- **Hydrostatic drive**
- **Combine power rear wheel drive system**
- **Torque converter**
- **Differential**
- **Final drives**
- **Power take-off**

OPERATION OF CLUTCH

The clutch provides the means of disconnecting the engine from its load while starting, shifting or idling. In Fig. 9 you can see how the standard dry clutch, found on most machines, operates.

In the *engaged* position, the pressure plate provides pressure against the clutch plate and forces the plate against the flywheel. Power is transmitted from the engine through the flywheel and clutch plate to the drive shaft or transmission input shaft.

The clutch is *disengaged* by applying pressure on the pedal which pushes the clutch release assembly against the release levers. The levers pull the pressure plate away from the clutch plate so that the clutch plate is no longer forced against the flywheel. Now the flywheel and pressure plate are free to rotate independently of the clutch plate and drive shaft.

Notice that in the engaged position, there is clearance (usually 1/16 to 3/16 inch; 1.6 to 4.8 mm) between the clutch release bearing and the clutch release levers. This is to allow for wear of the clutch plate facings.

As the facings wear, the release levers move closer to the clutch release bearing until, eventually, there is no clearance. Adjustment must then be made or the release levers will press continuously on the clutch release bearing and pressure will be reduced on the clutch plate.

This will cause the clutch release bearing to fail prematurely. And the clutch will slip also—resulting in a burned clutch and rapid facing wear.

To maintain this necessary clearance between the bearing and the release levers, the clutch pedal free travel must be maintained.

The free travel of the pedal (Fig. 9, left). The less free travel of the pedal-the less clearance between the clutch release parts. Too much free travel, however, can prevent the clutch from disengaging completely which will cause difficult shifting of the transmission and overheating of clutch plate. We will describe how to adjust free travel later.

Note that the standard clutch is a dry disk type and that no lubricant is found in the clutch compartment (except for the grease fitting to the release bearing). Because the clutch operates by friction, the disks and plates must be kept perfectly dry.

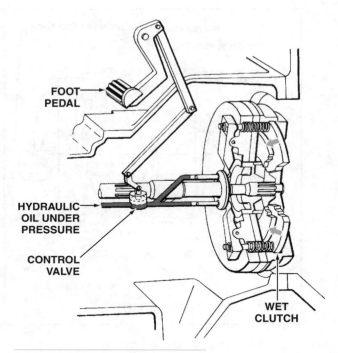

Fig. 10 — Operation of Hydraulic Clutch

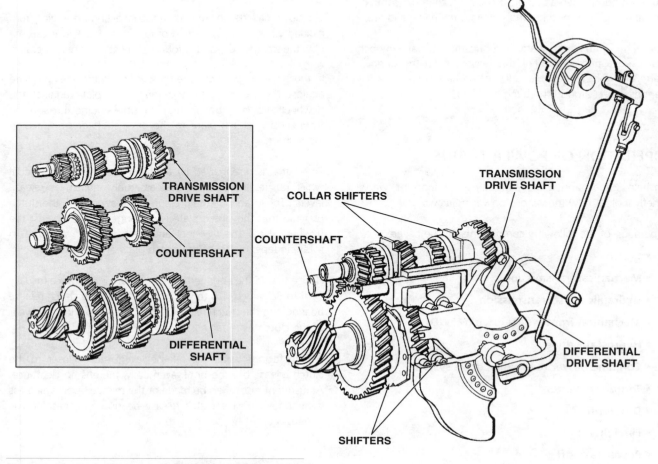

Fig. 11 — Mechanical Transmission in a Complete Power Train

Operation Of Hydraulic-Type Clutch

The hydraulic clutch (Fig. 10) is similar to the standard clutch except that the clutch plate operates *wet* in a transmission fluid and the clutch is engaged and disengaged hydraulically.

Hydraulic clutches don't normally require free travel or clearance adjustment.

OPERATION OF MECHANICAL TRANSMISSION

The mechanical transmission is a train of gears that transfers and adapts the engine power to the drive wheels of the machine.

The transmission does two jobs:

1) *Select speed ratios for various travel speeds.*

2) *Reverses the travel of the machine.*

The transmission can also power a special drive such as a PTO (power take-off).

Normally the transmission is located to the rear of the engine and clutch and in front of the differential or ring gear (Fig. 11).

Mechanical transmissions are of three major types:

- **Sliding Gear**
- **Collar Shift**
- **Synchromesh**

The SLIDING GEAR transmission has two or more shafts mounted in parallel or in line, with sliding spur gears arranged to mesh with each other and provide a change in speed or direction.

The COLLAR SHIFT transmission has parallel shafts with gears in constant mesh. Shifting is done by locking free-running gears to their shafts using sliding collars (see Fig. 11).

The SYNCHROMESH transmission also has gears in constant mesh. However, gears can be selected without clashing, by synchronizing the speeds of mating parts *before* they engage.

In all three cases, the transmission is shifted by hand or foot. So we call them *mechanical* transmissions.

The gear train for all these transmissions normally operates in a bath of gear oil. For special lubrication, oil sprays or feeder lines from oil pumps are sometimes used.

OPERATION OF HYDRAULIC ASSIST TRANSMISSION

The *hydraulic assist transmission* (Fig. 12) is a train of gears which can be shifted without interrupting the flow of power.

The gears are kept in constant mesh while two or more hydraulic clutches control the flow of power "on the go."

The parts work together as follows:

- **Hydraulic clutches-control the power flow**
- **Gear train-transmits the power flow**

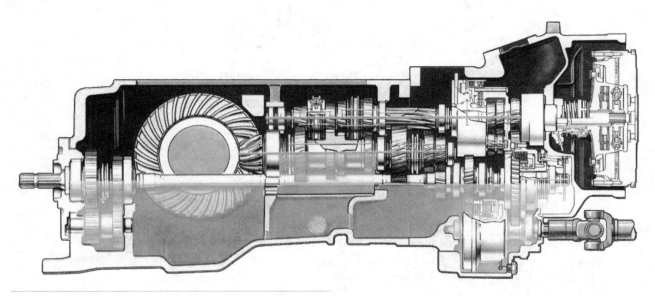

Fig. 12 — Hydraulic Assist Transmission in a Complete Power Train

When the operator shifts gears, hydraulic oil engages the clutches that route power to the selected gears.

A *hydraulic clutch* is normally an alternating pack of friction disks and plates (Fig. 13).

The clutch is *engaged* when pressure oil is sent to push the piston against the disks and plates, clamping them together. The disks are splined to the drum, while the plates are splined to the hub. As a result, input power through the hub is sent on through the hub to the output by the engaged clutch.

The clutch is *disengaged* when oil pressure is released and the piston moves away from the clutch pack. This frees the disks from the plates and the power flow is stopped. Spring action or oil pressure on the other side of the piston may be used to help release the disks and plates.

This hydraulic clutch unit replaces the standard clutch used on mechanical transmissions.

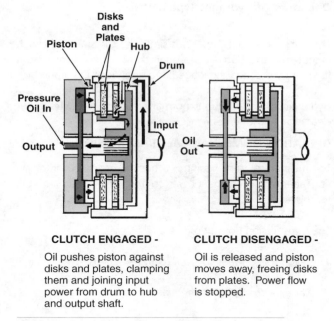

CLUTCH ENGAGED -
Oil pushes piston against disks and plates, clamping them and joining input power from drum to hub and output shaft.

CLUTCH DISENGAGED -
Oil is released and piston moves away, freeing disks from plates. Power flow is stopped.

Fig. 13 — Hydraulic Clutches Control the Power Flow in Hydraulic Assist Transmissions

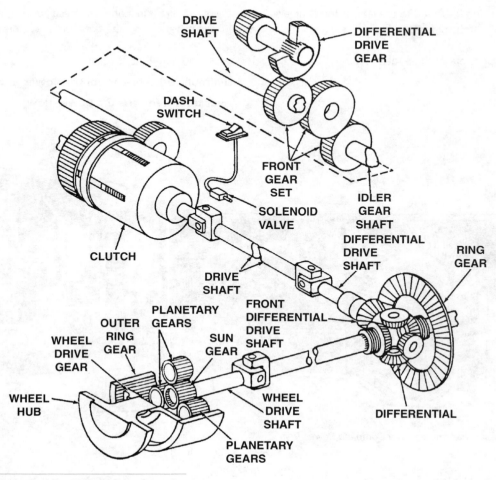

Fig. 14 — Mechanical Front Wheel Drive Operation

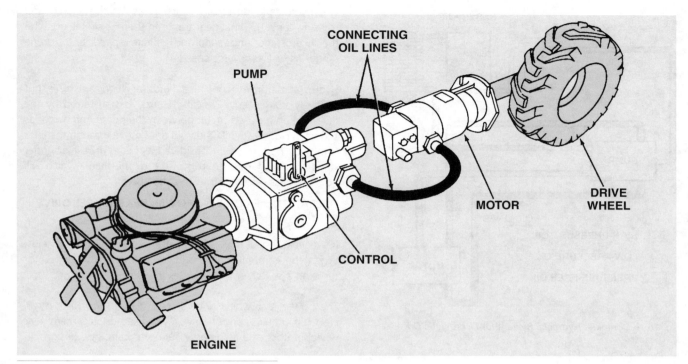

Fig. 15 — Hydrostatic Drive in a Complete Power Train

The *gear train* is usually either a *countershaft* or a *planetary* unit which feeds power to the output or drive wheels.

The gear train normally operates in an oil bath. This oil is usually the reservoir for the hydraulic circuit which operates the clutch units, so special transmission-hydraulic fluid must be used.

OPERATION OF MECHANICAL FRONT WHEEL DRIVE (MFWD)

When the dash switch is in the "engaged" position, spring pressure closes the solenoid valve preventing the flow of clutch control oil to the clutch. Springs force the clutch disk pack together and power flows forward through the U-jointed drive shaft to the front axle differential drive shaft. The shaft drive gear meshes with the ring gear, turning the limited slip differential unit as shown in Fig. 14. The differential supplies the required power to the left-hand and right-hand wheel drive shafts.

The wheel drive shaft powers the sun gear of the wheel hub planetary. The sun gear rotates the fixed planetary gears which walk around the outer ring gear. The planetary system reduces the drive shaft output speed and increases the torque at the front tires.

The wheel drive gear is meshed with the outer ring gear which is meshed to the wheel hub.

The front wheel housings are linked to a standard tractor steering system. Disengaging the MFWD provides a shorter turning radius.

When the MFWD dash switch is moved to the "disengaged" position, the solenoid valve directs pressure oil to release the MFWD clutch.

With the dash switch in the "auto" position, the MFWD is engaged and disengaged automatically. At speeds under 14 km/h (8.5 mph), the MFWD remains engaged until either brake pedal is depressed. If both brake pedals are depressed, the MFWD will remain engaged.

When the tractor speed exceeds 14 km/h (8.5 mph), a relay is activated which disengages the MFWD. If both pedals are depressed, the MFWD is automatically engaged to assist braking.

OPERATION OF HYDROSTATIC DRIVE

The *hydrostatic drive* is an automatic fluid drive which uses fluid under pressure to transmit engine power to the drive wheels of the machine.

Mechanical power from the engine is converted to hydraulic power by a pump-motor team (Fig. 15). This power is then converted back to mechanical power for the drive wheels.

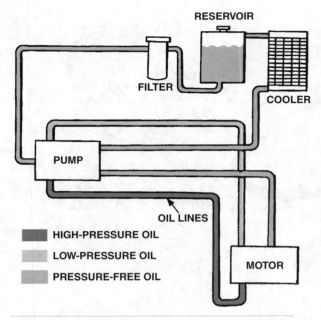

Fig. 16 — Complete Hydraulic System for Hydrostatic Drive

RESERVOIR

FILTER

COOLER

PUMP

OIL LINES

MOTOR

HIGH-PRESSURE OIL
LOW-PRESSURE OIL
PRESSURE-FREE OIL

The hydrostatic drive can function as both a clutch and transmission. The final gear train can then be simplified, with the hydrostatic unit supplying infinite speed and torque ranges as well as reverse speeds.

Hydrostatic transmissions use fluids at *high pressures* but relatively *low speeds*. Basically, energy is transferred by the fluid itself in a closed circuit between the pump and motor as shown in Fig. 16. While the fluid does move through the lines (shown in red), it is still considered as being at rest or under static pressure. The rise in pressure of the fluid—which will not compress—is what transfers the energy.

OPERATION OF COMBINE POWER REAR WHEEL DRIVE SYSTEM

Power rear wheel drive offers extra traction in muddy fields. When the combine needs additional traction, the operator turns on a switch which actuates this drive.

The power rear wheel drive system (Fig. 17) consists of an electro-hydraulic control valve, two fixed-displacement rear wheel motors of a planetary gearing or cam lobe design, an

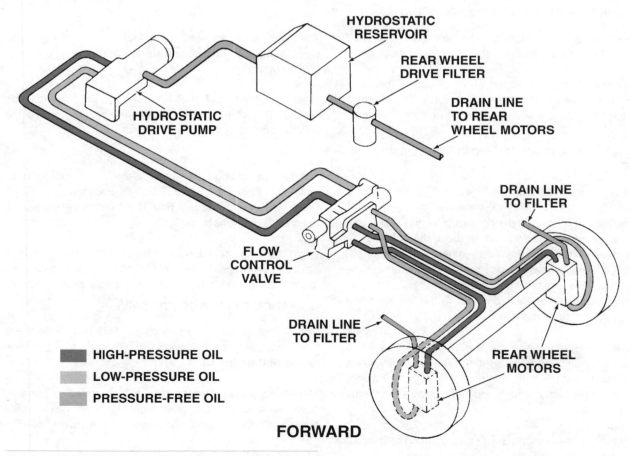

HYDROSTATIC RESERVOIR

REAR WHEEL DRIVE FILTER

DRAIN LINE TO REAR WHEEL MOTORS

HYDROSTATIC DRIVE PUMP

DRAIN LINE TO FILTER

FLOW CONTROL VALVE

DRAIN LINE TO FILTER

REAR WHEEL MOTORS

FORWARD

HIGH-PRESSURE OIL
LOW-PRESSURE OIL
PRESSURE-FREE OIL

Fig. 17 — Oil Flow Schematic of Power Rear Wheel Drive System

oil filter and connecting hydraulic lines. Hydraulic power for this system is taken from the hydrostatic drive to combine front wheels.

To engage the power rear wheel drive, the operator sends an electrical signal from the console control switch to the power rear wheel drive control valve. This valve responds by opening to allow flow of hydrostatic fluid to the rear wheel motors (Fig.17). The wheel motors convert this hydraulic energy into mechanical energy through a gear reduction to the wheel rims, propelling the combine.

OPERATION OF TORQUE CONVERTER

A *torque converter* is also an automatic *fluid* drive (Fig. 18). It transmits engine torque by means of hydraulic force, shifting smoothly through an infinite number of speeds.

Actually a gear train is used with the torque converter to give extra speed ranges. But no gear train could give the infinite variations in speed and torque of a torque converter.

Acting as a *clutch,* the torque converter connects and disconnects power between the engine and the gear train as a *transmission,* the converter gives many more speed ratios than are practical with a strictly mechanical gear box.

To compare a torque converter with a hydrostatic drive, use this rule of thumb:

Hydrostatic drives are driven by fluids at high pressure but at relatively low velocity, while torque converters are driven by fluids at low pressure but at high velocity.

Here are the formulas:

- *Hydrostatic DRIVE=HIGH pressure+LOW velocity*
- *Torque Converter=LOW pressure+HIGH velocity*

The basic torque converter system is shown in Fig. 18.

A fluid at high velocity strikes a turbine,and forces it to turn, driving the wheel. Thus, *torque is transmitted by a fluid.*

To change this torque, the velocity of the fluid is changed. At low velocity, the fluid will not even move the turbine. At high velocity, the turbine starts turning and the wheel picks up speed.

Inside an oil-filled housing (Fig. 18, left) are two parts: the driving half, or pump, and the driven half, or turbine.

As the pump is turned by the engine, centrifugal force causes oil to be forced radially outward, crossing over and striking the vanes of the turbine. This rotates the turbine in the same direction and so couples the power.

The torque or power from the turbines then flows through the gear train as shown to the power output.

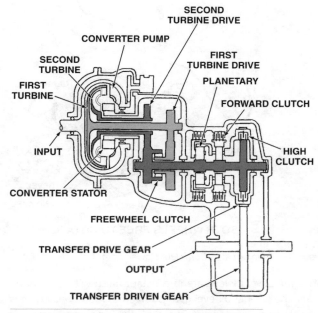

Fig. 18 — Torque Converter in Complete Power Train

OPERATION OF DIFFERENTIALS

The *differential* does two jobs:

- **Transmits power "around the corner" to the drive axles.**
- **Allows each drive wheel to rotate at a different speed and still propel its own load.**

The ring gear and bevel gears direct the power to the axles, while the bevel pinions give the differential action (Fig. 19).

When the machine is moving straight ahead, *both wheels are free to rotate* as shown in Fig. 19, left.

Engine power comes in on the pinion gear and rotates the ring gear. The four bevel pinions and the two bevel gears are carried around by the ring gear and all gears rotate as one unit. Each axle receives the same rotation and so each wheel turns at the same speed.

When the machine turns a sharp corner, only *one wheel is free to rotate,* as shown in Fig. 19, right.

Again engine power comes in on the pinion gear and rotates the ring gear, carrying the bevel pinions around with it. However, the right-hand axle is held stationary and so the bevel pinions are forced to rotate on their own axis and "walk around" the righthand bevel gear.

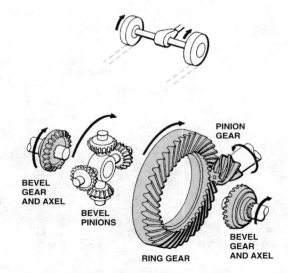

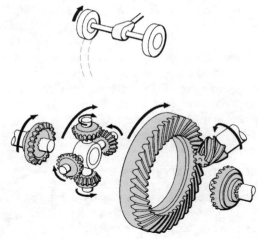

BOTH WHEELS FREE TO ROTATE

ONE WHEEL FREE TO ROTATE

Fig. 19 — Differential in Complete Power Train

Since the bevel pinions are in constant mesh with both bevel gears, the left-hand bevel gear is forced to rotate because it is subjected to the turning force of the ring gear which is transmitted through the bevel pinions.

During one revolution of the ring gear, the left-hand gear makes two revolutions—one with the ring gear and another as the bevel pinions "walk around" the other bevel gear.

As a result, when the drive wheels have unequal resistance applied to them, the wheel with the least resistance turns more revolutions. As one wheel turns faster, the other turns slower by the same amount. However, both wheels still propel their own loads—but at different speeds.

Differential action can be a disadvantage when the wheels slip. For example, when a farm tractor is plowing, - one wheel may lose resistance on slick ground and start spinning while the other wheel holds. Then the driving power is limited by the "wasted" power sent to the wheel that slips.

To prevent this loss of power, *differential locks* are often used.

OPERATION OF DIFFERENTIAL LOCKS

A **differential lock** directs power equally to both wheels by locking out the differential. This prevents the usual loss of traction when one wheel is slipping.

Three types of differential locks are used:

- *Mechanical*
- *Hydraulic*
- *Automatic (no-spin)*

The **mechanical differential lock** (Fig. 20) is the simplest. When the operator moves the control lever, a fork shifts a splined collar on the axle shaft to engage the collar with splines on the differential housing. This forces the axle and housing to rotate as a unit. The bevel gears are thus prevented from turning and so the differential is locked.

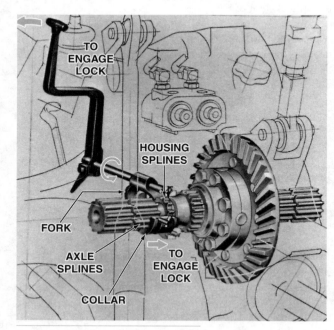

Fig. 20 — Mechanical Differential Lock

When drive wheels again have equal traction, the lock disengages automatically. The lock can be engaged on the go, but must be released before the machine is turned.

When the operator depresses the control pedal, a hydraulic clutch engages the **hydraulic differential lock.** When the pedal is released, oil pressure is cut off and the lock releases as soon as both wheels have equal traction. A safety release connects the control pedal to the tractor's brake pedals to unlock the differential whenever the brake pedals are used. This avoids the danger of making sharp turns with the differential lock still engaged.

The **automatic no-spin lock** (Figs. 21 and 22) is located inside the differential housing and replaces the bevel gears, bevel pinions and their shafts. The no-spin lock is normally engaged and still permits relative motion between the wheels on corners. When engaged, it prevents one wheel from spinning when it loses traction and thereby depriving the other wheel of full power.

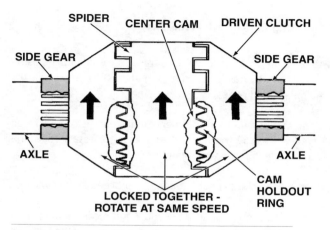

Fig. 21 — Automatic No-spin Lock (Driving Straight Ahead)

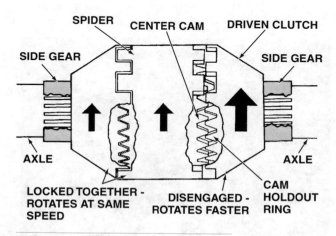

Fig. 22 — Automatic No-spin Lock (Left Turn)

However, the no-spin lock does not permit the inside wheel on a turn to slow down—only the outside wheel to speed up. It therefore tends to increase machine turning radius and, in a sharp turn, may prevent the machine from decelerating to a safe turning speed.

OPERATION OF FINAL DRIVES

The *final drive* is the last phase of the power train. It gives the final reduction in speed and increase in torque to the drive wheels (see Fig. 2).

Used on most large machines, the final drives are mounted near the drive wheels to avoid the stress of long axle shafts.

By reducing speeds, the final drives lower the stress and simplify the transmission, since extra gears and shafts can be eliminated.

Most final drives must support the weight of the machine as well as withstanding torque and shock loads.

OPERATION OF POWER TAKE-OFFS

The *power take-off (PTO)* is an attachment in the power train of a machine. It drives auxiliary equipment.

PTO's are normally gear-driven from the transmission and send power through a shaft to the PTO outlet where the driven equipment is coupled.

Most modern units are adjustable to drive equipment at standard speeds of either 540 or 1000 rpm.

The PTO is operated by a clutch release, which is sometimes part of the main engine clutch.

SERVICING OF POWER TRAINS

The power train requires important maintenance, as we will see now.

SERVICING OF ENGINE CLUTCHES

Because the foot clutch is the most commonly used on most machines today, we will cover its maintenance only. Hand-operated clutches require somewhat different service and are found on few modern machines. Therefore, refer to your operator's manual for maintenance procedures for this type of clutch.

The clutch on most machines requires two services:

1. *Lubricating the Clutch Release Bearing*

2. *Adjusting Clutch Pedal Free Travel*

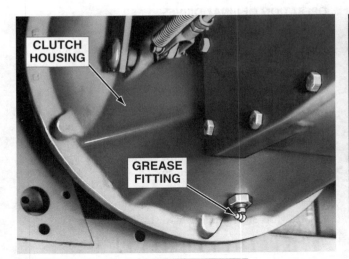

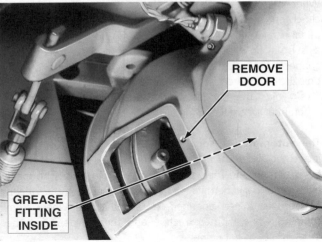

Fig. 23 — Clutch Release Bearing Grease Fitting

Lubricating The Clutch Release Bearing

On many of the newer machines, the clutch release bearing is a prelubricated, sealed bearing and requires no further lubrication until major service is performed on the clutch.

However, on some machines the bearing requires regular lubrication. Many manufacturers recommend that this be done every 250 hours. Refer to your operator's manual for suggested intervals.

If the bearing is lubricated too much or too often, excessive grease may be thrown onto the clutch facing and cause the clutch to "chatter" when engaged and may eventually damage the clutch facing.

Too little lubrication will cause the bearing to fail prematurely.

If the bearing on your machine requires periodic lubrication, proceed as follows:

1. Locate the grease fitting. It may be on the side or bottom of the clutch housing (Fig. 23).

   If an external grease fitting is not found, you may have to remove a cover plate to reach inside to lubricate the bearing.

2. Wipe grease fitting clean before attempting to apply grease.

3. Apply lubricant sparingly. One or two short strokes of the grease gun are usually sufficient. Excess grease might leak out and get on the dry clutch disks, causing them to slip.

4. Wipe off excess grease from fitting.

   NOTE: Some machines also have power take-off (PTO) clutches which require bearing lubrication.

Adjusting Clutch Pedal Free Travel

Adjustment of clutch pedal free travel is essentially the same for all non-hydraulic clutches whether they are single or multiple clutch plates, dry or wet type.

Many manufacturers recommend that you check pedal free travel every 250 hours and adjust if necessary. See the recommendations in your operator's manual.

To adjust the clutch pedal free travel, proceed as follows:

1. Refer to your operator's manual for recommended free travel distance. Usually, this may range from 1/2 to 2 inches (13 to 50 mm) or more depending on the machine and where the distance is measured. Also, determine where the measurement should be taken (for the next step).

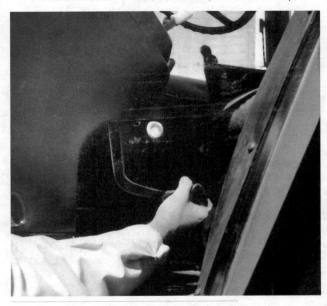

Fig. 24 — Measuring Pedal Free Travel at Pedal

2. Check clutch pedal free travel measurement (Fig. 24). This is the distance the pedal can be depressed before resistance is noticed. The resistance is caused by the clutch release bearing contacting the release levers.

3. If the measurement checks with those specified in your operator's manual, no adjustment is necessary.

4. If the measurement is different than those specified, proceed with the following steps.

5. Locate pedal adjusting mechanism (Fig. 25). Usually the adjustment is made near the pedal or it may be anywhere along the linkage leading to the clutch release mechanism.

6. Adjust the linkage, as. necessary, until the clutch pedal has the proper amount of free travel.

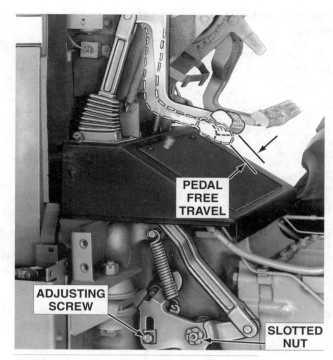

Fig. 25 — Adjusting Pedal Free Travel at Pedal Arm

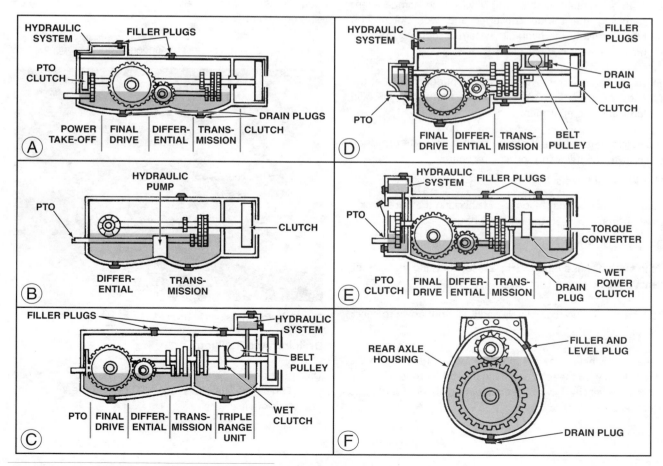

Fig. 26 — Basic Train Designs Showing Fluid Reservoirs

SERVICING TRANSMISSION, DIFFERENTIAL, AND FINAL DRIVES

Your machine may have a transmission that resembles one of those shown in Fig. 26 or it may have separate differential and final drives.

In Fig. 26, the transmission reservoirs are shown in blue, while the filler and drain plugs are shown in red. Here is an explanation:

(A) All gear drive units housed within one compartment. Hydraulic system separate.

(B) A one-compartment arrangement which also contains hydraulic pump and uses gear oil for hydraulic system.

(C) A two-compartment arrangement with one compartment supplying lubrication to the belt pulley and wet clutch and providing fluid for the hydraulic system.

(D) A four-compartment assembly with a separate hydraulic system but with only a partial division between the transmission and differential sections.

(E) A three-compartment assembly with one compartment supplying the torque converter and wet clutch with lubricant. Note the hydraulic system is supplied from the power take-off compartment.

(F) High-clearance tractors often use a spur-gear drive at the ends of the main axle. Each of these has its own lubricating compartment.

Regardless of its design, the maintenance of the transmission is similar to the following service procedures.

Checking Oil Levels

Operator's manual may recommend checking the transmission oil levels from every 50 to every 250 hours.

OIL LEVEL DIPSTICK

If the machine has a dipstick (Fig. 27) for checking the oil level, remove it and wipe off the excess oil.

Reinsert the dipstick completely and pull it out again to check the oil level.

If the level is below the full mark (or "safe" mark), fill to the proper level with the recommended oil of the proper viscosity. Make the level check with the engine running, or according to other recommendations.

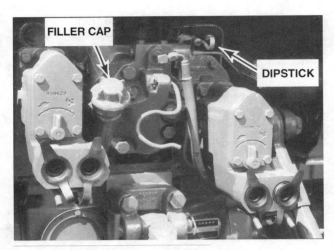
Fig. 27 — Transmission Oil Level Dipstick

OIL LEVEL PLUG

If your machine doesn't have a dipstick, remove the oil level plug (Fig. 28) form the transmission case.

On machines with separate final drives, remove the oil level plug (Fig. 29) from them also. Insert a finger to determine if oil is up to proper level.

If necessary, refill with the recommended oil of the proper viscosity.

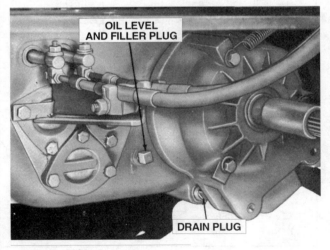
Fig. 28 — Transmission Oil Level Plug

Draining And Refilling

The usual draining and refilling period is at least once each year. Others recommend every 1000 hours or less. See your operator's manual.

Tools and Materials Needed

- **Wrenches for drain plug(s) and filter cap (inch or metric, as required)**
- **Clean, lint-free cloths**
- **Cleaning solvent (not gasoline)**
- **New oil of type and grade recommended by manufacturer**
- **New filter**
- **Container to catch waste oil**

To drain and refill the transmission, proceed as follows:

1. Drive the machine until you are certain the transmission fluid is well agitated and heated. This helps ensure that most of the sludge and dirt will drain out when the fluid is removed.

2. Park the machine on a level surface. This will ensure better draining position than if the machine is on a slight incline.

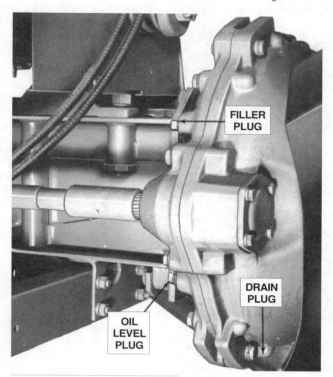

Fig. 29 — Final Drive Oil Level Plug

3. Remove drain plugs (Figs. 28 and 29) and catch the old fluid in a container.

If the transmission has the differential and final drives in the same housing, you will probably need to remove two plugs. If the final drives are separate, you may have to remove three plugs or more.

When the final drive is near the tire, use a metal shield to divert the oil away from the tire and into a container as shown in Fig. 30.

After all the fluid has drained out, clean the drain plugs; replace and tighten them. Be particularly careful to clean magnetic drain plugs of any metal particles.

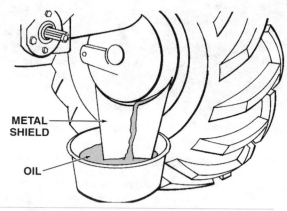

Fig. 30 — Using a Metal Shield to Divert Oil Away from Tire

4. Replace transmission oil filter if there is one (Fig. 31).

5. Clean dirt and grease from filler plug and surrounding area. Remove plugs.

6. Refill with the proper amount and type of transmission fluid or gear oil as specified in your operator's manual.

   Do not overfill; this will cause excessive agitation and foaming.

   IMPORTANT: If the machine has one common reservoir for both the transmission and hydraulic systems, use special care in cleaning and in replacing with transmission-hydraulic fluid of the correct type. Precision hydraulic parts can be seriously damaged by dirt or the wrong fluid.

7. Replace and tighten plugs.

8. If equipped, clean filler cap and breather (Fig. 27) in solvent (not gasoline). Shake out excess liquid. Add a small quantity of oil to filter and shake out excess. Replace cap.

Fig. 31 — Transmission-Hydraulic System Filter Covers

ADJUSTING TRANSMISSIONS

Transmission adjustments are usually performed at the time of major repairs. Gear trains are then adjusted for preload, backlash, or endplay (see Chapter 9 under "Gear Drives"). Other adjustments, as of shifting linkages, should be made per instructions in the machine operator's manual.

Adjustment of hydraulic power transmission units requires special test equipment and should be done only by a trained serviceman. The basic use of a hydraulic tester for diagnosis is given at the end of Chapter 8, "Hydraulic Systems".

PRECAUTIONS FOR TOWING MACHINES

On some machines the engine must be turning the transmission gears to obtain proper lubrication. Towing such a machine would result in poor lubrication and high shaft speed. The failure of many transmissions can be traced to towing.

It the transmission gears are operated at excessively high speeds, the gear lubricants will become overheated. Overheating a lubricant causes it to oxidize and thicken. Continuous overheating would result in transmission failure.

When towing a machine there is danger, too, that a brake may grab. The machine may bounce and be hard to steer. It the tires are filled with liquid, the high speed can also damage a tire.

If it becomes necessary to tow a farm machine, do so slowly. It is much better to haul the machine or drive it under its own power. Some machines have a lever that permits the transmission gears to be disengaged so they can be towed. Other machines must have the engine running to maintain power operation of steering and brakes for safety. Refer to the operator's manual for precautions.

TEST YOURSELF

QUESTIONS

1. Gear oil may have the same viscosity as engine oil.
   True_____   False_____

2. What three types of oils or fluids are used in transmissions?
   a. _____
   b. _____
   c. _____

3. If you must store lubricants in unprotected barrels, how should they be positioned to avoid contamination?

4. Why does clutch pedal free travel change periodically and require readjustment?

5. Hydraulic type clutches require periodic free travel or clearance adjustment.
   True_____   False_____

6. Name the three major types of mechanical transmissions.

7. When the ground speed on a MFWD tractor is below 14 km/h (8.5 mph) and the dash switch is in "auto" position, the MFWD disengages when both brake pedals are depressed.
   True_____   False_____

8. Hydraulic wheel motors convert hydraulic energy into mechanical energy.
   True_____   False_____

9. What may happen if you over-lubricate the clutch release bearing?

10. What should you do with the machine before draining old fluid from the power train?

HYDRAULIC SYSTEMS

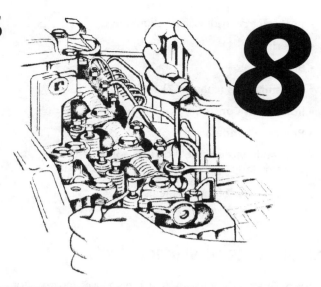

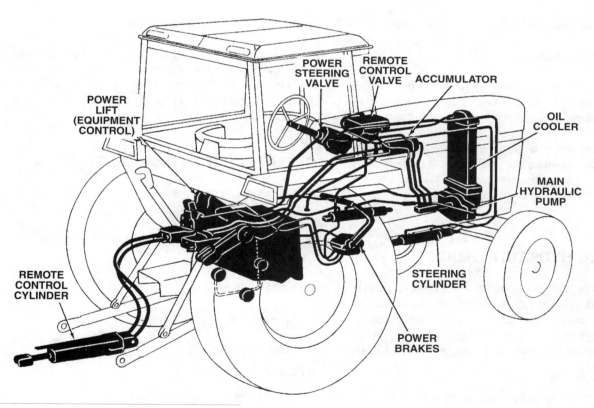

Fig. 1 — Modern Farm Tractor with Full Hydraulics

INTRODUCTION

Hydraulic systems (Fig. 1) provide the "muscles" for doing work. Some machines, like the tractor in Fig. 1, have a hydraulic system that performs several functions: steer, brake,

control implements, and operate remote functions. Other machines may have only one or two hydraulic functions. All the functions may share a common oil supply or they may have their own reservoirs.

The most common hydraulic functions are:

- **Steering**
- **Brakes**
- **Transmissions (chapter 7)**
- **Implement Control**
- **Remote Cylinders**
- **Hydraulic Motors We'll discuss some of these systems later.**

We'll discuss some of these systems later.

IMPORTANCE OF SERVICE

A well-maintained hydraulic system seldom gives the operator any trouble. Regular checks assure that the oil level is sufficient. Changing the oil and filters regularly helps prevent problems.

The oil in the hydraulic system is extremely sensitive to contamination. Dust, rust, moisture, and metal particles will damage the hydraulic system.

Hydraulic fluid lubricates and cools the entire hydraulic system. Any contaminant which builds up in the fluid can ruin the whole system.

Routine checks and repair of oil leaks will prevent excessive loss of fluid and overheating. Air leaks will cause the oil to oxidize rapidly, forming harmful gum and sludge. Check for air leaks and repair them promptly.

SELECTING HYDRAULIC FLUIDS

The fluid in a hydraulic system serves as the power transmitting medium. And as stated above, the fluid is also the system's lubricant and coolant. Selection of the proper oil is essential for satisfactory performance and life. Oil must be selected with care and from a reputable supplier. Be sure to use the manufacturer's recommended oil.

These are some common hydraulic system oils:

1. **Crankcase Oil** meeting API service classification CD or SF. The most severe classification is the key to proper selection of crankcase oils for mobile hydraulic systems.

2. **Antiwear Hydraulic Oil**—There is no common designation for oil of this type. However, they are produced by all major oil suppliers and provide the antiwear qualities of CD or SF crankcase oils.

3. **Certain Other Types Of Petroleum Oils** are suitable for mobile hydraulic service if they meet the following provisions:

   a. Contain the type and content of antiwear compounding found in CD or SF crankcase oils or have passed pump tests similar to those used in developing the antiwear-type hydraulic oils.

   b. Meet the viscosity recommendations for expected temperatures.

   c. Have the chemical stability for mobile hydraulic system service.

The following types of oil are suitable if they meet the above three provisions:

API CD Diesel Engine Oil

MIL-L-2104C

Type F and DEXRON II

Hydraulic Transmission Fluid Type C-3

When selecting hydraulic fluids, check the recommendations in the operator's manual. The manufacturer has picked a fluid which meets all the needs of the system, which may vary from simple cylinders to precision hydraulic pumps.

OPERATION OF HYDRAULIC SYSTEMS

A brief introduction to how hydraulic systems work will help you to understand why proper maintenance is so important.

The operation of three common hydraulic operations will be discussed:

1. *Hydraulic Steering*

2. *Power Brakes*

3. *Implement Control*

HYDRAULIC STEERING

Two types of hydraulic steering are used:

- **Hydraulic Assist Steering**
- **Full Power Steering**

HYDRAULIC ASSIST STEERING (not shown) is similar to mechanical steering, except for a hydraulic valve controlled by the steering wheel and hydraulic pistons which assist the steering mechanism in turning the wheels.

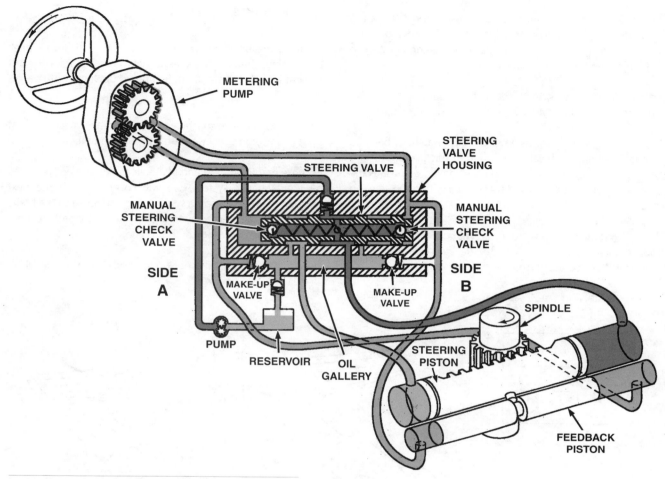

Fig. 2 — Metering-Pump Power Steering During a Right Turn

Since full power steering is the most popular today, we will discuss it more fully.

Fig. 2 shows a power steering system with a metering pump operating during a right turn.

NOTE: Indications of directions refer to those as seen from the operator's seat. Side A and B will help identify direction of movement in the steering valve housing.

When the operator turns the wheel to the right the gears in the metering pump direct oil in the steering system to the steering valve housing and to the left end of the feedback piston. This oil (under some pressure) moves the steering valve toward side B.

The movement of the steering valve opens the pressure oil circuit to the left end of the steering piston. Oil from the right end of the piston flows back to the steering valve oil gallery and to the reservoir.

Oil from the right end of the feedback piston cylinder is forced out, by piston movement, and returns through the steering valve housing to the metering pump.

This movement of the steering and feedback pistons from left to right causes the spindle to rotate clockwise and turn the front wheels to the right.

When the operator stops turning the steering wheel, the gears in the metering pump stop directing oil to the steering valve. Circuit pressure, from the right end of the feedback piston to the steering valve, (caused by movement of the feedback piston) acts against the side B of the steering valve. The valve moves toward side A, closing the pressure oil passage from the main hydraulic pump, and stops the turning movement. The valve becomes centered and traps oil in passages to both sides of the steering piston. The trapped oil holds the wheels in the right turn until the operator again turns the steering wheel.

If oil is lost from the control circuit, pressure in the control circuit drops. The reduced pressure causes the make-up valve to unseat and allow return oil from the steering piston to make up oil in the control circuit.

On articulated tractors, the steering and feedback pistons are replaced by hydraulic cylinders which control steering.

To protect against failure of power steering, a check ball and manual steering check valves are used in this power steering systems. If the oil supply fails and no incoming oil pushes the check valve open, it closes and traps all oil within the steering circuit.

This allows the operator to steer manually by using the trapped oil as a force to actuate the steering. Pressure is created as the operator turns the steering wheel.

For manual steering, see Chapter 9.

POWER BRAKES

On most machines, brakes are located on each drive wheel. For turning, the operator presses down the pedal for the left or right wheel. For stopping, he presses down on both pedals at once.

On four-wheel drive machines, a single brake mechanism at the transmission usually controls the whole unit.

Because manual brakes and hydraulic brakes are not powered by the hydraulic system, we will cover them in the next chapter. However, in some systems, oil is supplied to the brake reservoir by the tractor hydraulic system and bleeding these brakes will be covered later in this chapter.

Let's discuss the operation of *power brakes* in more detail.

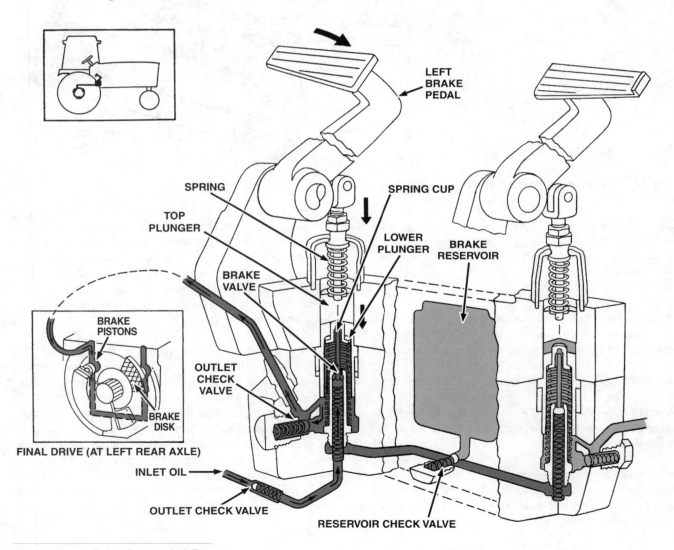

Fig. 3 — Power Brakes During a Left Turn

"Power" brakes mean that hydraulic force completely controls the braking of the machine, once the operator presses down the brake pedal to actuate the valving.

Full power brakes on a modern wheel tractor with a closed-center hydraulic system are shown in Fig. 3. Operation is shown during a left turn.

For a sharp left turn, the operator presses down on the left brake pedal. This causes a rod linkage to push down on the brake valve and open it. Inlet oil under pressure now rushes in through the open valve, forces the outlet check valve open, and flows on to the final drive at the left rear axle (see inset). Here the oil forces the brake pistons and pressure plates to press the revolving brake disk against a fixed plate and so brakes the left axle and wheel.

When the brake pedal is released, the brake valve is closed again by its spring, and inlet oil is shut off. This relieves pressure on the brake disk at the axle, and braking stops as some oil flows back to the brake valve area. This oil dumps into the brake reservoir after going past the valve and through the valve plunger. When both brake pedals are pressed down at once, oil is sent by both brake valves to both final drives. To assure equal braking, equalizing valves (not shown) are opened, connecting the two brake valves.

To protect the operator in case of failure of power brakes, oil trapped in the brake valve reservoir by the check valves allows temporary operation of the brakes. On large machines, a hydraulic accumulator stores "charges" of oil for emergency braking.

IMPLEMENT CONTROL

Two types of implement control systems are used on tractors:

- **Power Lift (Rockshaft)**
- **Remote Control**

The power lift is used to control mounted implements, while remote control cylinders are usually placed on a pull-type implement to control a function such as raising the plow bottoms.

Power Lift

The power lift usually is controlled either manually using a control lever or automatically by load sensing.

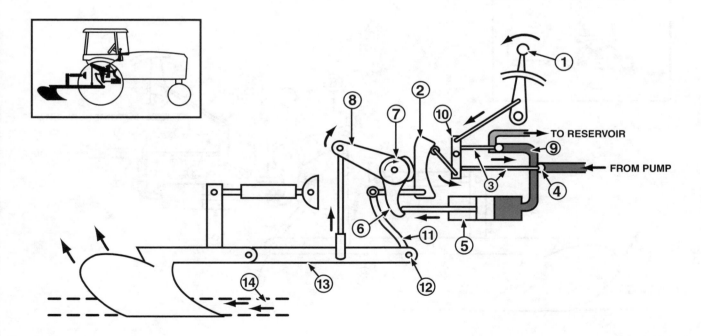

1—Control Lever
2—Cam Follower
3—Operating Rod
4—Valve Ball
5—Piston
6—Shaft Arm
7—Rockshaft
8—Lift Arm
9—Oil From Pump

Fig. 4 — Raising the Plow Using the Control Lever

RAISING PLOW USING CONTROL LEVER

In Fig. 4, the plow hits hard ground and the operator wants to raise it slightly. So he moves the control lever (1) to the front. This pivots the cam follower (2) forward and presses it against rod (3) which opens valve (4). Pressure oil is now admitted to the cylinder, forcing piston (5) to the rear. The piston pushes against the shaft arm (6), rotating rockshaft (7) and lift arm (8) upward. The lift arm is attached to the plow and so the plow is raised slightly to help it pass through the hard ground.

The plow stops rising when the valve (4) is closed again, trapping oil in the cylinder. This happens when the cam follower (2) working on the sloping cam of the rockshaft (7), is returned to the rear and releases the rod (3). The valve is then closed by its spring.

AUTOMATIC LOAD SENSING RAISES THE PLOW

In Fig. 5, the plow hits hard ground (1) and load control shaft (3) is pulled rearward by draft links (2). As a result, load control arm (12) is pivoted against cam follower (4). The cam follower pushes on rod (5) which opens valve (6) and admits

pressure oil to cylinder (7). The cylinder piston pushes against the arm (8), rotating rockshaft (9) and lift arm (10) upward. The lift arm is attached to the plow and so raises the plow slightly to help it pass through the hard ground.

With automatic load sensing, the plow will lower itself again when the hard ground is passed. This happens as the tension on the load control shaft (12) is partly released. It flexes forward and pulls back on the linkage to actuate other valves (not shown) which release some oil from the cylinder. This lets the lift arms (10) "settle," lowering the plow again.

The regular depth of the plow can be set at the control lever. The plow will stay at this depth unless a signal is given by the load sensing device.

We have just described full load sensing or *load control.*

Two other options are commonly available: If he wishes, the operator can lock out signals from the load sensing linkage by blocking the cam follower (4) at its lower end using a lever (not shown). This is called *depth control,* since the plow now stays at the depth set by the control lever. The other choice

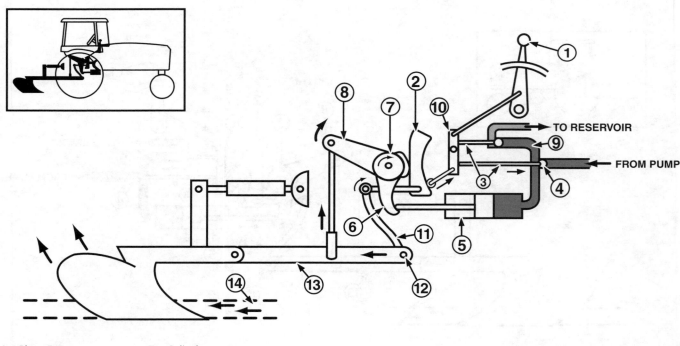

1—Plow Furrow	7—Cylinder
2—Draft	8—Shaft Arm
3—Load Sensing Shaft	9—Rockshaft
4—Cam Follower	10—Lift Arm
5—Operating Rod	11—Oil From Pump
6—Valve Ball	12—Load Control Arm

Fig. 5 — Automatic Load Sensing Raises the Plow

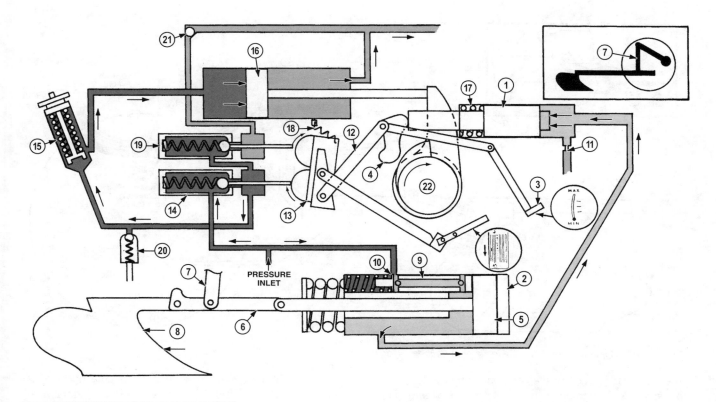

Fig. 6 — Hydraulic Load-Sensing Rockshaft

allows the operator to partially block the cam follower using the same lever. This is called *load and depth control,* since the load signals are now modified by the depth setting.

Some power lifts are designed for dual operations. Two hydraulic cylinders are normally used: one cylinder and valving controls the rear-mounted equipment, and the second operates a front-mounted tool or an attachment. However, the cylinders can be operated in parallel by opening valves which join them to the same pressure oil supply. Two control levers are also used, one for each function. But usually only one function (the rear one) has an automatic load sensing device.

ELECTRO-HYDRAULIC HITCH

Some newer tractors are equipped with an electrohydraulic 3-point hitch. It is electrically controlled and hydraulically operated.

The electro-hydraulic hitch uses electrical circuitry and solenoids to control hydraulic oil flow which activates the 3point hitch.

HYDRAULIC LOAD SENSING RAISES THE PLOW

The hydraulic load sensing system (Fig. 6) consists of a load control valve (1) and a sensing cylinder (2). The load control selector (3) is in a position at the top of the cam follower (4) to allow maximum load sensing. The rod end of the sensing cylinder piston (5) is attached to one draft arm (6). The two draft arms are connected by a shaft. The draft links (7) are attached to the draft arms.

As the plow hits hard ground (8), the soil resistance increases the draft load on the draft arms. The draft force is transmitted to the sensing cylinder (2) by the draft arms and pulls the sensing cylinder piston and valve (9) rearward. More oil then flows into the sensing cylinder through a variable orifice (10), causing sensing pressure on the front of the load control valve (1) to increase. The increase in sensing pressure results in rearward movement of the load control valve (1), cam follower (4), and valve operating link (112) which causes the valve operating cam (13) to rotate clockwise. Note that an orifice (11) allows some oil to escape from the front of the load control valve. This results in a variable pressure on the valve depending on the amount of oil that enters through the variable orifice (10).

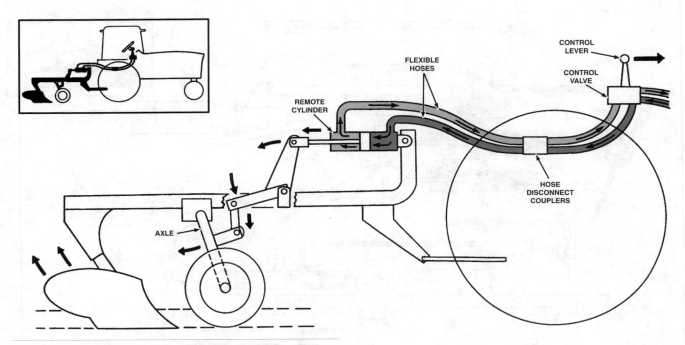

Fig. 7 — Raising a Pull-Type Plow Using Remote Cylinder Hydraulics

The clockwise rotation of the valve operating cam causes the pressure valve (14) to open and direct pressure oil through the throttle valve (15) to the backside of the rockshaft piston (16). The throttle valve controls the speed of oil flow to and from the rockshaft piston. The piston moves forward and causes the rockshaft (22) to rotate, lifting the draft links (7) and raising the plow. The check ball (21) prevents return oil from the front of the rockshaft piston from entering the return valve housing (19).

When the plow passes the hard ground, the draft force on the sensing cylinder decreases. The sensing cylinder piston (5) and valve (9) move forward permitting less oil to flow through the variable orifice, decreasing sensing pressure at the front of the load control valve. The spring in the load control valve housing (17) pushes the valve forward. The spring (18) causes the valve operating cam to rotate counterclockwise and forces the cam follower (4) forward, along with the load control valve. The pressure valve (14) closes and, if necessary, the return valve (19) opens to lower the plow.

When the pressure and relief valves are closed, oil trapped at the rear of the rockshaft may expand if the oil temperature rises. The thermal relief valve (20) senses thermal expansion of hydraulic oil in the system and opens if the expansion is too great.

REMOTE CONTROL OF EQUIPMENT

Tractors may operate equipment that is not mounted, but is pulled or pushed. To control this equipment with hydraulics, a remote actuator such as a cylinder or a motor is needed—separate from the tractor connected by flexible hoses.

Let's take the case of a plow again—this time one that is pulled behind the tractor (Fig. 7). The plow is pulling too hard and the operator wants to raise it. This is what happens:

The operator moves the hydraulic control lever to the front as shown. This actuates the control valve which sends pressure oil to the front of the remote cylinder. As this oil pushes the piston to the rear, the cylinder rod extends. Oil from the other side of the piston is forced out and returns through the valve to reservoir. As the cylinder rod extends, it pivots a linkage to the plow axle, rotating the bent axle to the rear and so raises the plow.

Remote cylinders have hundreds of uses on machines.

Another use of remote hydraulics is the *hydraulic motor*. For example, a small hydraulic motor can be mounted on a portable grain elevator as shown in Fig. 8. The motor converts fluid power into rotary motion which drives the elevating mechanism. Pressure oil supply usually comes from a machine hydraulic outlet.

We have, covered only the most common uses of hydraulics of modern machines. However, our primary aim is to describe maintenance.

SERVICING THE HYDRAULIC SYSTEM

There are four basic maintenance problems with hydraulic systems:

- **Not enough oil in the reservoir**
- **Clogged or dirty oil filters**
- **Leaking connections**
- **Incorrect oil in the system**

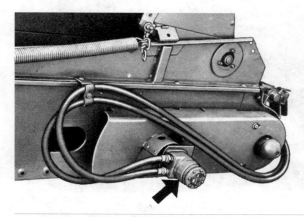

Fig. 8 — Small Hydraulic Motor Used to Drive Portable Grain Elevator

All these problems can be solved or prevented by knowing the system and maintaining it properly.

Let's discuss some of the practices which will keep the hydraulic system in top-notch condition.

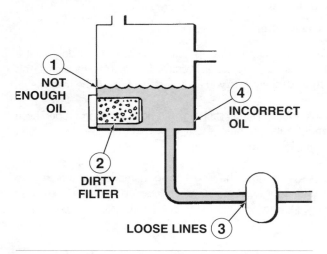

Fig. 9 — Basic Maintenance Problems with Hydraulic Systems

CHECKING OIL LEVEL

To check the oil level, most hydraulic systems have either a sight glass in the reservoir or a dipstick (Fig. 10). Check the oil level at least every 250 hours. Some manufacturers recommend daily checks.

If the oil level isn't up to the sight glass or the "Full" of "Safe" mark on the dipstick, fill the reservoir with the recommended hydraulic fluid. See *"Filling the System"* later in this chapter.

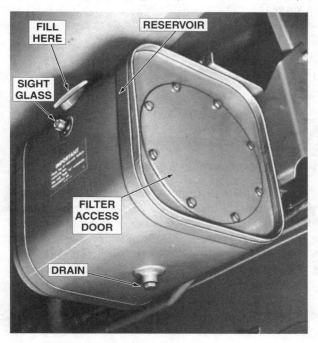

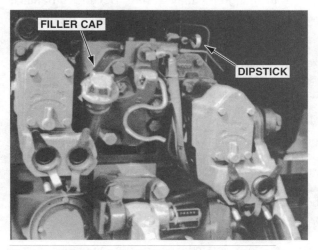

Fig. 10 — Two Methods of Checking Hydraulic Oil Level

At this time, also check for other malfunctions in the system. Look for:

1. **Oil Bubbles or Foaming Oil.** This may mean an air leak somewhere in the system.

2. **Changes in Oil Level.** If there is a noticeable change in the oil level from day to day, look for leaks or cracks in the external parts of the system.

3. **Milky Oil.** This indicates water in the system or in the oil used. Be sure that oil is stored properly.

If the reservoir has a breather cap, clean it in solvent.

CHECKING OIL COOLER

Check the oil cooler (Fig. 11) every 250 hours for accumulation of debris. Oil leaks are a problem as the oil attracts dirt. Anything that blocks air flow through the cooler can cause overheating of the hydraulic fluid.

CHECKING FOR LEAKS

 CAUTION: Escaping fluid under pressure can penetrate the skin causing serious injury. Avoid the hazard by relieving pressure before disconnecting hydraulic or other lines. Tighten all connections before applying pressure. Search for leaks with a piece of cardboard. Protect hands and body from high pressure fluids. If an accident occurs, see a doctor immediately. Any fluid injected into the skin must be surgically removed within a few hours or gangrene may result. Doctors unfamiliar with this type of injury should reference a knowledgeable medical source.

Excessive oil leakage can cause major damage to a hydraulic system if it goes unrepaired. Check all the hydraulic lines and connections for leaks every 50 hours or even daily if your operator's manual recommends it.

Some hydraulic systems are complex (Fig. 12) and have many lines and connections. With several connections in a hydraulic system, the chances are great that leaks will develop.

Look for:

1. **Pressure Oil Leaks.** Oil leaks in the pressure, side of the system can be located by examining the outside of lines and fittings.

2. **Air Leaks.** If the suction side of the system is drawing in air, the oil in the reservoir will bubble and foam.

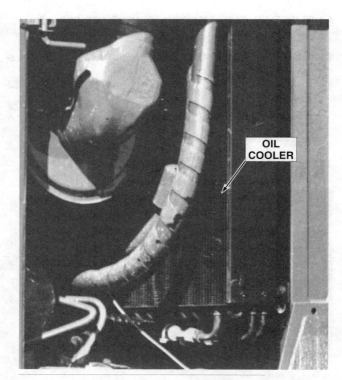

Fig. 11 — Location of a Typical Hydraulic Oil Cooler

3. **Pinched or Dented Lines.** This can cause oil foaming, overheating, and loss of hydraulic power. Replace damaged hoses or tubes at once. Wash lines inside and out with clean solvent before installing them.

Lower all units to the ground and inspect the machine completely. Tighten any leaking fittings using two wrenches to avoid twisting the lines (Fig 13). *Tighten only until snug and the leak stops. Do not overtighten.*

Hose Failures

While you are checking for leaks, examine hoses closely. If a hose fails, you may lose all hydraulic fluid in a few moments. This can be dangerous to you and cause damage to the machine.

Look for: cracking, splitting, pin-hole leaks, improper hose length, rubbing, heat, twisting, wrong hose selection, wrong fitting, or improper routing.

Replace any hose showing signs of damage with a new hose designed for exact replacement. *Don't economize!* Selecting a cheaper hose may result in premature failure of the hose.

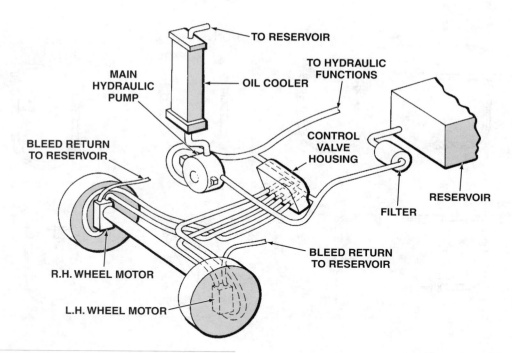

Fig. 12 — Hydraulic Systems Have Many Lines and Connections

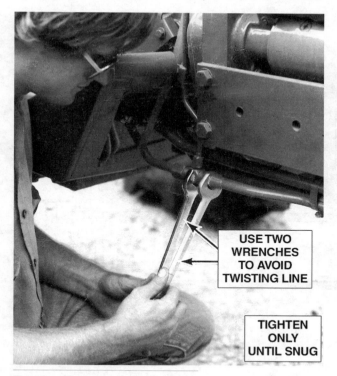

USE TWO
WRENCHES
TO AVOID
TWISTING LINE

TIGHTEN
ONLY
UNTIL SNUG

Fig. 13 — Tightening Hydraulic Fittings

Component Leaks

If a component of the hydraulic system is leaking, a defective seal may be the problem. Take the machine to a service shop for repair. Do not attempt to repair hydraulic components yourself. Special tools and knowledge are required to repair hydraulic systems.

Refer to *"General Maintenance"* later in this chapter for suggestions on preventing leaks and testing for internal leaks.

HOSE INSTALLATION

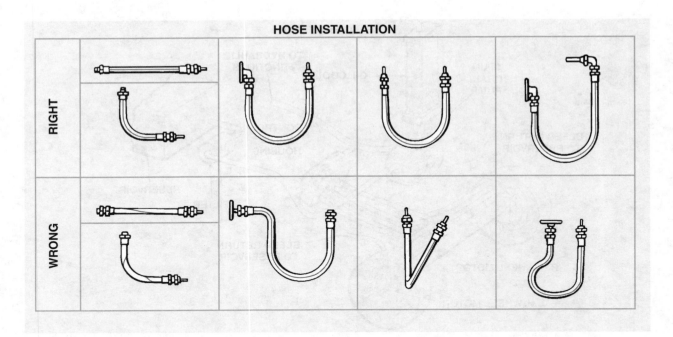

Fig. 14 — How to Route Hydraulic Oil Hoses

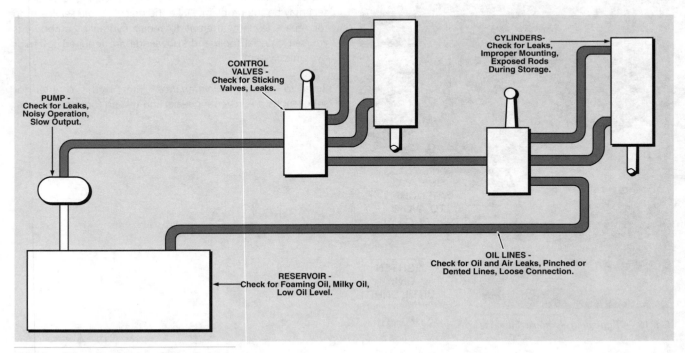

Fig. 15 — Where to Check for Hydraulic Leaks

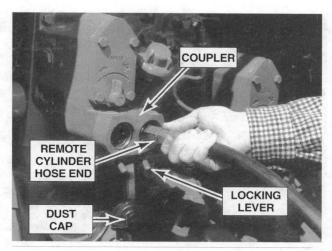

Fig. 16 — Connecting Remote Cylinder to Coupler on Machine

MAINTAINING REMOTE CYLINDERS

Remote cylinders require proper care for long service life. This includes correct connection, cleanliness and bleeding air when necessary.

Connecting Of Remote Cylinders

First install the remote cylinder on the implement as instructed in the operator's manual.

Plug the cylinder hoses into the machine couplers (Fig. 15). Some couplers have a rotating lever to lock the hose end into the coupler port.

When removing hoses from couplers, normally pull the hose straight out.

After hoses are removed, *be sure to insert dust plugs into the coupler ports.* Also place dust caps over the cylinder hose ends to protect them from dirt.

Bleeding Air From Remote Cylinders

Anytime a remote cylinder is plugged in the hydraulic circuit, all trapped air must be bled. This will prevent sluggish action of the cylinder.

1. First attach the cylinder to the circuit (see above).

 CAUTION: For personal safety, have one person on the tractor operating the hydraulic controls and a second person on the ground supporting the cylinder. Do not stand in front of or behind tractor wheels during this procedure.

2. Place the cylinder on the ground (or on a hanger) with the piston rod end down as shown in Fig. 16. (Or on mounted cylinders, place the head end of the cylinder in its working mount, allowing the rod end to move in and out freely.)

3. Start the machine and move the hydraulic control lever back and forth seven or eight times to extend and retract the cylinder. This will bleed the air. (On double-acting cylinders, you may have to turn the cylinder end-for-end and repeat the cycling of the control lever.)

Fig. 17 — Bleeding Air from Remote Cylinder

 CAUTION: Be sure machine is locked in PARK position before working around drive wheel.

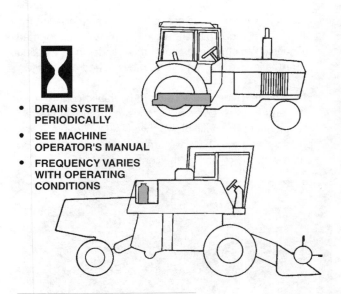

- DRAIN SYSTEM PERIODICALLY
- SEE MACHINE OPERATOR'S MANUAL
- FREQUENCY VARIES WITH OPERATING CONDITIONS

Fig. 18 — Drain the System Regularly

DRAINING, FLUSHING AND FILLING SYSTEM

These services are recommended at least once each year for most machines.

Tools and Materials Needed

1. Containers for old fluid

2. Hydraulic fluid (for flushing, if needed)

3. Clean, lint-free cloths

4. Box-end wrenches (inch or metric, as required)

5. Fresh hydraulic fluid (or type recommended)

6. Plastic tube (for bleeding)

Draining The Hydraulic System

Periodic draining of the entire hydraulic system is very important. This is the only positive way to completely remove contaminants, oxidized fluid, and other injurious substances from the system.

The frequency of draining depends on such things as the temperature of operation and the severity of working conditions. The operator's manual will tell the method to be used and the frequency, depending on conditions. Usually draining, flushing and refilling is recommended at least once each year.

Fig. 19 — Transmission-Hydraulic System Drain Plug

Tools and Materials Needed

1. Wrenches for drain plug(s) and filter cap (inch or metric, as required) .

2. Clean, lint-free cloths

3. Cleaning solvent (not gasoline)

4. New oil of type and grade recommended by manufacturer

5. New Filter

6. Container to catch waste oil

To drain the hydraulic system:

1. Operate the hydraulic system until it has reached normal operating temperature.

2. If the transmission case is the reservoir, also drive the machine until normal temperature is reached.

3. Remove drain plug from reservoir and catch oil in a container. See Figs. 9 and 18,

4. Replace drain plug.

5. If your operator's manual recommends flushing the system before refilling, refer to "Flushing The System," next.

Flushing The Hydraulic System

The nature and amount of deposits in a system may vary widely. Inspection may show any condition between a sticky, oily film and a hard, solid deposit (gum or lacquer formation) which completely chokes small oil passages.

If the system is drained frequently enough, the formation of gum and lacquer will be reduced.

When no gum or lacquer formation is suspected, clean the system as follows: After draining the system, clean any sediment from the reservoir, and clean or replace the filter elements.

It may be advisable to flush out the old oil remaining in the system after draining, particularly if the oil is badly contaminated. For this flushing, use the hydraulic fluid recommended for the system involved.

NOTE: Most solvents and chemical cleaners on the market today are NOT recommended for use in flushing hydraulic systems: 1) They are poor lubricants, resulting in damage to moving parts, especially the pump. 2) They are difficult to remove completely from the system. Just a trace of some of the commercial chlorinated solvents may be enough to break down the oxidation resistance of even the best hydraulic oils. Also, in the presence of a small amount of water, some of these solvents will corrode steel and copper.

To flush the system:

1. Operate the equipment to cycle the flushing oil through the system.

   It is important that the valves be manipulated so that the new oil goes through all lines. The time necessary to clean the system will vary, depending on the condition of the system.

2. Run the oil through the system until inspection shows the equipment to be in satisfactory condition, or until it is obvious that the system will have to be disassembled and cleaned manually by a service shop.

3. Drain out the flushing oil and refill the system with clean hydraulic oil of the recommended type.

4. Clean or replace the system filters before refilling the system.

For details, see "Filling the System," next.

Filling The Hydraulic System

Before filling the system, clean or replace the hydraulic oil filter. The filter may be located in the transmission case (Fig. 20) or in a separate reservoir (Fig. 21).

Fill the system as follows:

1. Clean the area surrounding the filter cover before removing cover.

Fig. 20 — Typical Transmission-Hydraulic System Filters

2. Remove the old filter and insert a new one (Fig. 20). Replace filter cover.

3. Fill the reservoir to the specified level with the recommended hydraulic oil. Use only clean oil and funnels or containers. Be sure to replace the filler cap before operating the equipment.

4. Start the engine and warm up the hydraulic system. Then operate the equipment through its working cycle several times to bleed air from the system. (Hydraulic brakes and steering must also be bled individually—see following.)

5. Shut off engine and check oil level again, Add oil if necessary.

Bleeding Brakes

When the brake system is part of the hydraulic system, the brakes must be bled whenever the hydraulic oil is drained and replaced. Also, whenever the pedals feel spongy or have excessive pedal free travel, you must bleed the air from them.

We will describe the procedures for bleeding hydraulic brakes connected to the hydraulic system; for procedures concerning conventional hydraulic brakes (trapped oil type), refer to chapter 9, "Other Components."

The machine may be equipped with either *hydraulic* brakes or *power* brakes. Read the following paragraphs on bleeding each type.

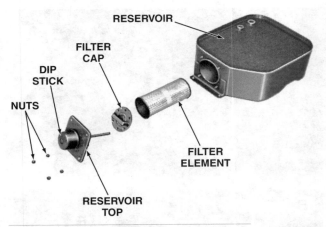

Fig. 21 — Typical Hydraulic Oil Reservoir and Filter

Tools and Materials Needed

1. Wrenches (inch or metric, as required)

2. Screwdriver (if needed)

3. Transparent plastic tube (long enough to reach from bleed valve to transmission filler hole)

BLEEDING HYDRAULIC BRAKES

To bleed the brakes, proceed as follows:

1. Start the engine and run it at fast idle for two minutes to make sure the brake reservoir is filled with oil.

A—Quad Range   C—Transmission Filter
    Equipped Tractors   D—Filter Cover
B—Power Shift   E—Packing
    Equipped Tractors   F—Housing

2. Locate the bleed screws. Usually they are located on top of the axle housing near the differential.

3. Attach a transparent plastic tube to the bleed valve as shown in Fig. 22.

4. If possible, insert the other end into the transmission oil filler hole as shown. Be sure the end of the tube is submerged in oil.

5. Unscrew the bleed valve 3/4 turn.

6. Slowly depress the brake pedal and allow it to return slowly.

7. Continue operating pedal in this manner until oil in the transparent tube is free of air bubbles.

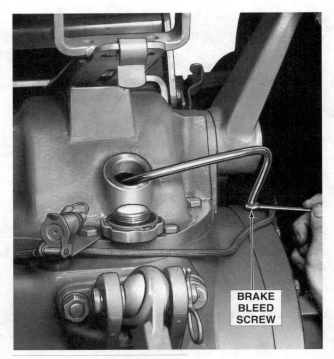

Fig. 22 — Bleeding Hydraulic Brakes

Fig. 23 — Bleeding Power Brakes

8. With the brake pedal still depressed, close the bleed valve securely.

9. Remove bleed tube and repeat this procedure for the other brake.

BLEEDING POWER BRAKES

If reserve power for braking is provided by a hydraulic accumulator, check the accumulator before bleeding brakes. To check the accumulator, depress brake pedals firmly several times with the engine stopped. The pedal should feel firm for five or six applications. If any trouble is suspected, contact your dealer for service.

To bleed the brakes, proceed as follows:

1. Start the engine and loosen the bleed screw locknut on both sides of the machine at the drive axle housing (Fig. 23), or follow instructions in your operator's manual.

2. Turn each bleed screw out two turns and tighten the lock nut. Tightening the lock nut prevents oil from leaking around the bleed screw.

3. Depress the brake pedals for a few minutes to bleed air from the brake system.

4. While holding the pedals down, loosen the bleed screw lock nuts and tighten the bleed screws.

5. Tighten the lock nuts, release the pedals and stop the engine.

6. Discharge the accumulator (if used) and check the pedal free travel. (The accumulator supplies oil pressure to apply the brakes for a short time after the engine has stopped.) If the travel is excessive (refer to your operator's manual), repeat the procedure again.

7. If bleeding the brakes does not correct the problem, take the machine to a service shop for testing and repair.

GENERAL MAINTENANCE OF HYDRAULIC SYSTEMS

We have covered specific maintenance of the hydraulic system, now let's look at general maintenance:

• **Importance of Cleanliness**

• **Preventing Overheating**

• **Preventing Leaks**

• **Safety Rules**

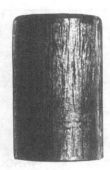

Fig. 24 — Pump Pistons Scored by Contaminated Fluid

IMPORTANCE OF CLEANLINESS

Cleanliness is No. 1 when it comes to servicing hydraulic systems. KEEP DIRT AND OTHER CONTAMINANTS OUT OF THE SYSTEM! Small particles can score valves, seize pumps, clog orifices and so cause expensive repair jobs.

How do you keep the hydraulic system clean? Let's put it this way:

• *Keep the oil clean*

• *Keep the system clean*

• *Keep your work area clean*

• *Be careful when you change or add oil*

PREVENTING OVERHEATING

Heat causes hydraulic oil to break down faster and lose its effectiveness. This why cooling of the oil is needed.

In many systems, enough heat is dissipated through the lines, the components, and the reservoir to keep the oil fairly cool. But on high-pressure, high-speed circuits, oil coolers are needed to dissipate the extra heat.

Overheating the system can:

• *Break down the oil*

• *Damage the seals*

• *Coat parts with varnish deposits*

• *Cause extra leakage past working parts*

• *Reduce the output of the system*

To help prevent overheating, keep the oil at the proper level, clean dirt and mud from lines, reservoirs, and coolers, check for dented or kinked lines, and keep relief valves adjusted properly. Also be careful not to overspeed or overload the system and never hold control valves in power position too long.

If the system still overheats, take the machine to a service shop for testing.

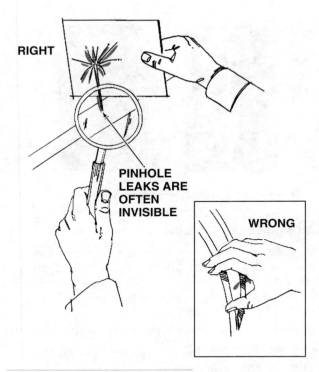

RIGHT

PINHOLE LEAKS ARE OFTEN INVISIBLE

WRONG

Fig. 25 — Checking Oil Lines for Leaks

PREVENTING LEAKS

What causes leaks? There are hundreds of causes, but leaks fall into two basic types:

- **External Leakage**
- **Internal Leakage**

Internal leakage does not result in actual loss of oil, but it reduces the efficiency of the system. External leakage does result in direct loss of oil and can have other undesirable effects as well.

External Leakage

External oil leaks not only look bad—they can be expensive and hazardous. A drop of oil every second from a leaking connector can cost you quite a lot of money.

A small leak can also be the signal for a hydraulic rupture that may injure a person as well as putting the machine out of operation.

Every joint in a hydraulic circuit is a potential point of leakage. This is why the number of connections in a system is kept to a minimum.

Components can leak, but care in assembly and use of new seals and gaskets during overhaul will help to reduce this problem.

The lines that connect the different parts of the system are the No. 1 source of external leaks. Here are a few key points:

1. If the reservoir oil level is lower than normal, check all external oil lines for leaks.

2. Pin-hole leaks are hard to detect, yet they can be dangerous. A "vapor" of oil from a small leak can create a fire hazard, or a fine spray of oil against a hot engine can ignite.

⚠ **CAUTION: Escaping fluid under pressure can penetrate the skin causing serious injury. Avoid the hazard by relieving pressure before disconnecting hydraulic or other lines. Tighten all connections before applying pressure. Search for leaks with a piece of cardboard. (Fig. 25) Protect hands and body from high pressure fluids. If an accident occurs see a doctor immediately. Any fluid injected~ into the skin must be surgically removed within a few hours or gangrene may result. Doctors unfamiliar with this type of injury should reference a knowledgeable medical source.**

3. The rubber cover on flexible hoses may crack or split without actually leaking. But check very closely for internal damage, The depth of the crack is the deciding factor.

4. Air leaks in suction lines are hard to locate. One way is to pour oil over the points where you suspect leaks. If the noise or bubbling in the system stops, you've located the leak.

5. If line connections are leaking, *tighten only until the leak stops.* If the connection will not stay tightened, the threads are probably stripped and the connector must be replaced. If the connector will tighten but still leaks, check for a cracked line flare or a damaged seal. But remember: *More damage has been done to line connectors by overtightening than from any other cause.*

After stopping leaks in a system, be sure to warm up the system and cycle the equipment, then recheck the trouble spots to be sure the leaks are stopped.

Recheck the system oil level and replace any oil lost through leaks or broken connections.

Internal Leakage

Slight internal leakage as a thin oil film is built into the working parts of a hydraulic system. This lubricates the mating surfaces of valve spools, cylinder pistons, and other moving parts. Oil is not lost through this normal internal leakage since it eventually returns to the system reservoir.

However, too much internal leakage will slow the operation of the system and waste power through the generation of heat. In some cases, it may cause cylinders to creep or drift. Or it may cause loss of oil control in the valves.

Internal leakage increases with the normal wear of parts. Leakage is accelerated by using oil which has too low a viscosity because this oil thins faster at higher temperatures. High pressures also force more oil out of leaking points in the system. This is one reason why excessive pressures can actually reduce the efficiency of the hydraulic system.

Internal leaks are hard to detect. Watch the operation of the system for sluggish action or creeping and drifting. When these signs appear, it's time to have a service shop test the system and pinpoint the trouble.

However, there are two components which can be checked without special hydraulic test equipment—the control valve, and the hydraulic cylinder.

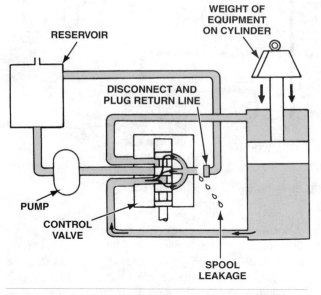

Fig. 26 — Checking Hydraulic System Control Valve for Internal Leaks

Checking Control Valve For Internal Leaks

If you suspect the system control valve is leaking internally, make the following check.

1. Raise the hydraulic equipment a few feet off the ground, return the control lever to neutral and shut off the engine.

2. Notice whether the equipment settles toward the ground. If the equipment settles, temporarily support it and disconnect the return line between the control valve and reservoir, then plug the line (Fig. 26).

3. Remove the support and examine the open port in the control valve as the equipment settles. If oil leaks from the port, the control valve spool is leaking. Take the equipment to a service shop for repair.

4. Remove plug and connect return line to the valve again.

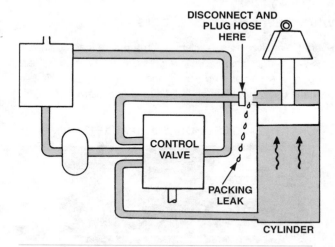

Fig. 27 — Checking Double-Acting Cylinder for Internal Leaks

Checking Hydraulic Cylinder For Internal Leaks

If no oil is leaking from the control valve, check the cylinder as follows:

1. To check a double-acting cylinder, run the cylinder to one end of its stroke. Support the equipment if it is raised, then shut off the engine.

2. Remove the hose from the end of the cylinder that was not pressurized (Fig. 27).

3. Start the engine again, pressurize the cylinder, and see if any oil comes out of the open port.

4. Repeat the test in the opposite direction since it may be possible for the cylinder to leak in only one direction.

5. If oil leaks out the open cylinder port, the packings in the cylinder must be replaced. Take the cylinder to a service shop for repair.

TESTING HYDRAULIC SYSTEMS

If you cannot locate troubles with the operational checks above, the system can be checked using a hydraulic analyzer or test gauges. Using this equipment, you can accurately measure oil flow, pressure, and temperature, and quickly isolate faulty components.

WHAT A HYDRAULIC TESTER DOES

Hydraulic analyzers are available with pressure loading valves, pressure gauges (high-and low pressure), flow meters, and temperature gauges to precisely analyze a complex hydraulic system. The test kit shown in Fig. 28 is one example.

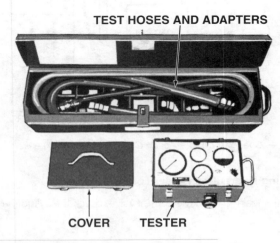

TEST HOSES AND ADAPTERS

COVER **TESTER**

Fig. 28 — Complete Hydraulic System Test Kit

In testing any hydraulic circuit, the following four checks are of prime importance:

1. **Temperature**—The oil should be checked for correct operating temperature to assure accuracy of the tests that follow.

2. **Flow**—The flow check determines if the pump is developing its rated output.

3. **Pressure**—These checks test relief valves for proper operation. (In a closed-center system, pressure checks indicate the operation of the main pump.)

4. **Leakage**—The leakage test isolates leakage in a particular component.

These basic checks may be made with most hydraulic testers. Before beginning, however, *read the instruction manual* furnished with the tester and review the system. You should have a thorough knowledge of the machine's specifications (relief valve pressures, pump output, engine rpm, and operating temperature) to accurately test the system.

To test a machine, you must disconnect some of the oil lines. But remember, DIRT IS THE WORST ENEMY OF A HYDRAULIC SYSTEM. Before disconnecting oil lines, steam clean the machine. And be sure to plug all openings to keep out dirt.

PUMP TESTING

The pump is the generating force for the whole hydraulic system. This is the place to start testing the system.

Installing The Hydraulic Tester

1. Relieve any pressure in the system and disconnect the pressure line between the pump and the control valve. Attach the pressure line to the hydraulic tester INLET port (Fig. 29).

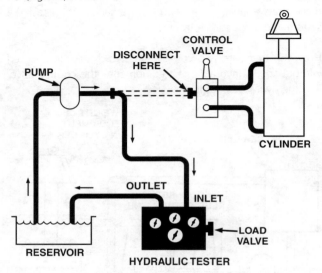

Fig. 29 — Testing the Hydraulic Pump

2. Connect hydraulic tester OUTLET port to the reservoir. Whenever possible, connect directly to the reservoir return line because it usually has a return filter. On a closed-center system, always return hydraulic tester oil to a point between the main hydraulic pump and the charging pump to maintain pressure in the system (or to be sure the main pump does not lose its charge).

3. Check the oil level and slowly close the tester load valve to load the system. (Do not exceed the system's maximum rated pressure.) Continue loading until the normal operating temperature of the system is reached (see machine specifications).

IMPORTANT: Be sure the tester load valve is OPEN before starting any tests. The load valve can develop tremendous pressure on a component if it is closed too far.

		GALLONS PER MINUTE (LITERS/MINUTE) @ PSI (kPa)									
		0	*250*	*500*	*750*	*1000*	*1250*	*1500*	*1750*	*2000*	*2250*
PUMP TEST		*31.0*	*28.0*	*25.0*	*22.0*	*19.0*	*16.0*	*13.0*	*10.0*	*7.0*	
CIRCUIT TEST	DIRECTION-CYLINDER TRAVEL										

OWNER _____   SERIAL NO. _____

TRACTOR MODEL _____   EQUIPMENT _____

COMMENTS _____

Fig. 30 — Sample Form for Recording Pump Test Results (Hand-Written Figures are Gallons and PSI)

Operating The Hydraulic Tester

1. With the tester load valve open, record maximum pump flow at zero pressure.

2. Slowly close the load valve to increase pressure and record the flow at 250 psi (1725 kPa) increments from zero pressure to maximum system pressure. Write down your test results so you can refer to them later. Use a test form such as the one shown in Fig. 30.

3. Open the hydraulic tester load valve until maximum pump flow is again at zero pressure.

4. Shut off the engine.

Pump Test Diagnosis

Pump flow at maximum pressure should be at least 75 percent of pump flow at zero pressure. (On modern variable displacement pumps of the radial piston type, 90 percent can be expected.) A lower reading like the one shown on the form in Fig. 30 indicates a badly worn pump.

If pump flow is poor during the free flow test as well as the pressure tests, the pump probably is not getting enough oil. This problem could be caused by low oil supply, air leaks, a restricted pump inlet line, or a dirty reservoir, filter or breather.

If the pump tests okay, then start checking the system components for trouble.

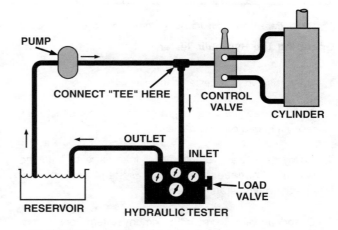

Fig. 31 — Testing the System Components

SYSTEM TESTING

Check the system components by the following procedures.

Installing The Hydraulic Tester

Install a tee fitting in the line between the pump and the control valve and attach the hydraulic tester INLET port to this tee (Fig. 31).

Leave the return line from the hydraulic tester OUTLET port connected in the same way as it was for the pump test.

		GALLONS PER MINUTE (LITERS/MINUTE) @ PSI (kPa)									
		0	250	500	750	1000	1250	1500	1750	2000	2250
PUMP TEST		32.0	31.7	31.4	31.0	30.6	30.2	29.8	29.3	28.8	
CIRCUIT TEST	DIRECTION-CYLINDER TRAVEL										
Boom Circuit	Lower	32.0	31.7	31.4	31.0	30.6	30.2	29.8	29.3	28.8	
	Raise	32.0	31.7	31.4	31.0	30.6	30.2	29.8	29.3	28.8	
Bucket Circuit	Dump	32.0	31.7	31.4	31.0	5.0	0.0				
	Roll-Bk.	32.0	31.7	31.4	31.0	30.6	30.2	10.0	0.0		

Inside this box, the following fields appear:

OWNER _____   SERIAL NO. _____

TRACTOR MODEL _____   EQUIPMENT _____

COMMENTS _____

Fig. 32 — Transmission-Hydraulic System Filter Covers

Operating The Hydraulic Tester

1. Open the hydraulic tester load valve.

2. Start the engine and adjust it to the manufacturer's recommended operating speed.

3. Slowly close the hydraulic tester load valve to load the system. Continue loading the system until normal operating temperature is reached.

4. Open load valve to record maximum system flow at zero pressure.

5. Operate the control valve and hold it in one of its power positions.

6. Slowly close the hydraulic tester load valve and record flow in 250 psi increments from zero pressure to maximum system pressure (Fig. 31).

7. Open the load valve until maximum flow is again at zero pressure and repeat the test in the rest of the control valve power positions.

Be sure to make all the tests at the same oil temperature to get readings that can be compared. If oil is too hot from the previous test, allow it to circulate through the system for cooling.

System Test Diagnosis

Here's how to judge the system tests:

1. *If flow at each pressure is same as for pump test:* All components are okay.

2. *If pressure begins to drop before full load is reached:* One of the circuits is bad. (Such as the bucket roll-back circuit in Fig. 32.)

The pressure drop is caused by leakage. To find out whether the leakage is in the control valve or the cylinder, disconnect the cylinder return line and move the control valve to a power position. If oil leaks from the cylinder return port, the cylinder is at fault and must be repaired. If no oil leaks out, the control valve is probably at fault.

3. *It flow drops the same with the control valve in all positions:* The system relief valve is probably at fault (see following). This condition could also indicate a leak in the control valve.

Relief Valve Diagnosis

If equipment with circuit relief valves is being checked, you can tell when the valves open because flow will suddenly drop about 3 gpm (11 Lpm) (or drop to zero gpm [Lpm] if a full-flow relief valve is used). Often the relief valves will start to "crack" open before they reach their full-pressure settings.

This can be noted by comparing the pressure and flow rate readings made in the circuit test above. Any great decrease in flow rate in these valves indicates a faulty valve.

As a general rule:

Faulty SYSTEM relief valves will affect readings in all tests.

Faulty CIRCUIT relief valves will affect only pressure readings in the Individual circuits.

SUMMARY: TESTING THE SYSTEM

The tests we have given you are only basic guidelines. Once you start testing actual machines, use your machine technical manual for detailed tests and test results. And remember that the best testing equipment has no value unless the person at the controls knows how to interpret the results.

SAFETY RULES FOR HYDRAULIC SYSTEMS

1. Always wear eye protection and proper clothing when doing maintenance work on hydraulic systems.

2. Always lower the hydraulic working units to the ground before leaving the machine.

3. Park the machinery where children cannot easily reach it.

4. Block up the working units when you must work on the system while raised. Do not rely on the hydraulic lift.

5. Never service the hydraulic system while the machine's engine is running unless absolutely necessary, as for bleeding the system.

6. Do not remove cylinders until the working units are resting on the ground or securely on safety stands or blocks. Also shut off the machine's engine.

7. When transporting the machine, lock the cylinder stops to hold the working units solidly in place.

8. Be sure all line connections are tight and lines are not damaged. Escaping oil under pressure is a fire hazard and can cause personal injury.

9. When washing parts, use a non-volatile cleaning solvent.

10. To insure control of the unit, keep the hydraulic system in proper adjustment.

TEST YOURSELF

QUESTIONS

1. List three maintenance problems that concern a hydraulic system.

2. Match the symptom on the left with its cause on the right.

   A. Oil bubbles or foaming oil

   B. Change in oil level

   C. Milky oil

   1. Water in the system

   2. Air leak somewhere in the system

   3. Leaks in the external parts of the system

3. Tighten leaking fittings as tightly as possible.
   True_____   False_____

4. What is the biggest enemy of hydraulic systems?

5. Give one safety rule which you should follow to avoid injury to yourself or others from the hydraulic system.

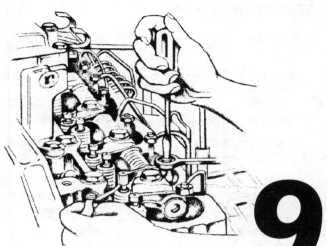

OTHER COMPONENTS

9

Fig. 1 — Transmission-Hydraulic System Filter Covers

INTRODUCTION

We have covered maintenance of the major basic components of the machine. Now let's look at maintenance of these other components:

- **Operator's Cab**
- **Manual Steering**
- **Steering Axis and Wheels**
- **Manual Brakes**
- **Tires**
- **Grease Fittings**
- **Belt Drives**
- **Chain Drives**
- **Gear Drives**
- **Lighting and Electrical Accessories**

Failure to service these components can:

- *Cause premature wear or damage to the machine*

- *Make the machine unsafe to operate*

- *Make operation of the machine uncomfortable*

In addition, we will show how to clean the machine exterior, which should be done at least once each year.

To maintain each of the above components properly, you must be familiar with the basic services which are covered on the following pages.

OPERATOR'S CAB

The operator's cab is designed to protect you against dust, cold and heat. Most cabs today also protect you in rollover accidents and help protect your hearing ability by reducing sound levels. Some even have radios and stereo tape players which give you up-to date news or soothing music.

If the cab has fresh air ventilation, heating and air conditioning, you have environmental controls which protect you against adverse operating conditions.

Following are typical cab services that should be performed at least every 250 hours or at intervals recommended in your operator's manual to maintain the maximum comfort in the operator's cab:

- **Air Filters**

- **Heater**

- **Air Conditioner**

Let's look at the maintenance required for each of these.

FILTERS

The cab may be equipped with either a fresh-air filter, a recirculating-air filter, or both (Fig. 2). Consult the operator's manual for detailed services.

Fresh-Air Filters

These are usually dry-type paper filters located in either the air intake or the filter cavity in the roof of the cab.

The following tools and materials are needed:

1. Compressed Air Source   3. Container of Warm Water

2. Water Pressure Source   4. Non-Sudsing Detergent

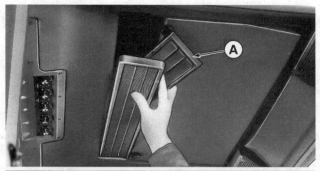

Fig. 2 — Air Filters in a Typical Cab

To clean **dry-type paper filter:**

1. Remove the filter from housing or access door (upper picture, Fig. 2)

2. Tap the filter gently on a flat surface-dirty side down (Fig. 3).

   Do not tap on uneven surfaces or the filter element may be damaged.

Fig. 3 — Tapping Filter on a Flat Surface

 CAUTION: Reduce compressed air to less than 30 psi (210 kPa) (2 bar) when using for cleaning purpose. Clear area of bystanders, guard against flying chips, and wear personal protection equipment including eye protection.

3. If you have a source of compressed air direct it through the filter in the opposite direction of the air flow (Fig. 4). Air flow is usually indicated by arrows.

4. If the filter is still dirty, wash it as follows.

5. Soak the filter (Fig. 5) for 15 minutes in warm water (not over 100°F; 40°C) with a special dry filter element cleaner (or a nonsudsing detergent, such as used in a dishwasher).

6. Rinse until clean with water from a hose (not over 40 psi; 275 kPa).

7. Shake excessive water from the filter and allow it to dry. Do not use compressed air to dry filter because this will rupture the wet element.

8. Reinstall filter. Be sure to install it with the arrows pointing in the direction of air flow.

Recirculating Air Filters

These filters are usually made of urethane foam and are located in the air recirculators (lower picture, Fig. 2).

To clean **urethane foam filters:**

1. Remove filter (see lower picture, Fig. 2) and clean by tapping or shaking filter.

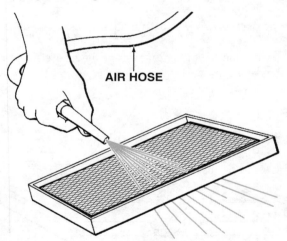

Fig. 4 — Directing Air Through Filter in Opposite Direction of Air Flow

2. If filter is still dirty, wash in clean water. Allow filter to dry thoroughly. Do not install wet filters in the air recirculators.

Fig. 5 — Soaking Filter in Warm Water and Cleaner

HEATER

The heater requires little maintenance. However, check the following:

1. Check the hoses and connections for leaks.

   Tighten clamps or replace hoses if necessary.

2. Open roof and check accumulation of dirt and debris in heater core. Clean if necessary. You may have to remove a cover to gain access to the core (Fig. 6).

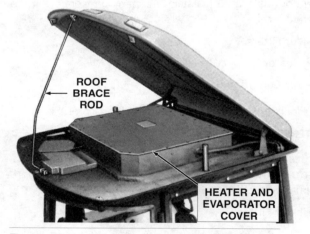

Fig. 6 — Heater and Air Conditioner Evaporator Location

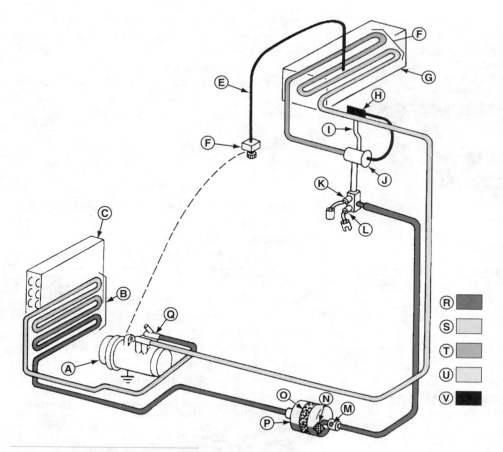

A. Magnetic Clutch
B. Heat Transfer from Refrigerant
C. Condenser
D. Temporary Control Switch
E. Sensing Tube
F. Heat Transfer from Cab Air to Refrigerant
G. Evaporator
H. Temperaure Sensing Bulb
I. External Equalizer Line
J. Thermal Expansion Valve
K. Hi-Pressure Sensing Switch
L. Low Pressure Sensing Switch
M. Sight Glass
N. Pickup Tube
O. Desiccant
P. Receiver-Drier
Q. Compressor
R. High Pressure Liquid
S. High Pressure Gas
T. Low Pressure Liquid
U. Low Pressure Gas
V. Sensing Tube Gas

Fig. 7 — Basic Air Conditioning System

AIR CONDITIONER

Service the air conditioning system periodically to maintain maximum cooling.

In Fig. 7, note how the refrigerant cycle operates.

From the **compressor,** high-pressure gas is sent to the **condenser,** where it is converted to liquid and heat is dissipated. The high-pressure liquid flows on to the **expansion valve,** where it is metered and its pressure is reduced. At the **evaporator,** the liquid is again converted to gas, absorbing heat from the air. The cycle is then repeated, starting at the compressor.

The air conditioner is a heat transfer unit. Failure of any element will interrupt the heat exchange cycle and cause the whole system to fail. Each basic element is engineered and balanced to the other parts of the system in order to move heat from the inside air to the outside air, where it is dissipated.

Servicing Air Conditioner

Service the system as follows:

1. Check evaporator core for accumulation of dirt and debris (see Fig. 6). Clean if necessary.

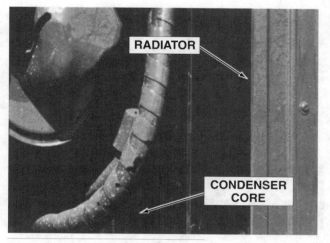

Fig. 8 — Air Conditioner Condenser Core

2. Check condenser core for accumulation of dirt and debris. It must be clean. The condenser is usually located near the radiator (Fig. 8).

3. Check refrigerant level. A sight glass (Fig. 9) is usually provided near the receiver-drier for this purpose. Your operator's manual will tell where it is located.

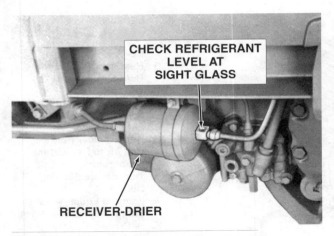

Fig. 9 — Sight Glass for Checking Refrigerant Level

4. The sight glass should be clear (free of bubbles) before starting the engine and operating the air conditioner.

5. Start the engine and run it at fast idle.

6. Turn on the air conditioner to the highest speed and turn the temperature control to the coldest temperature.

7. Bubbles will appear in the sight glass for a few minutes after starting the air conditioner.

   At temperatures above 70°F (21°C) the bubbles will disappear and the sight glass should be clear.

   If the bubbles do not stop flowing, the refrigerant level is low. See your service shop for recharging the system. Special equipment and safety are vital to this service.

8. Check the compressor drive belt for tightness (Fig. 10).

9. If the belt is too loose, tighten it as follows.

10. Loosen the compressor mounting bolts (B) and adjustment cap screw (A) (Fig. 10).

Fig. 10 — Compressor Belt Tension Adjustment
A—Adjusting Cap Screw
B—Mounting Bolts

11. Apply an outward force to the compressor until the belt is tightened as specified (usually deflecting the belt 1/4 inch [6 mm] with a 15- to 20-pound [65 to 90N] force on the belt midway between the compressor and crankshaft pulley is sufficient). See your operator's manual for exact specifications.

12. Tighten the compressor bolts in this position.

13. If water is not draining from the evaporator properly, check the evaporator drain tube trap (Fig. 11) for clogging or a dry trap.

14. If the water has evaporated from a trap, air will be drawn up the drain tube and may hold the condensed water in the evaporator housing. The trap must be primed. To do so, momentarily hold a garden hose against the bottom of the drain tube to fill the trap with water.

15. The receiver-drier (Fig. 9) is basically the filter for the air conditioner refrigerant. It removes condensation and other moisture, which can harm the system. While not replaced at regular intervals, it should be replaced when the system is in for major service, or whenever excessive moisture is a problem in the system.

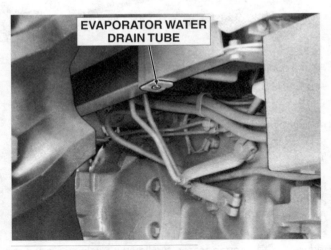

Fig. 11 — Evaporator Water Drain Tube

16. Compressor seals may dry out during cold weather when the air conditioner has not been operated for long periods of time. This will cause leaks which will allow refrigerant to escape. To avoid this problem operate the air conditioner for 5 to 10 minutes at a time at least once a month to prevent seals from drying out. If necessary, rotate the compressor crankshaft a few times by hand.

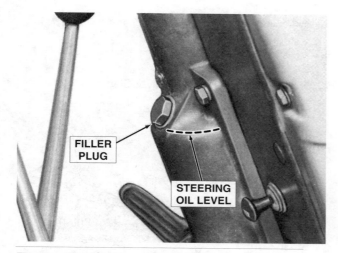

Fig. 12 — Checking Manual Steering Gear Housing Oil Level

HEATING AND AIR CONDITIONING PROBLEMS

If the machine cab does not heat or cool properly after regular maintenance has been performed, take it to a dealer for testing and service. Special test equipment and service tools are needed, especially for air conditioners.

MANUAL STEERING

The only maintenance required for manual steering gear is maintaining the oil level in the gear case every 250 hours and adjusting the gear backlash.

CHECKING MANUAL STEERING OIL LEVEL

Check the oil level in the steering gear housing every 250 or 500 hours, as recommended (Fig. 12). The operator's manual will indicate the proper level and type of lubricant.

ADJUSTING STEERING BACKLASH

When steering wheel backlash or "play" becomes excessive, adjust it as follows:

1. Turn the steering wheel from one extreme to the other and count the number of turns.

2. Turn the steering wheel back one half the number of total turns. This will position the mechanism in the midposition.

3. Loosen the jam nut on the steering gear adjusting screw (Fig. 13).

4. Tighten the adjusting screw until a very slight drag is felt when the steering wheel is turned back and forth through the mid-position.

5. Use a screwdriver to prevent adjusting screw from turning and tighten the nut. Recheck the adjustment.

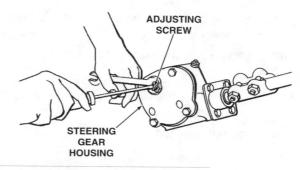

Fig. 13 — Adjusting Steering Gear Backlash

STEERING AXLE AND WHEELS

The steering axle and wheels require periodic adjustment and lubrication to prevent excessive wear and "play." Also, when the steering wheels are guided by tie rods and steering arms, toe-in must be adjusted annually or more frequently if recommended.

LUBRICATING STEERING AXLE AND WHEEL BEARINGS

Some steering axles and wheels require lubrication every 10 hours of operation. The exception is hand-packed bearings. These must be disassembled, cleaned, and hand packed every 1000 hours or annually. Also, wheel bearings with grease fittings must be cleaned and hand packed at the same intervals. When operating in extremely wet or muddy conditions, these services should be done more often.

Fig. 14 — Lubricating Grease Fittings on Steering Axle and Wheels (Wipe Clean First)

Shown in Fig. 14 is the location of grease fittings for typical steering axle and wheels. The operator's manual will show you where these are on the machine and how many strokes of lubricant to apply to each. Be sure to wipe fittings clean before applying grease gun.

CLEANING, REPACKING, AND ADJUSTING WHEEL BEARINGS

The following procedures describe typical cleaning, repacking and adjustment of most wheel bearings.

Tools And Materials Needed

1. Wrenches (inch or metric, as required)

2. Diagonal Pliers

3. Clean Cloths

4. Container Of Solvent (for cleaning, not gasoline)

5. Multipurpose Grease (or wheel bearing grease if recommended)

6. New Cotter Pins

7. Small Stiff-Bristle Brush

8. Hydraulic Jack

9. Support Stands

10. Source Of Compressed Air (if available)

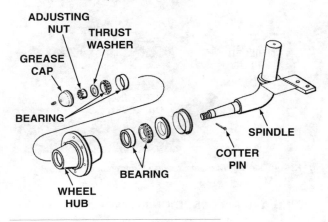

Fig. 15 — Spindle-Type Wheel and Bearings

Removing And Cleaning Bearings

Two typical types of wheel bearing assemblies are shown in Figs. 15 and 16. The spindle-type wheel is used on machines equipped with double tricycle wheels or wide axles. The axle-type wheel is usually used on machines with a single wheel.

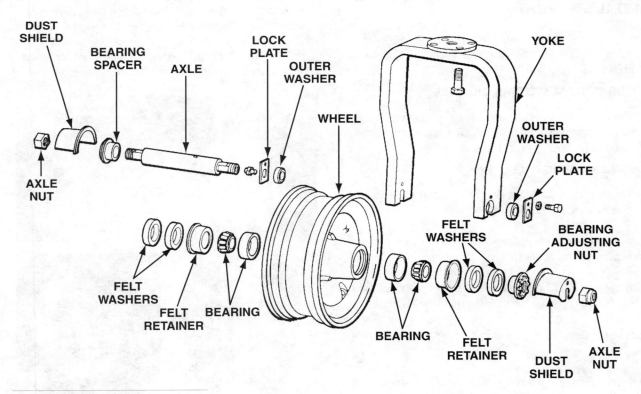

Fig. 16 — Axle-Type Wheel and Bearings

REMOVING BEARINGS ON SPINDLE-TYPE WHEELS

To remove the wheel bearings of a spindle-type wheel:

 CAUTION: Never rely on the jack alone to support the machine. Always use blocking under the machine in addition to the jack.

1. Jack up the machine so that the wheel is off the ground. Be sure to block the other wheels and set the parking brake so that the machine won't move and fall off the jack or support stands. Use blocks or support stands to securely support the machine. (On tricycle dual front wheels, run one wheel up on a block, freeing the other wheel for service.)

2. Clean dirt from wheel and hub cap.

3. Remove hub cap. It may be either screwed in, bolted on, or pushed into the hub. If bolted on, be careful not to damage the gasket under it. Lay cap, gasket and other parts as they are removed, in clean pan or container. Avoid laying parts on a dirty surface. Even the slightest amount of dust or dirt is difficult to remove from a bearing even in a cleaning solution.

4. Remove cotter pin with diagonal pliers. Straighten pin before removing it (Fig. 17).

5. Remove adjusting nut.

6. Remove thrust washer and outer bearing (Fig. 18). Shake the wheel gently if necessary to dislodge them. Do not allow the parts to fall to the ground.

7. Carefully pull the wheel off the spindle. Hold your hand behind the wheel to catch the inner bearing if it should fall off when the wheel clears the spindle.

   On some wheels the bearing and seal will come off with the wheel or remain on the spindle. If the bearing and seal cannot be removed easily from the spindle, leave them on. They can be cleaned while on the spindle.

8. If the grease seal remained in the hub, remove it with your fingers. Then remove the inner bearing.

Fig. 17 — Removing Adjusting Nut

Fig. 18 — Removing Thrust Washer and Outer Bearing

If the grease seal cannot be removed with your fingers, proceed with the next step as given below.

9. Turn the wheel over with the inner bearing down. Place a clean cloth or container under the hub to catch the bearing and seal when they fall out.

10. Use a brass drift punch or a wood dowel and gently tap the bearing cone from the hub (Fig. 19). Be careful not to tap on the bearing cage. You may damage the bearings.

Refer to cleaning the bearings later in this discussion.

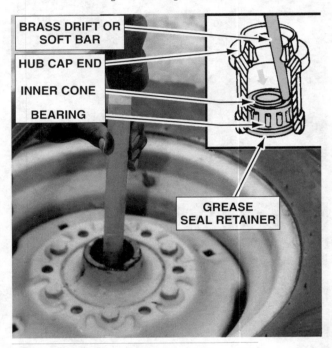

Fig. 19 — Removing Inner Bearing and Grease Seal

REMOVING BEARINGS ON AXLE-TYPE WHEELS

To remove the wheel bearings of an axle-type wheel:

1. Jack up the machine and support it as described in step 1 above.

2. Clean dirt from the wheel and hub areas.

3. Remove the screws from the bearing lock plates and bend the lock plates away from axle nuts (see Fig. 16).

4. Loosen axle nuts and remove dust shields.

5. Remove axle nuts and outer washers. Be careful that the wheel does not fall on you when you remove these parts. The wheel should now come off the yoke easily. Push down on the wheel if it does not come loose.

6. Disassemble axle, seals (felt washers and retainers), bearings, and any spacers and nuts remaining.

CLEANING WHEEL BEARINGS

To clean the wheel bearings and other parts:

1. Swirl the bearing in a container of clean solvent, using a brush to loosen grease deposits.

If you were unable to remove the inner bearing (spindle-type wheel), clean it and the grease seal while in place. Use a large brush and hold the container of solvent under the parts (Fig. 20). Dip the brush in the container and wash the bearing and seal thoroughly.

2. Clean the bearing cups also. It is not necessary to remove the cups from the hub. Also, clean the hub, cap and spindle or axle.

3. Remove solvent from all washed parts. If dry compressed air is not available, use a cloth free of dirt, dust and lint. Hold the bearings so the air blast won't spin the rolling elements or the cage (Fig. 21). Spinning a dry bearing can cause minute scoring of the bearing surfaces which will provide a rough enough surface to cause rapid wear.

NOTE: Do not use air which contains moisture. Moisture will cause the bearings to rust in a very short time.

Fig. 20 — Cleaning Inner Bearing on Spindle

4. Examine bearings for damage, wear, rust or corrosion. If it is apparent that any of these defects are serious enough, replace both the bearing race and cup of the affected bearing.

If the inner bearing (spindle-type wheel) requires replacement and you were unable to remove it before, use a wood dowel and hammer to tap off the bearing.

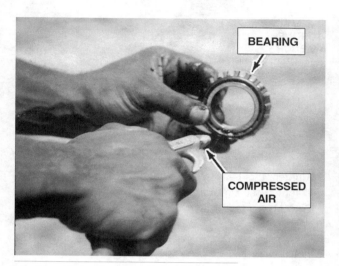

Fig. 21 — Drying Bearing with Compressed Air

5. Inspect the grease seals and retainers for excessive wear or damage. Replace any defective seals. The seal keeps out the dirt and moisture as well as retaining the grease.

If the seal is defective, the bearing life will be short. It is a good practice to replace seals and retainers each time the bearings are cleaned and repacked.

After you have determined which bearings can be reused and have replaced those that cannot, you are ready to repack the bearings.

Repacking And Assembling Bearings

To repack the bearings with grease and reassemble the wheels:

1. Use multipurpose grease or wheel bearing grease as specified by your operator's manual.

2. Rub a thin coating of clean crankcase oil on your hands to prevent the grease from sticking to them.

3. Place a small quantity of grease in the palm of your hand (Fig. 22). Push the grease into the elements of the bearing, press the bearing against the grease and rotate the bearing until grease has worked into the bearing thoroughly. Repeat this for each bearing.

4. If the inner bearing was left on the spindle, apply a thick coating of grease to the outer portions of the bearing. Wrap a clean cloth or piece of plastic around the bearing. Twist the ends of the cloth or plastic until it binds tightly around the bearing. This will press the trapped grease into the bearing (Bearing packer will do an even more thorough job, if available.)

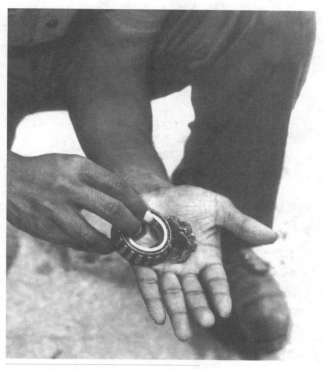

Fig. 22 — Packing Grease into a Bearing

5. Apply a coating of grease to the inside of the hub. This will help to prevent rust and prevent the entrance of dirt and water. Do not fill the entire cavity of the hub unless the operator's manual recommends it. Air space should be left in most hubs to permit the air to expand without building up pressure which can force grease past the seals (Fig. 23).

6. Reassemble the wheel bearings in the reverse order of disassembly. Be sure that grease seals are seated in the hub or retainers properly.

7. Install the wheel and be careful that dirt does not get into the bearing grease.

8. Adjust the wheel bearings as follows.

Adjusting Spindle-Type Wheels

1. Install thrust washer and slotted adjusting nut.

2. Tighten slotted adjusting nut until bearing is seated properly (Fig. 24). Be sure bearings are aligned with the spindle.

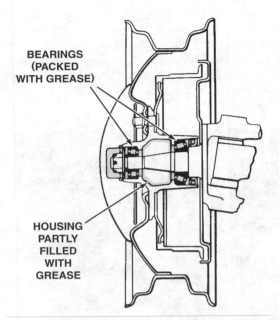

Fig. 23 — Wheel Hub Housing Partly Filled with Grease

3. Loosen the adjusting nut until the wheel can be turned easily; then turn the wheel and tighten the nut again until the wheel begins to turn with a slight drag.

NOTE: Some manufacturers recommend tightening the adjusting nut to a specific torque. You must use a torque wrench for this adjustment.

4. Loosen the adjusting nut until the nearest slot is aligned with the hole in the spindle. Check your operator's manual for its recommendations. Some manufacturers suggest loosening the nut as much as 1 /6 to 1 /3 turn.

5. *Always insert a new cotter pin.* Use diagonal pliers and bend one leg of the pin over the end of the spindle. Cut off any excess length of the other leg and bend it back against the nut. If the cotter pin is not installed properly, it could loosen and fall out allowing the wheel to come off.

6. Replace the hubcap.

Adjusting Axle-Type Wheels

1. Install the wheel on the yoke.

2. Slide outer washers onto axle until they seat into the hole in the yoke.

3. Attach the lock plates loosely with cap screws.

4. Screw on the axle nuts loosely.

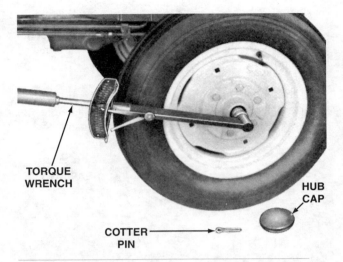

Fig. 24 — Adjusting Wheel Bearings on Spindle-Type Wheels

5. Tighten the bearing adjusting nut with a drift and a hammer (see Fig. 25) until a slight drag is felt when the wheel is rotated.

6. Back the nut off and lock the adjustment in the closest notch with the lock plate screw.

7. Tighten the axle nuts. The wheel should still rotate with a slight drag.

8. If the adjustment is correct, bend the corner of the lock plates against the axle nuts.

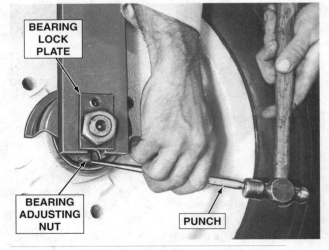

Fig. 25 — Adjusting Wheel Bearings on Axle-Type Wheels

ADJUSTING WHEEL TOE-IN (WIDE AXLE MACHINES)

Wheels which steer the machine must have proper toe-in so that the machine tracks in a straight line. This reduces wear on the tires and makes steering easier.

With wide steering axles, wheel toe-in must be checked periodically. "Toe-in" means that the wheels point slightly inward on the front or leading side.

Check the toe-in whenever:

- *Steering becomes difficult*
- *After hitting an obstacle*
- *After changing wheel spacing*
- *Before operating the machine at the beginning of the season.*

Checking And Adjusting Wheel Toe-in

To check the toe-in of the wheels which steer the machine:

1. Drive the machine straight ahead for a short distance on level ground. Stop the machine and shut off the engine.

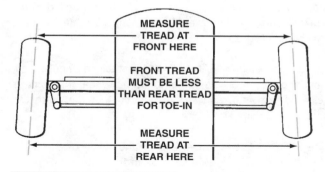

Fig. 26 — Measuring Wheel Toe-in

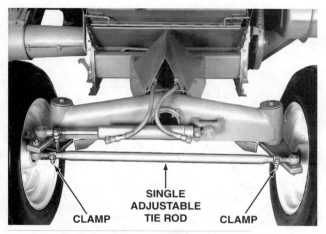

Fig. 27 — Machine with Single Tie Rod Adjustment

2. Measure the wheel tread at the front and rear of the wheels at hub level (Fig. 26). Usually, proper toe-in is 1/8 to 3/8 inch (3 to 10 mm) less in the front than in the rear. Check the operator's manual for specifications.

   If toe-in does not measure correctly, proceed with the following steps.

3. On machines with a single tie rod between steering wheels, loosen the tie rod clamps and turn the tie rod until the measurements are correct (Fig. 27). Tighten clamps.

4. On machines with a tie rod for each wheel, loosen both clamps on each tie rod (Fig. 28). Turn each tie rod an equal amount until toe-in measurements are correct. Tighten clamps. Both wheels must have equal toe-in.

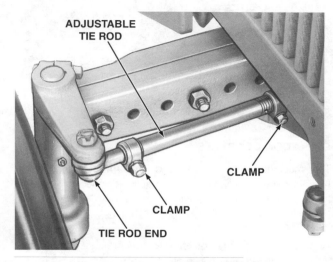

Fig. 28 — Machine with Tie Rod for Each Wheel

BRAKES

Most machines have two brake pedals (Fig. 29) which may be used for stopping (both pedals) or for turning (one pedal on either side to help turn machine).

To keep the machine safe to operate, be sure to maintain the brakes properly. Brakes that are out of adjustment can cause uneven braking or poor braking which may cause your machine to overturn or crash into something, injuring you or others and damaging the machine.

Knowing how brakes work will help you understand why they need adjustment.

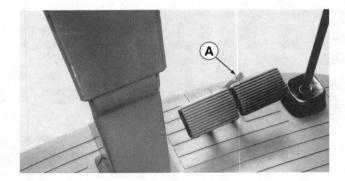

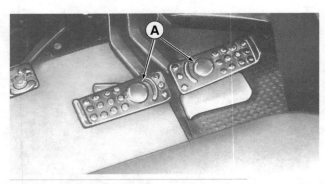

Fig. 29 — Most Machines Have Two Brake Pedals

OPERATION OF BRAKES

The machine may be equipped with mechanical brakes, hydraulic (power) brakes, or hydraulic (trapped oil) brakes. Hydraulic powered brakes were discussed in Chapter 8; here mechanical and hydraulic (trapped oil) brakes will be described.

Almost all agricultural machines have brakes for the drive wheels or drive train only.

Mechanical brakes are controlled and actuated by mechanical linkage. Control rods or cables provide the linkage between the brake pedals and the wheel brakes (Fig. 30).

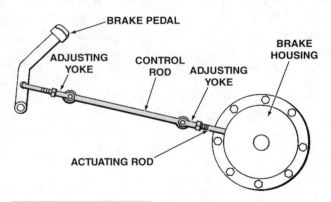

Fig. 30 — Mechanical Brakes

Thus far, only the brake controls have been described. The braking action itself is provided by one of the following methods:

- **Band Brakes (external contracting)**
- **Shoe Brakes (internal expanding)**
- **Disk Brakes**

For more information on hydraulic brakes, see Chapter 8.

Hydraulic brakes are controlled and actuated by hydraulic oil trapped between the brake master cylinder (controlled by the brake pedals) and the slave cylinders, which actuate the brake mechanism (Fig. 31).

The braking action of BAND BRAKES is obtained by pulling the band tightly around a rotating drum. When the force is released, a spring retracts the band so that the drum can rotate freely (Fig. 32).

The SHOE BRAKE is forced against the inside of the brake drum and slows or prevents the drum from turning (Fig. 33). This type of brake is popular on automobiles.

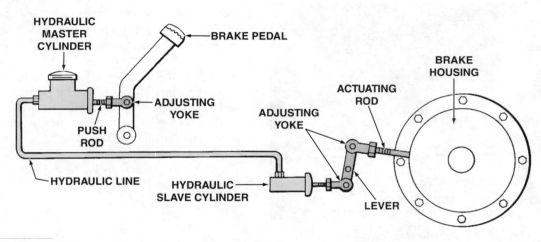

Fig. 31 — Hydraulic Brakes

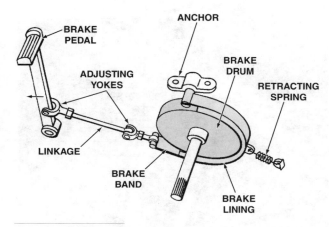

Fig. 32 — Band Brakes

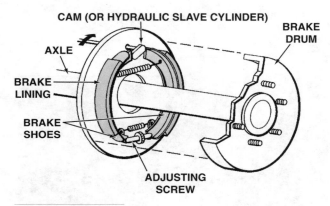

Fig. 33 — Shoe Brakes

DISK BRAKES are commonly used on agricultural machines; although, the other two types are found on some machines. Each brake mechanism consists of two driven brake disks which have friction facings attached to each side and two actuating disks which force the brake disks against a stationary braking surface (Fig. 34).

The driven brake disks are attached to either differential input shaft or to each drive axle within the differential housing.

Between the brake disks are two actuating disks which are held together by springs. Three steel balls are located in tapered cups on the inside of each actuating disk. When the actuating disks are rotated in opposite directions by levers, the steel balls ride out of their cups and force the brake disks apart (Fig. 34, right).

As the brake disks are forced farther apart, they bind against the stationary braking surfaces of the housing and slow or stop the shaft from turning.

All three of these brakes may be controlled by either mechanical or hydraulic action.

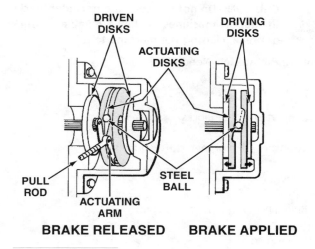

BRAKE RELEASED   BRAKE APPLIED

Fig. 34 — Disk Brakes

ADJUSTING THE BRAKES

Two things can indicate when brakes need adjustment:

1. *Too Much Pedal Free Travel*

2. *Poor Or Uneven Braking Action*

Typical adjustments are made as follows:

Before attempting to adjust the brakes on your machine, jack up the machine until the drive wheels clear the ground (Fig. 35). Support the machine securely with stands or blocks. Block the other wheels to prevent the machine from rolling off the supports. Be very careful. You could be seriously injured if the, machine should fall off the supports.

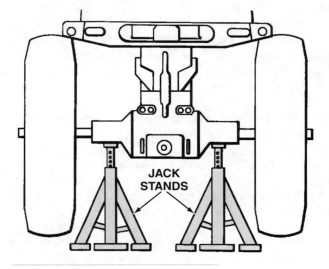

Fig. 35 — Raising Drive Wheels Off Ground

CAUTION: Do not use concrete or cinder blocks to support machines as they are liable to crack or break, causing the machine to fall.

Tools And Materials Needed

1. Jack

2. Support Stand Or Blocks

3. Wrenches (inch or metric, as required)

4. Screwdriver

5. Ruler (inch or metric, as required)

6. Brake Fluid

7. Clean Cloth

Adjusting Mechanical Disk Brakes

To adjust disk brakes:

1. Adjust brake pedal free travel (Fig. 36) at either the pedal or the brake housing, whichever is recommended in your operator's manual (see Figs. 30, 31 and 32).

   If the brake pedals have an interlock (Fig. 37) latching them together, adjust the pedal with the interlock first. Before adjusting, you must loosen a lock nut on the brake linkage at either the brake pedal or the brake housing.

2. Tighten or loosen the adjusting nut or yoke until the recommended free travel is obtained.

3. Repeat this procedure for the other brake pedal. This pedal must have the same amount of free travel as the other so that each pedal will cause the same amount of braking action when the pedals are interlocked. You must adjust brake pedals that are separated from each other in the same manner.

4. Check brakes for equal braking action while the machine is still raised off the ground (Fig. 38).

5. Latch the brake pedals together (Fig. 37).

6. Start the engine and run it at medium throttle. Check to be sure no one is near the machine.

7. Shift the transmission into a medium speed range and engage the clutch slowly to start the wheels rotating.

8. Disengage the clutch and shift into neutral.

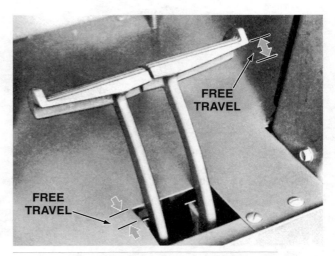

Fig. 36 — Two Methods of Measuring Pedal Free Travel

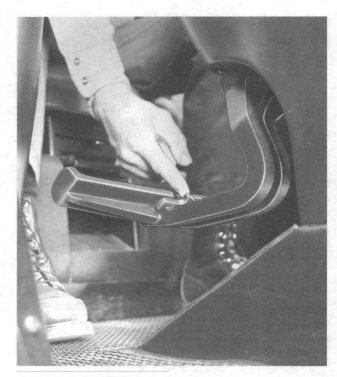

Fig. 37 — Brake Pedal Interlock

9. Apply the brakes slowly and observe the rate the wheels rotate (Fig. 38). If one wheel slows before the other, adjust the brakes until the two wheels brake evenly.

10. If the brakes cannot be adjusted evenly, new brake linings may be needed.

Adjusting Mechanical Shoe Brakes

To adjust shoe brakes, the machine should be on supports, drive wheels off the ground (see Fig. 38) then proceed as follows.

1. Remove the adjusting slot cover from each wheel cover (inside of wheel).

2. Insert a screwdriver into the slot to engage the adjusting screw teeth (Fig. 39).

3. Turn the adjusting screw until the wheel drags as you rotate it by hand. Back off the adjusting screw until little or no drag is felt. Repeat for the other wheel. Be sure to adjust it the same.

4. Check brake pedal free travel according to your operator's manual. If it isn't correct, adjust it by shortening or lengthening the linkage as required. Be sure that both pedals have exactly the same free travel.

5. Check the brakes for equal braking action while the machine is still off the ground. Follow the procedures described above for disk brakes, steps 5 through 11.

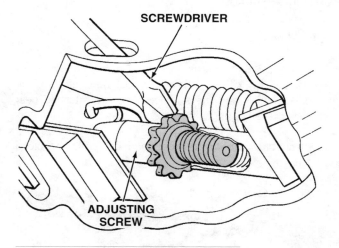

Fig. 39 — Turning Shoe Brake Adjusting Screw

Adjusting Mechanical Band Brakes

To adjust band brakes:

1. Adjust the brake pedal free travel at either the pedal or the brake band, which ever is recommended in the operator's manual.

2. Tighten or loosen the adjusting mechanism until the recommended free travel is obtained.

3. Check the brakes for equal braking action while the machine is still off the ground. Follow the procedures described above for disk brakes, steps 5 through 11.

4. Lower machine to ground. Never rock the machine from its blocks.

    The adjustments for mechanical brakes have been discussed earlier. The following discussion concerns hydraulic brakes.

Adjusting Hydraulic Brakes

Three procedures are required to adjust hydraulic (trapped oil) brakes:
*   *Bleeding Brakes*
*   *Adjusting Push Rods*
*   *Adjusting Brake Mechanism*

If brake pedal action feels soft or spongy, bleed the brakes using the following steps. The machine should not be raised off the ground.

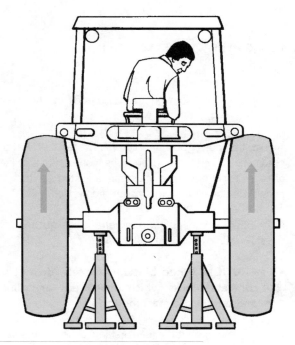

Fig. 38 — Checking for Equal Braking Action

BLEEDING HYDRAULIC BRAKES

To bleed brakes:

1. Locate the brake master cylinder (Fig. 40) and the slave cylinder (Fig. 41). The master cylinder is usually near the brake pedals and the slave cylinders are attached near each brake housing.

2. Clean dirt from the cylinders and especially the bleed screws.

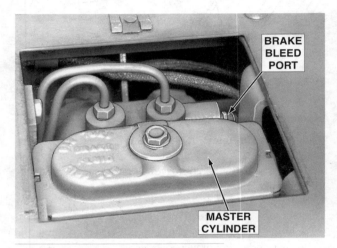

Fig. 40 — Brake Master Cylinder Bleed Port

3. Check the fluid level in the master cylinder. If necessary, fill the reservoir with the recommended fluid.

4. Have someone sit in the operator's seat to operate the brake pedals. Describe what you are about to do so that you work together.

5. If the master cylinder has a bleed valve, bleed it first (Fig. 41).

6. Have your assistant slowly depress the brake pedal for the right brake while you crack the bleed valve. Allow the fluid to escape slowly. If air is in the cylinder, bubbles will be released as you do this.

7. Close the bleed valve before the brake pedal is released. The pedal must be released slowly to avoid churning the fluid and creating more air pockets.

8. Repeat this procedure until no bubbles appear at the bleed valve. Also, repeat these steps for the other cylinder.

Check the master cylinder to be sure that sufficient fluid still remains in the reservoir. Fill again if necessary.

9. Now bleed the nearest slave cylinder in the same manner. Repeat for the other slave cylinder. Check the fluid level in the reservoir and fill if necessary.

10. Check the pedal action for a soft or spongy feel. If the pedal does not have a firm feel, there is still air in the lines and cylinders. Repeat the bleeding procedures.

11. Refill the reservoir to the proper level. Replace reservoir cover.

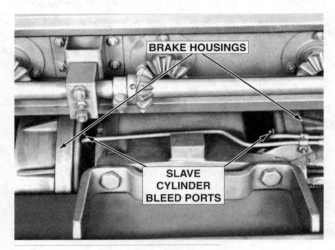

Fig. 41 — Brake Slave Cylinder Bleed Ports

ADJUSTING HYDRAULIC BRAKE PUSH RODS

To adjust the push rods:

1. Loosen the lock nuts on the push rods of the master cylinder (Fig. 42).

2. Adjust the push rods until proper pedal free travel is obtained or until the push rods contact the cylinder pistons. Each push rod must be adjusted so that the pedals are equal when the brakes are applied.

3. If the operator's manual recommends this adjustment for the slave cylinders, adjust them also.

 CAUTION: When blocking wheels, do not use concrete blocks which may break or crumble and permit the machine to fall.

4. Check the brakes for equal braking action. Do this by jacking up the machine so that the drive wheels are off the ground (see Fig. 38). Be sure to block the other wheels to prevent the machine from moving. Support the machine securely with stands or blocks.

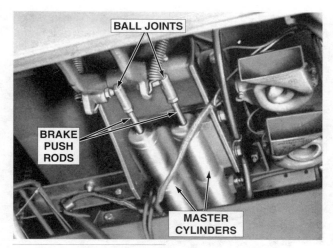

Fig. 42 — Adjust the Push Rods

ADJUSTING HYDRAULIC BRAKE MECHANISM

To adjust the brake bands, disks or shoes, follow the procedures described earlier for disk, band or shoe brakes, steps 5 through 11. If the brakes don't slow at the same rate, adjust the push rods or bleed the brakes again. When one side of the hydraulic system still contains air, it will not apply as much pressure to the brakes as the other side.

TIRES

Fig. 43 — Big Tires are Expensive—Take Care of Them

Tire replacement can cost thousands of dollars for larger machines. If tires are not properly inflated or are abused, their life can be shortened greatly. For example, underinflation can reduce tire life by up to one-quarter. This alone could cost hundreds of dollars. Tire abuse such as spinning wheels can wear tires even faster.

Maintaining tires properly takes only a few minutes periodically. Here are the key maintenance items:

- **Tire Inflation**
- **Ballast**
- **Tire Failures**
- **Safety Tips**

Let's look at each one.

TIRE INFLATION

Proper inflation is vitally important to proper service life of the tire. Tires are designed to operate with a certain sidewall deflection or "bulge." Correct air pressure helps provide proper traction, flotation, support of loads, and prevents excessive flexing of the tire which could cause sidewall cracking. See Fig. 44 for typical tire construction.

Overinflation

Overinflation prevents full contact of the tire tread with the ground or road (left, Fig. 45). This subjects the center of the tread to excessive wear. Because the tire is more rigid, it is more liable to damage by striking curbs, rocks, and other objects which could cause breakage of the cord plies.

Underinflation

Underinflated tires (center, Fig. 45) flex excessively at every turn of the wheel, resulting in high internal heat and premature failure. Underinflation is indicated by excessive wear of the sides of the tread while the center is relatively unworn.

NOTE: Radial tractor tires, even when properly inflated, appear to "squat" or bulge more than properly inflated conventional tires. Always check pressure with a gauge. Don't rely on tire appearance.

Proper Inflation

Correctly inflated tires (right, Fig. 45) permit all of the tread to contact the ground, yet are not soft enough to flex excessively.

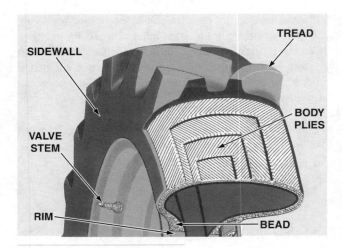

Fig. 44 — Typical Tire Construction

Tire Pressure Gauge

Proper inflation must be maintained at all times through all seasons. This makes it important that an *accurate pressure gauge* be used when checking inflation pressures. Also remember that tires gain pressure in hot weather and lose pressure in cold weather.

Two types of pressure gauges are usually available—*high-pressure* and *low-pressure*— for either dry or liquid testing.

Always use the proper type gauge when checking pressure. Normally, high-pressure gauges are not satisfactory for checking low-pressure tires as the gauges are usually calibrated in five-pound increments while low-pressure gauges are calibrated in one-pound increments.

Most important is that the gauge be *accurate*. Accuracy can only be determined by checking the gauge against a gauge of known accuracy.

Fig. 46 — Low-Pressure Tire Gauge

For this reason, keep one accurate gauge for the sole purpose of checking the accuracy of the gauge normally used. This is especially important with low-pressure gauges.

A low-pressure tire gauge is shown in Fig. 46.

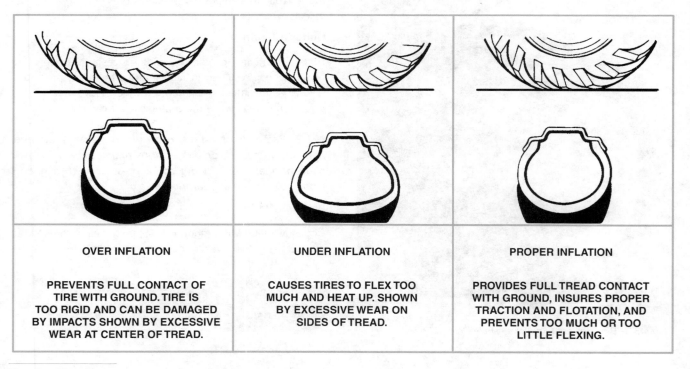

OVER INFLATION	UNDER INFLATION	PROPER INFLATION
PREVENTS FULL CONTACT OF TIRE WITH GROUND. TIRE IS TOO RIGID AND CAN BE DAMAGED BY IMPACTS SHOWN BY EXCESSIVE WEAR AT CENTER OF TREAD.	CAUSES TIRES TO FLEX TOO MUCH AND HEAT UP. SHOWN BY EXCESSIVE WEAR ON SIDES OF TREAD.	PROVIDES FULL TREAD CONTACT WITH GROUND, INSURES PROPER TRACTION AND FLOTATION, AND PREVENTS TOO MUCH OR TOO LITTLE FLEXING.

Fig. 45 — Tire Inflation

Tire Inflation Rules

Here are four rules that must be observed for proper tire inflation:

1. *Always check and inflate tires when they are cold.* This is very important because tires become heated through use and the air expands thus the pressure increases.

2. *Never "bleed" air pressure from warm or hot tires.* This always results in the tire pressure being too low when its temperature becomes normal and often results in tire damage when put under load. Instead of bleeding air from hot tires, reduce the load, the speed, or both.

3. *If a tire becomes low while operating, adjust pressure the same as other tires of the same size on the machine.* Recheck the pressure after about 30 minutes of operation to be sure it is still correct.

4. *Always use a liquid-type pressure gauge when checking pressure in tires with liquid ballast. Check pressure with the valve stem at the bottom.* Always wash the gauge with clean water after checking the tires.

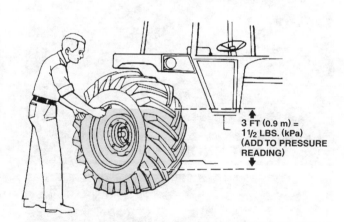

3 FT (0.9 m) = 1½ LBS. (kPa) (ADD TO PRESSURE READING)

Fig. 47 — Optional Method of Checking Air Pressure with Valve Stem at Top

If it is impossible or undesirable to check the pressure with the valve stem at the bottom, locate the stem at the top (Fig. 47).

For actual pressure, add about 1/2 psi (3.4 kPa) to the pressure gauge reading, as shown, for each foot the liquid is above the lower valve stem position.

Proper Amount Of Tire Inflation

Recommended tire inflation varies with size, ply, and load on tire (see tractor chart on next page). An average recommendation for a six-ply front tractor tire is 36 psi (250 kPa) (more with front-mounted equipment). An average six-ply rear tractor tire is 16 psi (110 kPa) (more with heavy ballast

TIRE INFLATION 6-PLY

Front tires	Lowest	Highest
All 7.50 sizes	20 psi (140 kPa)	36 psi. (250 kPa)
6.50	20 (140)	44 (300)
5.50 and 6.00	20 (140)	48 (330)

4-ply

Front tires	Lowest	Highest
All 7.50 sizes	20 psi (140 kPa)	24 psi. (165 kPa)
6.50	20 (140)	28 (195)
5.50 and 6.00	20 (140)	32 (220)
5.00	20 (140)	36 (250)
4.00	20(140)	44(300)

8 and 10-ply

Rear tires		Lowest	Highest
18.4	8-ply	16 psi. (110 kPa)	20 psi. (140 kPa)
23.1	8-ply	16 (110)	16 (110)
23.1	10-ply	16 (110)	20 (140)
24.5	10-ply	16 (110)	18 (125)

6-ply

Rear tires	Lowest	Highest
All 18.4	16 psi. (110 kPa)	16 psi. (110 kPa)
16.9	16 (110)	16 (110)
14.9	14 (95)	18 (125)
13.6	14 (95)	20 (140)
12.4	12 (80)	22 (150)
11.2	12 (80)	24 (165)

4-ply

Rear tires	Lowest	Highest
All 13.6	14 psi. (95 kPa)	14 psi. (95 kPa)
12.4	12 (80)	14 (95)
11.2	12 (80)	16 (110)
9.5	12 (80)	18 (125)

or rear-mounted equipment). Always follow your operator's manual for the exact tire pressure.

How To Inflate Tires

To check tire inflation:

1. If the tire contains ballast, be sure the valve stem is positioned correctly as described in the rules above, or use the method shown in Fig. 47.

2. Remove valve cap and check air pressure. Be sure to hold the gauge firmly against the valve stem to get a correct reading.

3. Check pressure again if you think a poor contact was made.

4. Add or release air as needed to obtain correct air pressure.

Do not exceed the maximum recommended air pressure. Some tire manufacturers recommend that you put a few more pounds in tires under the following conditions:

a. If mounted equipment puts most of the weight on one side of the machine, put a few extra pounds of pressure in the tires on that side, but do not exceed maximum pressure ratings.

b. If the tractor is used for plowing with one set of wheels in the furrow, inflate the furrow tires a few extra pounds (usually about 4 psi [30 kPa]) to avoid excessive buckling of tires (see Fig. 48). Again, do not exceed maximum pressure.

c. If the machine is to be operated on a paved or hard road for several hours, inflate all tires to the *maximum* recommended pressure.

Now let's take a look at how tire ballast affects traction and available horsepower.

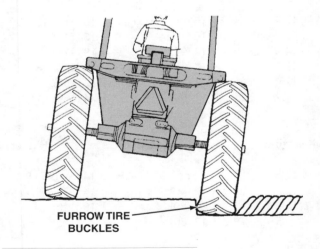

FURROW TIRE BUCKLES

Fig. 48 — Tire Tends to Buckle in Furrow

TIRE BALLAST

Tire ballast or weight can help give the most effective traction and power. The machine weight by itself may not be sufficient for full traction and drawbar pull. *However, improper tire ballast can cause premature tire wear.*

Farm tractors are the prime users of wheel ballast, so the discussion of ballast will refer mainly to them.

See *TRACTOR PERFORMANCE* on page 196.

TOO MUCH WEIGHT

NOT ENOUGH WEIGHT

PROPER SLIPPAGE

Fig. 49 — Tire Traction Patterns

Tire Traction

Tire traction can be judged by looking at the tire tread pattern after pulling under load as shown in Fig. 49.

Too Much Weight

When *too much weight* is used, the tire tracks will be sharp and distinct in the soil (Fig. 49, top) and there will be no evidence of slipping.

This is bad, as the tires are literally geared to the ground and do not allow the flexibility of engine operation that is obtained when some slippage occurs.

Too Little Weight

When the tires have *too little weight* they lose traction. The tread marks are entirely wiped out (Fig. 49, center) and forward progress is slowed. Not only is less work done but the tires wear excessively. Reduced speed caused by excessive slippage can also cause over-application of chemical pesticides.

Proper Weight

When the tires have *proper weight,* a small amount of slippage occurs (Fig. 49, bottom). Usually, between 10 and 15 percent slippage is considered ideal in the field. When the tire is properly weighted, the soil between the cleats will be shifted but the tread pattern is still visible in the tire track as shown. Proper weighting allows the engine to perform at its best with maximum flexibility.

Adding Ballast To Tires

See your local service shop for adding ballast to tires. The tires can be filled about three-fourths full of liquid to add weight. Usually a mixture of water and calcium chloride solution is used to prevent freezing. Dealers are equipped to mix and add solution to the tires. A special valve is needed to permit air to escape from the tire while the solution is being added.

If water is used instead of calcium chloride solution, it must be removed during winter in colder climates. Water also provides less weight per unit of volume than does calcium chloride solution.

Cast iron weights can also be attached to wheels for extra weight. Dual or triple tires are another way of improving traction and adding weight on larger tractors.

Remember that tire inflation should be higher when more ballast is added. See the operator's manual for recommended amounts under different operating conditions.

Dual And Triple Tires

Dual and triple tires are frequently added to improve traction and flotation of large tractors. Dual tires generally cost less than large single tires which would provide equal "footprint" or soil contact area. The extra weight of the added tires and wheels increases traction in adverse conditions. Extra tires also increase total load-carrying capacity (for more ballast, spray tanks, etc.). Total weight must not exceed load rating of the tires.

Tires used in dual or triple configurations must be matched in diameter and circumference to avoid uneven distribution of load. All drive tires on 4-wheel-drive machines should also be matched. Circumference of tractor drive tires, mounted and inflated, should not vary more than 11/2 inches (40 mm). Tires of uneven size can cause excessive tire slippage, axle breakage, difficult steering and other problems.

Adding dual or triple tires increases strain on axles and housings,and is not recommended on some tractor models. Check with your tractor dealer or manufacturer if the operator's manual does not indicate acceptability of extra tires.

We have discussed basic tire maintenance. Now let's look at some tire failures which are caused by poor maintenance or abuse.

TIRE FAILURES

As we have said, tire failures may be caused by abuse, underinflation, overinflation, or just plain careless operation.

If tires aren't inflated properly, they are more subject to damage than under any other condition.

Inspect tires regularly for the following signs of damage. If the machine is operated as it should be, you probably won't find any tire damage as described here. However, the following will reveal what kind of damage is caused by abuse, underinflation or overinflation.

Tire Abuse

Tire abuse is any operation or lack of attention that will cause damage to tires.

Avoid driving over objects, such as large rocks, tree stumps or anything that may penetrate the tire or break the tire cords. An impact break is shown in Fig. 50.

Avoid spinning the tires. Engage the clutch slowly to prevent the tires from spinning. Use ballast and weights when pulling heavy loads to prevent spinning damage shown in Fig. 50.

Adjust the tire spacing to avoid stubble damage (Fig. 50) when operating in harvested corn or soybean fields.

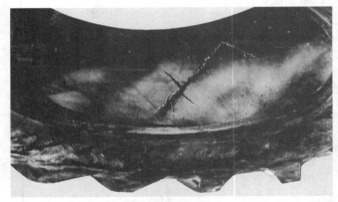

IMPACT BREAK

SPINNING WEAR

STUBBLE WEAR

EMBEDDED STONE

Fig. 50 — Damage Caused by Tire Abuse

Locate small cuts in the tire and bevel them to prevent stones and other small objects from embedding in the tire and causing leaks or broken cords (Fig. 50).

Check your machine for parts that may be rubbing or gouging the tires as they turn. Hitching or turning too short may cause this problem.

Underinflation

If your tires become underinflated, the sidewalls may buckle and break as shown in Fig. 51. This can occur when operating under heavy drawbar pull and when plowing with tires in the furrow. See the instructions on inflation described earlier.

Avoid operating on roads or other hard surfaces for long periods of time. If you must, inflate the tires to the *maximum* recommended pressure.

Overinflation

Avoid overinflating tires. Do not exceed the maximum pressure rating.

Breaks in the tire cord (Fig. 52) can occur much easier when striking an object with tires inflated above normal pressures.

Also, the center portion of the tire tread will become worn more rapidly than the outer portions.

SAFETY TIPS FOR TIRES

1. FOR YOUR SAFETY—Remember, an inflated tire can be very dangerous. Under pressure, for example, an 18-22.5 16 PR tire with 75 psi (515 kPa) pressure develops 103,789 Energy Foot-Pounds (140 717 J), and if it exploded, that energy could lift a 20,000 pound (9090.kg) tractor more than 5 feet (1.5 m) off the ground.

2. When inflating large tires, use a clip-on chuck and extension hose long enough to allow you to stand to one side and NOT in front of the tire assembly.

3. Before a jack is placed in position, block the tire and wheel on the *other* side of the machine. ALWAYS crib up with blocks or a stand just in case the jack should slip. NEVER use the jack alone.

4. Without proper tire repair equipment, tire service can be dangerous. Have tires serviced by a tire service shop that can do the job safer, easier and quicker.

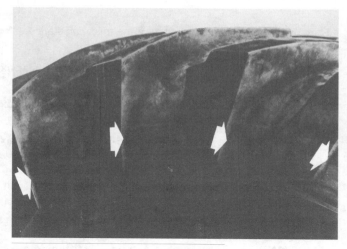

Fig. 51 — Damage Caused by Underinflation

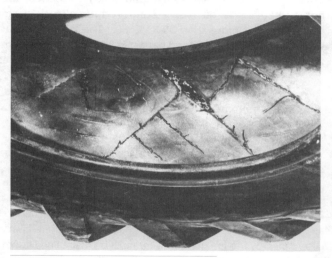

Fig. 52 — Damage Caused by Overinflation

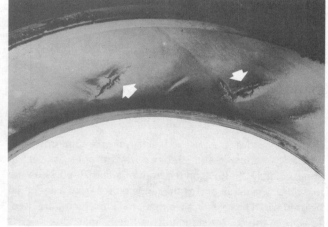

Fig. 53 — Large Farm Tires are Potential Safety Hazards

TRACTOR PERFORMANCE

A tractor will provide the best performance and power hop can be controlled when it is equipped with tires that are large enough relative to the tractor weight to provide a "soft" ride (low stiffness). In most situations, the tires should be inflated to operate at rated deflections. This means that they should be inflated to the minimum pressures required to support the static weight being carried on each axle. The bigger the tire air volume the better—best results will be obtained if there is more tire on the tractor than might have been thought necessary in the past. A tractor being set up for heavy tillage work should be thought of in terms of bigger tires and moderate to light weight instead of smaller tires and heavy weight. The three major items to be considered are:

- **Total tractor weight & static weight split (weight distribution on front and rear axles)**

- **Type of ballast used (cast and/or liquid weight)**
- **Tire inflation pressures**

No one item can be considered independent of the other two in order to achieve optimum tractor performance. A properly set up tractor will provide the following benefits:

- *Improved traction (reduced slip and higher fuel efficiency)*
- *Reduced compaction*
- *Improved flotation*

- *Improved ride*
- *Reduced tire wear*
- *Improved sidehill stability*
- *Better control of power hop on MFWD and 4WD tractors*

STATIC WEIGHT SPLIT AND BALLAST

Two-Wheel Drive Tractors

Two-wheel drive tractors will achieve optimum operating efficiency when static tractor weight split is set at approximately 25-35 % on the front axle and 75-65 % on the rear axle. The upper end of the range on the front axle should be used when heavy rear hitch mounted implements are used. To achieve the correct static tractor weight split, cast weights are recommended. Liquid ballast of up to 75 % fill can be used in the rear tires, but ride comfort is best if cast weights or a combination of liquid and cast weights is used.

IMPORTANT: Liquid ballast has a dramatic stiffening effect at low inflation pressures; therefore, a partial liquid fill used in combination with cast weights will provide the best ride. Do not exceed 75 % liquid fill (valve-stem level).

 CAUTION: Installing liquid ballast requires special equipment and training. Have the job done by a tractor dealer or a tire service store.

MFWD Tractor

Mechanical Front Wheel Drive (MFWD) tractors should have a static tractor weight split of 35-40 % on the front axle and 65-60 % on the rear axle. To achieve the recommended static tractor weight split, use cast weights on the rear and a combination of liquid and cast weights in the front.

IMPORTANT: Liquid ballast has a dramatic stiffening effect at low inflation pressures; therefore, liquid ballast in the rear tires should be avoided when a power hop condition exists. If rear liquid weight is used, do not exceed 40% fill (valve stem at four o'clock position) and preferably not more than 25-33 % fill. If front liquid weight is used, do not exceed 75% fill (valve-stem level). The liquid fill must be the same in all tires on the same axle.

 CAUTION: Installing liquid ballast requires special equipment and training. Have the job done by a tractor dealer or a tire service store.

Four-Wheel Drive Tractors

Four-wheel drive tractors should have the following static tractor weight split:

- **51-55 % on the front axle and 49-45 % on the rear axle for standard towed implements.**
- **55-60 % on the front axle and 45-40 % on the rear axle for hitch mounted implements.**
- **55-65 % on the front axle and 45-35 % on the rear axle for towed implements causing high down loads on drawbars.**

To achieve the recommended static tractor weight split, use combination of liquid and cast weights in the rear and cast weights o the front.

IMPORTANT: Liquid ballast has a dramatic stiffening effect at low inflation pressures; therefore, liquid ballast in the rear tires shoul not exceed 40 % fill (valve stem at four o'clock position) an preferably not more than 25-33% fill. The liquid fill must be th same in all rear tires. Added ballast is not normally required on th front axle; however, if required, cast weights are preferred.

 CAUTION: Installing liquid ballast requires specia equipment and training. Have the job done by a tracto dealer or a tire service store.

Verify the correct static tractor weight split by weighing each tractor ax or by consulting your tractor dealer.

INFLATION PRESSURE ADJUSTMENTS

The recommended tire inflation pressure is dependent upon static loa and the number of tires mounted on the axle. The "Rated Deflection" a determined by the tire manufacturer must be maintained in order for th tire to operate at optimum traction. The inflation pressure of large radi tires should be set to the pressure shown in the Extended Inflatio Pressure Table For Large Radial Tires. See Figure 54. For radial front tire and all bias tires, use the appropriate table provided by the tir manufacturer for the recommended inflation pressure.

IMPORTANT: All tires on the same axle must be inflated to th same pressure.

MONITORING TRACTOR PERFORMANCE

When performing field operations that load the tractor close to a tractio or power limit, closely monitor the following:

IMPORTANT: A radar monitor is recommended to precisel measure wheel slip and ground speed.

- **Wheel slip**—should not exceed 15% under normal conditions. Typical wheel slip is 5-12%.

EXTENDED INFLATION PRESSURE TABLE FOR LARGE RADIAL TIRES

CONVENTIONAL SIZE RADIAL DRIVE TIRES
FOR SPEEDS UP TO 25 MPH

Tire Size Designation	Infl psi / Load Per Tire	6	7	8	9	10	12	14	16	18	20	22	24
14.9R46	Single Lbs	2260	2470	2670	2860	3040	3380	3700	4000	4300	4560	4840	5080
	Dual Lbs	1990	2170	2350	2520	2680	2970	3260	3520	3780	4010	4260	4470
	Triple Lbs	1850	2030	2190	2350	2490	2770	3030	3280	3530	3740	3970	4170
18.4R38	Single lbs	2960	3240	3500	3760	3980	4440	4860	5260	5680	5980	6350	6600
	Dual Lbs	2600	2850	3080	3310	3500	3910	4280	4630	5000	5260	5590	5810
	Triple Lbs	2430	2660	2870	3080	3260	3640	390	4310	4660	4900	5210	5410
18.4R42	Single Lbs	3120	3420	3700	3960	4200	4680	5120	5540	6000	6300	6650	6950
	Dual Lbs	2750	3010	3260	3480	3700	4120	4510	4880	5280	5540	5850	6120
	Triple Lbs	2560	2800	3030	3250	3440	3840	4200	4540	4920	5170	5450	5700
18.4R46	Single Lbs	3280	3600	3880	4160	4420	4920	5400	5820	6150	6650	7000	7400
	Dual Lbs	2890	3170	3410	3660	3890	4330	4750	5120	5410	5850	6160	6510
	Triple Lbs	2690	2950	3180	3410	3620	4030	4430	4770	5040	5450	5740	6070
20.8R38	Single Lbs	3580	3920	4240	4540	4840	5380	5880	6350	6800	7250	7650	8050
	Dual Lbs	3150	3450	3730	4000	4260	4730	5170	5590	5980	6380	6730	7080
	Triple Lbs	2940	3210	3480	3720	3970	4410	4820	5210	5580	5950	6270	6600
20.8R42	Single Lbs	3780	4140	4480	4800	5100	5680	6200	6700	7150	7650	8100	8550
	Dual Lbs	3330	3640	3940	4220	4490	5000	5460	5900	6290	6730	7130	7520
	Triple Lbs	3100	3390	3670	3940	4180	4660	5080	5490	5860	6270	6640	7010
24.5R32	Single Lbs	4300	4700	5100	5460	5800	6450	7050	7650	8250	8700	9200	9650
	Dual Lbs	3780	4140	4490	4800	5100	5680	6200	6730	7260	7660	8100	8490
30.5LR32	Single Lbs	5140	5620	6100	6500	6950	7700	8450	9100	9650	10400	11000	11700
	Dual Lbs	4520	4950	5370	5720	6120	6780	7440	8010	8490	9150	9680	10300

METRIC SIZE RADIAL DRIVE TIRES
FOR SPEEDS UP TO 25 MPH

Tire Size Designation	Infl psi / Load Per Tire	6	9	12	15	17	20	23
420/80R46	Single Lbs	2910	3520	4080	4680	5360	5840	6400
	Dual Lbs	2560	3100	3590	4110	4710	5140	5630
	Triple Lbs	2390	2890	3340	3830	4390	4790	5240
710/70R38	Single Lbs	5360	6400	7400	8550	9650	10700	11700
	Dual Lbs	4710	5630	6500	7520	8490	9460	10280

Fig. 54 — Extended Inflation Pressure Table for Large Radial Tires

- **Engine speed**—The engine should operate in the speed range specified by the manufacturer. Under normal conditions at full throttle, the speed should be near rated rpm but may drop a few hundred rpm for short durations when operated under certain conditions such as a high draft load. You may also "shift up and throttle back" if this does not cause the engine to labor. Follow your tractor manufacturer's recommendations.

- **Ground speed**—5 mph or higher is preferred, but no less than 4 mph continuously. Follow your tractor manufacturer's recommendations.

If the tractor maintains engine and ground speed within the recommended limits but wheel slip is high, one or more of the following should be performed.

- **Reduce draft by reducing implement working depth or width.**

- **Add ballast but maintain correct tractor weight split.**

- **Consider larger diameter tire.**

If the tractor is able to maintain a minimum of 4 mph and the wheel slip is within the acceptable range, reduce implement draft by reducing depth or width.

POWER HOP

Under high drawbar loads, in certain soil conditions, MFWD and 4WD tractors may experience these simultaneous conditions:

- *Loss of traction*

- *Bouncing and pitching ride*

The occurrence of these two conditions at the same time is termed **power hop** (or wheel hop). Power hop may become so severe that the operator loses the ability to safely control the tractor. To regain control, the operator should reduce engine speed and/or reduce implement draft until power hop subsides. However, these actions are only a temporary measure. To permanently control power hop, the tractor ballast and tire inflation pressures should be adjusted as described under the previous TRACTOR PERFORMANCE section.

Power hop is strongly influenced by tractor weight split, amount and distribution of liquid ballast on each axle, and tire inflation pressures. If power hop is still present after following all the procedures outlined in the TRACTOR PERFORMANCE section, then the inflation pressure in the front tires should be raised in 2 psi increments until power hop subsides.

IMPORTANT: When raising the tire inflation pressure, do not exceed the tire manufacturer's recommended maximum inflation pressure rating. Make sure that all tires on an axle are inflated to the same pressure.

If power hop cannot be quelled following the previously outlined procedures, consult the tire manufacturer or the tractor manufacturer for additional guidance.

GREASE FITTINGS

Many of the bearings on today's machines are sealed with lubricant for the life of the bearing. Some bearings still require periodic lubrication, but these are few in relation to the number of lubrication points used on machines several years ago.

It is an easy task to grease your machine when it requires it (Fig. 55). Your operator's manual recommends how each bearing or shaft should be lubricated and how much. Usually, pictures tell you exactly where each fitting is located so that you will have no trouble finding them. Fittings on axles and wheels were covered earlier in this chapter.

Some grease fittings require daily or 10 hours service, while others are serviced at 50 or even 250 hour intervals. Common fittings which need daily service are on steering, clutch and brake mechanisms, especially the mechanical types.

If you don't lubricate the bearings or shafts when required, these parts will wear out prematurely. Grease is not expensive and repair costs will be saved by keeping the. machine properly lubricated.

Fig. 55 — Lubricating at Grease Fittings (Wipe Fitting Clean First)

OPERATION OF GREASE FITTINGS

When the grease gun is pushed down over the fitting, a seal is developed (Fig. 56). Pressure from the gun forces grease past a ball check valve in the head of the fitting. When the grease gun is removed, the check valve ball springs close to keep out dirt.

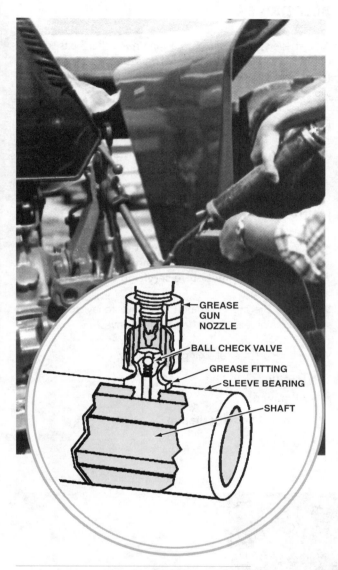

GREASE
GUN
NOZZLE

BALL CHECK VALVE

GREASE FITTING

SLEEVE BEARING

SHAFT

Fig. 56 — How Common Grease Fittings Operate

Some special fittings measure quantity or pressure, while others relieve excessive pressure, but these are not common on agricultural machines.

Grease Bank Systems

On some machines which have many fittings requiring regular lubrication, a central grease reservoir and pump is used. A few strokes of the pump forces grease through small individual tubes to each bearing. The reservoir must be kept filled, and each bearing should be inspected regularly to be sure grease is reaching all bearings.

To provide easier access for lubrication of some hard-to-reach bearings on certain machines, small tubes are installed from the bearings to a central easily-reached location on the machine. Individual grease fittings on each tube are filled with grease in the conventional manner. These systems cost less than the central-reservoir type, and it is easier to tell if each bearing is being greased.

Grease tubes in each of these systems must be protected from moving machine parts to avoid tube damage and loss of lubrication.

TYPES OF GREASE

The development of *multi-purpose grease* has made it possible for the machine operator to use one grease for almost all fittings and hand-packed bearings.

Many operator's manuals recommend wheel bearing grease for packing wheel bearings, but multi-purpose grease is now considered to be satisfactory for some wheel bearing lubrication.

RULES FOR LUBRICATING BEARINGS

If you follow the rules listed below, you can expect bearings and shafts to provide maximum service.

1. Always lubricate parts with recommended lubricant. Multi-purpose grease is satisfactory for most applications.

2. Use clean lubricants. Be sure to store lubricants in clean, air-tight containers.

3. Always wipe off dirt and grease fittings before attaching grease gun. After lubricating, wipe off excessive grease.

4. Hold grease gun directly in line with fitting while pumping slowly. Remove gun by swinging through a 30° arc.

5. Do not lubricate bearings too often. Sometimes excessive grease can leak onto other parts and damage them—for example, drive belts, brake linings and clutch linings.

6. Never apply too much pressure or lubricant to bearings with seals. You may rupture the seal, allowing grease to escape and dirt and moisture to enter bearing.

7. In cold weather, grease at the end of the day while the bearings are warm—they will accept grease more readily.

8. Make it a habit to grease your machine at the recommended intervals.

Fig. 57 — V-Belt Drive Using Multiple Belts

BELT DRIVES

Almost every power-driven machine has either belts, chains, or both. These drive components must be maintained to keep them from wearing out prematurely. Belts can stretch and slip — chains wear and rust.

First, let's look at the maintenance for belts.

⚠️ **CAUTION: Be sure to reinstall any guards or shields that are removed to adjust or replace belts.**

MAINTAINING V-BELTS

⚠️ **CAUTION: Never attempt to check or adjust belts while they are running. Always shut off the machine before servicing belts.**

V-belts are the most common belt drive today, so our main story on maintenance will be for these drives.

We will discuss the following about belts:

- **Tension**
- **Alignment**
- **Removal and Installation**
- **Wear**

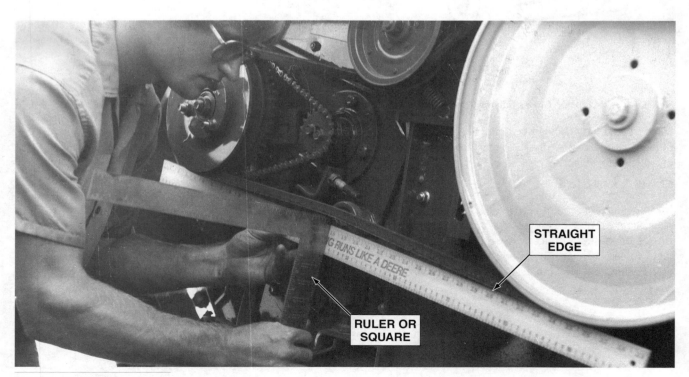

Fig. 58 — Checking Belt Tension

STRAIGHT EDGE

RULER OR SQUARE

Tools And Materials Needed

1. Wrenches (inch or metric, as required)

2. Straight Edge

3. Ruler (inch or metric, as required)

4. Spring Scale

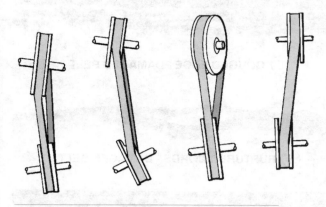

Fig. 59 — Sheaves Not Aligned Can Damage the V-Belt

Belt Tension

Proper belt tension is one of the most important things in maintaining belts.

Too little tension will cause slippage or slip-and-grab, causing the belt to break. If the belt does not break, slip will cause excessive cover wear, burned spots, and overheating.

Too much tension will cause belt heating and excessive stretch as well as damage to drive components, such as sheaves and shafts. The extra tightness will also place heavier loads on the bearings.

Remember that V-belts should ride on the sides of standard sheaves, not on the bottom of the groove.

Watch the tension on a new belt *during the first 24 hours of operation.* This is when the initial seating and stretch occurs.

Check belt tension by deflecting the belt on one side with a spring scale. Measure the deflection at the recommended pounds (kg) pull. Your operator's manual will give you this specification.

Another method is to depress the belt halfway between the sheaves and use a ruler at right angles to a straight edge to measure deflection (Fig. 58, right).

Fig. 60 — Check Alignment of Belt Sheaves

Belt And Sheave Alignment

Check sheave alignment regularly. Be sure that the shafts are parallel and the belt aligns with each sheave.

Common types of misalignment (exaggerated) are shown in Fig. 59. All are caused by shafts not parallel or sheaves not aligned.

To check alignment, place a straight edge between the sides of the sheaves (Fig. 60). The straight edge must touch the sheaves at the four arrows. Rotate the sheaves and check at different points. If variation is noticed, either the sheaves or shafts are bent. Replace the defective parts.

Belt Removal and Installation

Before removing any drive belt, loosen the tightener. *Do not force the belt off the sheaves.*

When installing any drive belt, loosen the tightener. Never force the belt onto the sheaves (Fig. 61). You may break the strength cords in the belt and weaken the belt so that it fails rapidly.

WRONG! NEVER FORCE BELT ON SHEAVE

Fig. 61 — Never Force a V-Belt onto a Sheave

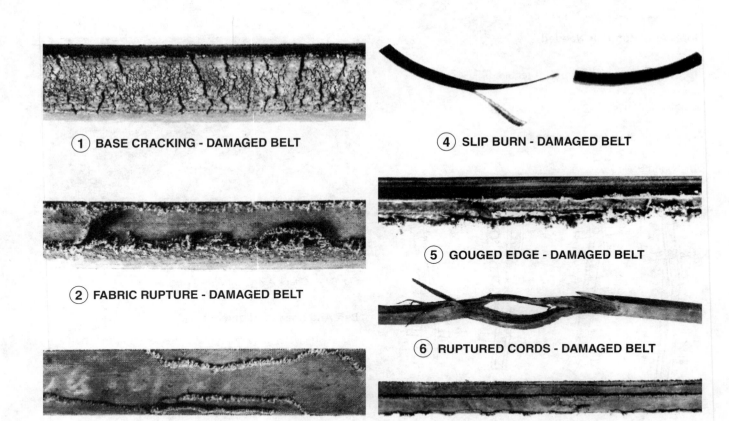

Fig. 62 — Examples of Wear on V-Belts

TROUBLESHOOTING V-BELT WEAR		
Symptom (Fig. 62)	Cause	Remedy
1. BASE CRACKING	Normal aging. Weather rotted inner fabric.	Replace belt.
2. FABRIC RUPTURE	Prying belt onto sheave. Worn Sheaves. Belt too tight.	Loosen belt tighteners before installing belt. Do not tighten belt too much. Also, replace belt.
3. COVER TEAR	Belt coming into contact with some part on machine.	Find interference and eliminate it.
4. SLIP BURN	Belt operated too loose. When operated under load, it finally grabbed and snapped.	Tighten belt properly. Also, replace belt.
5. GOUGED EDGE	Damaged sheave or interference from some part on machine.	Check condition of sheaves and check for interference. Also, replace belt.
6. RUPTURED CORDS	Driven sheave locked and drive sheave burned area of belt because belt would not rotate with sheave.	Avoid overloading drive and lubricate bearings to prevent bearing seizure. Also, replace belt.
7. WORN SIDES	Long operation without enough tension.	Check belt tension regularly and keep it properly tightened. Also, replace belt.

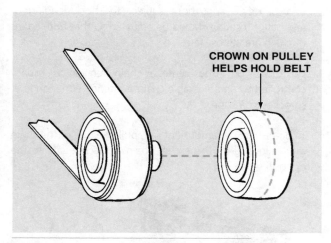

CROWN ON PULLEY HELPS HOLD BELT

Fig. 63 — A Crown Helps Keep Flat Belt on Pulley

Do not tighten the belt too much. Slight tension is always recommended on a V-belt.

On multiple belt drives, always replace all belts with a matched set of belts even though only one fails. Otherwise, the new belt may pull the whole load, because the older ones are probably stretched.

Troubleshooting V-Belt Wear

The examples shown in Fig. 62 will help you to recognize some of the signs of V-belt wear or damage.

The chart at right explains the causes of typical belt wear so that the problems can be corrected.

MAINTAINING FLAT BELTS

Many of the maintenance tips for V-belts also apply to flat belts.

Here are some of the rules:

1. Some flat belts, usually leather or canvas, may require belt dressings to prevent slippage and deterioration.

2. Flat belts normally need more tension than V-belts.

3. Pulley alignment is even more important with flat belts than for V-belts because flat belts can run off the pulley easier.

4. To install flat belts, move the power unit forward, place the belt on the pulleys, and back up carefully to tighten the belt. Start the belt slowly to make sure it is running straight before increasing the speed.

5. *Never force* a belt off a moving pulley.

CHAIN DRIVES

 CAUTION: Be sure to reinstall any guards or shields that are removed to adjust or replace chains.

Chain drives are used on some machines. They can eliminate the slippage that belt drives may give in some applications. Where timing is important, chains are often a must.

Because chains are under much stress, they must be maintained properly or they will fail in a short time.

Chain drives have one or more sprockets and an endless chain (Fig. 64).

One sprocket is normally mounted on a power shaft and is the driving sprocket for the complete drive. The second sprocket is driven in turn by the driving sprocket as shown.

A third sprocket may be used to adjust tension on the slack side of the chain.

We will discuss the following about chains:

* **Tension**

* **Lubrication**

* **Alignment**

* **Removal And Installation**

* **Wear**

* **Cleaning**

TOOLS AND MATERIALS NEEDED

1. Wrenches (inch or metric, as required)

2. Straight Edge

3. Lubricating Oil

4. Solvent

5. Container of Oil to Soak Chain

6. Chain Detaching Tool

CHAIN TENSION

Chain tension—or "slack"—is vital to the proper operation of chain drives. Unlike belts, chains require no initial tension and should *not* be tightened around the sprockets. Properly adjusted chain drives should permit slight flexing by hand in the slack strand of about two percent of the center distance (Fig. 65).

Too much tension causes the working parts to carry a much heavier load than is necessary and work much harder without delivering any more power. This causes rapid chain wear because of more pressures in the joints. In addition, shaft bearings are overloaded.

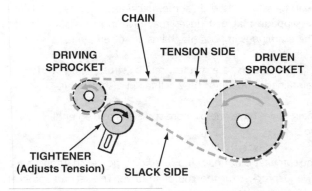

Fig. 64 — Parts of a Chain Drive

Too little tension is also harmful. On long centers, particularly, too much slack will cause vibration and chain whipping, reducing the life of the chain. On long centers, the slack strand should be supported or taken up by idler sprockets or guides.

Adjusting Chain Tension

 CAUTION: Never attempt to adjust chains while they are operating. Always shut off the machine before servicing chain.

To adjust chain tension:

1. For horizontal and inclined drives, should be about 1/4 inch per foot (2 mm shaft centers (with one side of chain taut).

2. Vertical drives and those subject to shock loading or reversal of rotation should be adjusted so that both spans of chain are almost taut.

3. For drives on fixed centers, chain tension is usually controlled by an adjustable chain tightener, either an idler sprocket or a shoe.

4. To determine the amount of sag, pull one side of the chain taut, allowing all the excess chain to accumulate in the opposite span.

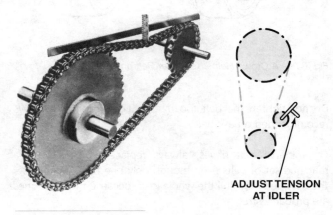

Fig. 66 — Adjusting Chains

5. Place a straight edge over the slack span and pull the chain down at the center (Fig. 66). Measure the amount of sag from the top of the chain to the underside of the straight edge.

6. If necessary, adjust the shaft centers or the tightener to provide the recommended amount of sag for proper chain slack.

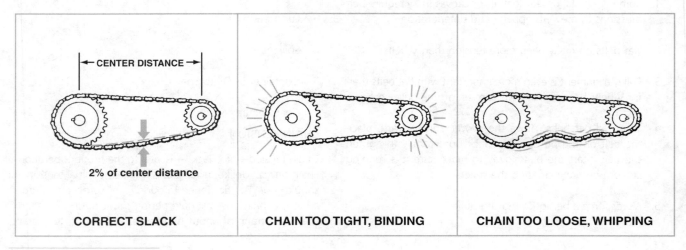

Fig. 65 — Chain Slack (Tension)

CHAIN LUBRICATION

Lubrication of chains is perhaps the most important factor in long service life. Running dry, exposed chains have been known to wear out in less than 200 hours. Manual lubrication can extend wear life three to ten times over life with no lubrication.

Dripping oil on the outside of the chain may not be enough. Oil must reach the vital bearing surfaces pointed out in Fig. 67, top. To do this, oil must penetrate the gap between the inside and outside plates of roller chains. This can be helped by oiling the chain while it is warm and then running it for a short time. Always oil the chain at quitting time each day, and let it set overnight.

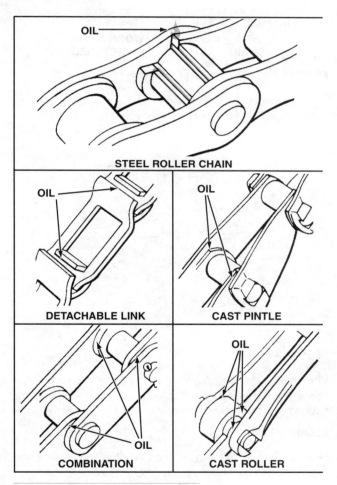

Fig. 67 — Lubrication Points on Chains

Chains which collect dirt and dust should still be oiled regularly. A "paste" of oil and dirt still wears less than dry dirt packed into the chain joints. Lubrication also helps prevent rust.

NOTE: For abrasive soil or sandy conditions, some manufacturers may not recommend lubrication of chains. However, this is the exception, not the rule.

CHAIN AND SPROCKET ALIGNMENT

Proper alignment of sprockets and shafts is necessary for maximum wear life. Rapid wear will result from misalignment due to rubbing of chain parts against sides of sprocket teeth and excessive friction wear in the joints caused by whipping and twisting of chains.

Align the sprockets axially on the shafts, using a straight edge (Fig. 68). Take care to apply the straight edge to a finished surface on the side of the sprocket. For long center distances, a stretched wire or cord can be used instead of a straight edge.

Fig. 68 — Alignment Sprockets Using a Straight Edge

CHAIN INSTALLATION

To couple the ends of a chain:

1. Loosen the tighteners to provide sufficient "working slack."

2. Bring the ends together over one sprocket, using the teeth to hold the chain.

3. Insert pin or pin link to couple chain into an endless strand (Fig. 69).

4. Adjust tighteners to provide proper tension for operation.

The above method is especially useful for coupling drive chains.

When it is necessary to couple long, heavy chain in the span between sprockets, draw the ends together with a block and tackle or other device. Then follow steps 3 and 4 above.

Keep chain straight when coupling. A link coupled when the chain is crooked may cause the chain to twist in operation.

To provide a solid back-up for the chain, assemble it in a straight line on the floor or a table. Then feed the chain onto its drive.

 CAUTION: Keep all chain guards and shields in place during operation.

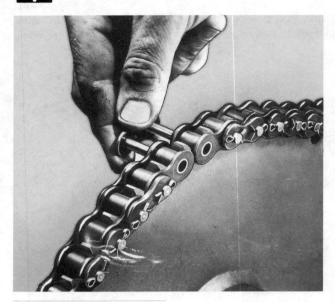

Fig. 69 — Installing Roller Chain

Chain Removal

The chain detacher is a convenient bench tool for uncoupling roller chain (Fig. 70). It is designed to prevent damage to the chain during disassembly.

The best rule when detaching any chain is: *Support the chain while detaching it.* This will avoid bending of links.

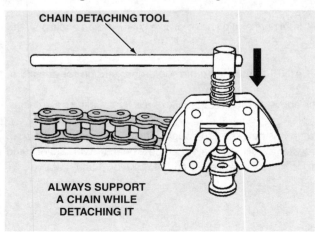

CHAIN DETACHING TOOL

ALWAYS SUPPORT
A CHAIN WHILE
DETACHING IT

Fig. 70 — Chain Detaching Tools for Roller Chain

CHAIN AND SPROCKET WEAR

As chains wear and stretch, they do not mate properly with their sprocket teeth. Badly worn roller chains ride so far out of the tooth pockets that they may be off the working faces (Fig. 71, right).

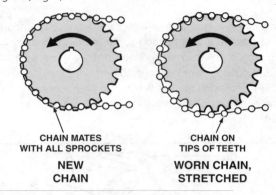

CHAIN MATES
WITH ALL SPROCKETS
**NEW
CHAIN**

CHAIN ON
TIPS OF TEETH
**WORN CHAIN,
STRETCHED**

Fig. 71 — Comparing New and Worn Roller Chains

As a rule, when a chain is worn until it has lengthened by three percent or more, it should be replaced.

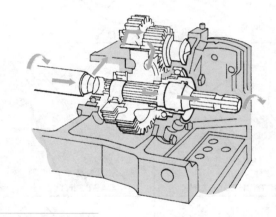

Fig. 72 — Gear Drive

When new chains are installed on excessively worn sprockets, the new chain will wear rapidly. Sprockets should be replaced or reversed if possible when the teeth develop a *hooked* appearance.

CLEANING CHAINS

Periodic cleaning of chains is good economy under even the best operating conditions. Follow these steps:

1. Remove chain from sprockets.

2. Wash chain in solvent.

3. Drain solvent and soak chain in oil.

4. Hang chain to drain off excess lubricant.

5. Install chain.

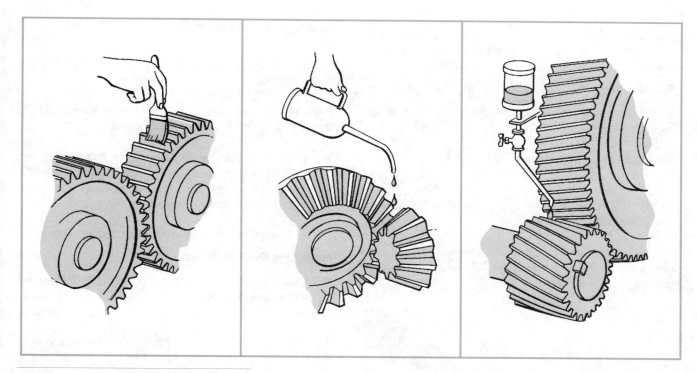

Fig. 73 — Three Ways of Lubricating Open Gears

GEAR DRIVES

Gears are the most common way to transmit power for heavier loads. With gears in mesh, all slippage is gone. Even the linkage of the chain is eliminated giving more power potential.

OPERATION

Chapter 7 on "Power Trains" covers the basic gear types and their uses. Refer to that chapter for the basics of gear drive operation.

This discussion will cover only the small open gear drives which require special lubrication or adjustment.

LUBRICATION OF GEARS

Gear lubricants range from simple mineral oils to complex formulas containing many ingredients.

For the type of oil to use, consult your machine operator's manual.

Common gear lubricants are:

SPUR GEARS—may use a good grade of petroleum oil—but not always.

BEVEL GEARS—may use an extreme-pressure (E.P.) lubricant.

WORM GEARS—may use an SCL lubricant, which offers even greater lubricant qualities.

Methods Of Lubricating Gears

Enclosed Gears (Chapter 7) are usually lubricated by the gears moving through a sump of oil and may have additional run-off troughs to lubricate the upper gears.

Open gears can be lubricated by:

1. Splash pan which the gears run through.

2. Hand lubrication by brushing or squirting with oil can (Fig. 73).

3. Automatic lubrication by a drip oiler.

Check the operator's manual for the proper intervals and types of lubricant.

ADJUSTING THE GEAR DRIVE

When a gear drive is operated, reaction loads from gears, etc. are transmitted to the bearings and the various parts deflect.

For this reason, the gear drive may periodically require adjustment for the proper fit between parts.

Three kinds of adjustments are used:

• **Backlash**—clearance or "play" between gears in mesh

• **Endplay**—end-to-end movement in a gear shaft due to bearing clearances

• **Preload**—a load within the bearings set up by adjustment

These adjustments should only be made following instructions in the machine service manual and using proper tools and equipment.

Backlash In Gears

Too much backlash in gear trains is the result of: 1) improper mesh between gears or 2) lack of support in bearings.

The result of too much backlash can be broken gear teeth or bouncing of gears under impact forces.

Backlash is often adjusted to a specified reading on, assembled gears (Fig. 74).

The dial indicator is mounted so that it registers the full rotary movement of the ring gear shown. To adjust the backlash reading, shims are often used.

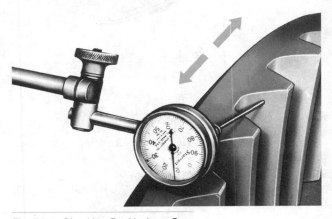

Fig. 74 — Checking Backlash on Gear

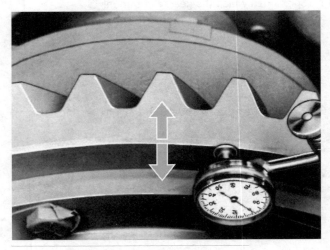

Fig. 75 — Checking Endplay on Gears And Shafts

Endplay In Gears And Shafts

Too much endplay is caused by lack of bearing support for the thrust produced by the gears rotating.

Preloading is often used to take up the slack and load the bearings.

To check endplay (Fig. 75), a dial indicator is mounted against the side of a gear or the end of a shaft. The gear or shaft is then pried in both directions and the readings noted. The difference between the two readings is the endplay.

Shims or adjusting nuts are widely used to adjust endplay.

Preloading Of Gear Drives

If the loads are heavy or the thrust too great, gear trains are often preloaded to reduce the deflection of parts. This preload must fit the design of the bearings and the strength of the parts.

If bearings are preloaded too tight, they will heat up and fail. If they are set too loose, the supporting parts will deflect too much, causing them to wear rapidly.

Gear drives are preloaded by shims, thrust washers, adjusting nuts, or by double-race bearings.

LIGHTING AND ELECTRICAL ACCESSORIES

This section covers some of the extra equipment which completes the electrical system on machines.

The basic electrical system was covered in Chapter 6 on batteries and charging, starting, and ignition circuits.

Now let's fill in the remainder of the system with the lighting and other electrical accessories:

- **Lighting Circuits**
- **Circuit Breakers and Fuses**
- **Wiring Harnesses**
- **Gauges**
- **Meters**
- **Switches**
- **Electric Motors**
- **Cigarette Lighters**
- **Stereo Tape Players**

Fig. 76 — Lighting on a Combine

FLOOD LAMP

WARNING LAMPS

DUAL-BEAM
HEADLIGHTS

JOHN DEERE

WARNING LAMPS

FLOOD
LAMPS

TAIL LIGHTS

Fig. 77 — Lighting on a Tractor

Let's take a closer look at each of these accessories.

LIGHTING CIRCUITS

Lights are used on most modern agricultural machines. They are required by state or local governments for night driving or towing in most areas. To avoid trouble, know your local regulations.

On modern machines, the lights are often two or four headlights and one taillight (Fig. 77). This usually requires a 12-volt system.

In addition, a flashing warning lamp or lamps is required in most states. This lamp warns other traffic that a slow-moving vehicle is on the road. A slow-moving vehicle (SMV) emblem is also required in many states (Fig. 77).

On many agricultural implements, special lighting is used for night work in the field. On a self-propelled combine, for example, a special flood lamp is used to light up the area where the grain is being cut and fed into the combine (Fig. 76). Another flood lamp shows the operator when the grain tank is full of grain.

Layout Of The Lighting Circuit

The lighting circuit is normally a part of the complete electrical system. It operates on power from the battery with help from the charging circuit.

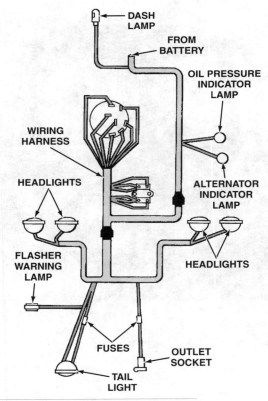

Fig. 78 — Layout of a Typical Lighting Circuit

The parts of a typical lighting circuit are shown in Fig. 78. They are the various *lamps* which are operated by a *light switch*. The switch is connected to the battery or charging circuit by the *wiring harness*. Other accessories shown are an electrical outlet socket and indicator lamps. The circuit is protected from a current overload by the *circuit breakers* and *fuses*.

On most machines, the starter switch must be turned on before the lights can be operated by light switch.

Also, some machines have indicator lamps which light up when the starter switch is turned on and then go out when the engine is running, showing that the alternator, oil pressure, etc., are normal.

On machines with two or four batteries, a "split-load" lighting circuit is sometimes used. This divides the load equally between both batteries, when the lights are turned on.

Lamps

Lamps used for lighting of modern machines are:

- *Sealed-beam units (for headlights and flood lamps)*
- *Light bulbs (for other lights)*

Sealed-Beam Units

Headlights and flood lamps are normally sealed-beam units.

The headlights throw out a high-intensity beam and should always be dimmed when approaching a vehicle at night.

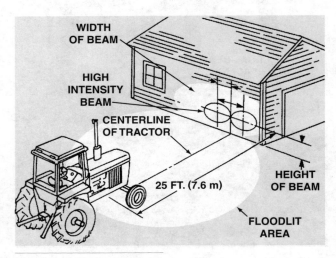

Fig. 79 — Adjusting Headlights

Adjusting Headlights

When headlights are used on public roads, be sure they are adjusted so that the glare of the lights will not shine into the eyes of approaching drivers.

Adjusting the headlights on a typical tractor is shown in Fig. 79. This procedure ban be used for other machines also.

Position the machine, as shown, on level ground squarely facing a wall 25 feet (7.5 m) away.

Turn the headlights on "bright" and check the height of the beams on the wall. The centers of the light beams should be I to 4 feet (0.3 to 1.2 m) high, depending upon the height of the headlights. Keep the intense part of the beams at least 5 inches (15 cm) below the center of the light from which it comes.

The headlights should also be parallel to the tractor centerline. Look down the center of the machine to see if the centers of the beams are at equal distances from the centerline (about four feet [1.2 m] apart or two feet [0.6 m] off center on most tractors).

On machines with dual headlights, also check the outer flood lamps on "dim" to see that they shine downward and outward to illuminate the desired area as shown in Fig. 79.

To adjust the lights, loosen the lamp mounting bracket and rotate them as desired. Then retighten the mounting bracket. *Remember: Only the lamp mounting bracket is adjustable-not the sealed-beam unit itself.*

On other machines with headlights mounted higher than those on a tractor, always adjust the lamps downward far enough to avoid glare to oncoming traffic.

Light Bulbs

Miscellaneous lights such as tail lights, dash lamps, and indicator lamps are normally equipped with single- or double-contact bulbs.

When replacing bulbs, use the same style and part number as the old one. Otherwise, the system can be damaged or the bulb may burn out rapidly.

Special light bulbs for special lighting effects may be required for some tail lights, flasher lamps, or indicator lamps.

Indicator lamps are often used in place of gauges for generator, oil pressure, and temperature checks.

If the indicator lamp lights up or glows while the engine is running this shows a failure in the system being monitored. For example, an oil pressure light may glow when the engine is low on oil.

When an indicator lamp comes on, be sure to stop the engine at once and check out the possible causes. But also remember that a burned-out indicator lamp never lights up, even while the engine is being ruined!

Failures of Lamps

Failure of lamps may be caused by a defective unit a broken wire, a disconnected wire, a corroded connection, a switch failure or an open circuit breaker.

To check a light bulb, visual inspection is best. A good bulb will be clear while a burned-out bulb may be dark. Where the bulb glass is not dark, the filament wire will be visible. If it is broken, the bulb is defective.

To check a lighting circuit, test the faulty part for voltage drop. If you don't have a voltmeter, take the machine to a service shop for testing.

If the voltage is correct but the lamp is dim, look for a poor wiring connection between the lamp and the main wiring harness. Also check for a poor ground at the lamp mounting. Remember that the frame of the machine serves as the ground and good contact must be made to complete the circuit.

If there is no voltage across the lamp, look for a broken wire, poor contact in the light switch, or a disconnected wiring connector. Replace or repair any defective parts.

If the lights all go out suddenly, check for a tripped circuit breaker or a blown fuse. For details, see "Circuit Breakers" and "Fuses" later in this section.

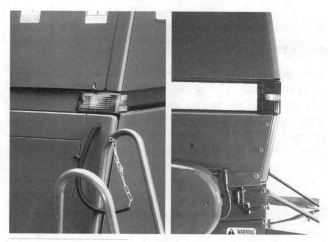

Fig. 80 — Flashing Lamp

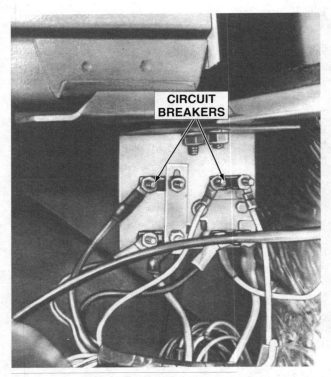

Fig. 81 — Circuit Breakers for a Lighting Circuit

Flashing Lamps

When a flashing warning lamp (Fig. 80) is prohibited by local regulations, disconnect the flasher unit and the short wire connected to the flasher. (See the operator's manual.) If you want to burn the warning lamp continually, connect the wire from the lamp directly into the lighting circuit wiring harness.

CIRCUIT BREAKERS

A circuit breaker (Fig. 81) protects an electrical circuit from current overload. The breaker acts as a switch and opens when the current passing through the circuit exceeds the rated level. The breaker may close automatically, after the switch is shut off for a short period. Some breakers have to be closed manually. Both automatic and manual reset circuit breakers are used in electrical systems.

In general, circuit breakers are used when heavy loads may be instantly placed on the circuit.

To check for a defective circuit breaker, use an ohmmeter or a voltmeter. If an ohmmeter is used, a good circuit breaker will show zero resistance.

A defective breaker will show full resistance. If a voltmeter is used, and the circuit breaker is defective, the battery side will show voltage and the load side will not.

Again, if you don't have these instruments, take the machine to a service shop for testing.

Some circuit breakers are equipped with a reset opening. When the breaker trips, it may be reset by inserting a small wire in the opening and pushing against the spring tension (Fig. 82).

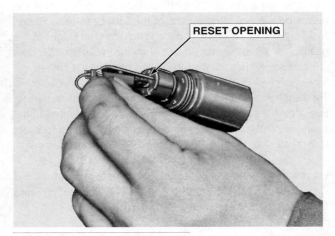

Fig. 82 — Resetting a Circuit Breaker

FUSES

Fuses protect an electrical circuit from current overload. When too much current passes through the circuit, the fuse blows, breaking the flow of current and preventing damage to the circuit.

A fuse consists of fine wire or thin metal strip enclosed in glass or fire-resistant material. Most fuses used for modern agricultural and industrial equipment are automotive blade types. They have a contact on each end and are held in place in a fuse holder or panel (Fig. 83). The holder is usually a two-piece tube which can be easily separated for installing or replacing fuses. The fuse panel is a plastic or fiber board which contains many fuses. The panel keeps the fuses in one place and aids in fuse replacement.

Blown fuses are usually caused by:

1. A short circuit in the electrical circuit caused by defective wiring or a defective component (lights, motor, etc.).

2. An overload in the circuit caused by a surge of electricity passing through the circuit.

3. Poor contacts in the electrical circuit or the components.

4. Overheating in the circuit caused by overloads or poor contacts.

5. Use of incorrect size fuses in the circuit.

6. Fuse located too near a hot area such as an engine or a heater.

7. Vibrations near the fuse, causing the contacts to come loose.

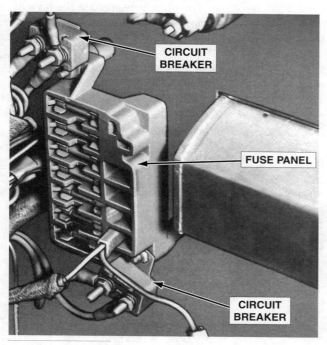

Fig. 83 — Fuse Panel

Types of Fuses

Two types of fuses are widely used in machine electrical circuits:

- *Quick-blowing fuses*
- *Slow-blowing fuses*

A QUICK-BLOWING fuse blows instantly whenever a too-heavy load occurs.

A SLOW-BLOWING fuse will allow an overload for a short period before it blows.

Finding Cause Of Blown Fuse

By looking at a blown fuse, you can often tell what failure in the circuit caused it to blow.

Refer to Fig. 84 for a general check for causes of blown out fuses-whether from overload or from short circuit.

QUICK-BLOWING FUSES:

If an *overload*—glass case will be clear because fuse link overheats and simply melts away.

If a *short circuit*—glass will be dark, stained by the fuse link which suddenly "burns up."

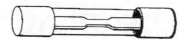

QUICK-BLOWING FUSE

- **If blown from overload glass will be clear.**
- **If blown from short circuit glass will be dark.**

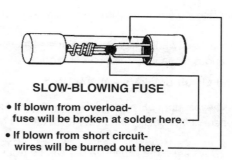

SLOW-BLOWING FUSE

- **If blown from overload-fuse will be broken at solder here.**
- **If blown from short circuit-wires will be burned out here.**

Fig. 84 — Determining the Cause of a Blown Fuse

SLOW-BLOWING FUSES:

If an *overload*—fuse link will break at solder, which has melted.

If a *short circuit*—fuse link will break at small wires because of sudden heat.

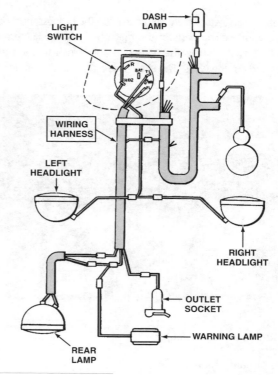

Fig. 85 — Wiring Harness

Remember that a fuse is meant to protect against overloads. It will also protect against short circuits, but these are abnormal and should be repaired at once.

If a quick-blowing fuse tends to blow out frequently due to small overloads, replace it with a slow-blowing type of the same size.

If the fuse still keeps on blowing, the circuit is overloaded and is not meant to handle the loads being placed on it.

Always replace a blown fuse with one of the same size.

Never use a fuse with a higher amperage rating as it may result in serious damage to the circuit it protects.

Fuses And Circuit Breakers—Where Used

Fuses are cheaper but not reusable. So they are used mainly in circuits where "blow outs" from heavy loads are not common.

Circuit breakers are more expensive but can be reset without replacement. So they are used in heavy-duty circuits where sudden heavy loads are expected—or where safety is a factor.

WIRING HARNESSES

A wiring harness is the trunk and branches which feed the electrical circuit. Wiring leads from one part of the circuit enter the trunk or sheath, joining other wires, and then emerge at another point in the circuit (Fig. 85). The harness sheath is normally made of rubber, cloth, electrical tape, or plastic tubing.

Be careful when installing a wiring harness. The harness must not interfere with moving parts of the machine. Also make certain that the clips which hold the harness do not pinch through the harness and cut the wires. This can cause a short in the circuit.

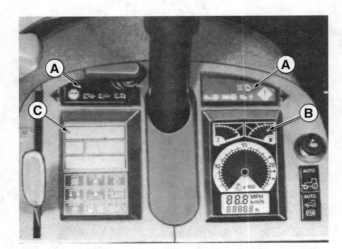

A—Warning Indicator Lamps
B—Tachometer
C—Performance Monitor

Fig. 86 — Transmission-Hydraulic System Filter Covers

Individual wires in a harness may be replaced by cutting off the defective wire at each end of the harness. Discard the removed ends of the wire. Run the new wire around the harness; do not try to thread the wire through the harness. Place the new wire in clips with the harness or attach to the harness with electrical tape.

The proper gauge or size of an electrical wire depends upon:

1. *Total length of the wire in circuit.*

2. *Total amperes that the wire will carry.*

But when replacing a defective wire in a circuit, remember:

Always use the same or heavier gauge of wire for replacement. Never use an undersized wire because it will not carry the required load and will overheat.

GAUGES

Gauges are used on modern machines to keep the operator informed on the various functions of the machine systems (Fig. 86).

Examples of these gauges are: fuel gauge, water temperature gauge, and oil pressure gauge.

The fuel gauge is controlled by a sensing unit located in the fuel tank and the water temperature gauge and oil pressure gauge are controlled by sensing units located in the engine radiator and cylinder block.

The sensing units are all variable resistance types and operate the gauges as follows:

The higher the water temperature, oil pressure, or level of fuel, the lower (or higher) the resistance in the sensing unit. This change in resistance causes more (or less) current to pass through the connecting wire to the gauge coil, which in turn causes a new reading on the gauge.

Diagnosis Of Gauge Failures

Circuits for three common gauges are shown in Fig. 87.

Diagnose the failures of gauges as given below.

If a gauge does not register, the cause could be:

1. Lack of current to the gauge.

2. Poor ground connection.

3. Connecting wire grounded to implement.

4. A defective sensing unit or gauge.

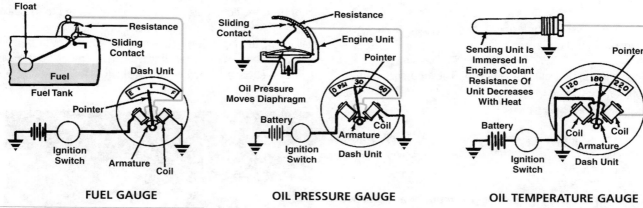

FUEL GAUGE **OIL PRESSURE GAUGE** **OIL TEMPERATURE GAUGE**

Fig. 87 — Three Gauges And Their Circuits

If a gauge consistently registers too high, the cause could be:

1. Poor connection between gauge and connecting wire.

2. Broken connecting wire.

3. Poor ground at sensing unit.

4. Failure of gauge or sensor, usually the sensor.

If you cannot determine the cause of the failure, take the machine to a service shop for testing. If you find that a gauge or sensing unit is defective, replace it.

Indicator lamps often use small light bulbs which glow to tell of a failure.

If these lamps do not glow when the starter switch is turned on before starting the engine, first check for a defective bulb. Then, if necessary, check out the other causes given above. (Normally, the lamps should glow when the switch is turned on, then go out shortly after the engine starts—unless there is a problem.)

METERS

Ammeters

The ammeter is an instrument for measuring the strength of an electrical current in terms of amperes.

Normally the ammeter is connected directly to the regulator in series to measure the flow of current through the electrical system.

A typical ammeter consists of a moving magnet with attached needle placed close to a conductor between the ammeter terminals. Current flow through the conductor creates a magnetic field that deflects away from zero on the meter scale.

If an ammeter does not register correctly, replace it with a new ammeter. Do not attempt to repair a defective ammeter.

Voltmeters

Voltmeters are used to indicate the voltage of the electrical input in a circuit (see Fig. 86).

A typical voltmeter consists of a needle attached to a moving iron vane placed inside two stationary coils. The coil winding is parallel with the needle pivot and one winding tends to keep the needle at zero while the other tends to move the needle to the full scale deflection.

Voltmeters are connected in parallel with the voltage to be measured. Since the voltmeter has a high resistance, adding this component to the circuit will change the total circuit current very little, and the voltage reading obtained shows the true voltage present without the meter in the circuit.

If a voltmeter does not function properly, a new voltmeter must be installed. A defective voltmeter cannot be repaired.

Electric Hour Meter

Electric hour meters are used to show the operating time of a machine while the engine is operating at its rated speed (see Fig. 86).

The hour meter records the time in hours and only operates when the engine is running.

Do not attempt to repair a defective hour meter or its sending unit. When they fail, new components must be installed.

SWITCHES

A switch is a device which opens, closes, or directs current in an electrical circuit.

All switches do basically the same job. The difference is in the way they are operated.

Servicing of Switches

If a switch is defective, always replace it with a new switch. *Do not try to repair a defective switch. It is usually cheaper and safer to replace it.*

IMPORTANT: Always be sure to replace a defective switch with a switch of the same electrical rating. A switch with too high or too low a rating can bum out an electrical circuit.

ELECTRIC MOTORS

Small d.c. electrical motors are used to perform auxiliary functions on some machines. For example, motors are used to operate air conditioner blower, ventilating and heating fans (Fig. 88) and windshield wipers.

Take defective motors, to a good electrical shop for servicing by trained technicians.

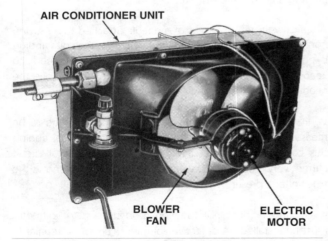

Fig. 88 — Electric Motor Used to Operate Air Conditioner Blower Fan

CIGARETTE LIGHTERS

The cigarette lighter contains a heating element which contacts the electrical circuit when the lighter is pushed in. This causes the element to heat up and glow. The element will remain heated long enough to permit lighting a cigarette or cigar.

The lighter employs a circuit breaker to cut off the electrical current to the lighter element when it has heated to its peak.

Failure of the cigarette lighter may be caused by a broken wire, disconnected wire, burned-out element, defective lighter shell, or a tripped circuit breaker.

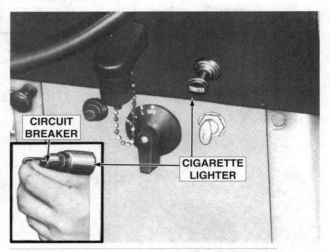

Fig. 89 — Resetting Circuit Breaker on Cigarette Lighter

Some circuit breakers on lighters are equipped with a reset opening (Fig. 89). If the lighter fails to operate, the circuit breaker may be open and must be reset.

To do this, insert a small wire in the small hole in the end of the lighter as shown and push in against the spring tension.

If a lighter has a burned-out element or a defective shell, these parts must be replaced.

STEREO TAPE PLAYER

1. It the operator's cab is equipped with a stereo tape player, clean the tape head occasionally. After many hours of operation, brownish colored oxides from the tapes will accumulate on the tape head (Fig. 90).

2. To remove this accumulation, use a non-abrasive cleaning cartridge as instructed on the cartridge.

3. If a cleaning cartridge is not available, use a cotton swab soaked with isopropyl (rubbing) alcohol.

4. Press on the motor switch with a pencil when cleaning the capstan. Clean the channel switch contacts also.

IMPORTANT: Do not use any other solvents or cleaners unless they are specifically designed for cleaning tape heads. **NEVER** use anything that would scratch or mar the tape head. Do not use a magnetized tool on the switch. The tape head may become magnetized and increased background noise and loss of high frequency response will result. When this happens, use a demagnetizer at the tape head as instructed by the manufacturer.

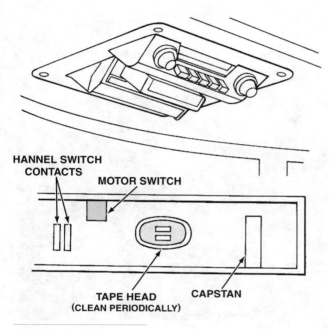

HANNEL SWITCH
CONTACTS
MOTOR SWITCH
TAPE HEAD
(CLEAN PERIODICALLY)
CAPSTAN

Fig. 90 — Tape Player Head

CLEANING THE MACHINE

The operator's manual may not mention cleaning the machine. However, regular cleaning will pay off in pride, protection against dirt and chemicals, extra safety, and in general longer life for the equipment.

Paint can be damaged by long exposure to oil, grease, fertilizers, and sprays.

Grease and oil can accumulate and collect dirt which works its way into bearings and other precision parts. Grease on steps and handholds is also a safety hazard.

Cleaning also helps reveal leaks in the cooling system, engine blocks, hydraulic lines, and other parts.

Thoroughly clean the entire machine at least once each year or at the end of the working season. Also clean the machine when it gets very dirty or muddy or when it has been used around chemicals such as fertilizers or crop sprays.

TOOLS AND MATERIALS NEEDED

1. Commercial degreaser, (solvent)

2. Small spray gun

3. Putty knife

4. Screwdriver

5. Cleaning cloths

6. Paintbrush and soap

7. Set of open-end wrenches (inch or metric, as required)

8. Pail

9. Water hose equipped with nozzle

10. Wire brush

11. Face and eye protection

HOW TO CLEAN THE MACHINE

IMPORTANT: Never pressure spray or hose a diesel engine while the engine is running as the injection pump can be damaged.

There are two ways of cleaning the machine on the farm:

- **Commercial degreaser (solvent)**
- **Diesel fuel**

Either method is effective, but the degreaser is somewhat faster and does a better job of cleaning the hard-to-reach places. Neither means is satisfactory for removing mud or other substances that do not contain oil or grease. *(Do not use gasoline. It is an extremely bad fire hazard.)*

Degreasers are available in small spray cans, or you can buy a more concentrated form in quantities of a quart to a gallon or more (Fig. 91). The concentrated degreaser is by far the least expensive since you can dilute it with five to ten parts of diesel fuel. The cleaner your machine, the more dilution you can use. A gallon of the concentrate is enough to clean your machine several times.

SMALL PRESSURE SPRAY CAN

BULK CONCENTRATE (DILUTE BEFORE APPLICATION)

Fig. 91 — Degreasers are Available in Small Pressure Cans or Bulk Concentrate

If you are using a degreaser, check the instructions on the can. Some are flammable and are dangerous if used in a closed building or near a flame. Materials under pressure also have additional hazards. Such chemicals could be hazardous to skin or eyes. Wear rubber gloves and eye protection.

The procedures for using degreasers or diesel fuel are as follows:

1. Allow machine to cool, if it has been running.

   A hot engine will evaporate the cleaning solvent, but an engine that is warm to your touch can be cleaned most easily.

2. Remove hood, side panels, and PTO shields if necessary to reach accumulated dirt.

   This may not be necessary if most of your machine engine is exposed.

Fig. 92 — Use a Putty Knife to Remove Heavy Accumulations of Grease and Grime (PTO Shields Removed for Cleaning)

3. Use a putty knife to remove heavy accumulations of grease and grime (Fig.92).

   This will save time and solvent.

4. Apply solvent on areas that need cleaning (Fig. 93).

   If you are using a *degreaser* (unless it is in a pressure-type can) apply it with a paint sprayer or insect spray gun in order to get a thin well-distributed film. Apply liberally until the surface has a moist appearance.

   If you are using a *diesel fuel* without a degreaser, apply with a paintbrush to help get penetration.

Fig. 93 — Apply Solvent on Areas that Need Cleaning (PTO Shields Removed for Cleaning)

5. Let solvent set approximately 15 minutes.

   This gives the solvent time to do an effective job of penetrating and loosening the grease and oil particles.

6. Remove solvent from engine and other surfaces.

   With a *degreaser* use a strong stream of water (Fig. 94). Avoid spraying into vents and air intakes. Continue to flush until all milky substance is removed from machine.

   If you use *diesel fuel*, remove it with a strong soap and water solution applied with a paintbrush, then flush it off with water.

7. Check for places you have missed.

You may have to use a rag or wire brush to remove some accumulations that did not flush off. Small spots that look dirty while the machine is wet may appear clean enough after drying.

8. Replace the hood and panels that were removed originally.

9. Wipe the machine surfaces dry.

Fig. 94 — Degreaser is Removed with a Strong Water Spray

TEST YOURSELF

QUESTIONS

1. Paper air filters may be cleaned in any good detergent.
   True_____ False_____

2. (Fill in the blanks.) If _____ appear in the sight glass of an air conditioner, the refrigerant level is low.

3. Explain how a wheel bearing should be adjusted for tightness.

4. Match the following items covering tires with the correct corresponding item.
   A. Overinflation   1. Spinning Wear
   B. Underinflation   2. Center Tread Wear
   C. Operator Abuse   3. Side Tread Wear

5. When rear tractor tires have the proper weight, what is the correct slippage rate?

6. Name the three major items that must be considered in order to properly set up a tractor?

7. The tire inflation pressure does not need to be the same in all tires on the same axle in order for optimum tractor performance to be achieved.
   True_____ False_____

8. What should you do just before attaching a grease gun to a grease fitting?

9. What are two effects of tightening a belt drive excessively?

10. Name three reasons for lubricating chains.

11. Which one of the reasons shown below may have caused a quick-blowing fuse to blow if the glass of the fuse is clear?
    A. Overload   B. Short Circuit   C. Open Circuit

12. (Fill in the blanks.) The proper gauge or size of an electrical wire depends upon the _____ of the wire in circuit and the _____ that the wire will carry.

TUNE-UP AND STORAGE

ENGINE TUNE-UP

Engine tune-up is probably the most important preventive maintenance that can be performed on a machine. However, most operators make the *mistake of performing tune-up only when the engine is not running satisfactorily.* This is often a costly error because at this point the engine may be worn or damaged until it requires major repair or overhaul. Not only could these costly repairs be avoided by good maintenance, but operating costs could also be saved.

WHAT IS TUNE-UP?

Tune-up is the process of making checks and minor adjustments to improve the operation of the engine.

Tune-up is also *preventive maintenance.* Troubles can be caught early and prevented by checking out the engine before it actually fails.

WHEN SHOULD AN ENGINE BE TUNED?

Regularly! The intervals for tune-up may vary from 500 to 1000 hours or each spring and fall, depending upon the operating conditions. But *regularity* is the key to tuning the engine so that major problems are prevented.

A badly worn engine cannot be tuned up. This is why the engine should first be checked to see if:

1) *A tune-up will restore it, or*

2) *Major overhaul is needed.*

Let's go through a visual inspection and dynamometer test first and then we'll see how tune-up follows it.

VISUAL INSPECTION

By inspecting the engine before tuning it, you can learn a lot about its general condition.

Check out the following items:

1. **Oil and Water Leakage**

   Inspect the engine for any oil or water leaks. If the engine has been using too much oil, this often means an external oil leak. If the engine overheats, look for leaks in the cooling system.

2. **Electrical System**

   Inspect the *battery* for corrosion, cracked case, or leaks at the cell covers.

   Remove the cell caps and examine the tops of the battery plates (Fig. 2). If they are covered with a. chalky deposit, this means one of three things:

   1) Electrolyte level has been too low.

   2) Battery charge has been too low, causing sulfation.

   3) Battery was charged at too high a rate, boiling out water.

   Any of these conditions can reduce the life of the battery. If they have gone too far, the battery must be replaced.

   Check the *battery cables and connections* for damage and looseness.

Fig. 1 — Tune-Up is Making Checks and Minor Adjustment

Fig. 2 — Visual Inspection Helps Indicate Whether a Tune-Up or Overhaul is Needed

Be sure the cables are the right size. Many complaints of poor starting can be traced to battery cables that are too small.

To check for this, operate the starter with the engine cold. If the battery cable gets hot, the cable is probably too small.

Inspect the *wiring harnesses*. If they are too oil-soaked, frayed, or corroded, replace them.

On spark-ignition engines, check the *distributor* for a cracked cap, excessive grease, or other damage.

Check the operation of the alternator or generator *gauge* or *voltmeter*. It should light or register when the starter switch is turned on.

Failure can be due to a burned-out bulb, an incomplete circuit, or the alternator or generator is not producing current; (Lack of current to the battery will show up as a discharged battery.)

If the oil pressure light does not go out, or the gauge doesn't register normal when the engine is running, stop the engine at once and find the cause. Check for low oil level in the crankcase, or a short circuit in the line from sensor to gauge or light.

Stop the engine at once and find the cause.

Lack of engine oil pressure can result in failure of expensive parts inside the engine due to lack of lubrication.

3. Cooling System

Wait until the engine has been idle for several hours and the crankcase oil is cold; then loosen the crankcase drain plug and carefully turn it out to see if any water seeps out. If water is present, locate the cause of the cooling system leak.

Inspect the cooling system for leaks, deteriorated hoses, bent or clogged radiator fins, slipping fan belt, or any other condition which could result in improper cooling.

4. Air Intake System

Inspect the air intake system for possible leaks or restrictions. If the proper amount of clean air does not reach the engine, performance and durability will be affected.

VISUAL INSPECTION CHECKLIST

❐ **OIL AND WATER LEAKAGE**

❐ **ELECTRICAL SYSTEM**
- **Battery**
- **Cables**
- **Wiring**
- **Indicator Lights**

❐ **COOLING SYSTEM**
- **Water in Crankcase**
- **External Leaks**
- **Clogging**

❐ **AIR INTAKE SYSTEM**
- **Air Leaks**
- **Restrictions**

❐ **FUEL SYSTEM**
- **Leaks**
- **Restrictions**
- **Clogged Filter**

❐ **STEAM CLEANING**

---

5. Fuel System

Check the fuel system for leaks and for bent or dented lines, which might cause a restriction.

Check the fuel transfer pump sediment bowl. On diesel engines, inspect the fuel filters for dirt, water, or other foreign matter.

6. Steam Cleaning

After checking for leaks, steam clean the engine. This not only helps to recondition the engine, it makes tune-up easier and troubles easier to spot.

DYNAMOMETER TESTS

If possible, test the engine on a dynamometer both *before* and *after* it is turned. Before tune-up, this test gives you the horsepower (kilowatt) output and fuel consumption of the engine as it is. This will help you to determine if a tune-up can restore the engine or whether an overhaul is needed. After tune-up, a dynamometer test will also let you measure the engine's improvement.

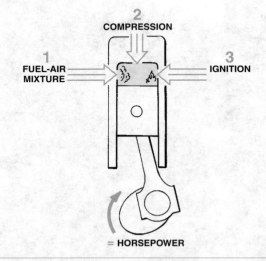

Fig. 3 — Three Basic Things are Needed to Produce Engine Horsepower

Good performance by the engine depends on these basic things:

1) **Adequate supply of clean air and fuel**

2) **Good compression**

3) **Proper valve and ignition timing for good combustion.**

Failure or low performance on any of these factors (Fig. 3) makes it impossible to fully restore the engine.

Therefore, if the dynamometer test shows that any of these three factors is bad—as shown by low power—the engine will have to be reconditioned.

Make the dynamometer test as follows:

1. Connect the machine to the dynamometer (Fig. 4) using the manufacturer's instructions.

2. Operate the engine at about one-half load until the coolant and crankcase oil temperatures are up to normal. (This will take about 30 minutes—*but is very important to a good test.*)

3. Gradually increase the load on the engine until its speed is reduced to rated load speed as given in the engine Technical Manual.

4. Read the horsepower (kilowatts) on the dynamometer.

5. Compare the power with that given in the engine Technical Manual.

However, do not expect engines to always equal these specifications. But if the engine rates much lower than normal, this is a signal that service is needed.

NOTE: Shop dynamometers cannot be expected to give results on tractors which match the Nebraska tests, for these tests are run under only the most ideal conditions.

While the engine is operating under load, note the outlet of the crankcase ventilating system. If too much vapor appears, also remove the crankcase oil filler cap.

If an excessive amount of vapor or smoke appears here as well as at the vent, there is blow-by in the engine cylinders and they must be reconditioned before the engine will perform at its best.

NOTE: Instruments are available to measure the flow of air and gases through the crankcase ventilating system.

The normal rate of engine vapor flow is specified in the engine Technical Manual.

Any increase in flow over the specified amount indicates crankcase blow-by.

If the blow-by is excessive, have the engine reconditioned for good operation.

Even though the engine develops its rated power using a normal amount of fuel, a tune-up may still improve its efficiency. Consider both hours of operation and the conditions under which the engine has been operated. It is far more economical in the long run to tune the engine *before* a lack of performance makes it mandatory.

Remember: Most manufacturers suggest a regular period of operation between tune-ups, such as spring and fall, or every 500 or 1000 hours of operation.

Fig. 4 — Dynamometer Tests Before Engine Tune-Up

ENGINE TUNE-UP CHART

The following chart gives a capsule of the steps necessary to tune your engine at the recommended intervals. Where they apply, the chapter and page in this text is given for the details of the procedure.

If, after performing these tune-up steps, the engine fails to respond properly, have a service shop make further tests. The engine may require adjustments or repairs that you are not able to perform because of the special tools and knowledge required.

Step No.	Operation	Chapter	Page
1. AIR INTAKE AND EXHAUST SYSTEM			
	❐ Clean out precleaner (if used)	2	12
	❐ Remove and clean air cleaner	2	12
	❐ Inspect exhaust system and muffler	2	22
	❐ Check crankcase ventilating system for restrictions	2	25

Fig. 5 — Dynamometer Tests After Engine Tune-Up

DYNAMOMETER TESTS AFTER TUNE-UP

The dynamometer test is the final check of overall engine performance after tune-up. It will tell you whether the tune-up has been adequate. Compare it with the dynamometer test made before tune-up.

Test for the following things:

1. *Engine Horsepower (kilowatts)*

2. *Exhaust Analysis*
   Smoke Analysis (Diesel)
   Carburetor adjustment (spark-ignition)

3. *Fuel Consumption*

4. *Crankcase Blow-By*

Most dynamometer manufacturers have instruments to be used with the dynamometer for checking the above items.

Use the engine Technical Manual for procedures and specifications.

NOTE: If the engine fails to produce the desired power, and an air cleaner restriction test was not made at the beginning, make one now. It is possible that an air restriction is causing the loss of horsepower.

A completely tuned engine should pass the dynamometer test with no problems.

However, the engine should not put out *more power* than it was designed for. Tampering, with the engine to get extra power will shorten engine life and raise operating costs. It may also void the engine warranty.

SUMMARY: ENGINE TUNE-UP

Tune-up of an engine may seem like a long ordeal.

Actually, most of the items can be checked in a minute or two.

But why check out so many items if the engine has not actually failed?

The answer is that **tune-up is preventive maintenance.**

Before the engine fails, we keep it tuned up so that causes of future failures are corrected early, and possible causes are prevented.

Tune-up catches the problems early—in the farm shop, not in the field.

Shop costs are much cheaper than field costs, and by scheduling the tune-up during a lull in operation, costly downtime at peak periods can be prevented.

Tune-up means that the engine is ready to go and the operator can depend on it for some long and productive hours on the job.

WHY REGULAR TUNE-UP PAYS

Tune-Up Will Not Restore A Badly Worn Engine-Only Major Overhaul Will

BUT:

- **Tune-up Improves The Engine**
- **And Also Prevents Later Problems**

HOW?

- **Catching Problems Early Means Fewer Service Calls In The Field**
- **Shop Service Is Cheaper Than Field Calls**
- **And Shop Service Can Be Scheduled To Avoid Peak Operations**

RESULTS:

- **Tune-Up Means That The Engine Is Ready To Go**
- **And Is Dependable For Long, Productive Hours**

Fig. 6 — Why Regular Engine Tune-Up Pays

STORAGE OF MACHINES

When your machine is not going to be used for several months, it must be prepared for storage to prevent damage to components. Some manufacturers offer storage kits for these long periods of storage. The kits may include rust and corrosion preventives and plastic bags and tape to seal off openings.

For suggested storage procedures, use the charts that follow. They will indicate what steps to perform when preparing your machine for storage and when removing it from storage. *Be sure to observe all safety precautions.*

Where applicable, a chapter and page reference are given for details on each step.

PREPARING MACHINE FOR STORAGE

Step No.	Operation	Chapter	Page
1.	Clean exterior of machine.	9	211
2.	Perform engine tune-up.	10	214
3.	Check coolant for antifreeze protection to minimum anticipated temperature. *For those who don't drain and flush each season.*	5	75

Step No.	Operation	Chapter	Page
4.	Drain and refill transmission (warm up before draining oil).	7	140
5.	After refilling transmission, add corrosion and rust inhibitor to oil, if recommended. Operate transmission until oil is thoroughly circulated.	7	140
6.	Clean and repack wheel bearings.	9	174
7.	Drain and refill hydraulic system with fresh oil.	8	156

NOTE: Operate hydraulic system until oil is thoroughly heated before draining.

Step No.	Operation	Chapter	Page
8.	After refilling hydraulic system, add corrosion and rust inhibitor to oil, if recommended. Operate the system until oil is thoroughly circulated.	8	157
9.	Park machine in selected storage location.	10	220
10.	Drain fuel tank (gasoline and diesel only.) CAUTION: Check with LP-Gas dealer about emptying LP-Gas fuel tank.	3	39,49
11.	Remove, clean and replace fuel sediment bowl and filters.	3	43,50
12.	Add two gallons of fuel (mixed with rust inhibitor, if recommended) to the fuel tank.		
13.	Run engine for several minutes and then drain tank again.		
14.	Drain fuel lines and carburetor.		
15.	If recommended, add rust inhibitor to engine crankcase and to air intake.		
16.	With plastic bags and tape, seal ends of air inlet pipe, exhaust pipe, crankcase breather pipe, and hydraulic system breather pipe.		220

Step No.	Operation	Chapter	Page
17.	Remove battery. (Check electrolyte level and specific gravity each month while the battery is in storage. Charge battery when necessary.)	6	97
18.	Remove any weights from machine.		
19.	Remove weights from tires. (Drain water if there's danger of freezing.)	9	187
20.	Remove tires if machine is not to be supported off the ground during storage. If you do not wish to remove the tires, raise machine so that tires are off the ground.		

NOTE: Support machine securely with support stands or blocks.

Step No.	Operation	Chapter	Page
21.	Check and inflate tires to normal pressures.		185
22.	On machines with conventional dry clutch, block clutch pedal in the disengaged position.		
23.	Release tension on all drive belts and chains.		195,199
24.	Apply grease or rust preventive to chains.		199
25.	Coat all exposed metal surfaces, such as axles and hydraulic piston rods, with grease or a rust and corrosion preventive.		193
26.	Lubricate all points normally requiring lubrication.		

Step No.	Operation	Chapter	Page
27.	Check machine over carefully and make a list of parts or repairs needed to make the machine ready for operation when removed from storage. Make these repairs as soon as possible so that little time will be wasted when you remove the machine from storage to use during the next season.		
28.	Clean off rust, then prime and paint these areas to prevent further rusting.		
29.	Cover machine with a tarpaulin if it is not being stored in a building.		

REMOVING MACHINE FROM STORAGE

Step No.	Operation	Chapter	Page
1.	Remove all protective coverings from the machine, including plastic bags on all openings.		
2.	Remove clutch pedal block and allow clutch to engage.		
3.	Check tire inflation pressures.		183
4.	Install tires on machine if they where removed.		
5.	Remove supports from machine and lower machine to ground.		
6.	Install battery. Check specific gravity of electrolyte and add water if necessary. Charge battery if specific gravity too low.	6	97
7.	Check crankcase oil level.	4	67

NOTE: Check operator's manual to see if machine can be operated with rust inhibitor in systems. If not, drain and refill.

Step No.	Operation	Chapter	Page
8.	Check hydraulic system oil level.	8	151
9.	Check oil level in transmission, differential, and final drives.	7	140
10.	Adjust tension of belt and chain drives.	9	195,199
11.	Fill fuel tank with proper fuel.	3	32
12.	Check coolant level.	5	78
13.	Start the machine and let it idle for a few minutes. Check to be sure the machine is operating properly before using it.		

TEST YOURSELF

QUESTIONS

1. A badly worn engine can be restored by a complete tune-up.
   True_____ False_____

2. Before tuning up an engine, what should be done?

3. When should dynamometer tests be made?

TROUBLESHOOTING

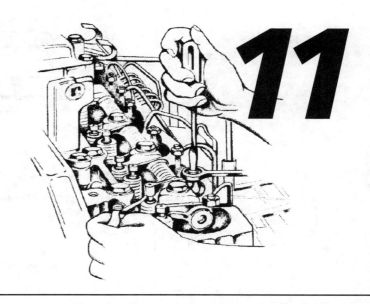

OPERATIONAL CHECKOUT

Several machinery manufacturers provide a new approach to finding the cause of the most common malfunctions without the use of complicated diagnostic gauges and instruments. These operational checkout procedures are based on the maintenance person's ability to Look, Listen and Feel.

On the following two pages you will find samples of operational check-outs. Of course, each machine will require it's very own specific procedure.

Use this procedure to check all systems and functions on the machine. It is designed so you can make a quick check of the operation of the machine while doing a walk around inspection and performing specific checks from the operator's seat.

Should you experience a problem with your machine, you will find helpful diagnostic information in this checkout that will pinpoint the cause. This information may allow you to perform a simple adjustment which will reduce the downtime of your machine. Use the table of contents to help find adjustment procedures.

The information you provide after completing the operational checkout will allow you or your dealer to pinpoint the specific test or repair work needed to restore the machine to design specifications.

A location will be required which is level and has adequate space to complete the checks. No tools or equipment are needed to perform the checkout.

Complete the necessary visual checks (oil levels, oil condition, external leaks, loose hardware, linkage, wiring, etc) prior to doing the checkout. The machine must be at operating temperature for many of the checks.

Start at the top of the left column and read completely down column before performing check, follow this sequence from left to right. In the far right column, if no problem is found (OK), you will be instructed to go to next check. If a problem is indicated (NOT OK), you will be referred to either a section in this manual or to your dealer.

TURN SIGNAL AND FLASHER CHECK	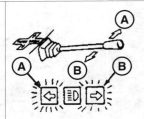 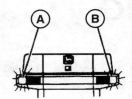	Move turn signal lever to left turn position (A) and then right turn position (13). *LOOK. Left front and rear amber lights and dash indicator (A), then right front and rear amber lights and dash indicator (B) must be flashing.*	**OK:** Go to next check **NOT OK:** If turn signals do not work, check turn signal fuse. **IF OK:** Go to your dealer
WARNING FLASHER CHECK	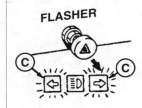 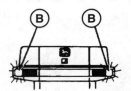	Pull out warning flasher switch knob. *LOOK. Front (A) and rear (B) amber fights and both dash indicators (C) must be flashing.*	**OK:** Go to next check **NOT OK:** Check turn signal fuse. **IF OK:** Go to your dealer.
BRAKE LIGHT CHECK	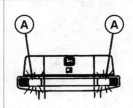	Depress brake pedal and observe brake lights (A). *LOOK: Brake lights must come on.*	**OK:** Go to next check **NOT OK:** Check brake light fuse. **IF OK:** Go to your dealer.
HORN CIRCUIT CHECK Key ON.	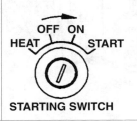	Push button. *LISTEN: Horn (A) must sound*	**Ok:** Go to next check **NOT OK:** Check fuse number 5. **IF OK:** Go to your dealer.

MECHANICAL FRONT WHEEL DRIVE (MFWD) DRIVING CHECKS

MFWD LIMITED-SLIP DIFFERENTIAL AND CONTROL LINKAGE CHECK	Shift transaxle to 1st reverse. Engage MFWD and drive machine. Run engine at approximately 1200 rpm. Turn steering wheel for a full left or right turn and observe how the front tires attempt to slide sideways (side load), and the amount of tire scuffing. Disengage MFWD. *LOOK. Tire side loading and scuffing must stop when MFWD Is disengaged* *NOTE: If tires attempt to slide sideways and tire scuffing is seen with MFWD engaged, limited-slip differential is working and power is being transmitted to MFWD.*	**OK:** Go to next check. **NOT OK:** Move MFWD control linkage to feel engagement detents. if no detents, inspect linkage to transfer case. If OK, go to Troubleshooting chapter, MFWD, No Power To MFWD. Go to your dealer.
ENGINE AND TORQUE CONVERTER CHECK	 With loader bucket level, and cutting edge at the centerline of front wheels, position machine against a dirt bank or immovable object. Engage MFWD and differential lock. Shift transaxle to 1st forward. Increase engine speed to fast idle. *LOOK: All four wheels must turn.*	**OK:** Go to next check. **NOT OK:** If all wheels stop, a torque converter problem is indicated. If the front wheels stop, a MFWD problem is indicated. Go to Troubleshooting chapter, Power Train, Machine Lacks Power Or Moves Slow. Go to your dealer.
MFWD GEAR AND PINION CHECK	Drive machine at transport speed with MFWD engaged, then disengaged. *LISTEN: MFWD MUST NOT whine.*	**OK:** Go to next check. **NOT OK:** If MFWD whines, check oil levels and fill to correct levels. If OK, check backlash. Go to your dealer.

TROUBLESHOOTING

Troubleshooting is a form of *preventive maintenance* which can help you find and correct minor problems before they become major ones.

The basic procedures for maintaining the machine properly have been covered. However, all machines will fail from time to time. The following charts will help you to identify problems so that you can determine the possible causes and remedies.

These charts list causes of typical failures of the engine, power train, hydraulic system, electrical system, brakes and operator's cab. Where they apply, the chapter and page number is given to guide you to the remedy described in this book.

In most cases, these charts show only problems that you as an operator can remedy. Many problems require expert diagnosis and repair by a service shop. If you can't eliminate the problem, take the machine to a service shop for testing and repair, The charts are arranged in the following order:

- **Engine**
- **Electrical Systems**
- **Power Train**
- **Hydraulic System**
- **Brakes**
- **Operator's Cab**

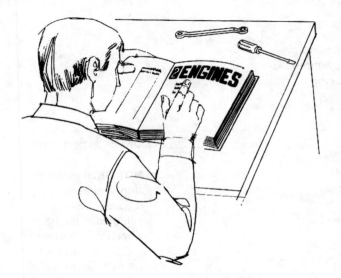

TROUBLESHOOTING CHART

ENGINE

Problem	Cause	Remedy	Chap.	Page
1. ENGINE HARD TO START OR WILL NOT START	No fuel or improper fuel.	Fill tank. If wrong fuel, drain and refill with proper fuel.	3	32
	Water or dirt in fuel or dirty filters.	Check out fuel supply. Replace or clean filters.	3	50
	Air in fuel system (Diesel).	Bleed air from system.	3	51
	Low cranking speed.	Charge or replace battery, or service starter as necessary.	6	102
	Improper timing.	Check distributor (Spark-Ignition).	6	113
		Have service shop check injection pump (Diesel).		
	Defective coil or condenser (Spark-Ignition).	Replace coil or condenser.	6	111
	Pitted or burned distributor points (Spark- Ignition).	Clean or replace points.	6	115
	Cracked distributor cap or eroded rotor (Spark-Ignition).	Replace cap or rotor.	6	110
	Distributor wires loose or installed in wrong order (Spark-ignition).	Push wire into sockets. Install wires in correct firing order.	6	118
	Fouled or defective spark plugs (Spark-ignition).	Clean and regap plugs or replace them.	6	108
	Poor injection nozzle operation (Diesel).	Have service shop clean or repair nozzles.		
	Liquid fuel in-lines (LP-Gas).	Always turn on vapor valve when starting the engine.		44
	Engine flooded.	Wait several minutes before attempting to start engine. Do not choke engine again.		
2. ENGINE STARTS BUT WILL NOT RUN PROPERLY	Fuel problem-dirt, air restrictions, or clogged filters.	Check fuel supply, bleed system (Diesel), check for line restrictions, and clean or replace fuel and air filters and screens.	3	50
	Carburetor needs adjustment (Spark- Ignition).	Adjust idle and load air-fuel mixtures.	3	41

TROUBLESHOOTING CHART

ENGINE
(Continued)

Problem	Cause	Remedy	Chap.	Page
2. ENGINE STARTS BUT WILL NOT RUN PROPERLY (cont'd)	Defective coil or condenser (Spark-Ignition).	Replace as necessary.	6	111
	Defective ignition resistor or key switch (Spark-Ignition).	Replace resistor or switch.		
	Pitted or burned distributor points (Spark-Ignition).	Clean or replace points.	6	115
	Fouled or defective spark plugs (Spark-Ignition).	Clean and regap plugs or replace them.	6	108
	Cracked distributor cap or eroded rotor (Spark-Ignition).	Replace cap or rotor.	6	110
3. ENGINE DETONATES (Gasoline)	Wrong type of fuel.	Use proper octane fuel.	3	31
4. ENGINE PRE-IGNITES (Gasoline)	Distributor timed too early. Distributor advance mechanism stuck.	Retime distributor. Free mechanism.	6 6	111 111
	Faulty spark plugs or spark plug heat range too high.	Install new plugs that have proper heat range.	6	106
5. ENGINE BACKFIRES - (Spark-Ignition)	Spark plug cables installed wrong.	Install in correct firing order.	6	109
	Carburetor mixture too lean.	Adjust carburetor.	3	46
6. ENGINE KNOCKS	Improper distributor/timing (Spark-Ignition).	Time distributor.	6	118
	Improper injection pump timing (Diesel).	Have service shop check injection pump.		
	Worn engine bearings or bushings.	Have service shop replace.		
	Loose bearing caps.	Have service shop tighten to proper torque		
	Foreign matter in the cylinder.	Have service shop remove material and repair engine.		
7. ENGINE OVERHEATS	Defective radiator cap.	Replace cap.	5	84
	Radiator core plugged with dirt and debris.	Clean radiator core.	5	79
	Defective thermostat.	Replace thermostat.	5	84

ENGINE
(Continued)

	Problem	Cause	Remedy	Chap.	Page
7.	ENGINE OVERHEATS (cont'd)	Loss of coolant.	Check for leaks and correct.	5	79
		Loose fan belt.	Adjust tension.	5	83
		Cooling system has scale deposit build-up.	Use cooling system cleaner to remove scale.	5	81
		Overloaded engine.	Reduce load or shift into a lower gear.		
		Incorrect engine timing.	Time distributor (Spark Ignition).	6	118
			Have service shop time injection pump (Diesel).		
		Engine low on oil.	Add oil to the proper level.	4	67
		Wrong type of fuel.	Use recommended fuel.	3	32
8.	LACK OF POWER	Air cleaner dirty or obstructed.	Clean or replace air cleaner. Remove obstruction.	2	12
		Restriction in fuel lines, filters or carburetor.	Clean plugged parts.	3	
		Wrong type of fuel.	Use recommended type.	3	31
		Frost at fuel-lock strainer (LP-Gas).	Clean strainer.	3	45
		Governor not operating properly.	Have service shop adjust or repair.		54
		Valves in engine head leaking.	Have service shop recondition.		47
		Incorrect valve clearance.	Adjust clearance.	2	18
		Low engine compression.	Have service shop check and repair engine.		27
		Incorrect timing.	Time distributor (Spark Ignition).	6	118
			Have service shop time injection pump (Diesel).		
		Carburetor improperly adjusted or dirty (Spark-Ignition).	Have service shop clean and adjust carburetor.		40
		Wrong spark plugs or plugs fouled (Spark-Ignition).	Clean, regap or replace spark plugs.	6	109

TROUBLESHOOTING CHART

ENGINE
(CONTINUED)

Problem	Cause	Remedy	Chap.	Page
8. LACK OF POWER (cont'd.)	Distributor points burned (Spark-Ignition).	Replace points and condenser.	6	115
	High engine operating temperature.	See "ENGINE OVERHEATS" above.		
	Low engine operating temperature.	Check thermostat.	5	84
	Vent on fuel tank plugged (Gasoline and Diesel).	Check fuel tank cap.	3	45
9. ENGINE USES TOO MUCH OIL	Crankcase oil too light.	Use recommended weight of oil.	4	65
	Worn pistons and rings.	Have service shop recondition.		
	Worn valve guides or stem oil seals.	Have service shop replace.		
	External oil leaks.	Eliminate leaks.	4	70
	Oil pressure too high.	Have service shop adjust pressure.	4	70
	Restricted air intake system.	Check system and relieve restriction.	2	16
10. OIL PRESSURE TOO LOW	See "ENGINE USES TOO MUCH OIL" above.			
11. ENGINE USES TOO MUCH FUEL	Clogged or dirty air cleaner.	Clean or replace air cleaner.	2	12
	Improper type fuel used.	Drain fuel tank and fill with recommended fuel.	3	32
	Engine overloaded.	Reduce load or shift into lower gear.		
	Improper valve clearance.	Adjust valve clearance.	2	20
	Engine out of time.	Time distributor (Spark Ignition).	6	118
		Have service shop time injection pump (Diesel).		
	Incorrect carburetor adjustment.	Adjust carburetor.	3	46

TROUBLESHOOTING CHART

ENGINE
(Continued)

Problem	Cause	Remedy	Chap.	Page
11. ENGINE USES TOO MUCH FUEL (cont'd.)	Engine not operating at proper temperature.	Check thermostat.	5	84
	Choke in closed position.	Open choke or adjust linkage if necessary.		
12. ENGINE EXHAUSTS BLACK OR GRAY SMOKE	Improper type of fuel.	Drain fuel tank and fill with recommended fuel.	3	32
	Clogged or dirty air cleaner.	Clean or replace air cleaner.	2	12
	Defective muffler.	Replace muffler.	2	22
	Engine overloaded.	Reduce load or shift into a lower gear.		
	Fuel injection system faulty.	Have service shop determine cause and repair.		
	Engine out of time.	Time distributor (Spark Ignition).	6	118
		Have service shop time injection pump (Diesel).		
	Incorrect carburetor adjustment.	Adjust carburetor.	3	46
13. ENGINE EXHAUSTS WHITE SMOKE	Improper type fuel.	Drain fuel tank and fill with recommended fuel.	3	32
	Low engine temperature.	Allow engine to warm up to normal temperatures before operating under load,		
	Defective thermostat.	Replace thermostat.	5	84
	Engine out of time.	Time distributor (Spark Ignition).	6	118
		Have service shop time injection pump (Diesel).		

TROUBLESHOOTING CHART
ELECTRICAL SYSTEMS

Problem	Cause	Remedy	Chap.	Page
1. LOW BATTERY OUTPUT	Low electrolyte level.	Add distilled water to proper level.	6	97
	Low specific gravity.	See "LOW BATTERY CHARGE" below.		
	Defective battery cell.	Replace battery.	6	106
	Cracked or broken case.	Replace battery.	6	106
	Low battery capacity.	Replace battery with one of recommended capacity.	6	106
2. BATTERY USES TOO MUCH WATER	Cracked battery case.	Replace battery.	6	106
	Overcharged battery.	Apply load to battery and have voltage regulator checked.	6	102
3. LOW BATTERY CHARGE	Excessive loads from added accessories.	Remove excessive loads or install larger alternator.		
	Excessive engine idling.	Allow engine to idle only when necessary.		
	Continuous drain on battery.	Clean battery top.	6	97
		Check for component grounded or shorted.		
	High resistance in circuit.	Clean and tighten connections. Replace faulty wiring.		
	Faulty charging operation.	See "LOW CHARGING CIRCUIT OUTPUT"		
4. LOW CHARGING CIRCUIT OUTPUT	Slipping drive belts.	Adjust belt tension.	9	193
	Excessively worn or sticking brushes in alternator or generator.	Replace brushes.	6	120
	Defective alternator or generator.	Replace unit or have service shop repair.		
5. NOISY GENERATOR OR ALTERNATOR	Defective or badly worn belt.	Replace belt.		194
	Generator brushes not seated.	Seat brushes.	6	120
	Generator commutator worn too much.	Have service shop recondition.		
	Worn or defective bearings.	Have service shop replace bearings.		

TROUBLESHOOTING CHART

ELECTRICAL SYSTEMS
(Continued)

Problem	Cause	Remedy	Chap.	Page
5. NOISY GENERATOR OR ALTERNATOR (cont'd.)	Loose mounting or loose pulley.	Tighten mounting and pulley.		
	Misaligned drive belt and pulley.	Realign belt and pulley.	9	195
6. SLUGGISH STARTING MOTOR OPERATION	Low battery charge.	Charge battery.	6	102
	High resistance in circuit.	Clean and tighten wiring connections.		
	Defective starting motor.	Have service shop repair.		
	Starting motor bearings dry .	Lubricate bearings or replace sealed bearings.		120
	Engine oil viscosity too high.	Drain oil and replace with viscosity of oil recommended for cold temperatures.	4	63
7. STARTING MOTOR WILL NOT OPERATE	Low battery charge.	Charge battery.	6	102
	High resistance in circuit.	Clean and tighten connections.		
	Starter safety switch open.	Move shift lever to neutral or park position.		
	Defective or improperly adjusted starter safety switch.	Have service shop adjust or replace switch.		
	Defective starter switch.	Replace switch.		
	Defective starter.	Have service shop check, repair or replace starter.		
8. MISFIRING OF ENGINE	Improper spark plug heat range.	Replace plugs with hotter or colder range plugs as required.	6	106
	Bad plug wiring.	Replace plug wires.	6	109
	Worn spark plug electrodes or fouled plugs.	Clean plugs and regap. Replace plugs if necessary.	6	108
	Defective spark plugs.	Replace plugs.	6	108
	Incorrect distributor timing.	Retime distributor.	6	118
	Insufficient voltage available to spark plugs.	See "LOW VOLTAGE AT SPARK PLUG", below.		
9. LOW VOLTAGE AT SPARK PLUG	Worn or improperly spaced distributor points.	Adjust point gap.	6	115

Problem	Cause	Remedy	Chap.	Page
9. LOW VOLTAGE AT SPARK PLUG (cont'd.)	Dirty, burned, or pitted points.	Clean or replace points and condenser.	6	115
	Defective condenser.	Replace condenser.	6	115
	Dirt or moisture in distributor cap.	Clean distributor cap.	6	110
	Cracked distributor cap.	Replace cap.	6	110
	Eroded distributor rotor.	Replace rotor.	6	110
	Defective spark plug cables.	Replace cables.	6	108
	Defective ignition coil.	Replace coil.		
	Loose wire connections.	Tighten all connections.		
10. BUILD-UP OF MATERIAL ON DISTRIBUTOR POINTS	Condenser has improper capacity.	Replace with proper condenser.	6	115
11. EXCESSIVE WEAR ON DISTRIBUTOR POINTS RUBBING BLOCK	Inadequate lubricant.	Use cam lubricant to prevent wear.	6	112
12. BURNED DISTRIBUTOR POINTS	Loose lead wire or high resistance in condenser.	Tighten lead or replace condenser.		
	Wrong method of cleaning distributor points.	Use point file and lintless cloth.	6	115
	Oil or foreign material on points.	Clean or replace points.	6	115
13. DIM LIGHTS	High resistance in circuit or poor ground on lights.	Clean and tighten all connec-. tions. Replace faulty wiring.	6	109
	Low battery charge.	Charge battery.	6	102
	Defective light switch.	Replace switch.		
14. GENERATOR OR ALTERNATOR INDI-CATOR LAMP GLOWS INTERMITTENTLY	Excessive resistance in battery lead to unit or regulator.	Clean and tighten all connec-tions. Replace faulty wiring.	6	109
	Excessive internal resistance in generator or alternator.	Replace brushes or take to service department.	6	120
		Have unit repaired or replaced.		

TROUBLESHOOTING CHART

ELECTRICAL SYSTEMS
(Continued)

Problem	Cause	Remedy	Chap.	Page
15. OIL PRESSURE INDICATOR LAMP FAILS TO LIGHT	Burned-out bulb.	Replace bulb.		
	Open circuit or excessive resistance in wiring.	Clean and tighten all connections. Replace faulty wiring.	6	109
	Defective lamp body.	Replace lamp body.		
	Faulty oil pressure switch.	Replace switch.		
16. OIL PRESSURE LAMP REMAINS ON WITH STARTING SWITCH OFF	Defective lamp body.	Replace lamp body.		
	Grounded wire to oil pressure switch.	Repair or replace wiring.	6	109
	Faulty oil pressure switch.	Replace switch.		

TROUBLESHOOTING CHART
POWER TRAIN (CLUTCH)

Problem	Cause	Remedy	Chap.	Page
1. CLUTCH SLIPS	Too little clutch pedal free travel.	Adjust clutch pedal free travel.	7	138
	Operator riding clutch pedal.	Do not ride clutch pedal.	7	129
	Worn clutch disks.	See dealer for repair.		
2. CLUTCH GRABS OR CHATTERS		Take the machine to a service shop for repair or adjustment.		
3. CLUTCH SQUEAKS	Clutch release bearing dry.	Lubricate bearing.	7	138
	Clutch actuating mechanism dry.	Lubricate linkage and shafts.	7	138
4. CLUTCH RATTLES AND VIBRATES		Take the machine to a service shop for repair or adjustment.		

TROUBLESHOOTING CHART
POWER TRAIN (MECHANICAL TRANSMISSION)

Problem	Cause	Remedy	Chap.	Page
1. TRANSMISSION NOISY	Transmission oil level low.	Fill transmission with proper lubricant.	7	140
	Worn or broken gears.	See dealer for repair.		201
2. TRANSMISSION HARD TO SHIFT		Take machine to service shop for repair or adjustment.		
3. TRANSMISSION STICKS IN GEAR	Clutch not releasing.	Adjust clutch pedal free travel.	7	138
	Shift linkage binding.	Free linkage.		
	Worn shift linkage.	Have dealer repair.		
4. TRANSMISSION SLIPS OUT OF GEAR		Take machine to service shop for repair or adjustment.		
5. TRANSMISSION LEAKS OIL	Oil level too high.	Drain to proper level.	7	140
	Gaskets damaged or missing.	Have dealer install new gaskets.		
	Drain plug loose.	Tighten drain plug.		
	Lubricant foaming excessively.	Use recommended lubricant.		

TROUBLESHOOTING CHART

POWER TRAIN (HYDRAULIC ASSIST TRANSMISSION)

Problem	Cause	Remedy	Chap.	Page
1. MACHINE WON'T MOVE	Cold weather starting clutch disengaged.	Engage clutch.		129
	Park lock engaged.	Release lock.		
	Control linkage binding or disconnected.	Free linkage or connect linkage.		
	Oil filter plugged.	Replace oil filter.		67
2. SHIFTS ERRATICALLY	Shift control disconnected or binding.	Free controls or connect disconnected parts.		
3. LOW SYSTEM PRESSURE	Plugged oil filter.	Replace filter.		67
	Low oil level.	Fill to proper level.	7	140
4. TRANS.MISSION OVERHEATING	Reservoir oil level too low or too high.	Bring oil level to proper level.	7	140
	Plugged oil filter.	Replace filter.	7	67
	Plugged core in oil cooler.	Clean core.		

TROUBLESHOOTING CHART
POWER TRAIN (TORQUE CONVERTER)

Problem	Cause	Remedy	Chap.	Page
1. OVERHEATING	Oil level too low.	Fill to proper level.	7	140
	Machine overloaded.	Reduce load.		
	Plugged oil cooler core.	Clean core.		
2. NOISY	Major failure or maladjustment.	Take machine to service shop for repair or adjustment.		
3. OIL LEAKS	Loose bolts or damaged gaskets.	Tighten bolts. Have service shop replace gaskets.		
	Loose fittings or oil lines.	Tighten fittings and lines.		
4. MACHINE LACKS POWER OR ACCELERATION	Major failure or maladjustment.	Take machine to service shop for repair or adjustment.		

TROUBLESHOOTING CHART
POWER TRAIN (HYDROSTATIC TRANSMISSION)

Problem	Cause	Remedy	Chap.	Page
1. MACHINE WILL NOT MOVE	System low on oil.	Fill to proper level.	7	140
	Faulty control linkage.	Free linkage.		
	Disconnected oil line.	Reconnect oil line,		
	Mechanical failure.	See dealer for repair.		
2. NEUTRAL HARD TO FIND	Faulty speed control linkage.	Adjust control linkage.		
3. SYSTEM OVERHEATING	Oil level too low.	Fill to proper level.	7	140
	Oil cooler core plugged.	Clean core.		
	Engine fan belt slipping or broken.	Tighten or replace belt.		
4. SYSTEM NOISY	Air in system.	Check oil supply; fill if low. Check for loose fittings and tighten.		
5. SLUGGISH ACCELERATION AND DECELERATION	Air in system.	Check oil supply; fill if low. Check for loose fittings and tighten.		
6. HARD SHIFTING	Speed control lever not in neutral.	Position lever in neutral.		

TROUBLESHOOTING CHART
POWER TRAIN (DIFFERENTIAL)

Problem	Cause	Remedy	Chap.	Page
1. NOISY	Oil level too low.	Fill to proper level.	7	140
2. TURNING DIFFICULTY	Differential lock won't release, brakes dragging, or differential lock stuck.	Take machine to service shop for repairs.		136
3. MECHANICAL LOCK DOESN'T HOLD	Linkage not in adjustment.	Take machine to service shop for repairs or adjustment.		
4. HYDRAULIC LOCK DOESN'T HOLD	Valve malfunction or linkage not in adjustment.	Take machine to service shop for repairs or adjustment.		

TROUBLESHOOTING CHART
HYDRAULIC SYSTEM

Problem	Cause	Remedy	Chap.	Page
1. SYSTEM DOESN'T OPERATE	Little or no oil in system.	Fill to proper level. Check system for leaks.	8	151
	Oil of wrong viscosity.	Drain and refill system with proper oil.	8	157
	Oil filter plugged.	Replace filter.	8	67
	Restriction in system.	Take machine to service shop for repairs.		
	Oil leaks.	Tighten fittings and lines.	8	152
	Slipping or broken pump drive belt.	Tighten or replace belt.		
2. SYSTEM OPERATES ERRATICALLY	Air in system.	Check for leaks and tighten fittings and lines.	8	152
	Cold oil.	Allow system to warm up.		
3. SYSTEM OPERATES SLOWLY	Cold oil.	Allow system to warm up.		
	Oil viscosity too heavy.	Drain and refill system with proper viscosity of oil.	8	157
	Engine speed too slow.	Operate engine at recommended speed.		
	Low oil supply.	Fill to proper level.	8	151
	Air in system.	Check for leaks and tighten fittings and lines.	8	152
4. SYSTEM OPERATES TOO FAST	Adjust cylinder ram speed.	See operator's manual.		
	Adjust or repair.	Adjust per operator's manual. For repair, see dealer.		
5. SYSTEM OVERHEATING	Operator holding controls in power position too long.	Return controls to neutral when not in use.		
	Incorrect oil viscosity.	Use recommended viscosity of oil.	8	64,144
	Low oil level.	Fill to proper level. Check for leaks.	8	151
	Dirty oil.	Drain and refill with clean oil.	8	157
	Oil cooler core plugged or dirty.	Clean core.		

Problem	Cause	Remedy	Chap.	Page
6. FOAMING OIL	Low oil level.	Fill to proper level. Check for leaks.	8	151
	Water in oil.	Drain and replace oil.	8	157
	Wrong kind of oil.	Drain and replace with recommended oil.	8	157
	Air leak.	Tighten lines and fittings.	8	152
7. NOISY PUMP	Low oil level.	Fill to proper level. Check for leaks.	8	151
	Air in oil.	Check for leaks. Tighten lines and fittings.	8	151
8. COMPONENTS LEAKING	Failure of major parts.	Take machine to service shop for repairs.		

TROUBLESHOOTING CHART
BRAKES

Problem	Cause	Remedy	Chap.	Page
1. BRAKES NOT HOLDING	Glazed, greasy or worn linings.	Replace linings.		
2. BRAKES NOT RELEASING	Cables or linkage binding.	Adjust linkage and cables.	9	180
	Foreign material lodged in brake mechanism.	Remove material.		
3. PEDAL BOUNCES OR SPONGY	Hydraulic brakes: air in system.	Bleed brakes.	8, 9	159,182
4. NO BRAKES	Hydraulic brakes: air in system.	Bleed brakes.	8, 9	159,182
	Manual brakes: linings worn or linkage out of adjustment.	Replace linings or adjust linkage.	9	180
	Power brakes: accumulator discharged.	Take machine to service shop for repairs.		
5. MACHINE PULLS TO ONE SIDE	Brakes adjusted unevenly.	Adjust brakes.	9	180
6. HYDRAULIC BRAKES OPERATE ERRATICALLY	Contaminated fluid.	Drain and clean system. Refill system with proper fluid. Bleed brakes.	8, 9	159,182

TROUBLESHOOTING CHART
OPERATOR'S CAB

Problem	Cause	Remedy	Chap.	Page
1. BLOWER NOT KEEPING DUST OUT	Defective seal around filter.	Check seal condition. Check filter for proper installation.		
	Defective or dirty filter.	Replace or clean filter.	9	167
	Air leaks into cab.	Check cab for leaks. Plug leaks.		
	Blower air flow too low.	See "BLOWER AIR FLOW TOO LOW".		
2. BLOWER AIR FLOW TOO LOW	Clogged filter or air intake screen.	Clean filter or intake screen.	9	167
3. HEATER WILL NOT HEAT	Air trapped in heater core.	Bleed air from heater.	9	168
	Defective thermostat in engine.	Replace thermostat.	5	74
	Air conditioner turned on.	Turn off air conditioner.		
4. HEATER WILL NOT SHUT OFF	Heater hoses connected improperly.	Change hose connections.	9	168
5. AIR CONDITIONER WILL NOT COOL	Blower air flow too low.	See "BLOWER AIR FLOW TOO LOW".		
	Compressor belt slipping.	Tighten belt.	9	170
	Lack of refrigerant in system.	Check sight glass and have system recharged.	9	169
	Evaporator core plugged.	Clean core.	9	169
	Condenser core clogged.	Clean core.	9	169
	Heater turned on.	Turn off heater.		
	Compressor not running.	Check fuse.		

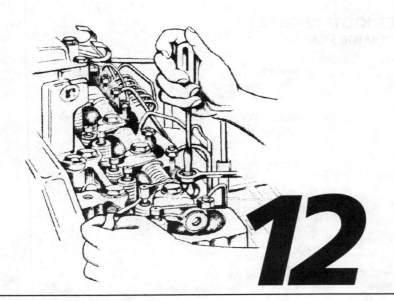

SAFETY

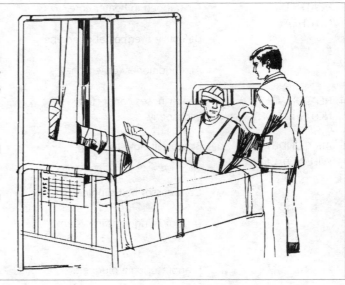

INTRODUCTION

Each year 500 people die in machinery related accidents in North America, many more around the world. Many thousands receive serious injuries that disable them for the rest of their lives.

Many factors can cause an accident: carelessness, haste, poor judgment, lack of experience, and even mechanical failure created by lack of maintenance.

Don't become a statistic; learn and practice **safe** operating and maintenance procedures.

RECOGNIZE SAFETY INFORMATION

This is the safety-alert symbol. When you see, this symbol on your machine or in this manual, be alert to the potential for personal injury.

Follow recommended precautions and **safe** operating practices.

UNDERSTAND SIGNAL WORDS

A signal word—DANGER, WARNING, or CAUTION— is used with the safety-alert symbol. DANGER identifies the most serious hazards.

DANGER or WARNING safety signs are located near specific hazards. General precautions are listed on CAUTION safety signs. CAUTION also calls attention to safety messages in this manual.

⚠ DANGER

⚠ WARNING

⚠ CAUTION

FOLLOW SAFETY INSTRUCTIONS

Carefully read all safety messages in this manual and on your machine safety signs. Keep safety signs in good condition. Replace missing or damaged safety signs. Be sure new equipment components and repair parts include the current safety signs. Replacement safety signs are available from your dealer.

Learn how to operate the machine and how to use controls properly. Do not let anyone operate without instruction.

Keep your machine in proper working condition. Unauthorized modifications to the machine may impair the function and/or safety and affect machine life.

If you do not understand any part of this manual and need assistance, contact your dealer.

STOP AND THINK

Stop and think about the maintenance procedures. What could happen? How could it happen? What is the safest way? Read all safety instructions and follow them every time.

GET FAMILIAR WITH EACH MACHINE

Don't rush into a maintenance job. Get very familiar with the specific functions and potential safety hazards of each machine. Always refer to the operator's manual of each machine. Even similar machines do not always have identical systems. So be very careful. Follow all safety instructions...every time. Remember: You are protecting yourself and others by being careful.

PRACTICE SAFE MAINTENANCE

Understand service procedure before doing work. Keep area clean and dry.

Never lubricate or service machine while it is moving. Keep hands, feet and clothing from power-driven parts. Disengage all power and operate the controls to relieve pressure. Lower equipment to the ground. Stop the engine. Remove the key. Allow machine to cool.

Securely support any machine elements that must be raised for service work.

Keep all parts in good condition and properly installed. Fix damage immediately. Replace worn or broken parts. Remove any buildup of grease, oil or debris.

Disconnect battery ground cable(s) (-) before making adjustments on electrical system or welding on machine.

REMEMBER: Always turn off the engine before you work on a machine.

WEAR PROTECTIVE CLOTHING

Wear close fitting clothing and safety equipment appropriate to the job.

Prolonged exposure to loud noise can cause impairment or loss of hearing.

Wear a suitable hearing protective device such as earmuffs or earplugs to protect against objectionable or uncomfortable loud noises.

PROTECT YOUR EYES

Eyesight is one of the most precious abilities we have. So protect your eyes very carefully. Wear safety glasses or face shields, when you are using a chisel or punch. Wear a welding shield or a helmet when you are welding. Keep shield in place when you are chipping slag.

EYE PROTECTION

WEAR GOGGLES UNDER HELMET

USE CLEAR LENS IN WELDING HELMET

PROTECT YOUR HEARING

Machines that are running make a lot of noise. Prolonged exposure to noise will damage your ability to hear. Therefore you should always wear hearing protection such as ear plugs or muffs.

PREPARE FOR EMERGENCIES

Be prepared if a fire starts.

Keep a first aid kit and fire extinguisher handy.

Keep emergency numbers for doctors, ambulance service, hospital and fire department near your telephone.

WORK IN VENTILATED AREA

Engine exhaust fumes can cause sickness or death. If it is necessary to run an engine in an enclosed area, remove the exhaust fumes from the area with an exhaust pipe extension.

If you do not have an exhaust pipe extension, open the doors and get outside air into the area.

WORK IN CLEAN AREA

Before starting a job:

• Clean work area and machine.

• Make sure you have all necessary tools to do your job.

• Have the right parts on hand.

• Read all instructions thoroughly; do not attempt shortcuts.

SERVICE MACHINE SAFELY

Tie long hair behind your head. Do not wear a necktie, scarf, loose clothing or necklace when you work near machine tools, or moving parts. If these items were to get caught, severe injury could result.

Remove rings and other jewelry to prevent electrical shorts and entanglement in moving parts.

USE TOOLS THAT FIT

Many serious accidents happen, when the wrong tools are used or when tools are used that don't fit. Make sure you use metric dimensioned tools on metric products, and inch-dimensioned tools on products of customary design. Also, don't use tools for purposes they are not designed for.

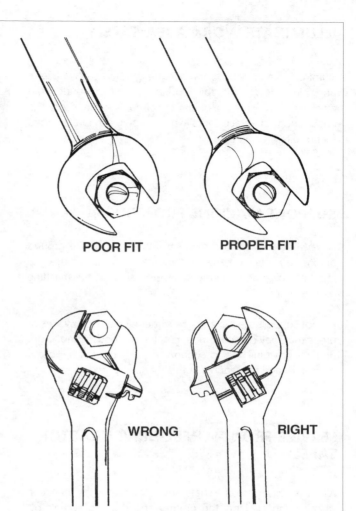

POOR FIT   PROPER FIT

WRONG   RIGHT

PARK MACHINE SAFELY

Before working on the machine:

• Lower all equipment to the ground.

• Stop the engine and remove the key.

• Disconnect the battery ground strap.

• Hang a "DO NOT OPERATE" tag in operator station.

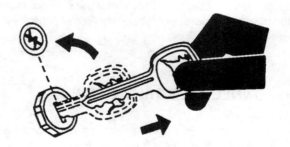

ILLUMINATE WORK AREA SAFELY

Illuminate your work area adequately but safely. Use a portable safety light for working inside or under the machine. Make sure the bulb is enclosed by a wire cage. The hot filament of an accidentally broken bulb can ignite spilled fuel or oil.

SUPPORT MACHINE PROPERLY

Always lower the attachment or implement to the ground before you work on the machine. If you must work on a lifted machine or attachment, securely support the machine or attachment.

Do not support the machine on cinder blocks, hollow tiles or props that may crumble under continuous load. Do not work under a machine that is supported solely by a jack. Follow recommended procedures in this manual.

SERVICE FRONT-WHEEL-DRIVE TRACTOR SAFELY

When servicing front-wheel-drive tractor with the rear wheels supported off the ground and rotating wheels by engine power, always support front wheels in a similar manner. Loss of electrical power or transmission/hydraulic system pressure will engage the front driving wheels, pulling the rear wheels off the support if front wheels are not raised. Under these conditions, front drive wheels can engage even with switch in disengaged position.

DISCONNECT ELECTRICAL CIRCUIT

Disconnect battery ground strap(s) before carrying out any electrical repairs or welding on the machine.

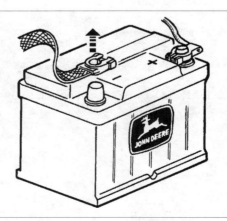

HANDLE BATTERIES SAFELY

Sulfuric acid in battery electrolyte is poisonous. It is strong enough to burn skin, eat holes in clothing and cause blindness if splashed into eyes.

Avoid the hazard by:

1. Filling the batteries in a well-ventilated area.

2. Wearing eye protection and rubber gloves.

3. Avoiding breathing in the fumes when electrolyte is added.

4. Avoiding spilling or dripping electrolyte.

5. Using the proper jump start procedure.

If you spill acid on yourself:

1. Flush your skin with water.

2. Apply baking soda or lime to help neutralize the acid.

3. Flush your eyes with water for 10 - 15 minutes.

Get medical attention immediately.

If acid is swallowed:

1. Drink large amounts of water or milk.

2. Then drink milk of magnesia, beaten eggs or vegetable oil.

3. Get medical attention immediately.

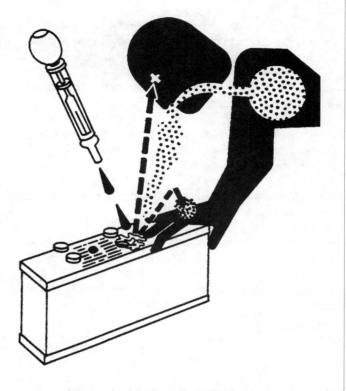

PREVENT BATTERY EXPLOSIONS

Keep sparks, lighted matches, and open flame away from the top of battery. Battery gas can explode.

Never check battery charge by placing a metal object across the posts. Use a volt-meter or hydrometer.

Do not charge a frozen battery; it may explode. Warm battery to 16°C (60°F).

AVOID HIGH-PRESSURE FLUIDS

The hydraulic system and the fuel injection system contain fluids under very high pressure. Small leaks in these systems will allow oil or fuel to escape with high velocity.

Escaping fluid under pressure can penetrate the skin causing serious injury.

Avoid the hazard by relieving pressure before disconnecting hydraulic or other lines. Tighten all connections before applying pressure.

Search for leaks with a piece of cardboard. Protect hands and body from high pressure fluids.

If an accident occurs, see a doctor immediately. Any fluid injected into the skin must be surgically removed within a few hours or gangrene may result. Doctors unfamiliar with this type of injury should contact other knowledgeable medical sources.

AVOID HEATING NEAR PRESSURIZED FLUID LINES

Flammable spray can be generated by heating near pressurized fluid lines, resulting in severe burns to yourself and bystanders. Do not heat by welding, soldering, or using a torch near pressurized fluid lines or other flammable materials. Pressurized lines can be accidentally cut when heat goes beyond the immediate flame area.

SERVICE COOLING SYSTEM SAFELY

Danger of scalding!

With the engine shut off, first loosen the radiator cap or expansion tank cap only to the first stop to relieve the pressure before removing the cap completely.

Top off cooling system with coolant only when engine is shut off.

AVOID HARMFUL ASBESTOS DUST

Avoid breathing dust that may be generated when handling components containing asbestos fibers. Inhaled asbestos fibers may cause lung cancer.

Components that may contain asbestos fibers are brake pads, brake band and lining assemblies, clutch plates and some gaskets. The asbestos used in these components is usually found in a resin or sealed in some way. Normal handling is not hazardous as long as airborne dust containing asbestos is not generated.

Avoid creating dust. Never use compressed air for cleaning. Avoid brushing or grinding of asbestos-containing materials. When servicing, wear an approved respirator. A special vacuum cleaner is recommended to clean asbestos. If not available, wet the asbestos-containing materials with a mist of oil or water.

Keep bystanders away from the area.

Please note designations on spare parts.

STAY CLEAR OF ROTATING DRIVELINES

Entanglement in rotating driveline can cause serious injury or death. When operating with the PTO, no-one must be allowed to remain in the vicinity of the rotating PTO stub shaft or drive shaft. Always ensure that the guards for PTO drive shaft, PTO stub shaft and driveshaft guards are in position and that rotating shields turn freely.

Wear close-fitting clothing. Stop the engine and be sure PTO driveline is stopped before making adjustments, connections or cleaning out PTO-driven equipment.

As soon as PTO drive shaft has been removed, reinstall guard over PTO stub shaft.

BE AWARE OF STORED ENERGY

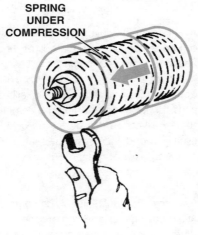

SPRING UNDER COMPRESSION

Stored energy can work for you, or it can be carelessly released and cause injury.

In many farm machines, energy is stored so it can be released at the right time, in the right way for you. Here are some components that store energy. You should recognize them as you use and service equipment.

• Springs

• Hydraulic Systems

• Compressed Air

• Electricity

• Raised Loads

• Loaded Mechanisms

Always release or disconnect the stored energy before you begin maintenance work.

SERVICE TIRES SAFELY

Explosive separation of a tire and rim parts can cause serious injury or death.

Do not attempt to mount a tire unless you have the proper equipment and experience to perform the job.

Always maintain the correct tire pressure. Do not inflate the tires above the recommended pressure. Never weld or heat a wheel and tire assembly. The heat can cause an increase in air pressure resulting in a tire explosion. Welding can structurally weaken or deform the wheel.

When inflating tires, use a clip-on chuck and extension hose long enough to allow you to stand to one side and NOT in front of or over the tire assembly. Use a safety cage if available.

Check wheels for low pressure, cuts, bubbles, damaged rims or missing lug bolts and nuts.

STORE ATTACHMENTS SAFELY

Store attachments such as dual wheels, cage wheels and loaders can fall and cause serious injury or death.

Securely store attachments and implements to prevent falling. Keep playing children and bystanders away from storage area.

OBSERVE ENVIRONMENTAL PROTECTION REGULATIONS

Be mindful of the environment and ecology.

Before draining any fluids, find out the correct way of disposing of them.

Observe the relevant environmental protection regulations when disposing of oil, fuel, coolant, brake fluid, filters and batteries.

DISPOSE OF WASTE PROPERLY

Improperly disposing of waste can threaten the environment and ecology. Potentially harmful waste used with equipment include such items as oil, fuel, coolant, brake fluid, filters, and batteries.

Use leakproof containers when draining fluids. Do not use food or beverage containers that may mislead someone into drinking from them.

Inquire on the proper way to recycle or dispose of waste from your local environmental or recycling center. Do not pour waste onto the ground, down a drain, or into any water source.

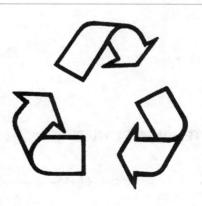

AVOID BEING CRUSHED

There are many crush points on a machine. A crushing injury or death is caused, if you get between two parts that move towards each other, like the front and rear portions of a fourwheel-drive articulated tractor.

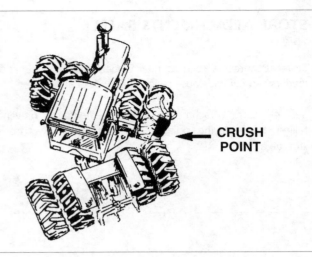

← CRUSH
POINT

You can also get crushed, if you get between a stationary part and a moving part, like between the 3-point hitch and the tractor. Another way to get crushed is to be under a machine that is not well blocked and the machine falls on you.

**WORKING UNDER HEAVY OBJECTS
THAT AREN'T SECURELY BLOCKED
MAY RESULT IN CRUSHING INJURIES**

RETIGHTEN WHEEL NUTS

Retighten machine wheel nuts at the intervals specified in the machine operators manual.

HANDLE FUEL SAFELY-AVOID FIRES

Handle fuel with care: it is highly flammable. Do not refuel the machine while smoking or when near open flame or sparks.

Always stop engine before refueling machine. Fill fuel tank outdoors.

Prevent fires by keeping machine clean of accumulated trash, grease, and debris. Always clean up spilled fuel.

HANDLE STARTING FLUID SAFELY

Starting fluid is highly flammable.

Keep all sparks and flames away when using it. Keep starting fluid away from batteries and cables.

To prevent accidental discharge when storing the pressurized can, always keep the cap on the container and store in a cool, protected location.

Do not incinerate or puncture starting fluid containers, even when empty.

KEEP CAB/ROPS INSTALLED PROPERLY

Make certain all parts are reinstalled correctly if the cab or rollover protective structure (ROPS) is loosened or removed for any reason. Tighten mounting bolts to specified torque.

Protection offered by cab or ROPS will be impaired if subjected to structural damage, involved in an overturn incident or altered in any way by welding, bending, drilling or cutting. A damaged cab or ROPS should be replaced, not reused.

PREVENT MACHINE RUNAWAY

Avoid possible injury or death from a machine runaway.

Do not start the engine by starting across starter terminals. Machine will start in gear if normal circuitry is bypassed.

NEVER start engine while standing on ground. Start engine only from operator's seat, with the transmission in neutral or "Park".

OBSERVE ROAD TRAFFIC REGULATIONS

Always observe local road traffic regulations when using public roads.

Replace the Slow-Moving-Vehicle Emblem (SMV) if it is missing.

USE SAFETY LIGHTS AND DEVICES

Slow moving tractors, self-propelled equipment and towed implements or attachments can create a hazard when driven on public roads. They are difficult to see, especially at night. Avoid personal injury or death resulting from collision with a vehicle.

Flashing warning lights and turn signals are recommended whenever driving on public roads. To increase visibility, use the lights and devices provided with your machine. For some equipment, install extra flashing warning lights.

Keep safety items in good condition. Replace missing or damaged items.

LIVE WITH SAFETY

Follow safe maintenance procedures. Make sure the machine is functioning properly, especially the safety systems. Install all guards and shields and ensure they work properly. Replace damaged or missing safety signs on the machine. Live with safety.

SUMMARY

Safety is the most important consideration when you perform maintenance on a machine. A very small careless act can result in a major injury... possibly death. Whatever you do... safety comes first.

TEST YOURSELF

QUESTIONS

1. (Fill in the blank) Approximately _____ people die in machinery related accidents in North America per year.

2. Name the three signal words.

3. Unless so instructed within a diagnostic procedure, the engine should always be stopped before performing service.
   True_____ False_____

4. Name four of the six components that store energy.

5. Loose fitting clothing is not a safety hazard.
   True_____ False_____

6. (Fill in the blank) A frozen battery should be warmed up to _____ °F prior to charging.

7. The high-pressure fluids within a fuel injection system or hydraulic system can escape with enough velocity to penetrate the skin.
   True_____ False_____

8. (Fill in the blank) A _____ should be worn when working around materials containing asbestos.

9. A lot of noise for a prolonged period will increase your hearing ability.
   True_____ False_____

10. (Fill in the blank) Applying heat to a wheel and tire assembly will cause the air pressure in the tire to _____.

APPENDIX

UNIFIED INCH BOLT AND CAP SCREW TORQUE VALUES

SAE Grade and Head Markings	NO MARK	1 or 2[b]		5 5.1 5.2		8 8.2
SAE Grade and Head Markings	NO MARK	2		5		8

	Grade 1				Grade 2b				Grade 5, 5.1, or 5.2				Grade 8 or 8.2			
Size	Lubricated[a]		Dry[a]		Lubricated[a]		Dry[a]		Lubricated[a]		Dry[a]		Lubricated[a]		Dry[a]	
	N•m	lb-ft	N•m	lb-ft	N•m	lb-ft	N•m	lb-ft	N•m	lb-ft	N•m	lb-ft	N•m	lb-ft	N•m	lb-ft
1/4	3.7	2.8	4.7	3.5	6	4.5	7.5	5.5	9.5	7	12	9	13.5	10	17	12.5
5/16	7.7	5.5	10	7	12	9	15	11	20	15	25	18	28	21	35	26
3/8	14	10	17	13	22	16	27	20	35	26	44	33	50	36	63	46
7/16	22	16	28	20	35	26	44	32	55	41	70	52	80	58	100	75
1/2	33	25	42	31	53	39	67	50	85	63	110	80	120	90	150	115
9/16	48	36	60	45	75	56	95	70	125	90	155	115	175	130	225	160
5/8	67	50	85	62	105	78	135	100	170	125	215	160	215	160	300	225
3/4	120	87	150	110	190	140	240	175	300	225	375	280	425	310	550	400
7/8	190	140	240	175	190	140	240	175	490	360	625	450	700	500	875	650
1	290	210	360	270	290	210	360	270	725	540	925	675	1050	750	1300	975
1-1/8	470	300	510	375	470	300	510	375	900	675	1150	850	1450	1075	1850	1350
1-1/4	570	425	725	530	570	425	725	530	1300	950	1650	1200	2050	1500	2600	1950
1-3/8	750	550	950	700	750	550	950	700	1700	1250	2150	1550	2700	2000	3400	2550
1-1/2	1000	725	1250	925	990	725	1250	930	2250	1650	2850	2100	3600	2650	4550	3350

DO NOT use these values if a different torque value or tightening procedure is given for a specific application. Torque values listed are for general use only. Check the tightness of fasteners periodically.

Shear bolts are designed to fail under predetermined loads. Always replace the shear bolts with an identical grade.

Fasteners should be replaced with the same or higher grade. If higher grade fasteners are used, these should only be tightened to the strength of the original.

Make sure fastener threads are clean and you properly start thread engagement. This will prevent them from failing when tightening.

Tighten plastic insert or crimped steel-type lock nuts to approximately 50 percent of the dry torque shown in chart. Tighten toothed or serrated-type lock nuts to full torque

[a] "Lubricated" means coated with a lubricant such as engine oil, or fasteners with phosphate and oil coatings. "Dry" means plain or zinc plated without any lubrication.

[b] Grade 2 applies for hex cap screws (not hex bolts) up to 152 mm (6-in.) long. Grade 1 applies for hex cap screws over 152 mm (6-in.) long, and for all other types of bolts and screws of any length.

METRIC BOLT AND CAP SCREW TORQUE VALUES

	4.8	8.8	9.8	10.9	12.9
Property Class and Head Markings	4.8 / 4.8	8.8 / 8.8	9.8 / 9.8	10.9 / 10.9	12.9 / 12.9

	5	10	10	12
Property Class and Head Markings	5 / 5 / 5	10 / 10 / 10	10 / 10 / 10	12 / 12 / 12

Size	Class 4.8				Class 8.8 or 9.8				Class 10.9				Class 12.9			
	Lubricated[a]		Dry[a]		Lubricated[a]		Dry[a]		Lubricated[a]		Dry[a]		Lubricated[a]		Dry[a]	
	N•m	lb-ft	N•m	lb-ft	N•m	lb-ft	N•m	lb-ft	N•m	lb-ft	N•m	lb-ft	N•m	lb-ft	N•m	lb-ft
M6	4.8	3.5	6	4.5	9	6.5	11	8.5	13	9.5	17	12	15	11.5	19	14.5
M8	12	8.5	15	11	22	16	28	20	32	24	40	30	37	28	47	35
M10	23	17	29	21	43	32	55	40	63	47	80	60	75	55	95	70
M12	40	29	50	37	75	55	95	70	110	80	140	105	130	95	165	120
M14	63	47	80	60	120	88	150	110	175	130	225	165	205	150	260	190
M16	100	70	125	92	190	140	240	175	275	200	350	225	320	240	400	300
M18	135	100	175	125	260	195	330	250	375	275	475	350	440	325	560	410
M20	190	140	240	180	375	275	475	350	530	400	675	500	625	460	800	580
M22	260	190	330	250	510	375	650	475	725	540	925	675	850	625	1075	800
M24	330	250	425	310	650	475	825	600	925	675	1150	850	1075	800	1350	1000
M27	490	360	625	450	950	700	1200	875	1350	1000	1700	1250	1600	1150	2000	1500
M30	675	490	850	625	1300	950	1650	1200	1850	1350	2300	1700	2150	1600	2700	2000
M33	900	675	1150	850	1750	1300	220	1650	2500	1850	3150	2350	2900	2150	3700	2750
M36	1150	850	1450	1075	2250	1650	2850	2100	3200	2350	4050	3000	3750	2750	4750	3500

DO NOT use these values if a different torque value or tightening procedure is given for a specific application. Torque values listed are for general use only. Check tightness of fasteners periodically.

Shear bolts are designed to fail under predetermined loads. Always replace the shear bolts with identical property class.

Fasteners should be replaced with the same or higher property class. If higher class fasteners are used, these should only be tightened to the strength of the original.

Make sure the fastener threads are clean and that you properly start thread engagement. This will prevent them from failing when tightening.

Tighten the plastic insert or crimped steel-type lock nuts to approximately 50 percent of the dry torque shown in the chart, applied to the nut, not to the bolt head. Tighten the toothed or serrated-type lock nuts to full torque value.,

a *"Lubricated" means coated with a lubricant such as engine oil, or fasteners with phosphate and oil coatings. "Dry" means plain or zinc plated without any lubrication.*

MEASUREMENT CONVERSION CHART

Metric to English

LENGTH
1 millimeter = 0.039 37 inches ....in
1 meter = 3.281 feet ....ft
1 kilometer = 0.621 miles ....mi

AREA
1 meter^2 = 10.76 feet^2 ....ft^2
1 hectare = 2.471 acres ....acre
  (hectare = 10,000 m^2)

MASS (WEIGHT)
1 kilogram = 2.205 pounds ....lb
1 tonne (1000 kg) = 1.102 short ton ....sh tn

VOLUME
1 meter^3 = 35.31 foot^3 ....ft^3
1 meter^3 = 1.308 yard^3 ....yd^3
1 meter^3 = 28.38 bushel ....bu
1 liter = 0.028 38 bushel ....bu
1 liter = 1.057 quart ....qt

PRESSURE
1 kilopascal = .145/in^2
  (1 bar = 101.325 kilopascals)

STRESS
1 megapascal or
1 newton/millimeter^2 = 145 pound/in^2 (psi) ....psi
  (1 N/mm^2 = 1 MPa)

POWER
1 kilowatt = 1.341 horsepower (550 ftlb/s) ....hp
  (1 watt = 1 Nm/s)

ENERGY (WORK)
1 joule = 0.000 947 8 British Thermal Unit ....BTU
  (1 J = 1 W s)

FORCE
1 newton = 0.2248 pounds force ....lb force

TORQUE OR BENDING MOMENT
1 newton meter = 0.7376 pound-foot ....(lb-ft)

TEMPERATURE
$t_C = (t_F - 32)/1.8$

English to Metric

LENGTH
1 inch = 25.4 millimeters ....mm
1 foot = 0.3048 meters ....m
1 yard = .9144 meters ....m
1 mile = 1.608 kilometers ....km

AREA
1 foot^2 = 0.0929 millimeters ....mm
1 acre = 0.4047 hectare ....ha
  (hectare = 10,000 m^2)

MASS WEIGHT
1 pound = 0.4535 kilograms ....kg
1 ton (2000 lb) = 0.9071 tonnes ....t

VOLUME
1 foot^3 = 0.028 32 meter^3 ....m^3
1 yard^3 = 0.7646 meter^3 ....m^3
1 bushel = 0.035 24 meter^3 L
1 bushel = 35.24 liter L
1 quart = 0.9464 liter L
1 gallon 3.785 liters L

PRESSURE
1 pound/inch2 = 6.895 kilopascals
        = 0.06895 bars

STRESS
1 pound/in^2 (psi) = 0.006 895 megapascal ....MPa
     or newton/mm^2 ....N/mm^2
  (1 N/mm^2 = 1 MPa)

POWER
1 horsepower (550 ftlb/s) = .7457 kilowatt ....kW
  (1 watt = 1 Nm/s)

ENERGY (WORK)
1 British Thermal Unit = 1055 joules ....J
  (1 J = 1 W s)

FORCE
1 pound = 4.448 newtons ....N

TORQUE OR BENDING MOMENT
1 pound-foot = 1.356 newton-meters ....Nm

TEMPERATURE
$t_F = 1.8 \times t_C + 32$

GLOSSARY

A

ABRASION

Wearing or rubbing away of a part.

ACCUMULATOR

A container which stores fluids under pressure as a source of hydraulic power. It may also be used as a shock absorber.

ADDITIVE

A substance added to oil to give it certain properties. For example, a material added to engine oil to lessen its tendency to congeal or thicken at low temperatures.

AIR CLEANER

A device for filtering, cleaning, and removing dust from the air admitted to an engine.

AIR CONDITIONING

Absolute control of temperature and humidity; air conditioning in true sense used only in some laboratories and manufacturing plants where temperature and humidity control are very critical. Ordinary usage in homes, buildings, and vehicles means control of temperature and removal of moisture by condensation; more correct designation is refrigeration.

ALIGNMENT

An adjustment to a fine or to bring into a line.

ALTERNATOR

A device which converts mechanical energy into electrical energy.

ALTERNATING CURRENT (A.C.)

A flow of electrons which reverses its direction of flow at regular intervals in a conductor.

AMBIENT TEMPERATURE

Temperature of surrounding air. In air conditioning, it refers to *outside* air temperature.

AMMETER

An instrument for measuring the *flow* of electrical current in amperes. Ammeters are usually connected in series with the circuit to be tested.

AMPERE

A unit of measure for the flow of current in a circuit.

AMPERE-HOUR

A unit of measure for battery capacity. It is obtained by multiplying the current (in amperes) by the time (in hours) during which current flows. For example, a battery which provides 5 amperes for 20 hours is said to deliver 100 ampere-hours.

ANTIFREEZE

A material such as ethylene glycol, alcohol, etc., added to water to lower its freezing point.

AUTOMATIC TRANSMISSION

A transmission in which gear or ratio changes are self-activated.

AXIAL

Parallel to the shaft or bearing bore.

AXLE

The shaft or shafts of a machine upon which the wheels are mounted.

B

BACKFIRE

Ignition of the mixture in the intake manifold by flame from the cylinder such as might occur from a leaking inlet valve.

BACKLASH

The clearance or "play" between two parts, such as meshed gears.

BACK-PRESSURE

A resistance to free flow, such as a restriction in the exhaust line.

BAR

A unit of pressure equal to 100 kiloPascals or 1.02 kg /CM2. Approximately equal to 14.5 psi.

BATTERY

See "STORAGE BATTERY"

BEARING

The supporting part which reduces friction between a stationary and rotating part.

BLEED

The process by which air is removed from a fuel or hydraulic system.

BLOW-BY

A leakage or loss of compression past the piston ring between the piston and the cylinder.

BOILING POINT

The temperature at which bubbles or vapors rise to the surface of a liquid and escape.

BREAK-IN

The process of wearing in to a desirable fit between the surfaces of two new or reconditioned parts.

BRUSH

A device which rubs against a rotating slip ring or commutator to provide a passage for electric current to a stationary conductor.

BYPASS

An alternate path for a flow of air or liquid.

C

CAMSHAFT

The shaft containing lobes or cams to operate the engine valves.

CARBURETOR

A device for automatically mixing gasoline fuel in the proper proportion with air to produce a combustible vapor.

CARBURETOR "ICING"

A term used to describe the formation of ice on a carburetor throttle plate during certain atmospheric conditions.

CENTIMETER

A unit of length equal to 0.01 meter, or approximately 0.39 inches (symbol: cm).

CETANE

Measure of ignition quality of diesel fuel—at what pressure and temperature the fuel will ignite and burn.

CHARGE

To restore the active materials in a battery by the passage of direct current through it.

CHOKE

A device such as a valve placed in a carburetor air inlet to restrict the volume of air admitted.

CIRCUIT BREAKER

A device to protect an electrical circuit from overloads.

CLEARANCE

The space allowed between two parts, such as between a shaft and its bearing.

CLUTCH

A device for connecting and disconnecting the engine from the transmission or for a similar purpose in other units.

COIL (IGNITION)

A transformer which steps up voltage to produce ignition sparks.

COLD RATING

The cranking load capacity of a battery at low temperatures.

COMBUSTION

The process of burning.

COMBUSTION CHAMBER

The volume of the cylinder above the piston with the piston on top center.

COMPRESSION

The reduction in volume or the "squeezing" of a gas. As applied to metal, such as a coil spring, compression is the opposite of tension.

COMPRESSION RATIO

The volume of the combustion chamber at the end of the compression stroke as compared to the volume of the cylinder and chamber with the piston on bottom center. Example: 8 to 1.

CONDENSATION

Process of changing a gas to a liquid.

CONDENSER

An automotive term which describes a capacitor.

CONDUCTOR

A substance or body through which an electrical current can be transmitted.

CONSTANT MESH TRANSMISSION

A transmission in which the gears are engaged at all times, but shifts are made by sliding collars which lock together two or more gears.

CONTRACTION

A reduction in mass or dimension; the opposite of expansion.

CONVERTER

As used in connection with LP-Gas, a device which converts or changes LP-Gas from a liquid-to a vapor for use by the engine.

COOLANT

A liquid circulated through an engine to absorb and release heat. Usually a mixture of water and antifreeze or rust inhibitor.

COOLER (OIL)

A heat exchanger which removes heat from a fluid. (See "Heat Exchanger.")

COUPLING

A connecting means for transferring movement from one part to another; may be mechanical, hydraulic or electrical.

CRANKCASE

The lower housing in which the crankshaft and many other parts of the engine operate.

CRANKCASE DILUTION

When unburned fuel finds its way past the piston rings into the crankcase oil, where it dilutes or "thins" the engine lubricating oil.

CRANKSHAFT

The main drive shaft of an engine which takes reciprocating motion and converts it to rotary motion.

CURRENT

Movement of electricity along a conductor. Current is measured in amperes.

CYLINDER

A round hole which receives the engine piston. Also a device for converting fluid power into linear or circular motion.

CYLINDER HEAD

A detachable portion of an engine fastened securely to the cylinder block which contains all or a portion of the combustion chamber.

D

DEAD CENTER

The extreme top or bottom position of the crankshaft throw at which the piston is not moving in either direction.

DETERGENT

A compound of a soap-like nature used in engine oil to remove engine deposits and hold them in suspension in the oil.

DETONATION

A too-rapid burning or explosion of the fuel-air mixture in engine cylinders. It becomes audible through a vibration of the combustion chamber walls and is sometimes confused with a "ping" or spark "knock."

DIAGNOSIS

In engine service, the use of instruments to "trouble shoot" the engine parts to locate the cause of a failure.

DIAL INDICATOR

A type of micrometer where the readings are indicated on a dial rather than on a thimble as in a micrometer.

DIESEL ENGINE

Named after its developer, Dr. Rudolph Diesel. This engine ignites fuel in the cylinder from the heat generated by compression. The fuel is an "oil" rather than gasoline, and no spark plug or carburetor is required.

DIFFERENTIAL GEAR

The gear system which permits one drive wheel to turn faster than the other.

DILUTION

See Crankcase Dilution.

DIRECT CURRENT (D.C.)

A steady flow of electrons moving steadily and continually in the same direction along a conductor from a point of high potential to one of lower potential. It is produced by a battery, generator, or rectifier.

DIRECT DRIVE

Direct engagement between the engine and drive shaft where the engine crankshaft and the drive shaft turn at the same rpm.

DISCHARGE

To remove electrical energy from a charged body such as a capacitor or battery.

DISPLACEMENT

The volume displaced by one complete stroke or revolution (of a pump, motor, or engine cylinder).

DISTRIBUTOR (IGNITION)

A device which directs the ignition of an engine.

DRAWBAR HORSEPOWER (Kilowatts)

Measure of the power of a machine at the drawbar hitch point.

DRIVE LINE

The universal joints, drive shaft and other parts connecting the transmission with the driving axles.

DYNAMOMETER

A test unit for measuring the actual power produced by an engine.

E

ELECTRICITY

The flow of electrons from atom to atom in a conductor.

ELECTROLYTE

Any substance which, in solution, is dissociated into ions and is thus made capable of conducting an electrical current. The sulfuric acid-water solution in a storage battery is an electrolyte.

ELECTRONIC IGNITION

An ignition system for spark-ignition engines which uses a reluctor, sensor, and ignition controller to control the timing of the spark.

ENDPLAY

The amount of axial or end-to-end movement in a shaft due to clearance in the bearings.

ENGINE

The prime source of power generation used to propel the machine.

ENGINE DISPLACEMENT

The sum of the displacement of all the engine cylinders. See "Displacement."

EVAPORATION

The process of changing from a liquid to a vapor, such as boiling water to produce steam. Evaporation is the opposite of condensation.

EXHAUST GAS ANALYZER

An instrument for determining the efficiency with which an engine is burning fuel.

EXHAUST MANIFOLD

The passages from the engine cylinders to the muffler or exhaust pipe which conduct exhaust gases away from the engine.

EXPANSION

An increase in size. For example, when a metal rod is heated it increases in length and perhaps also in diameter. Expansion is the opposite of contraction.

F

FEELER GAUGE

A metal strip or blade finished accurately with regard to thickness used for measuring the clearance between two parts; such gauges ordinarily come in a set of different blades graduated in thickness by increments of 0,001 inch (or mm).

FILTER

A device which removes solids from a fluid.

FLOW METER

A hydraulic testing device which gauges either flow rate, total flow, or both.

FLUID DRIVE

A pair of vaned rotating elements held in position close to each other without touching. Rotation is imparted to the driven member by the driving member through the resistance of a body of oil. (See Chapter 6 on Torque Converters.)

FOOT-POUND (ft-lb)

This is a measure of the amount of energy or work required to lift one pound a distance of one foot; approximately equal to 1.36 joule.

FOUR-CYCLE ENGINE

Also known as Otto cycle, where an explosion occurs every other revolution of the crankshaft; a cycle being considered as 1/2 revolution of the crankshaft. These strokes are (1) intake stroke; (2) compression stroke; (3) power stroke; (4) exhaust stroke.

FREE-WHEELING CLUTCH

A mechanical device which will engage the driving member to impart motion to a driven member in one direction but not the other, Also known as an "overrunning clutch."

FUEL KNOCK

Same as Detonation.

FUSE

A replaceable safety device for an electrical circuit. A fuse consists of a fine wire or a thin metal strip encased in glass or some fire-resistant material. When an overload occurs in the circuit, the wire or metal strip melts, breaking the circuit. Also see "Circuit Breaker."

G

GAS

A substance which can be changed in volume and shape according to the temperature and pressure applied to it. For example, air is a gas which can be compressed into smaller volume and into any shape desired by pressure. It can also be expanded by the application of heat.

GEAR

A cylinder- or cone-shaped part having teeth on one surface which mate with and engage the teeth of another part which is not concentric with it.

GEAR RATIO

The ratio of the number of teeth on the larger gear to the number of teeth on the smaller gear.

GENERATOR

A device which converts mechanical energy into electrical energy.

GOVERNOR

A device to control and regulate engine speed. May be mechanical, hydraulic, or electrical.

GROUND

A ground occurs when any part of a wiring circuit unintentionally touches a metallic part of the machine frame.

GROUNDED CIRCUIT

A connection of any electrical unit to the frame, engine, or any part of the tractor or machine, completing the electrical circuit to its source.

H

HECTARE

A measurement of area equal to 10,000 square meters, or approximately 2.47 acres (symbol: ha).

HORSEPOWER (hp)

The energy required to lift 550 pounds one foot in one second; approximately 0.746 kilowatts.

HYDRAULIC PRESSURE

Pressure exerted through the medium of a liquid.

HYDROMETER

An instrument for measuring battery specific gravity. A hydrometer is used to test the specific gravity of the electrolyte in a battery.

I

IDLE

Refers to the engine operating at its slowest speed with the machine not in motion.

INHIBITOR

A material to restrain some unwanted action, such as a rust inhibitor which is a chemical added to cooling systems to retard the formation of rust.

INJECTION PUMP (Diesel)

A device by means of which the fuel is metered and delivered under pressure to the engine injector.

INJECTOR (Diesel)

An assembly which receives a metered charge of fuel from another source at relatively low pressure, then is actuated to inject the charge of fuel into a cylinder or chamber at high pressure and at the proper time. Also called "injection nozzle."

INPUT SHAFT

The shaft carrying the driving gear by which the power is applied, as to the transmission.

INSULATOR

A substance or body that resists the flow of electrical current through it. Also see "Conductor."

INTAKE MANIFOLD

The passages which conduct the fuel-air mixture from the carburetor to the engine cylinders.

INTAKE VALVE

A valve which permits a fluid or gas to enter a chamber and seals against exit.

INTERNAL COMBUSTION

The burning of a fuel within an enclosed space.

J

JOULE

A unit of energy or work approximately equal to 0.102 kg•m, or about 0.7377 ft-lbs (symbol: J).

K

KILOGRAM

A unit of mass (weight) approximately equal to 2.2 pounds (symbol: kg).

KILOMETER

A unit of distance equal to 1000 meters, or approximately 0.62 miles (symbol: km).

KILOPASCAL

A unit of pressure equal to 0.01 bar, or approximately 0.145 psi (symbol: kPa).

KILOWATT

A measurement of work equal to 1000 watts, or approximately 1.34 horsepower (symbol: kW).

KNOCK

A general term used to describe various noises occurring in an engine; may be used to describe noises made by loose or worn mechanical parts, preignition, detonation, etc.

L

LINKAGE

Any series of rods, yokes, and levers, etc., used to transmit motion from one unit to another.

LITER

A unit of volume equal to 1000 cubic centimeters, or approximately 0.26 gallons (symbol: L).

LOW SPEED

The gearing which causes the greatest number of revolutions of the engine as compared to the driving wheels.

LP-GAS, LIQUEFIED PETROLEUM GAS

Made usable as a fuel for internal combustion engines by compressing volatile petroleum gases to liquid form. When so used, must be kept under pressure or at low temperature in order to remain in liquid form, until used by the engine.

M

MANIFOLD

A pipe or casting with multiple openings used to connect various cylinders to one inlet or outlet.

MANOMETER

A device for measuring a vacuum. It is a U-shaped tube partially filled with fluid. One end of the tube is open to the air and the other is connected to the chamber in which the vacuum is to be measured. A column of Mercury 30 in. high equals 14.7 lbs. per square in. which is atmospheric pressure at sea level. Readings are given in terms of inches of Mercury.

MECHANICAL EFFICIENCY (Engine)

The ratio between the indicated horsepower and the brake horsepower of an engine.

METER

A unit of length equal to 100 centimeters, or approximately 39.4 inches (symbol: m).

MISFIRING

Failure of an explosion to occur in one or more cylinders while the engine is running; may be a-continuous or intermittent failure.

MOTOR

This term should be used in connection with an electric motor and should not be used when referring to the *engine* of a machine. An electric motor-converts electrical energy to mechanical energy. A hydraulic motor converts hydraulic energy to mechanical energy, usually rotation.

MUFFLER

A chamber attached to the end of the exhaust pipe which allows the exhaust gases to expand and cool. It is usually fitted with baffles to porous plates and serves to subdue much of the noise created by the exhaust.

N

NEWTON

A unit of force equal to approximately 9.8 kilograms, or 4.45 pounds force (symbol: N).

O

OCTANE

Measurement which indicates the tendency of a gasoline or LP-Gas fuel to detonate or knock.

OHMMETER

An instrument for measuring the *resistance* in ohms of an electrical circuit.

OPEN OR OPEN CIRCUIT

An open or open circuit occurs when a circuit is broken, such as by a broken wire or open switch, interrupting the flow of current through the circuit. It is much like a closed valve in a water system.

OUPUT SHAFT

The shaft or gear which delivers the power from a device, such as a transmission.

P

PINION

A small gear having the teeth formed in the hub.

PISTON

A cylindrical part closed at one end which is connected to the crankshaft by the connecting rod. The force of the expansion in the cylinder is exerted against the closed end of the piston, causing the connecting rod to move the crankshaft. A cylindrical part of a hydraulic cylinder which is attached to the rod. Oil entering the cylinder under pressure moves the piston thus extending the rod. If oil pressure can be applied to both sides of the piston, it is called a double-acting cylinder and it can provide a force in two directions.

PISTON RING

An expanding ring placed in the grooves of the piston to seal off the passage of fluid or gas past the piston.

PLANETARY GEARS

A system of gearing which is modeled after the solar system. A pinion is surrounded by an internal ring gear and planet gears are in mesh between the ring gear and pinion around which all revolves.

POLARITY

A collective term applied to the positive (+) and negative (-) ends of a magnet or electrical mechanism such as a coil or battery.

POUR POINT

The lowest temperature at which a fluid will flow under specific conditions.

POWER HOP

The occurrence of loss of traction and a bouncing, pitching ride at the same time when a mechanical front wheel drive or four-wheel drive tractor is under high drawbar loads in certain soil conditions. Also called wheel hop.

POWER SHIFT TRANSMISSION

A transmission in which gear changes are selected manually but are power actuated; no master clutch is involved.

PREIGNITION

Ignition occurring earlier than intended. For example, the explosive mixture being fired in a cylinder as by a flake of incandescent carbon before the electric spark occurs.

PRELOAD

A load within the bearing, either purposely built in, or resulting from adjustment.

PRESSURE

Force of a fluid per unit area, usually expressed in pounds per square inch (psi), bar, or kilopascals (kPa).

PUMP

A device which converts mechanical force into hydraulic fluid power. Basic design types are gear, vane, and piston units. Or, a mechanical device for moving fluids such as fuel.

R

RATED HORSEPOWER

Value used by the engine manufacturer to rate the power of his engine, allowing for safe loads, etc.

RATIO

The relation or proportion that one number bears to another.

REGULATOR

A device which controls the flow of current or voltage in a circuit to a certain desired level.

RELAY

An electrical switch which opens and closes a circuit automatically.

REMOTE

A hydraulic function such as a cylinder which is separate from its supply source. Usually connected to the source by flexible hoses.

RESERVOIR

A container for keeping a supply of working fluid in a hydraulic system.

RING GEAR

A gear which surrounds or rings the sun and planet gears in a planetary system. Also the name given to the spiral bevel gear in a differential.

S

SCALE

A flaky deposit occurring on steel or iron. Ordinarily used to describe the accumulation of minerals and metals accumulating in an engine cooling system.

SENDING UNIT

A device, usually located in some part of an engine or other system, to transmit information to a gauge on an instrument panel.

SHIM

Thin sheets used as spacers between two parts, such as the two halves of a bearing.

SHORT (OR SHORT CIRCUIT)

This occurs when one part of a circuit comes in contact with another part of the same circuit, diverting the flow of current from its desired path.

SLIDING GEAR TRANSMISSION

A transmission in which gears are moved on their shafts to change gear ratios.

SLUDGE

A composition of oxidized petroleum products along with an emulsion formed by the mixture of oil and water. This forms a pasty substance and clogs oil lines and passages and interferes with engine lubrication.

SOLVENT

A solution which dissolves some other material. For example, water is a solvent for sugar.

SPARK PLUGS

Devices which ignite the fuel by a spark in a spark-ignition engine cylinder.

SPECIFIC GRAVITY

The ratio of a weight of any volume of a substance to the weight of an equal volume of some substance taken as a standard, usually water for solids and liquids. When a battery electrolyte is tested, the result is the specific gravity of the electrolyte.

STORAGE BATTERY

A group of electrochemical cells connected together to generate electrical energy. It stores the energy in a chemical form.

STRAINER

A coarse filter.

STROKE

The distance moved by the piston in an engine or hydraulic cylinder.

SUCTION

Suction exists in a vessel when the pressure is lower than the atmospheric pressure; also see Vacuum.

SULFATION

The formation of hard crystals of lead sulfate on battery plates. The battery is then "sulfated."

SYNCHROMESH TRANSMISSION

Transmission gearing which aids the meshing of two gears by causing the speed of both gears to coincide at the same time.

SYNCHRONIZE

To cause two events to occur at the same time. For example, to time a mechanism so that two or more sparks will occur at the same instant.

T

TACHOMETER

An instrument for measuring rotary speed; usually revolutions per minute.

THERMOSTAT

A heat-controlled valve used in the cooling system of an engine to regulate the flow of water between the cylinder block and the radiator.

TORQUE

The effort of twisting or turning.

TORQUE CONVERTER

A turbine device utilizing a rotary pump, one or more reactors (stators) and a driven circular turbine or vane whereby power is transmitted from a driving to a driven member by hydraulic action. It provides varying drive ratios; with a speed reduction, it increases torque.

TORQUE WRENCH

A special wrench with a built-in indicator to measure the applied turning force or torque.

TRANSMISSION

An assembly of gears, or other elements which gives variations in speed or direction between the input and output shafts.

TROUBLESHOOTING

A process of diagnosing the source of the trouble or troubles through observation and testing.

TUNE-UP

A process of accurate and careful adjustments to obtain the best performance from a machine.

TURBOCHARGER

A blower or pump which forces air into the engine cylinders at higher-than-atmospheric pressure. The increased pressure forces more air into the cylinder, thus enabling more fuel to be burned and more power produced.

V

VACUUM

A perfect vacuum has not been created as this would involve an absolute lack of pressure. The term is ordinarily used,to describe a partial vacuum; that is, a pressure less than atmospheric pressure; in other words a Suction.

VACUUM GAUGE

An instrument designed to measure the degree of vacuum existing in a chamber.

VALVE

A device which controls either 1) pressure of fluid, 2) direction of fluid flow, or 3) rate of flow.

VALVE CLEARANCE

The air gap allowed between the end of the engine valve stem and the valve lifter or rocker arm to compensate for expansion due to heat.

VAPOR LOCK

A condition wherein the fuel bolls in the engine fuel system, forming bubbles which retard or stop the flow of fuel to the carburetor.

VENT

An air breathing device in a fluid reservoir.

VISCOSITY

The measure of resistance of a fluid to flow. An engine oil rating.

VOLATILITY

The tendency for a fluid to evaporate rapidly or pass off in the form of vapor. For example, gasoline is more volatile than kerosene as it evaporates at a lower temperature.

VOLTAGE

That force which is generated to cause current to flow in an electrical circuit. It is also referred to as electromotive force or electrical potential. Voltage is measured in volts.

VOLTMETER

An instrument for measuring the force in volts of an electrical current. This is the difference of potential (voltage) between different points in an electrical circuit. Voltmeters are connected across(parallel to) the points where voltage is to be measured.

VOLUME

The amount of fluid flow per unit time. Usually given as gallons per minute (gpm), or liters per minute (L/min).

W

WATT

Work done at the rate of the joule per second, or the rate of work represented by an electric current of one ampere under a pressure of one volt (symbol: W).

WIRING HARNESS

The trunk and branches which feed an electrical circuit. Wires from one part of the circuit enter the trunk, joining other wires, and then emerge at another point in the circuit.

ABBREVIATIONS

API—American Petroleum Institute (develops designations for various petroleum products)

ASAE—American Society of Agricultural Engineers (sets standards for many components for agricultural use)

BDC—bottom dead center (of an engine piston)

BTU—Abbreviation for British Thermal Unit. Amount of heat required to raise temperature of one pound of water (approximately one pint) 1°F. All substances are rated in relation to water as standard of measurement.

°C—degrees Celsius (of temperature) (formerly called centigrade)

cm—centimeter (length)

cm²—square centimeters (area)

cu. in.—cubic inch

°F—degrees Fahrenheit (of temperature)

ft.—feet

ft.-lbs—foot-pounds (of torque or turning effort)

gpm—gallons per minute (of fluid flow)

ha—hectare (area)

hp—horsepower

I.D.—Inside diameter (as of a hose or tube)

in.—inch

J—joule (work or energy)

kg—kilogram (mass or weight)

km—kilometer (distance)

kPa—kilopascal (pressure)

kW—kilowatt (work or power)

L—liter (volume)

m—meter (length)

mph—miles per hour

N—Newton (force)

N•m—Newton•meter (torque)

mph—miles per hour

O.D.—outside diameter (as of a hose or tube)

psi—pounds per square inch (of pressure)

rpm—revolutions per minute

SAE—Society of Automotive Engineers (sets standards for many components for both automotive and agricultural use)

sq. ft.—square feet

sq. in.—square inch

TDC—top dead center (of an engine piston)

W—watt (work or power)

SUGGESTED READINGS

TEXTS

Farm Power and Tractors; Jones, Fred R. and Aldred, W.H.; 5th Edition; McGraw-Hill Book Company, 1980.

Farm Tractor Tune-up and Service Guide; American Association for Agricultural Engineering and Vocational Agriculture, Agricultural Engineering Center, Athens, Georgia 30601.

Farm Tractors; American Oil Company, Engineering Bulletin No. FT-53A, 910 South Michigan Ave., Chicago, Illinois 60680.

Fundamentals of Semiconductors; Delco Remy, Anderson, Indiana.

How to Get Extra Service From Farm Tires; The Rubber Manufacturers Association, Inc., 444 Madison Avenue, New York.

I & T Shop Service; Intertec Publishing Corp., Overland Park, Kansas 66215.

Optimum Tractor Tire Performance Handbook; The Goodyear Tire & Rubber Company, Akron, Ohio 44316.

Tractor and Small Engine Maintenance; Brown, Arlen D. and Strickland, R. Mack; 5th Edition; The Interstate Printers and Publishers, 1983.

Tractor Maintenance Principles and Procedures; American Association for Vocational Instruction Materials, Engineering Center, Athens, Georgia 30601.

Tractor Tips; Champion Spark Plug Company, Toledo, Ohio.

Tractors and Their Power Units; Liljedahl, J.B., et al; 4th Edition; Van Nos Reinhold, 1989.

Transistor Regulators; Delco Remy, Anderson, Indiana.

Fundamentals of Service: Engines; John Deere Publishing, 5440 Corporate Park Drive, Bettendorf, IA 52807, 1-800-522-7448.

Fundamentals of Service: Electronic and Electrical Systems; John Deere Publishing, 5440 Corporate Park Drive, Bettendorf, IA 52807, 1-800-522-7448.

Fundamentals of Service: Hydraulics; John Deere Publishing, 5440 Corporate Park Drive, Bettendorf, IA 52807, 1-800-522-7448.

Fundamentals of Service: Power Trains; John Deere Publishing, 5440 Corporate Park Drive, Bettendorf, IA 52807, 1-800-522-7448.

Fundamentals of Service: Air Conditioning; John Deere Publishing, 5440 Corporate Park Drive, Bettendorf, IA 52807, 1-800-522-7448.

Fundamentals of Service: Fuels, Lubricants and Coolants; John Deere Publishing, 5440 Corporate Park Drive, Bettendorf, IA 52807, 1-800-522-7448.

Fundamentals of Service: Tires and Tracks; John Deere Publishing, 5440 Corporate Park Drive, Bettendorf, IA 52807, 1-800-522-7448.

Fundamentals of Service: Belts and Chain; John Deere Publishing, 5440 Corporate Park Drive, Bettendorf, IA 52807, 1-800-522-7448.

Fundamentals of Service: Bearings and Seals; John Deere Publishing, 5440 Corporate Park Drive, Bettendorf, IA 52807, 1-800-522-7448.

Fundamentals of Service: Shop Tools; John Deere Publishing, 5440 Corporate Park Drive, Bettendorf, IA 52807, 1-800-522-7448.

Fundamentals of Service: Identification of Parts Failures; John Deere Publishing, 5440 Corporate Park Drive, Bettendorf, IA 52807, 1-800-522-7448.

Fundamentals of Service: Fiberglass and Plastics; John Deere Publishing, 5440 Corporate Park Drive, Bettendorf, IA 52807, 1-800-522-7448.

Fundamentals of Machine. Operation: Tractors; John Deere Publishing, Corporate Park Drive, Bettendorf IA 52807, 1-800-522-7448.

Fundamentals of Machine Operation. Combine Harvesting; John Deere Publishing, 5440 Corporate Park Drive, Bettendorf, IA 52807, 1-800-522-7448.

Fundamentals of Machine Operation: Hay and Forage Harvesting; John Deere Publishing, 5440 Corporate Park Drive, Bettendorf, IA 52807, 1-800-522-7448.

Fundamentals of Machine Operation: Machinery Management; John Deere Publishing, 5440 Corporate Park Drive, Bettendorf, IA 52807, 1-800-522-7448.

Farm Business Management: Farm and Ranch Safety Management; John Deere Publishing, Corporate Park Drive, Bettendorf IA 52807, 1-800-522-7448.

VISUALS AND FILMS

Preventive Maintenance Comprehensive Slide Set. 35 mm color. Matching set of 240 slides for illustrations in FMO "Preventive Maintenance" text. John Deere Publishing, 5440 Corporate Park Drive, Bettendorf, IA 52807, 1-800-522-7448.

INSTRUCTOR'S GUIDE AND WORKBOOK

Preventive Maintenance Instructor's Guide (John Deere Publishing, 5440 Corporate Park Drive, Bettendorf, IA 52807, 1-800-522-7448) contains corresponding chapter units based on FMO Preventive Maintenance text, teaching tips, answers to chapter quizzes, transparency masters and suggested script for transparencies.

Preventive Maintenance Student Guide (John Deere Publishing, 5440 Corporate Park Drive, Bettendorf, IA 52807, 1-800-522-7448) contains corresponding chapter units based on FMO Preventive Maintenance text, with chapter quizzes, study and discussion activities, and laboratory exercises.

ANSWERS TO TEST YOURSELF QUESTIONS
CHAPTER 1

1. It reduces failures, saves on operating costs, and keeps equipment safe to operate.

2. Preventive maintenance pays for itself, and it saves money by reducing repairs and fuel consumption, and by increasing efficient performance.

3. Because it is written specifically for your machine.

4. Before starting your machine each day, perform daily maintenance and check the machine for damage and potential failures.

5. Always think about what you are going to do before you do it.

ANSWERS TO TEST YOURSELF QUESTIONS
CHAPTER 2

1. a. <u>E</u>   d. <u>N</u>
   b. <u>I</u>   e. <u>B</u>
   c. <u>B</u>   f. <u>I</u>

2. All of these

3. None of the items apply to dry element type air cleaners.

4. A-2; B-1

5. Compression

6. True

7. True

8. 1-2-4-3 or 1-3-4-2

9. TDC or Top Dead Center

10. Straight through and reverse flow

ANSWERS TO TEST YOURSELF QUESTIONS
CHAPTER 3

1. Knock.

2. A-2; B-1.

3. A.

4. 1, C; 2, B; 3, A.

5. The four parts are: (1) fuel tank (pressurized), (2) Fuel strainer, (3) converter, and (4) carburetor.

6. The two gases are: (1) Butane and (2) Propane.

7. Dirt.

8. The three jobs are: (1) maintains a selected speed, (2) limits the slow and fast speeds, and (3) shuts down the engine when it overspeeds.

9. Fuel tank, fuel filters, and transfer pump.

10. Fuel filters.

ANSWERS TO TEST YOURSELF QUESTIONS
CHAPTER 4

1. (1) reduce friction and wear, (2) cool moving parts, (3) seal the cylinders, (4) keep the parts clean.

2. Viscosity.

3. False. When the crankcase oil becomes black, it shows that the oil is doing its job of keeping contaminants suspended.

4. False. Oil additives do wear out. Follow operator's manual for specified oil change recommendations.

5. Contamination.

6. (1) circulating splash, (2) internal force feed and splash, (3) full internal force feed .

7. Bypass system and full-flow system.

8. Daily.

9. This permits the dirt or contaminants to be agitated in the oil so that the contaminants will drain-out with the old oil.

10. False. Tighten oil filters until the seal just touches, then tighten no more than another 1/2 turn. If the filter is tightened too tightly, the seal may become distorted and leak.

ANSWERS TO TEST YOURSELF QUESTIONS

CHAPTER 5

1. To prevent overheating; to regulate temperatures.

2. Without inhibitors it will rust, corrode, and leave deposits in the engine.

3. C and D.

4. Rust or scale.

5. -34°F. (-37°C)

6. One-third (1/3).

7. False. The thermostat maintains a minimum temperature.

8. False. You could be burned seriously. Wait until the engine coolant has cooled.

9. First blank - "hot"; second blank - "cold".

10. Blow-by (of engine gases).

ANSWERS TO TEST YOURSELF QUESTIONS

CHAPTER 6

1. A and D.

2. False. The <u>distributor</u> affects the timing.

3. The <u>charging</u>, <u>starting</u> and <u>ignition</u> circuits.

4. Corroded terminals and acid deposits on the top of the battery provide a circuit for current to flow out.

5. Hydrogen gas is released by the battery when it is charging. This gas is very explosive.

6. False. An engine operating under these conditions should use a <u>colder</u> plug.

7. A and B.

8. Solder deposits on the inside of the housing.

9. Always <u>polarize</u> it.

10. A-2, B-1.

ANSWERS TO TEST YOURSELF QUESTIONS
CHAPTER 7

1. True. For example, SAE 80 gear oil has about the same viscosity as SAE 20 engine oil. (Only the numbers are different)

2. a) gear oil
   b) automatic transmission fluid
   c) transmission-hydraulic fluids

3. The barrel should be tilted.

4. Because the clutch facings wear down as they operate.

5. Excessive grease may be thrown onto the clutch facing and cause the clutch to "chatter" when engaged.

6. Drive the machine until the transmission fluid is well agitated and heated.

ANSWERS TO TEST YOURSELF QUESTIONS
CHAPTER 8

1. Any of the following:
   A. Not enough oil in the reservoir
   B. Clogged or dirty oil filters
   C. Leaking connections
   D. Incorrect oil in the system

2. A-2; B-3; C-1

3. False. You may damage the connection. Tighten the connection only until the leak stops.

4. Dirt

5. Compare your answer to any of the rules listed under "Safety Rules for Hydraulics" in the FMO Preventive Maintenance student text.

ANSWERS TO TEST YOURSELF QUESTIONS

CHAPTER 9

1. False. Clean only in any good non-sudsing detergent.

2. "Bubbles".

3. Tighten the adjusting nut and turn the wheel until the wheel drags slightly, then back off the nut to the next slot.

4. A-2; B-3; C- 1.

5. The correct slippage rate is 10 to 15 percent.

6. Wipe off dirt and grease from the fitting.

7. 1-belt heating; 2-excessive stretch; 3-damage to drive components, such as sheaves and shafts. The extra tightness will also place heavier loads on the bearings. (Any two of the three above)

8. Any three of the following:
   1. Reduce wear
   2. Protect against rust, corrosion, and heat
   3. Prevent seizing of pins and bushings
   4. Cushion shock loads

9. A. Overload

10. First blank - "length"; second blank - "amperes".

ANSWERS TO TEST YOURSELF QUESTIONS

CHAPTER 10

1. First blank, "operating"; second blank, "repairs".

2. Any four of the following: Intake System, Exhaust System, Fuel System, Electrical System, Lubrication System, or Cooling System.

3. Remove ballast or weights;
   Remove from ground or raise from ground;
   Inflate to normal pressure.

4. Check specific gravity;
   Add water (if necessary);
   Charge (if necessary)

ANSWERS TO TEST YOURSELF QUESTIONS

CHAPTER 12

1. 500

2. Danger
   Warning
   Caution

3. True

4. Springs
   Hydraulic Systems
   Compressed Air
   Electricity
   Raised Loads
   Loaded Mechanisms

5. False

6. 60°F (16°C)

7. True

8. An approved respirator

9. False

10. Increase resulting in a tire explosion.

INDEX

W